Vintage Port

The Wine Spectator's Ultimate Guide for Consumers, Collectors and Investors

By James Suckling

Published by Wine Spectator Press
A division of M. Shanken Communications, Inc./West
Opera Plaza Suite 2014
601 Van Ness Avenue
San Francisco, CA 94102
(415) 673-2040, (415) 673-0103 (fax)

M. Shanken Communications, Inc. also publishes *The Wine Spectator, Impact, Impact International, Market Watch, Food Arts, Impact Research Reports, Leaders, Impact Yearbook, Impact International Directory, Market Watch Creative Adbook, The Wine Spectator's Wine Country Guide,* and sponsors the Impact Marketing Seminars and the California and New York Wine Experiences. Headquarters office at 387 Park Avenue South, New York, NY 10016, (212) 684-4224, (212) 684-5424 (fax).

First Edition

Book and jacket design by Kathy McGilvery
Decanter illustration by Dorothy Reinhardt

Distributed to the Book Trade by Sterling Publishing Co., New York, NY

Manufactured in the United States of America
ISBN 0-918076-80-3

TO CATHERINE

FOREWORD

If you ever have had the opportunity to share a fine, old vintage Port with good friends, then you can understand the excitement, fascination and ceremony that this elegant, fortified wine has evoked throughout its history. In *Rich, Rare and Red*, Ben Howkins has gone as far as asserting that vintage Port is an essential ingredient for the maintenance of the quality of life. This sentiment has guided British Port consumption for centuries, and with the 1980s, an ever-growing number of people in the United States and around the world have come to appreciate its appeal.

Arguably, nothing in the wine world offers the complexity and intensity of flavor capable of rounding out an evening of fine food and stimulating after-dinner conversation like a great Port.

The best vintage Ports are undoubtedly among the finest and, in some circles, the most sought-after wines in the world. These are highly collectible and, because of their relatively small production, long life and history of price appreciation, can make great investments. Appreciation of the inherent value of Port as a fine wine, however, is only the start. The development of Port is more closely tied to the history of its native country than any other wine, and it is a rich and colorful history. For hundreds of years the story of these wines has been totally intertwined with the histories of Portugal and Britain, the Douro Valley, the cities of Oporto and London, and the British and Portuguese people.

One of the most interesting aspects of vintage Port — and the entire Port wine trade — is that it has, for the most part, somehow avoided the technological revolution that is transforming the world's wine regions. The Douro Valley offers one of the last glimpses into a world gone by, where wines, winemaking techniques and the wine industry are largely still a part of the 19th century.

A number of books have been written on the subject of Port. Most of these books deal only with parts of the story — one author writes mostly about the history of the region, another on selected profiles of certain Port shippers, and still another discusses viticultural and enological techniques. Very few contain all of the above. And none actually reviews the wines from each house, giving the reader tasting and buying recommendations. The lack of a comprehensive reference was the impetus for this book.

In *Vintage Port*, James Suckling, senior editor and European bureau chief for *The Wine Spectator*, focuses his training as a reporter, journalist, and wine taster on writing a complete book on Portugal's great dessert wine, creating a reference and tasting guide to this special wine. This book is the culmination of five years of his research and tasting.

Vintage Port is a complete reference covering all facets of the wines and their development: History — the story of vintage Port and its development in the Douro Valley; The Vineyard — viticultural practices, grape varieties and the top vineyards; The Winery — from pressing to fermentation to fortification; The Lodge — the aging process to bottling and release; The Vintages — this century's declared vintages rated with listings of the top wines' score and price; A Classification of Vintage Port — how the top house rank in a system of five tiers; Buying and Investing — how to buy vintage Port in the auction market, including collectibility ratings and price performance data of well-known wines at auctions; and Serving and Storing — advice on topics from storing vintage Port properly to decanting and proper service.

The heart of the book concentrates on profiles and in-depth tasting notes of more than 50 of the finest Port producers. For each producer there are ratings and evaluations of wine quality, discussions on wine style and individual vineyard and winery practices, careful direction as to when to drink the wines, pricing information for older vintages in the market today and advice as to which wines are best for investment.

Nearly all of the previous books on vintage Port have been written by members of the wine trade, or have been sponsored by one Port house or another. This book is a completely independent effort. *Vintage Port* by James Suckling, along with the just-published *California's Great Chardonnays* by James Laube, joins *California's Great Cabernets* in *The Wine Spectator*'s "Ultimate Guide" series of comprehensive books for consumers, collectors and investors where our only interest is that of the reader.

Wines evolve and change with time, and so must any book like this one. It is our intention to revise this book periodically, with updated tasting notes, rankings and price data so that it continues to be the most current and comprehensive reference on the subject.

Finally, this book would not have been possible without the team spirit and commitment of members of the entire staff of *The Wine Spectator*.

Marvin R. Shanken
Editor and Publisher
The Wine Spectator
New York, NY
August 1990

ACKNOWLEDGMENTS

This book would have never been possible without the enthusiasm and support of my family, friends, colleagues and members of the wine trade.

I wish first to thank my wonderful wife, Catherine. We first met through the Port trade when she was working for the British agents of Quinta do Noval, and her genuine interest and enjoyment of the subject was a never-ending source of sustenance to finish this book. Her love and devotion kept me going. My parents were another reservoir of motivation. My father, John, an avid wine collector, has always been a close confidant on all of my endeavors, while my mother, Beverly Reordan, an accomplished artist, has been an inspiration for my creative energies as a writer and photographer.

Members of *The Wine Spectator* staff have always been supportive of this project. Everyone from the editors to the production staff has given me help. In particular, Greg Walter, president of *The Wine Spectator* and project director, has offered me much guidance and encouragement through the writing, and Lisa King, the copy editor of the project, has provided me with the invaluable service of improving my prose when necessary. Kathy McGilvery and Liza Gross were equally irreplaceable for their help in designing and producing this book. Thanks also to *Wine Spectator* wine research coordinator Mark Norris for gathering pricing data and crunching all the numbers. My assistant in London, Maree Oxnard, was also an important member of the team, working diligently behind the scenes.

It is difficult to list all the friends and wine trade members who have aided me in my research. As for friends, the encouragement of Stephen Browett, Tim and Stephanie Johnston, Richard Mayson, Robert Nicholson and Thomas and Sara Matthews has been uplifting in many a down period when I thought this book would never be finished. We also shared a good decanter or two of fine vintage Port. I wish to thank others for passing their Port my way, including many extremely rare bottles: John Avery, John Barratt, Lindsay Hamilton, Peter Leaver, Tim Stanley-Clarke and Richard Torin. Other important sources included: Skinkers wine bar, London;

Christie's auctions, London; The White Horse Inn, Chilgrove, England; and Farr Vintners, London.

Members of the Port trade were just as helpful in opening bottles and providing information. Nearly all the Port shippers encouraged me to write this book and welcomed my views and opinions — both positive and negative. Particularly helpful were: Tim Bergqvist, Sophia Bergqvist, Jeremy Bull, David Baverstock, Peter Cobb, David Delaforce, Bruce Guimaraens, Gordon Guimaraens, Ben Howkins, David Orr, Robin Reid, Alistair Robertson, David Sandeman, James Symington, Peter Symington, Cristiano van Zeller, Dirk van der Niepoort, Rolf van der Niepoort, and William Warre.

In conclusion, I wish to thank Marvin Shanken, editor and publisher of *The Wine Spectator*. He is a devoted wine collector, and his passion for vintage Port was infectious. He urged me from our early years working together at the *The Wine Spectator* to learn more about vintage Port, and later, to write this book. This book would have never been possible without his support.

James Suckling
London, England
August 1990

CONTENTS

INTRODUCTION

After tasting a 1948 Fonseca or 1945 Croft, it is hard to believe better wines exist. The layers of concentrated aromas and flavors in such fine vintage Ports offer a kaleidoscope of sensations. Each sip seems better than the last, as your taste buds react to this nectar called vintage Port. It is perplexing how such a civilized drink can come from one of the most unsophisticated wine regions in Europe.

Vintage Port is great in spite of itself, and cannot be compared to any other wine in the world. It originates from remote vineyards in Portugal's Douro Valley, which have little in common with the well-manicured vines of renowned châteaux in Bordeaux. It is made under conditions that most high-tech winemakers of California or Australia would consider a mockery of enology, and then is transported more than 100 miles to be aged in dusty old warehouses. Yet vintage Port remains one of the world's greatest wines.

In spite of such physical obstacles, vintage Port continues to gain in popularity, defying such social barriers as a growing anti-alcohol lobby, a decline in consumption of fortified wine, and a general move away from high-alcohol drinks. More and more, people are serving vintage Port at the end of a meal. George Saintsbury's words on Port in his 1924 edition of *Notes on a Cellar Book* are still true: "It has not the almost feminine grace and charm of Claret; the transcendental qualities of Burgundy and Madeira; the immediate inspiration of Champagne; the rather unequal and sometimes palling attractions of Sauternes and Mosel and Hock. But it strengthens while it gladdens as no other wine can do."

The Port trade is still an anachronism, although it has seen more advances in viticulture and winemaking in the 1980s than in the past two centuries. A new generation is taking over and bringing new ideas to the production and marketing of Port. Yet some Port producers still refuse to become part of the 20th century. Could their reluctance be well founded? How much of the quality in a great vintage Port can be attributed to traditional methods? What have changes in winemaking and viticulture actually achieved? Who makes the best vintage Port and why? I have tried to answer these questions and many others in this book.

WHAT IS VINTAGE PORT?

Port is a sweet, fortified wine, high in alcohol due to the addition of a neutral spirit during fermentation. Port-style wines are produced in many countries and wine regions around the world — France, the United States, Australia and South Africa to name a few — but the strict usage of the term "Port" should refer to wine produced in the Douro Valley east of Oporto in Portugal. There are two basic types of Port or Porto as it is labeled in the United States: wood aged and bottle aged. Wood-aged Port includes such styles as white, ruby, tawny, vintage character and late-bottled vintage, as well as old tawnies and *colheita* (vintage-dated) tawnies. Each is made from Ports that have been aged in wood and treated to remove any solids in the wine before bottling. Bottle-aged Ports include crusted, traditional late-bottled vintage and vintage. Although they are made from Ports also aged in wood, they are not stabilized, fined or filtered before bottling and throw a sediment or "crust" while improving with age in the bottle.

White Port is made from a range of white grape varieties grown in the Douro Valley, such as Malvasia Fina and Rabigato. It is made in the same way as a red Port, although consumed primarily as an ap é ritif or mixer. Ruby Ports are red, young, fruity wines while a standard tawny is lighter in color and softer in flavor. Both are usually bottled when three years old. The main difference between the two is that ruby Ports are made from darker, richer wines while tawnies are made from lighter ones. Vintage character is similar to a standard ruby but made from richer, more powerful wines. Late-bottled vintage, by comparison, is also a premium ruby but made from a single vintage.

Old tawnies and *colheitas* are a step up in quality. These are the limited-quantity wood Ports upon which many shippers pride themselves. Old tawnies, that are 10, 20 or 30 years old, are blends of various fine-quality Ports matured in wooden cask. The year denotes the average age of the blend. *Colheita* Ports are old tawnies produced from single vintages, such as 1967, 1957 or 1934. Crusted Port and traditional late-bottled vintage Port very closely resemble a full-fledged vintage Port. They improve with age in the bottle while developing a crust. A crusted Port is a blend of rich, young wines from various vintages bottled after three to four years in wood. A traditional late-bottled vintage is virtually the same but made from a single vintage. These last two wines are very difficult to find today.

This book is about vintage Port, clearly the king of all Port. These Ports are produced from the wine of a single vintage and bottled after two to two and a half years in wood. They may be a blend of wines from various vineyards or produced from a single estate or *quinta*. The best vintage Ports are deeply colored, massive wines with plenty of fruit and tannin to give them great longevity. They usually need at least 10 to 15 years of bottle age before drinking.

HOW THE WINES WERE CHOSEN AND TASTED

This book is the result of my obsession with one of the world's great wines. I have tried to taste as many vintage Ports and interview as many Port producers as possible. The research for this book goes back to 1985, when I visited London and Portugal to write a story on America's growing interest in vintage Port. Since then, I have returned to Oporto, Vila Nova de Gaia and the Douro Valley more than a dozen times, and I have lived and worked in London since late 1986. Most of the work for this book, however, was done between September 1989 and June 1990, and I spent nearly two months in Portugal during that period.

This book was written from hundreds of tasting notes, dozens of interviews and numerous documents. None of this information was gathered through trips paid for by the producers or through any form of industry sponsorship, with the exception of representatives of various Port houses who kindly opened bottles of their vintage Ports to be tasted. Many of the older vintage Ports, such as the 1935s, 1934s and 1927s, were bought at auction and from other sources to be tasted. From the outset, I wanted this to be an independent book on Port, since nearly all the others before it have been written by members of the wine trade or under its auspices.

The tasting notes are an accumulation of five years of research. I have notes on nearly every vintage Port I have tasted since 1985. My vintage Port tasting notes total nearly 2,000, although only about 504 were used in this book due to duplication. I have tasted some vintage Ports from leading houses such as Taylor, Graham, Fonseca and Dow dozens of times, looking at my notes after each tasting to check the wines' development. Tasting more obscure wines, particularly those from pre-1950 vintages, was more difficult. I tasted many of these rare vintages only once or twice, although I have conferred with respected Port tasters about my conclusions including the most respected palates in the Port trade. It is not easy to find accomplished vintage Port tasters. Most proficient wine tasters spend little time on vintage Port.

All the tasting notes in this book are my own. A large percentage of the tastings were done blind in Oporto and London. The major houses — Cockburn, Croft, Dow, Ferreira, Fonseca, Graham, Quinta do Noval, Sandeman, Taylor and Warre — were all tasted blind against one another at least once in almost every vintage back to 1927. Among the other houses I evaluated in blind tastings were Borges & Irmão, C á lem, Churchill, Delaforce, Fonseca-Guimaraens, Gould Campbell, Graham's Malvedos, Hooper, Martinez, Niepoort, Offley Forrester, Quarles Harris, Quinta do Bomfim, Quinta da Cavadinha, Quinta da Eira Velha, Quinta da Roêda, Quinta de Vargellas, Rebello Valente, Royal Oporto and Smith Woodhouse. I would have preferred to taste all of the vintage Ports in this book blind because I believe it is the fairest way to evaluate them, but often it was simply impossible.

Most of my evaluations of producers and wines were made in 1989 and 1990, making them as current as possible. Inevitably, these judgments will change as the wines evolve. For example, a very young vintage Port might receive a score of 90 for its great aging potential. In 15 to 25 years, it might receive a higher or lower score based on its drinkability and potential improvement. At 30 to 50 years, it might start to decline in quality and would be marked much lower. There are numerous examples of old vintage Ports tasted for this book. Many of the 1960s, 1958s and 1950s may have received scores in the 90s or high 80s about 10 or 15 years ago, but they have long since reached their peaks and have begun to decline.

Wine tasting is not a science but a totally subjective evaluation of an ever-changing product. My tasting notes reflect this and should only be used as a guide to the potential quality of a vintage Port. There may be less variance in my evaluations of wines younger than 1963 because I have tasted most of them numerous times. I may be less accurate on more mature vintage Ports since some I only tasted once. Bottle variation and other variables are unavoidable.

I judged all the vintage Ports in this book in the same way as I evaluate other wines. The analysis focused on four areas: color, nose, taste and finish. I wrote a descriptive note on each wine, and then gave each a numerical score reflecting the wine's overall quality. I used *The Wine Spectator's* 100-point scale:

95-100 Classic, a great wine
90-94 Outstanding, a wine of superior character and style
80-89 Good to very good, a wine with special qualities
70-79 Average, a drinkable wine that may have minor flaws
60-69 Below average, perhaps drinkable but not recommended
50-59 Poor, undrinkable, not recommended

In general, I was most impressed by the bigger, more powerful vintage Ports, whether a young 1985 or a mature 1948. These are the wines that scored the highest — normally from 86 to 100 — and they are the vintage Ports I would buy for my own cellar. For me, a great vintage Port by definition must have the potential to improve for decades. In essence, the difference between a fine wine and an ordinary one is that the former improves with age. Aging potential is crucial in rating young vintage Ports; therefore, I gave the highest scores to those wines with deep colors, rich aromas and concentrated flavors. For me, a young vintage Port must have what shippers call "grip" — an impressive intensity of fruit and a firm tannin structure. When looking at more mature vintage Ports with 15 to 30 years of bottle age, I assessed how well they were evolving. Were they balanced? Were they still youthful? How much longer would they improve? Vintage Ports more than 30 years old were evaluated in a similar way, but I was less critical about how much longer they would continue to improve with age. With extremely old wines, such as those from the 1930s, 1920s and 1910s, I gave good marks to those that were still relatively drinkable even though they may have resembled a tawny more than a vintage Port.

How the Book Is Organized

This book is written for anyone interested in Port, even though it focuses on vintage Port. I hope it offers readers a useful picture of the Port trade past and present.

Chapter I is a look at the history of vintage Port and the industry that developed around it. Chapter II looks at the vineyard estates and viticultural practices. Chapter III is an examination of the harvest and winemaking techniques prevalent in the Douro. Chapter IV follows the wine down the Douro Valley to the century-old aging lodges at Vila Nova de Gaia. Chapter V is a brief synopsis of nearly all the vintages of Port from 1900 to 1987. It rates the vintages on a 100-point scale and gives as much relevant information on the year as possible. Chapter VI describes the people behind vintage Port. It is a compendium of timely profiles of some of the Port trade's most colorful and interesting personalities and companies. Chapter VII is a classification of the top vintage Port houses based on quality. Chapter VIII gives recommendations on buying and investing in Port. Chapter IX should help you enjoy your vintage Port by discussing the proper serving and storage for these wines. Chapter X is the heart and soul of the book; it includes profiles and tasting notes of 58 vintage Port producers.

I hope Chapter X will be a helpful reference for vintage Port lovers. The vintage Port producers are presented in alphabetical order. Each profile includes the following information:

Classification: From first to fifth tier, houses are ranked according to the overall quality of their vintage Ports in a manner similar to Bordeaux's 1855 classification.

Collectibility rating: The houses are placed in one of three categories — AAA, AA and A — according to their attractiveness to wine collectors and investors. The top-rated vintage Ports, AAA and AA, are the ones that will increase the most in quality and value while aging.

At a glance: Here are the vital statistics, including each producer's founding date, ownership and production.

Tasting notes: Each wine tasted includes a concise tasting note describing the overall quality of the wine as well as its style and structure. These assessments are then translated into a numerical score on *The Wine Spectator* 100-point scale. Each note also includes information on when to begin drinking the vintage Port, and its current U.S. and United Kingdom retail and auction prices.

WHY A BOOK ON VINTAGE PORT?

As a wine lover, I have marveled over the intensity and complexity of flavors of a fine vintage Port. As a journalist, I have always been fascinated by the story of vintage Port. It remains a throwback in a world of advanced technology. Tasting a glass of vintage Port or researching an article on the subject has always made me feel as if I were experiencing history firsthand. The Port trade serves as a living example of how great wine was once made, long before the days of university-trained enologists and stainless steel, temperature-controlled vats.

Vintage Port helps one understand wine better. It still proves that making fine wine is not a question of high finance and ultra-modern technology. Of course, vintage Port represents only a tiny segment of the total Port trade, equaling 3 percent to 4 percent of the harvest in a declared year, or about 300,000 cases. But vintage Port remains the flagship of the Port trade, and learning more about it helps one understand the ambitions and the objectives of the various houses and the Port trade itself. I only hope fascination with and enthusiasm for this unique wine is infectious.

CHAPTER I

THE HISTORY OF VINTAGE PORT

T he origins of today's vintage Port are closely tied to the geopolitics of 17th-century Europe, in particular the influence of the Dutch and the British and their common enemy at the time, France.

Within a decade of each other, both Holland and Britain declared war on France. Both needed an alternative to supplement their respective citizenry's substantial appetite for French wines. The Dutch, early giants in worldwide trade, ventured up the Douro Valley from Oporto in 1672 to the village of Lamego — today the beginning of the prime area for vintage Port — in search of red wines for their home market. The British, already trading their textiles with Portugal, also saw the merits of the wines produced in the outlying regions around Oporto.

These 17th-century vintage wines from northern Portugal bore little resemblance to the powerful fortified vintage Ports of today. They were most likely simple red table wines, perhaps akin to today's slightly unfinished and bubbling red *vinhos verdes*. The practice of fortifying wines with neutral spirits to stop fermentation was virtually unknown. The only brandy to come in contact with the rough and raw reds of Oporto was added before shipping in cask, in hopes of giving stability to the wines.

Fortification of Port as we know it today did not come into vogue until the mid-1700s. The addition of large doses of brandy (and sometimes other products such as elderberry juice) to wines was widespread by 1756, when the Marquês de Pombal, the strong-willed Portuguese prime minister, established the Companhia Geral da Agricultura dos Vinhos do Alto Douro to regulate the Oporto wine trade. The Old Wine Co., as it was called then, had a monopoly on the Port trade for more than 130 years, and was also given a monopoly on the distribution of brandy, which undoubtedly encouraged the spirit's use in wine. Pombal financed much of the rebuilding of Lisbon, which had been devastated in 1755 by an earthquake, through such nationalized trading companies as the Old Wine Co.

Some observers at the time believed that this period was the beginning of the debasement of the potentially great wines of the Douro. Cyrus Redding wrote in 1833 in his book *A History and Description of Modern Wines*, "In 1756, began the era of deterioration of these wines." He lambasted the Old Wine Co. for not maintaining the quality of Douro wines at the same level as those from France, and went on to blame the monopoly for promoting adulteration, which it originally was established to combat.

Redding wrote: "They then began their own career of amendment, by buying or making brandy, and pleading the necessity for its use in adulterating the wines in a greater degree than before. They charged the taste of Englishmen as their excuse, and gradually proceeded to encourage the mixing together of all sorts of grapes and fermenting their must carelessly, with a view to quantity…They did not spare brandy in the operation, nor elderberries, nor burnt corn nor anything that would answer to colour the wine when it was not thought deep enough."

THE FIRST VINTAGE PORT

The debate continues over what was truly the first vintage Port. The House of Sandeman claims it produced the first in 1790, shipping it in cask to England a few years later. Sarah Bradford, in her authoritative historical perspective on the Port trade, *The Story of Port*, last published in 1983, stated that in 1775, "Oporto produced 'the first wine which could worthily claim the title to vintage Port.' It was the pioneer, the first in a long and glorious line of vintage wines; in 1787, the French followed suit with the first bottled vintage claret, Château Lafite, but the glory of the discovery belongs to the Port trade."

It is doubtful that the discovery of vintage bottled wines can be credited to the Port trade in light of the discovery, in the 1980s, of a handful of vintage bottled clarets and Sauternes dated before 1787. A half bottle of 1784 Margaux believed to have been the property of Thomas Jefferson was sold at a 1987 Bordeaux wine auction. In 1988 a group of wine collectors opened a bottle of 1747 Château d'Yquem in Austria. German wine collector Hardy Rodenstock says that he knows where a cache of bottled Hungarian Tokay from the mid-1600s lies in Poland. To date, Rodenstock has produced no evidence to support his claim.

These early vintage Ports from the 18th century were clearly not the prototypes of modern vintage Port. The writings of T.G. Shaw in *Wine, the Vine and the Cellar* in 1863 indicate that vintage Ports until the 1810s were lighter and slightly less fortified than those of modern times. They were produced primarily in the Baixo Corgo, the area known today for its standard Port production, rather than in the Cima Corgo, where nearly all the great vintage Port estates are now located. More importantly, Shaw's writings indicate that the wines were probably handled more severely and bottled later than vintage Ports of the 20th century.

Shaw wrote: "They were usually kept for two or three years (in cask) before shipment, being carefully fined and racked during that period. On arrival (in London), the shipping houses placed those which were not already sold in their bonded cellars; and those who bought them placed them in their own cellars, where they again racked or treated them according to their judgment." It was common for London wine merchants to fine their wines with egg whites, which could strip the body and some of the color from a young Port if used excessively. Merchants often waited another two or three years before bottling the wines; some waited even longer.

According to Shaw, the popular 1820 vintage may have marked the beginning of the two- or three-year bottlings of vintage Port with little or no fining. He wrote that 1820 produced grapes "so ripe and luscious that the wine was much too sweet and clammy." The 1820 was quickly snapped up by the British wine trade, since the four preceding vintages had been extremely poor. What Shaw described as bad treatment of the 1820 wines was in fact very close to the methods of handling today's vintage Ports: "It was put into the bottle at once, on the argument, as I remember, of some of the so-called wise men of the docks — 'Get it into glass, get the cork on the top of it, and then you will keep in all the good.' " Copies of Christie's wine auction advertisements from the period publicizing the sale of parcels of 1820 vintage Port confirm Shaw's reports of three- and five-year bottlings of the vintage.

Not all consumers were pleased with these early bottlings, and Shaw described their dismay when they opened bottles of 1820 with four or five years of bottle age and found "plenty of 'crust' and plenty of colour in the wine, and a 'well-stained cork,' but their 1820 (was) very much the same as on the day when it was bottled." Shaw applauded the merchants and wine consumers who a few years after bottling their 1820s decided to uncork and blend them with older vintages before rebottling. He said the blend was a much better Port. "I am convinced that the sweet 1820, succeeding so many bad years, and followed by the two similar though not such very saccharine years, was the origin of the bad repute into which Port has gradually fallen since that period."

The trend toward bottling some of the wines early and laying them down continued. Shaw wrote about an excellent 1847 but again complained about early-bottled stocks. "Some of that vintage, early bottled, is scarcely fit for use even now, and will never be equal to those which were allowed to get rid of their coarse parts in the wood," he wrote in a subsequent edition of his book.

As much as critics like Shaw wrote against deeply colored, powerful vintage Ports, there was a growing circle of British wine consumers who sought these wines with the purpose of laying them away in their cellars. They enjoyed watching their young vintage Ports evolve over the years into balanced, intensely fruity wines. This interest in aging vintage Port acted as an impetus for collecting and cellaring other wines.

In his chapter on Port in *Notes on a Cellar-Book*, George Saintsbury, the archetypal wine writer, underlined the influence Port had on wine collectors at the time: "My cellar, if not exactly my cellar-book (which, as has been said, did not begin till some years later) was founded in this eminent respect on a small supply of 1851 (I think, but am not sure, Cockburn's)…"

THE CORK AND BOTTLE

The evolution of the glass wine bottle and cork was significant in the progression of vintage Port. The concept of retaining wines from a particular vintage and cellaring them had not existed since Roman times, and the practice was reborn primarily in Great Britain. Before, the bottle was merely used as a decanter to be filled with wine from a cask in its owner's or a wine merchant's cellar before arriving at the table. Some were made of fragile glass, although metal, clay, leather and wood were also used. It was not until the 1630s, according to Hugh Johnson in *Vintage: The Story of Wine*, that Sir Kenelm Digby, "the father of the modern wine bottle," improved the process of glass bottle making, which made them durable and inexpensive enough to be considered more than a decanter. In the meantime, corks began to be used again after being forgotten since Roman times.

Johnson wrote about a drinks writer, Worlidge, who in his *Treatise of Cider*, published in 1676, described how to handle bottled cider properly. Much of what he wrote could have been applied to wine or Port. Worlidge wrote of the necessity of choosing good corks and soaking them in hot water before inserting them firmly into bottles, and then "lying bottles sideways to be commended, not only for preserving the corks moist, but for that the air that remains in the bottle is on the side of the bottle from which it can neither expire." This suggests that the notion of laying down one's ciders, fine wines and Ports may have started much earlier than the mid-1700s.

The development of the cylindrical bottle would eventually facilitate laying down wines and Ports. According to Margaret Pigott, curator of Harveys Wine Museum in Bristol, England, wine bottles went through five design periods, the name of each period aptly describing the shape of the bottle: shaft and globe, onion, bladder, mallet and finally cylinder. The first of these periods began in the late 1600s and slowly evolved into the cylinder by the 1740s. "With the cylindrical bottles, it was thus now possible to stack several rows of bottles one on top of the other in a horizontal position…vintage wine, unknown since Roman times, was thus rediscovered," Pigott wrote in a John Harvey & Sons price list in 1990.

These straight-side bottles enabled more people to stock wines at home in bottles rather than in casks. British consumers were not allowed by law to buy pre-bottled wines from the mid-17th century to the early 19th century. Since they had to buy wine by the cask, the average person generally consumed wine or Port in pubs or restaurants. Vintage wines were primarily the hobby of the affluent.

In *Vintage: The Story of Wine*, Johnson described well the wine and Port buying habits of the British: "Before the 18th century, the cellar of a house (if it had one) was identical in function with the cellar of an inn. Barrels (in England they would generally be of cider and beer) stayed in them until they were emptied, by daily drawing off. Mansions at first, then rapidly smaller town-houses, manors and farms, adapted their cellars for storing the new bottles. The standard arrangement was open shelving of brick, stone or slate, often vaulted, in 'bins' that held 25 dozen bottles, the contents of a hogshead. To buy a pipe of Port (enough to fill two bins) became almost a convention among country gentlemen with plenty of room in their cellars. Usually the merchant would send two men to bottle the wines in the customer's cellar and lay it down in the bins."

THE BRITISH AND PORT

Port as we know it today would never have come into existence without the British. The Romans probably planted the first vineyards in the Douro Valley, and from the 13th to the 16th century wines were being shipped down river to Oporto and then sold throughout Portugal, to the Dutch and to the British.

But it was the British who brought fame first to the wines of the Douro and subsequently to Port, and their thirst for Port, especially vintage, has lasted for centuries. The history of vintage Port coincides with the development of and changes in the British Port market, since only recently have other countries begun buying vintage Port in any quantities.

In 1678 Britain went to war with France, thus cutting off supplies of the wines the British loved most. Portugal was a devoted ally and trading partner of the British, and the trade in wines from Oporto began in earnest as an alternative to French wines.

Throughout the 17th and 18th centuries, the British demand for Portuguese wines, primarily Port, fluctuated with Great Britain's volatile relationship with France. The worse their rapport became with the French, the better the exports of Port to Britain.

The Methuen Treaty of 1703 is generally regarded as marking the beginning of the Port trade. British diplomat John Methuen negotiated a treaty with Portugal stating that its wines could be imported to his country at two-thirds the tax rate of French wines if certain tariffs on British textiles were relaxed. The significance of this treaty in developing a climate for a brisk trade in Port was not immediately apparent. Thousands of pipes of wines from the Douro Valley and other regions within striking distance of Oporto were being shipped annually well before that date. Moreover, British merchants were already well entrenched in Oporto when the treaty was signed, trading British textiles for such goods as dried codfish, cotton and fruits as well as wines.

The 1720s were a good decade for the Port trade, which grew in strength as exports of wines increased to Great Britain. In 1727 the British merchants in Oporto formed an association or guild — then called a "factory" — in hopes of improving their bargaining power with Portuguese growers and wine brokers. In the late 1730s, prices in Britain began to decline as the wine market softened. Moreover, the Portuguese government had imposed a levy on all Port shipped to Great Britain. The move may have prompted the first substantial shipments to America, because some British merchants circumvented the tax by shipping their wines first to the colonies and then to England.

By the 1750s the Port business was extremely depressed. British merchants in Oporto began to complain about the quality of wines they were buying as a way to vent their frustration. Their association wrote an open letter to the growers explaining that they would not buy any more wine unless the quality improved. A copy of the correspondence fell into the hands of the Marquês de Pombal, who as a consequence established the Old Wine Co. The British merchants had shot themselves in the foot. Not only was the Port market in England and other parts of the United Kingdom depressed, the British now had to buy their wines and later their brandy at fixed prices from the Portuguese government.

Although the British were unhappy with the arrangement, the establishment of the Old Wine Co. in 1756 gave rise to the first demarcation of the Douro Valley for wine production. The region was divided into two wine areas: the *ramo* for Portuguese and Brazilian consumption and the *freitoria* for export to other markets. The Old Wine Co. had powers similar to those of today's Instituto do Vinho do Porto and the Casa do Douro, controlling nearly all aspects of viticulture, winemaking and sales. In 1761 it took over the monopoly for brandy sales to the trade.

For the next four decades, the Port trade grappled with maintaining its market in Great Britain. Annual shipments varied from 25,000 pipes to 50,000 pipes (3.47 million to 6.94 million gallons). Prices remained stable in both Portugal and Britain. By the end of the 18th century, most of the leading names in vintage Port were well established: Warre, Croft, Taylor, Sandeman, Offley Forrester, Kopke, van Zeller and Burmester. All were prosperous traders in Ports as well as in textiles and various agricultural products.

By this time, some foreign shippers had already bought *quintas* up the Douro, starting a tradition of owning key vineyards in the region that has continued today. Job Bearsley, who founded the firm of Taylor, Fladgate & Yeatman, was the first, buying in 1744 Casa dos Alambiques at Salgueiral near the village of Regua in the Baixo Corgo. The property still belongs to Taylor, which runs a vinification center there. Quinta do Roriz was another property owned by foreigners, and Kopke bought the estate in 1760 after its Scottish owner went bankrupt.

In addition, many British shippers had gained the respect of the Portuguese by this time, and they were no longer viewed simply as opportunists taking wealth and goods away from Portugal. Joseph James Forrester exemplified this new breed of British wine merchant. He spoke fluent Portuguese and enjoyed the company of both peasant and nobleman. He was even made a baron by the Portuguese monarchy. Working for the house of Offley Forrester, he was a man of many talents who could paint beautiful watercolors of the region, draw detailed maps of the Douro and write eloquent papers on the Port trade. He was most famous for his pamphlet called *A Word or Two About Port*, in which he condemned the Port trade for promoting the fortification of wines from the Douro. He viewed this as the corruption of a wine that he believed had the potential to be as fine a table wine as those from Bordeaux or Burgundy.

Forrester came to Oporto in 1831, and had a great influence on the Port trade until his death in May 1861. He died during a visit to one of the period's other great characters, Dona Antónia Ferreira, the Portuguese "empress of the Douro" who owned thousands of acres of vineyards. Forrester drowned after his boat capsized in rapids west of Quinta de Vargellas and Quinta do Vesùvio, and it is said that he was carrying a money belt full of gold coins to pay farmers, which pulled him down to the bottom of the murky Douro River. His body was never found. Ferreira and her friend Baroness Fladgate survived the disaster; according to folklore, their crinolines kept them afloat.

THE FACTORY HOUSE

Located in Oporto just across the bridge to Vila Nova de Gaia, the Factory House stands as a monument to the perseverance and dedication of the British Port trade. Its Georgian exterior was completed in 1790 under the guidance of British consul John Whitehead, although the handful of British merchants had already formed the British Factory of Merchants nearly a century before. "Factory" comes from the British usage of the word factor, meaning merchant. Members used to meet in the street where the Factory House stands today to discuss business. That street later became the Rua Nova dos Inglezes, or the new street of the English. It is now called the Rua do Infante Dom Henrique.

The Factory House was built using funds from two self-imposed levies on British merchants: one on Port exports and the other on goods imported. The British only enjoyed the use of their superbly constructed granite building from 1790 to 1807, because most of the British fled Portugal in 1807 after the French, under Napoleon's Marshall Soult, took control of Lisbon. In March 1809, the French captured Oporto and the Factory House. Two months later, the British recaptured Oporto, but the Factory House was not reinstated as the center of the British Port trade for another two years. At one point during this period, the Factory even functioned as a coffee house. On Nov. 11, 1811, a dinner was held to celebrate the reopening of the Factory House, and in June 1990 the grand old mansion commemorated its 200th anniversary.

"There were once British factories all over the world," said David Delaforce, whose father, John, wrote the definitive history of the Factory House in his book *The Factory House*. "It is the only factory that is still serving in the world. It is unique."

The Factory House has remained relatively unchanged for nearly two centuries although the British Association replaced the Factory of Merchants in 1814. There was a failed attempt to change its "British Port shippers only" membership requirements in 1825, and the building itself survived cannon fire during the Portuguese Civil War in the late 1820s and early 1830s.

The current member firms are Churchill Graham, Cockburn, Croft, Delaforce, W. & J. Graham, Fonseca-Guimaraens, Martinez Gassiot, Robertson Brothers (Rebello Valente), Sandeman, Silva & Cosens (Dow), Taylor and Warre. Offley Forrester, which was once a member, is now owned by Martini & Rossi, and no longer qualifies. Sandeman and Robertson, owned by Canadian drinks giant Seagram, only remain members because the majority of their shares are held in Britain.

The Factory House hasn't changed much since Henry Vizetelly visited in 1876. In his book published in 1880, *Facts About Port and Madeira*, he wrote that the Factory House "of recent years seems to have subsided into a kind of sleepy club, limited to a very few members, but liberally provided with English newspapers and magazines."

CONTINUED SUCCESS

By the mid-19th century the Port trade had a stable business with Great Britain, with shipments averaging between 20,000 and 25,000 pipes (2.77 million and 3.47 million gallons) per year. New houses had been established — Graham, Guimaraens, Cockburn and Dow, which merged with Silva & Cosens in 1877 — all catering to a growing demand in Britain for wines with "colour! colour! colour!" as T.G. Shaw wrote in *Wine, the Vine and the Cellar.*

There were some great vintages during this period, which could be described as the Golden Age for vintage Ports. The good to great years included 1847, 1851, 1853, 1854, 1858, 1859, 1863, 1868, 1870, 1871, 1872, 1873, 1875 and 1878. The 1878 was the last great vintage before the root louse phylloxera devastated the Douro. George Saintsbury tasted and chronicled many of these vintages in his book: "The much talked-about 1820 I do not think that I ever drank *securus*, that is to say, under circumstance which assured its being genuine. Some '34, with such a guarantee, I have drunk, and more '47, the latter from when it was about in perfection (say, in 1870) to date the other day when it was some 60 years old and little but a memory, or at least a suggestion. But '51 in all its phases, dry, rich and medium, was, I think, such a wine as deserved the famous and *pios encomum* (slightly altered) saying that the Almighty might no doubt have caused a better wine to exist, but that he never did."

What brought the end of this series of excellent vintages was the same culprit that lay waste to Bordeaux, Burgundy, Champagne and the rest of Europe's vineyards. Phylloxera arrived in Portugal in the late 1860s, and by 1871 it had been identified in the Douro Valley. The region had already been under attack from oidium, a fungus that primarily affects the foliage of the vine. The phylloxera louse, which destroys the root system of the vine, was a far more lethal pest. According to George Robertson in *Port*, "By 1881, the Port shippers were predicting the end of the Port trade; the entire production of that year amounted to some 6,000 pipes in an area planted to produce 250,000 pipes" (of Port and table wine).

As in France and the rest of Europe, growers in the Douro found that through planting American vines and then grafting the European *Vitis vinifera* onto them, they could combat the phylloxera. By the late 1880s, most of the key vineyard sites up the Douro were either replanted or in the process of being rejuvenated. Some terraces, nonetheless, were never replanted, and these skeleton vineyard sites, still evident today, bear witness to the difficulty of the period.

Nonetheless, there were some good vintages in the 1890s, such as 1890, 1896 and 1897. Saintsbury was extremely impressed with the 1890 and wrote that " '51, '70 and '90 supplied the three best Ports I have ever had." But there is something special about the vintage Ports produced before phylloxera. Like the great wines of Bordeaux and Burgundy from the same period, some of these vintage Ports are still amazingly youthful and powerful. It is difficult to say why they are so superior in quality, and perhaps such great modern vintages as 1963 or 1977 will eventually equal or best 1868, 1870 and 1878.

THE TURN OF THE CENTURY

As Port shippers welcomed the 20th century, business was going well and new export records were being set. World War I had some effect on business, since shipments to Great Britain were limited to 50 percent of those before the war, but shippers remained bullish. They had three excellent vintages to sell — 1900, 1904 and 1908. In addition, the opening decade of the 1900s may have been the beginning of the selective shipping of a vintage based on its quality. From the 1900 vintage onward, Port houses began to declare fewer vintages — about three to four per decade — an average continued to this day.

At this time two- and three-year bottlings became the industry standard. According to Ernest Cockburn in *Port Wine and Oporto*, "In olden times 'Vintage Port' was not seen as it is known to-day, as it was then the practice to sell it bottled in the autumn of the third year of its existence after it had been shipped to the United Kingdom in the second autumn. It is doubtful whether it became the general practice to bottle it during the second autumn much before the early 1890s." Many more Port houses had gained control of their key *quintas* for vintage Ports by this time. The shipper-owned wine estates included Taylor's Quinta de Vargellas, Dow's Quinta do Bomfim, Croft's Quinta da Roêda, Graham's Quinta dos Malvedos and A.J. da Silva's Quinta do Noval.

In 1916 Port became popular in pubs when taxes were raised on spirits. The drink of Port and lemonade came into fashion. Sandeman was the only shipper to declare 1911, to commemorate the coronation of George V; although I have seen Croft 1911 in Christie's auctions. The 1911 Sandeman is still good today. The 1912 vintage is far better, producing outstanding wines. Some, such as the 1912 Cockburn, are still classics today, with wonderfully elegant fruit flavors and a tight finish. Other declared vintages were 1917 and 1919.

The decade of the 1920s was, for the most part, a buoyant period for the world, and the Port trade also prospered. But when the Depression hit in 1929, Port had already fallen slightly out of fashion and had been relegated to merely an after-dinner drink. Even vintage Port was becoming hard to sell, and while there were some good vintages declared, such as 1920, 1922 and 1924, the market could only absorb so much.

When shippers declared the fabulous 1927 in 1929, many of their wine merchant clients in Britain were wondering where they were going to sell the wines. To make things worse, 1927 was perhaps the largest first-class vintage ever produced. Many houses made more than 40,000 cases of the 1927. Not only did the 1927 lay to waste the rule that vintage Port was always a limited product, it presented the wine trade with a problem. Many wine merchants had to hold large stocks of the 1927, so cellars along the Thames River near the Tower of London were full, as were those in the city. Some merchants even decided to use part of their 1927s as components in their blended wood Ports.

The outstanding quality of the 1931 vintage complicated the situation, and with plenty of stocks of 1927 still on the market, few shippers could bear declaring another vintage. The exceptions were Quinta do Noval, Rebello Valente and Burmester. Noval made its reputation on its 1931, of which it made about 100 pipes (13,800 gallons). Since then, Noval has been considered the equal of nearly all the British houses. Burmester and Rebello Valente never rose as high. Other houses had bigger problems than deciding whether to declare a vintage in the mid-1930s. Some were not financially strong enough to weather the difficult market, and firms like Feuerheerd, Hutcheson and Tuke Holdsworth were sold to other houses.

In 1933 the Portuguese government decided to regulate Port again, and established three organizations to oversee the trade: the Instituto do Vinho do Porto, the Casa do Douro, and the Gremio dos Exportadores do Vinho do Porto. The system remains two-thirds unchanged today. The IVP controls the production and marketing of Port, while the Casa do Douro handles viticulture and represents the 28,000 growers in the Douro. The Gremio was abolished in 1974, although the Port shippers created the Associção dos Exportadores do Vinho do Porto, or the Port Shippers Association to look after their interests. The most important function of the IVP and Casa do Douro is to set the level of Port production and prices for grapes each harvest.

The Port market was still slightly depressed when the excellent split vintages of 1934 and 1935 were declared. Wyndham Fletcher described the situation in his book *Port*: "The 1935 vintage was offered in 1937, but interest was very patchy. Half the trade had already offered the 1934s and stocks of older vintage Port were enormous. Little did we know that within four or five years most of this wine would either be bombed out of existence or drunk as wood Port, in default of anything else available."

The demand for vintage may have been light, but the overall Port market showed some signs of recovery in the late 1930s. Other markets, such as France and Belgium, were developing. Even Americans were buying Port, although in tiny amounts compared to European markets. A positive change in the United Kingdom wine trade did help some houses. British Customs & Excise altered the rules for bottling in the late 1930s, allowing shippers themselves to bottle in bond. This caused many Port houses with offices and cellars in London to bottle and store vintages themselves if demand was light — which was the case with 1935.

The start of World War II brought a quick halt to the increase in Port shipments to most European markets. Britain was still the main market for Port, but the British found Port a luxury they did not need during the war. Moreover, many of the shippers themselves went off to war, and the trade remained very quiet. Some houses in Vila Nova de Gaia were open only a few days a week. It was much livelier in London, however, and some shippers' offices there, such as Cockburn Smithes, were damaged or destroyed in bomb raids. There were stories about streams of 1927, 1934 and 1935 vintage Port running down the streets near the London Bridge as warehouses full of Port were hit by the bombing raids.

Fletcher wrote that some houses, such as Cockburn, shipped stocks of Port to America in case Hitler invaded Portugal. These stocks would have acted as a basis to rebuild their business if Gaia was destroyed. This, of course, never happened, but these stocks may have helped develop the American market for Port after the war. World War II also encouraged Oporto bottling since the British government imposed an import quota from 1944 to 1949. Most wine merchants were not interested in using their import quotas for vintage Port, so the shippers themselves bottled the excellent war vintages of 1942 and 1945 and held them for the trade. Fletcher also wrote that the quota system required an "identifying mark on the bottle and the first Cockburn label was therefore designed. When things got back to normal these labels were supplied for wine in bulk."

After the war and the end of the quota system, the Port market remained stable at best. Shipments never climbed back to pre-war levels, although there was some interest in old stocks of vintage Port for a period. According to William Warre of Symington Port Shippers, the demand was so great for older vintage Port at one point just after the war that they shipped reserve wines that had been held back for family consumption. This is why vintage Ports from undeclared years, like 1944 Dow or 1943 Sandeman, can sometimes be found on the market. The rest of the Port market was depressed. According to Fletcher, "There was no new business…we spent our time examining stock; in other words tasting through our old vintage Ports."

It was a difficult market for more than 15 years after the war. Many firms simply could not recuperate from the lost business during the war, even though many managed to make some excellent vintage Port in 1947 and 1948. Most even declared the lighter but useful 1950. Some houses just could not carry on, however, and were sold, like Guimaraens in 1948 and Morgan in 1952. Others merged with competitors; Smith Woodhouse joined W. & J. Graham. Many simply went out of business, like Hunt Roope. Well-established Port families such as the Yeatmans of Taylor and the Symingtons of Silva & Cosens and Warre were barely hanging on by the end of the 1950s. "It was difficult to hold things together at the time," recalled Ian Symington, whose family now controls Graham, Dow (Silva & Cosens) and Warre, among others. "We were simply trying to survive."

Most houses declared the 1955, but it was almost impossible to sell. Few firms offered

1958, even though the wines were perfectly good. Former managing director John Smithes of Cockburn said they still had too much 1955 unsold to consider declaring the 1958. Fonseca's Bruce Guimaraens remembered the late 1950s: "We didn't declare 1958 because in those days you couldn't give vintage Port away." To make the situation worse, the IVP announced in 1959 that Port shippers had to have a stock ratio of three to one, meaning for every cask shipped a house needed two in its cellar. Shippers were scrambling to acquire stocks and many further extended themselves financially to stay in business.

There was some relief in the 1960s, but prices were still low. Most shippers declared the 1960 vintage, and the sublime 1963 followed; however, they were both difficult to sell. The British market was still primarily interested in private label (buyer's-own-brand Port) and vintage Port had failed to increase in price. About this time, however, France and other continental markets began to open up. By 1963 France had bypassed Britain as the number one export market, and total Port shipments reached about 3.3 million cases. As is still true today, France and Belgium primarily drank Port as an apéritif, so they preferred light Ports such as tawnies. They certainly were not interested in the excellent vintage Port declarations of 1963, 1966 and 1967.

Regardless of the improvements in the market, the 1960s were another period of mergers and sellouts of various houses. This decade also was the beginning of large drinks companies buying into Port, although wine and spirits merchants Gilbey had done so with Croft in 1910. Wine merchants John Harvey & Sons of Bristol, which would later become part of Allied Lyons, bought Cockburn and Martinez Gassiot in the early 1960s, while in 1962 Croft joined United Wine Traders, which later became International Distillers and Vintners, now part of Grand Metropolitan. Delaforce sold to the same group in 1968. Even Graham could not persevere and sold to the Symingtons in 1970. "It was a bad time," recalled Taylor's Robertson. "By the late 1960s, nearly everyone (family-run British houses) was gone, with the exception of the Symingtons and ourselves."

Although there were some positive moments in the 1960s, such as the declarations of the excellent 1963 and 1966 vintages, it was not until the early 1970s that business picked up. "It was (with) the 1970 vintage that there was a spark," said Robertson. "Only suddenly we were clobbered on the head with the revolution and oil crisis." Many shippers say that the Portuguese revolution was not a trying time for the Port trade, and it was business as usual, but according to Fernando van Zeller, who was the head of the Port Shippers Association in 1974 and 1975, "The Port trade was very close to being nationalized. I saw the papers on the minister's desk waiting to be signed. If it was not for the British, the entire trade would have been nationalized."

Only one company, Real Companhia Velha, was directly nationalized, although the revolution had a more profound effect on vintage Port. It was at this time that mandatory Oporto bottling for vintage Port was put into effect. Vintage Port had always been shipped in cask, except during the 1940s, but with the stroke of a bureaucratic pen, that tradition was finished. The mid-1970s were also difficult for Port shippers after it was revealed that most of the 1972, 1973 and 1974 Ports were fortified with synthetic alcohol (see Chapter III), but as a whole, most Port shippers were glad to be in business still when the 1970s came to a close.

Another impact of the volatile 1970s was an increased interest in vintage Port in America. During the oil crisis in the early 1970s, some of the major wine merchants and drinks groups in Britain decided to sell their stocks of vintage Ports at auction to raise cash. Wines from years like 1963 and 1966 were sold at about £10 to £15 ($18 to $27) a case. Many of the buyers were small merchants with clients in America, and large shipments of vintage Ports were re-exported to the United States and Canada. "I am sure that this opened up America to vintage Port," said Port shipper James Symington.

THE 1980S AND THE FUTURE

After decades of trials and tribulations, Port shippers found themselves in a boom period in the 1980s. In the first five years of the decade, world shipments for all Port increased 26 percent from 6.8 million cases to 8.6 million. By 1986, sales had more than doubled 1975's figure of 4.2 million cases. Everyone was buying more Port, from the French and Belgians in their bistros to the British and Germans in their pubs and bars. The Europeans accounted for more than 90 percent of all Port consumption, with the French drinking more than one in every three bottles sold. Said John Burnett, managing director of Croft, in 1987, "We feel very confident in Port. Against all the odds — anti-alcohol, taxes and many others — Port is growing healthily."

It was not until 1989 that world Port shipments declined, but only slightly. Exports dropped about 2 percent to 7.81 million cases, while the domestic market fell 4 percent to 1.2 million. A large part of the decline was due to price increases and a general move by the Port trade to upgrade the image of its product in some markets. In addition, some shippers attempted to reduce their sales of bulk Port, meaning Port exported in container and then bottled by the buyer. In isolated instances such moves have worked, but consumers in France, Belgium and Holland still view Port as nothing more than a cheap apéritif, buying primarily on price. Premium products such as mature tawnies and vintage Ports are virtually unknown in these markets.

Sales of vintage Port still rely on two markets, Britain and the United States. Americans have become some of the most ardent drinkers of vintage Port — often to the dismay of the British. Said British Port shipper David Sandeman in 1985, "God forbid when the Americans start buying more vintage Port than the British, but it will probably happen one day."

Americans are already on the march. In 1987 and 1988, when most of the 1985 vintage was sold, the United States imported 76,600 cases of vintage while the British bought 104,700. American demand is still behind, but the increase in shipments of vintage Port is significant when comparing figures for the 1983 vintage: in 1985 and 1986, the U.S. market imported 51,400 cases while the British bought 150,900. Americans prefer vintage Port, which accounts for one of every three bottles of Port shipped there. In addition, the U.S. market for all types of Port has grown immensely, from 36,000 cases in 1981 to 129,000 in 1988. Demand is still tiny compared to France, which imported 3.15 million cases of Port in 1988, but it is a market to be reckoned with.

Other markets have slowly continued to trade up to vintage and other premium Ports. It is not uncommon now to be offered a glass of vintage Port at a Michelin one- or two-star restaurant in France, Belgium or Germany when the Cognac and Armagnac is rolled out. "Before the 1980s, vintage Port was a one-country market," said Taylor's Robertson. "It still is a very serious product. Nothing changed that, but now more people are becoming more affluent and they are now prepared to spend money on fine table wine and vintage Port. With the 1980s, vintage Port was a serious classic wine in the same context as the great wines of France."

The growing demand for premium Ports, including vintage, aged tawnies and fine rubies, has prompted many shippers to strive for better quality in all their Ports. Programs to increase vineyard planting in the Cima Corgo with financial backing from the World Bank and the European Economic Community (discussed further in Chapter II) should improve the supply of first-class wines. Some say their vintage Port production could increase 20 percent to 30 percent. In addition, many houses have been investing in technology and improving their methods to enhance the quality of their wines. "People are more confident now," said Ben Howkins of Taylor Fladgate in London, author of *Rich, Rare and Red*. "Before, they just sold their Ports and hoped for the best. Now, people are in better control and they have a good long-term view."

CHAPTER II

THE VINEYARD:
UP THE DOURO

It is hard to imagine that anything can grow in the Upper Douro Valley, the source of vintage Port. It is one of the most difficult wine-producing regions in the world. The climate is tough and uncertain. Weather forecasts are usually of little use. Summers are blistering hot, with temperatures often reaching above 110 degrees, while in winter it can get well below zero. A warm summer day may bring a disastrous hail storm, and the usually wet winter may be as dry as a desert.

The Douro's terrain is almost lunar in its ruggedness and desolation. The soil is a hard, schistous type, similar to some of West Germany's slate vineyards along the Rhine and Mosel rivers. It retains little water and offers few nutrients, amplifying the cold of winter and the heat of summer. When the soil crumbles, it becomes a fine powder that can choke those working in the vineyards. Most of the vineyard work is still done by hand, although mechanization is increasing.

Settlements of any sort are sparse. The handful that do exist could be compared to American boom towns at the turn of the century, consisting of nothing more than a post office and a few dusty bars, rustic restaurants and poorly stocked stores.

Transportation and communication are limited at best. It takes two hours to travel 30 to 40 miles by car along bumpy asphalt roads. Even on a good day, telephoning Oporto from the heart of the Upper Douro can take hours. International calls can take days. The single-track train, which travels up and down the valley a few times a day, takes more than three hours to reach the village of Pinhão from Oporto. The rather grimy train cars are usually filled with peasants returning from shopping in the gray city of Oporto. Port shippers are found at the head of the train in the slightly more civilized first-class section.

Growing vines in sections of the Upper Douro is like trying to establish vineyards in parts of America's Grand Canyon. But somehow vines flourish along the steeply terraced banks of the Douro River and its various tributaries.

Port producers often joke about the difficulty of the region, but usually with a certain reverence. Growing vines and making wine here are a challenge every day, taxing both the mind and body.

"In its virginal state, it is impossible to think something can grow here. It really is another world," said David Sandeman, chairman of the Port house bearing his family's name, as he overlooked new plantings at one of his properties, Quinta do Vau, in late 1989.

The extreme conditions of the region produce a hardy determination in its inhabitants, in everyone from peasant farmers to university-trained vineyard managers and enologists. "It is a tough place to be," said Bruce Guimaraens, who oversees production at Taylor and Fonseca. "But I am dedicated to quality. I would do anything for a few pipes of top-quality Port."

THE DOURO VALLEY

The official Douro Valley region encompasses about 617,500 acres in northeastern Portugal. Its current boundaries were established in 1921, although the Portuguese began demarcating the area as early as 1756. Some say it was the first officially demarcated wine region in the world.

The Douro Valley begins about 50 miles up river from Oporto, near the town of Barqueiros just west of Regua, and carries on eastward for another 65 miles to the Spanish border at Barca d'Alva. The Douro River, or River of Gold, flows through the center of the region, from the Spanish province of León to the Atlantic at Oporto. About 75 percent of the 560-mile-long Douro River flows through Spain, where it influences fine winemaking in the regions of Ribera del Duero and Rueda. Ribera del Duero is particularly well known for the fine red wines made at the properties of Vega Sicilia and Pesquera.

Once a fierce and treacherous river, the Douro was used for about a century to transport wine and other goods by large sailboats, or *barcos rabelos*. A series of hydroelectric dams built in the late 1950s has tamed the river, and it is no longer a vital transportation route. But the murky, brown, silt-laden Douro plays an irreplaceable role in creating the microclimates unique to the Douro Valley.

Some growers believe the dams, which have raised the height of the river, have slightly increased the temperature and humidity in the valley. Photographs taken before the dams were built show the river level 100 to 200 feet lower in many places; its waters now cover many good vineyard sites.

About 13.2 percent of the Douro Valley, or about 81,510 acres, is under vine, according to figures from the Instituto do Vinho do Porto. The area is divided into three subregions — the Baixo Corgo, Cima Corgo and Douro Superior. The Baixo Corgo is the smallest, with 111,150 acres. About one-third is planted to vines, and about 46 percent of the Douro's total vineyards are found here. The Cima Corgo is larger in total area, with 234,650 acres. About 14 percent is planted to vines, and the area accounts for about 40 percent of the total vineyards. The Douro Superior is the largest subregion, with 271,700 acres. Only 4.4 percent is planted, representing 14.5 percent of the total.

The annual wine production of the Douro Valley averages approximately 1.37 million hectoliters, or 15.2 million nine-liter cases of wine. Port makes up an average of 65 percent of the production, the remainder being table wines. The government strictly regulates the yield of Port, setting a production quota a few months before each harvest.

Traditionally, the best wines — vintage Ports in particular — have come from the Cima Corgo and Douro Superior. All of the top-quality *quintas*, or vineyard estates, are there. The best region in the Cima Corgo is near the village of Pinhão, about 80 miles east of Oporto. There are more great vineyards here than anywhere else in the Cima Corgo.

One of the best parts of this region is in the Pinhão Valley. This area is to Port what Pauillac is to claret. Here the tiny Pinhão River flows southward to meet the Douro River. There are dozens of outstanding *quintas* along this small tributary, including Quinta do Cruzeiro and Quinta do Santo António, which produce Fonseca; Quinta de Terra Feita, which goes into Taylor; Quinta da Cavadinha, the backbone of Warre; and Quinta do Noval.

If the Pinhão Valley is Pauillac, the Rio Torto is Margaux. Most Port shippers agree that this winding valley on the south bank of the Douro River about a mile from Pinhão makes equally great wines. Vintage Ports such as Graham and Croft are made primarily from *quintas* here.

There are some other areas that produce great wines, such as the Ribalonga and Tua and the region near Quinta de Vargellas and Quinta do Vesùvio. Even *quintas* along the river lowlands near the village of Pinhão, terrain not traditionally successful in quality Port production, make excellent wines.

THE ROLE OF THE QUINTA

Regardless of its location, it is the *quinta* — the vineyard estate — that gives serious vintage Port its character. There are more than 83,000 different vineyards sites in the Douro Valley registered with the government, and about 28,000 growers. Not all produce Port, and even fewer make wines good enough for vintage Port.

The average Douro winemaker makes less than 12 pipes (1,600 gallons) of Port each year. This may be part of the huge production of one of numerous Douro cooperatives — an association of growers who share winery facilities — or the crop may be sold to larger vintners as grapes, must or finished Port. Some of these *quintas*, however, do make outstanding Ports, good enough to be used for vintage in a first-class year. These *quintas* are wine estates just like the great châteaux of Bordeaux or the legendary domaines of Burgundy. Nearly all the great *quintas* have ties with certain houses. These include Quinta do Bomfim (Dow), Quinta do Cruzeiro (Fonseca), Quinta do Noval, Quinta dos Malvedos (Graham) and Quinta de Vargellas (Taylor).

These *quintas* may encompass anything from a dozen acres to several hundred, and their wines serve as the backbones of vintage Port blends. Many also represent the source of single-*quinta* vintage Ports, which are made in undeclared years. A *quinta*'s entire production may not be used in a house's vintage blend. Only the best wines are selected for a vintage lot in a declared year. Wines from some sections of the vineyards at a large *quinta* like Vargellas or Noval may not be good enough to go into a vintage lot. This could be due to the youth of the vines or to an inferior microclimate or soil type.

"The *quintas* are where the style of our vintage Ports comes from," said Alistair Robertson, majority shareholder and head of Taylor Fladgate and Fonseca. "There is no doubt that the style of Taylor comes from Vargellas and Terra Feita, and Fonseca comes from Cruzeiro and Santo António. Mostly by luck, we have been able to buy the major *quintas* that have been the backbones of our vintage. So it is very tidy."

Other key vintage Port producers have only recently managed to buy important estates. For instance, Sandeman paid $3.5 million for 195-acre Quinta do Vau in mid-1988, while Cockburn bought Quinta dos Canais in late 1989 for $2.6 million. Both companies agreed that buying these properties was essential to secure quality grapes for their best wines. Prestige was another reason for the rush to buy *quintas* in the late 1980s.

"It is important for a quality Port shipper to have a property in the Douro," said José Teles Dias da Silva, the young managing director of Osborne who in 1990 still did not own a *quinta*. "We are rather young in the trade and we need to make a statement about our dedication to quality. We will find a property to buy one day."

These *quintas* are much more than simple vineyard sites. Most include production facilities as well as accommodations for workers, owners and guests. Some *quintas*, such as the grandiose Quinta do Vesùvio, have extensive plantings of olive trees, fruit and nut orchards and vegetable gardens. Farm animals are also raised at many *quintas*.

The everyday life at a *quinta* centers around the main house on the property. Many of these stone and timber buildings resemble something one might have found a hundred years ago on plantations in any number of countries. The exteriors, with shaded verandas and elegant courtyards, are as well kept as the pristine sitting rooms and guest bedrooms. Some, such as Quinta de Vargellas, are temples to public relations. Its owners proudly liken it to a French chalet, although Vargellas is more reminiscent of some elegantly designed winery in California's Napa Valley — complete with swimming pool, lavish dining room and tastefully decorated guest rooms.

Such grandeur is rare in the Douro, however. Most of the 28,000 growers in the region own only an acre or two of vineyards, making a meager living out of growing grapes.

The growers are essential to the Port trade, since most major shippers only have enough vineyards to cover about one-tenth of their total production. Shippers have contracts — usually verbal — with dozens of different growers to buy their must or Port production. Growers remain incredibly loyal to Port shippers and often sell grapes, must or wine to a particular shipper for generations. "We have a grower in the Ribalonga area that has been supplying us with wine for over 200 years," said John Burnett, managing director of Croft.

There is always discussion among shippers about where they bought a particular wine or what they think of a certain grower. They remain rather cagey, not wanting to give away too much information. Although it seldom happens, a grower may switch to another shipper. Port houses are continually trying to lure away competitors' growers, even though they may have been selling to the same house for decades. Others simply try to buy them out, a practice very common in the late 1980s. "All that does is raise the prices for all of us," said Burnett. "A grower will generally stay with a shipper as long as they are given the same offer."

The amount of growers' wines used in vintage Port varies from house to house. Noval and Offley use only wine from their own *quintas*, while Sandeman bought all of its wines until 1988. Small, super-premium houses like Niepoort and Burmester still buy everything, although Niepoort purchased *quintas* in 1989. Taylor and Fonseca supply 80 percent to 85 percent of the grapes for their vintage lots from their own *quintas*. "You have to supply most of your own grapes for your vintage. How else can you guarantee the quality of your vintage?" said Cristiano van Zeller, head of Quinta do Noval.

REGULATED PORT CROP

The quantity and price of grapes for Port are strictly set each year before the harvest by a governmental organization, the Instituto do Vinho do Porto. The Port harvest averages between 8.5 and 9 million cases. In 1989, prices ranged from $625 per ton (100 escudos per kilo) to $940 per ton (150 escudos per kilo) for the best quality.

The production and prices are set according to the classification of the vineyard, which can range from A to F. This ranking is carried out by another quasi-governmental institution, the Casa do Douro, which oversees all matters concerning viticulture in the Douro and is also the association for growers in the Douro. In late July 1990, the Casa do Douro also bought a 40 percent interest in the Port house of Real Companhia Velha. A and B vineyards are considered the best quality and are the source of vintage and other premium Ports. Grapes from such vineyards receive the best prices. Official permits, or *cartões*, are issued for each *quinta*, stating how many liters of grape must may be made into Port per 1,000 vines. The amount changes each vintage, but on average A and B are allowed to produce 600 liters of Port, C and D vineyards can make 550 liters, and E vineyards are permitted 500 liters. Vineyards with F ratings are usually not authorized to make Port. Since vineyards up the Douro can make between 500 to 1,650 liters of wine per 1,000 vines, growers may also produce a large amount of table wine as well as Port. According to Croft's Burnett, an A or B vineyard makes about one pipe of wine per 1,000 vines, while lower-ranked vineyards in the Baixo Corgo produce around three pipes.

Shippers normally must buy both the grower's table wine and his Port. This is less of a burden with A or B vineyards, since their yields are extremely low, while their counterparts with D classifications and young vines might make 60 percent table wine. Most of this wine is sold to merchants who need cheap table wines for the domestic market, although a few shippers, such as Ferreira, Ramos-Pinto, Cockburn and Sandeman, have been making and bottling good table wines from this excess production. In addition, Quinta do Noval and the Symington group have been experimenting with making table wines.

Vineyards must meet various minimum requirements to receive a classification. For example, vineyards situated at more than 600 meters in elevation or less than five years old will not be considered. After a vineyard meets these prerequisites, 12 criteria are reviewed to make the ranking. Each criterion is given a numerical score, or *ficha cadastral*, which can be positive or negative. The maximum total is 1,630 points. The criteria include productivity (150 points), altitude (120), soil composition (100), location (600), pruning and training methods (100), vine types and rootstock (150), degree of slope (100), exposure (50), vine density and spacing (50), rock type (80), shelter (60), and age of vines (70).

Vineyards awarded more than 1,200 points receive A ratings, and the ratings descend in alphabetical rank every 200 points. F is the lowest ranking, for vineyards receiving fewer than 400 points. Nearly all the A and B vineyards are in the Cima Corgo and Douro Superior.

Recent developments and improvements in viticulture and enology have brought the classification's validity into question. Most Port producers believe it is basically correct but that the ranking system needs updating to take these changes into account. The classification system has been controversial since it began in 1947. Receiving a poor classification means producing less Port and making less money, since table wine is sold at substantially lower prices than Port. Perhaps more importantly, some vintners believe that the ranking is inaccurate and does not reflect the true quality of the vineyards. For example, Cockburn's nearly 4,000 acres of vineyards in the valley of Vilarica in the Douro Superior are rated C, "but we think it is A-B quality," said Miguel Corte Real Gomes of Cockburn. "It is all planted by variety and we know we can make very good vintage-quality wines here." Moreover, the system simply does not provide enough quality Port for the trade. Why should a grower with an A classification be limited to making only 60 percent of his harvest into Port?

The problem is compounded in short vintages like 1988. This has led many vintners to stretch their authorizations, creating a virtual black market for permits. Some growers sell

THE DUORO VALLEY

The following maps outline the officially demarcated Port regions of the Duoro Valley. The three sub-regions—Baixo Corgo, Cima Corgo and Douro Superior are highlighted.

MAP LEGEND

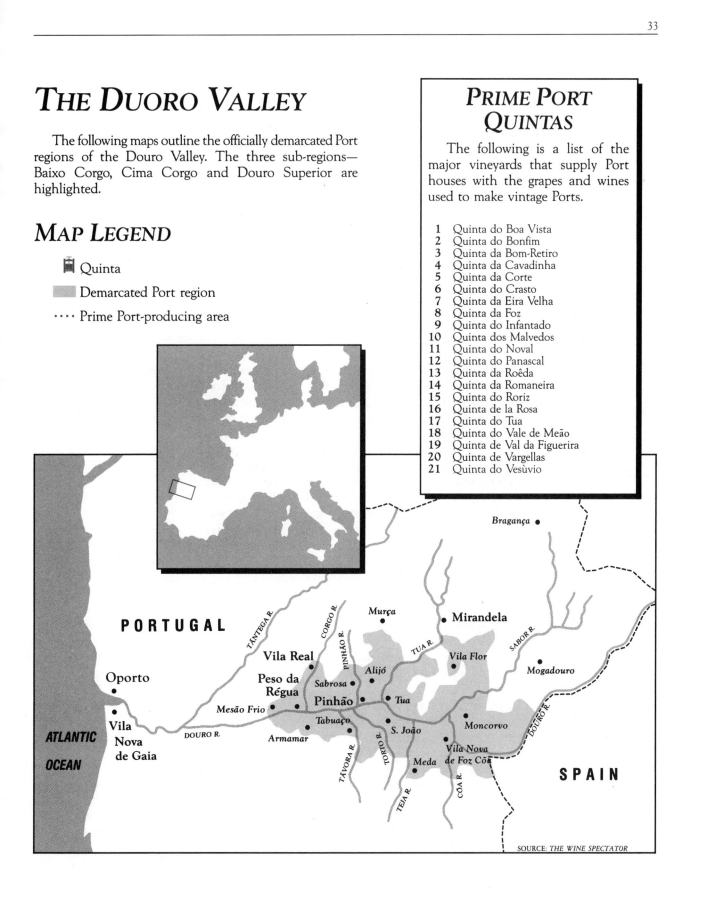

Quinta

Demarcated Port region

Prime Port-producing area

PRIME PORT QUINTAS

The following is a list of the major vineyards that supply Port houses with the grapes and wines used to make vintage Ports.

1 Quinta do Boa Vista
2 Quinta do Bonfim
3 Quinta da Bom-Retiro
4 Quinta da Cavadinha
5 Quinta da Corte
6 Quinta do Crasto
7 Quinta da Eira Velha
8 Quinta da Foz
9 Quinta do Infantado
10 Quinta dos Malvedos
11 Quinta do Noval
12 Quinta do Panascal
13 Quinta da Roêda
14 Quinta da Romaneira
15 Quinta do Roriz
16 Quinta de la Rosa
17 Quinta do Tua
18 Quinta do Vale de Meão
19 Quinta de Val da Figueira
20 Quinta de Vargellas
21 Quinta do Vesùvio

SOURCE: *THE WINE SPECTATOR*

their permits, while others take the authorization for one *quinta* and use it for the surplus production of another. "At the moment, something to the effect of 15 percent of the total production of Port is top-notch. We are always competing for the best wines," said Jeremy Bull, a consulting winemaker for Cálem who was formerly with Taylor.

"In the end you want more licenses to make more Port," added Bruce Guimaraens. "We cannot find enough quality wines to fill the demand. In the Douro, it is all a matter of licenses."

WORLD BANK PLANTINGS

New plantings in the Cima Corgo and Douro Superior coming into production in the 1990s should help the situation. Under a scheme financed through the World Bank, each grower could qualify to plant up to 24 acres of vineyards with financing at rates 3 percent to 4 percent lower than those commercially available in Portugal. The terms were for 16 years.

The program began in 1982, offering about $10 million in loans. The new plantings total about 6,000 acres, with an additional 2,400 acres of existing vineyards being replanted. The potential increase in top-quality Port production could reach 6,000 pipes, or 367,000 cases. It represents a total increase of 3 percent to 4 percent in annual Port production.

"They are going to be very, very good for the trade as a whole, these new plantings," said Peter Cobb, a director of Cockburn. "We consider it a very positive development that will be extremely beneficial to the maintenance, even improvement, of all plantings in the prime areas."

Douro growers can also receive money under a restructuring of vineyards program organized by the European Economic Community, but this only applies to vineyards already planted.

The World Bank program is important for all top-quality wines made in the Upper Douro but especially for vintage Port. At the moment, a serious house's vintage Port production in a declared year may range from 7,000 to 25,000 cases. The average is more like 12,000 to 16,000 cases. Increasing the number of high-quality vineyards could help increase the production of vintage Port, providing more wine for a growing international demand. The only drawback would be if these larger volumes of vintage Port translate into lower quality — a situation that has already occurred in some instances. Royal Oporto claimed to make more than 100,000 cases of vintage Port in 1983, and the wine is not in the same league as that of most other houses. Another example was when Croft allegedly doubled the production of its 1982 vintage, making a much lighter wine compared to its other fine vintages.

There have been exceptions to the "more quantity means less quality" rule. Many of the top houses made between 40,000 and 50,000 cases of the fabulous 1927 vintage, which is generally still beautiful to drink today. The fact remains, however, that vintage Port is a limited product. It can only be made in the best years and from the best grapes. "Vintage Port is like the cream in a bottle of milk," said Robin Reid, former managing director of Croft. "The rest is just jolly good milk."

Most quality-conscious producers believe they will increase their vintage Port production by one-fourth to one-third with the World Bank plantings. Only growers who already owned vineyards classified A or B were allowed to apply. There were strict rules on how and where the new vineyards could be planted, including minimum and maximum altitudes and slopes, terrace styles, rootstocks and grape varieties. For instance, growers could plant their vines up and down the hillside, as in West Germany, as long as the slopes were no more than 30 percent. Otherwise, the vineyards had to be terraced.

Some Port trade members remain cautious, nonetheless. They argue that while these new plantings will meet the demand for quality Ports like vintage, they wonder what will become

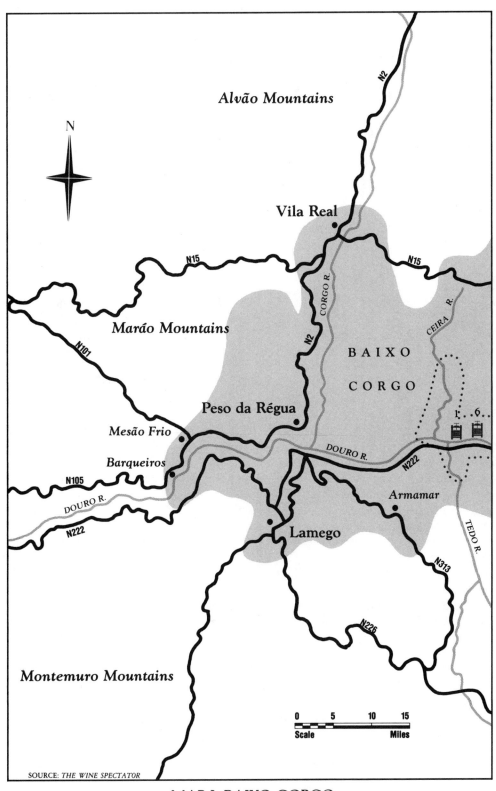

MAP I: BAIXO CORGO

of the growers who supply grapes and wine for the bread-and-butter Ports of the industry, the cheap tawnies and rubies. Wines coming from A-B vineyards are usually too intensely colored and powerful for these wines. Growers in the Baixo Corgo may find it difficult to make money with the increased competition from the higher regions.

"The scheme was not well received," said Cobb. "It was designed to help what is the poorest region in the EEC. But there are problems."

Many of the small growers are already defaulting on their loans. They were not well versed in finances and the loans only covered about 40 percent or 50 percent of their costs for establishing a vineyard. Unfinished terraces and half-planted hillsides are already a common site in the Douro.

"If we are not careful, there could be problems like we had in Jerez," said David Sandeman, whose company also makes Sherry. The area experienced financial problems due to overproduction in the early 1980s. "There has been an enormous amount of planting in recent years, and there will not be a shortage of grapes. We would like to buy more vineyards, but in five years from now. We want to wait and see what happens."

A FOCUS ON VARIETALS

These new plantings in the 1980s have focused a great deal of attention on grape varieties. Port, vintage included, has always been a blend of numerous grape varieties. It is not as simple as single-variety regions like Burgundy with Pinot Noir and the northern Rhône Valley with Syrah. Even California winemakers might find the number of varieties here overwhelming.

Most vine growers in the Douro Valley still have little or no idea which grape varieties grow in their vineyards. Most are a hodge-podge of grape types — white planted next to red, Touriga Nacional next to Tinta Amarela. Asking a Douro farmer what grape types he has in his vineyard will usually elicit only a shrug.

Part of this confusion is due to tradition. Until recently, growers and shippers paid scant attention to their vineyards or what was planted there, attaching little importance to the proper time to prune or the right moment to pick.

There are more than 80 identified varieties currently planted in Douro Valley vineyards, and there are dozens more unnamed. Most are *Vitis vinifera*, the same family that includes classic French varieties such as Cabernet Sauvignon and Chardonnay. References to various grapes grown in the Douro and other wine-producing regions of Portugal can be found as far back as the 16th century, according to a 1986 paper written by José António Rosas and João Nicolau de Almeida, both from the Port house of Adriano Ramos-Pinto. In the 1500s, 16 varieties had been identified, some of which are still found today: Mourisco, Ferral, Malvasia, Bastardo and Donzelinho.

In 1853 Baron Forrester called for the identification and separation of the various varieties. He wrote in *Portugal Its Capabilities*: "What an infinite variety of delicious wines might be made in the Alto Douro if proper separations of the grapes were studied." Official registration of varieties for Port production came in 1940, when the government approved and rated 88 types.

Today five varieties are favored for vintage Port and other premium Ports. They are Tinto Cão, Tinta Roriz, Touriga Francesa, Tinta Barroca and Touriga Nacional. The World Bank scheme stipulates that these five grape varieties must be used for the new plantings.

This is not to say that other varieties such as Sousão, Mourisco or Tinta Francisca are poor in quality, but studies begun in 1967 by Ramos-Pinto under the auspices of the Centro Nacional de Estudos Vitivinicolas suggest that the five varieties stipulated for World Bank plantings are clearly the most outstanding for Port. This was the first in-depth study under-

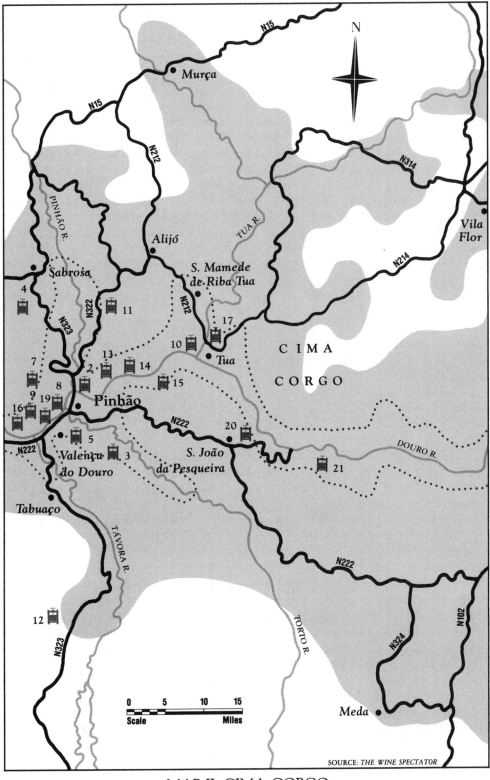

MAP II: CIMA CORGO

taken on Port varieties, although shippers such as Dick Yeatman of Taylor Fladgate and John Smithes of Cockburn dabbled in the subject in the late 1950s and early 1960s.

"There are over 80 identified varieties here," said Guimaraens of Taylor and Fonseca. "And God knows how many other unidentified ones are around. Thank God we must use only five varieties now for the new plantings."

Nearly all the grapes planted in the Douro are indigenous to Portugal, although Roriz is the same as Spain's Tempranillo. Tinta Francisca is said to be Pinot Noir brought to Portugal by Comte Henri de Bourgogne in 1095, but research has proven that this is nothing more than folklore.

Guimaraens gave a quick synopsis of the five leading varieties and their specific traits during a visit in 1989: Tinta Barroca is good for planting on north- or east-facing slopes. It is healthy and less susceptible to diseases. Tinta Roriz is also very tough and a vigorous grower. It needs south-facing slopes and produces meaty wines. Tinto Cão is better in cool areas. It has many bunches, but its wines lack body. Touriga Francesa is good all around and grows especially well in hot areas. It is a big producer and popular with small growers. By comparison, Touriga Nacional gives the smallest yields and is sensitive to diseases. But it produces superb Port with lots of color and body.

A popular tasting Port shippers often host for journalists and other visitors shows the characteristics of key varieties from a recent vintage. The exercise of tasting the individual wines clearly illustrates the uniqueness of each variety and how they interplay with one another in a blend.

Touriga Nacional is the classiest of the five grape types. With a deep ruby-purple color, it has an intensely aromatic nose of raspberries and tea. The palate is well balanced but powerfully rich in fruit and tannins. It is a solid base for a vintage Port. The Roriz is less balanced but more tannic and acidic, providing backbone to the Port.

Tinta Barroca is more like the Nacional but softer and less intense. It can give a little more flesh to the blend. Tinto Cão is rather light but its lovely fruity and floral nose adds character to a Port. Touriga Francesa has a distinctive earthy and floral nose and is full-bodied, with plenty of fruit and alcohol.

Some Port shippers have considered releasing commercially a vintage Port made from a single grape variety. Touriga Nacional would be the most likely candidate. But most shippers agree that a vintage Port must be a blend, which gives a complexity of character and style to the wine.

This has not kept people from planting by variety, however. Ramos-Pinto began the trend at its Quinta da Ervamoira in the late 1960s. *Quintas* like Cockburn's Tua and Taylor's Vargellas had smaller such plantings almost a decade before. Now, nearly all the new planting in the Douro is done by variety.

Australian enologist David Baverstock, who began with Croft in 1982 and now works with the Symington family, believes the emphasis on varieties can only improve the quality of Port in general. "We are just scratching the surface here," he said. "We are taking the parameters of quality vintage Port and trying to fine-tune it a bit. Maybe in 20 years we won't find a difference, and we will replant the varieties all together again. But I don't think so."

The vineyard at Cockburn's Vilarica is a fine example of varietal planting. The company bought the property in 1979. A large map of the vineyards on a wall at Cockburn's headquarters there denotes each parcel and its corresponding grape type. It shows plantings of Touriga Nacional, Tinta Barroca, Malvasia Preta, Tinto Cão, Tinta Roriz, Mourisco, Touriga Nacional and Malvasia Fina. This group of varieties accounts for about 90 percent of the planting. The rest is spread among dozens of other types and hundreds of different clones. There are even 2,000 vines of Chardonnay.

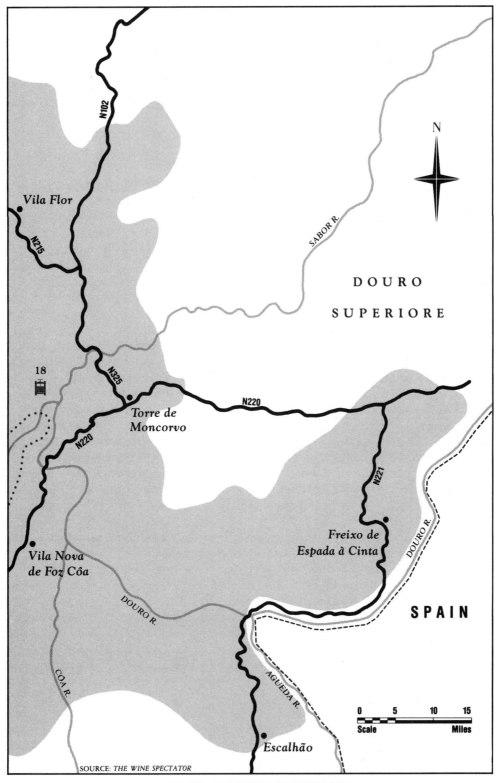

N

DOURO

SUPERIORE

SABOR R.

N102

Vila Flor

N215

18

N325

N220

Torre de
Moncorvo

N221

Freixo de
Espada à Cinta

DOURO R.

Vila Nova
de Foz Côa

DOURO R.

SPAIN

AGUEDA R.

COA R.

0   5   10   15
Scale   Miles

Escalhão

SOURCE: *THE WINE SPECTATOR*

MAP III: DOURO SUPERIOR

"Everything we have planted now has been through experimentation," said Cockburn's vineyard manager, Miguel Corte Real Gomes, during the harvest of 1989.

At the beginning of the project, he spent three years studying the characteristics of each key variety according to the various soil types, microclimates and rootstocks. He continues his research, and he is currently working closely with the University of Vila Real.

"We have several plantings with the 150 different clones, but we won't know much for another five or six years," he said. "We are sure we have the best 150 clones of Touriga Nacional, but then we will take the best 10. We already see 20 that are better than the rest."

Rootstocks and Grafting

Attention to rootstocks is just as important as properly selecting varieties. With a few exceptions, vines in the Douro are grafted to American rootstock, as are vinifera vines in winemaking regions elsewhere in Europe and in California. Native American vines are resistant to phylloxera, the grape root louse that destroyed the vineyards in California in the 1860s and Europe in the 1870s, 1880s and 1890s.

Phylloxera and other diseases such as oidium were so bad at the time that many growers simply abandoned their vineyards. These pre-phylloxera terraced vineyards are a common site in the Douro. Dilapidated and falling down, they are overrun with bushes and weeds. Only an occasional olive or cork tree gives any indication that these terraces were once cultivated.

The phylloxera devastates a vine by sucking nutrients from its roots. Various methods have been tried to eradicate the louse, including flooding the vineyards and fumigating the soil with carbon disulfide, but once a vineyard is infested, it is difficult to get rid of the pest.

The American rootstocks used for grafting usually come from one of three types: *Vitis riparia*, *Vitis rupestris* or *Vitis berlanderi*. A very popular rootstock in the Douro is 99R, a cross between *berlanderi* and *rupestris*. Others include Rupestris du Lot, 110, 140RA, 3309 and 1103.

Since all of these rootstocks are resistant to phylloxera to varying degrees, a grower tries to select a rootstock that is best suited to the variety to be planted and the vineyard's microclimate and soil. For instance, 99R may grow better with Touriga Nacional while 3309 may be better in drier areas because of its deep root system. It is like choosing a surrogate mother; a poor carrier can be a disaster.

"In very fertile soil, getting the rootstock right is not that important, but in difficult soils like the Douro, you need good, vigorous rootstocks," said Corte Real Gomes.

The soil of the Douro is desert-like, with few nutrients for the vine. Dan Stanislawski, an American professor of geography, studied the soils of Portugal in his book *Landscapes of Bacchus*. In his chapter on the Douro, he described the region: "The Upper Douro Valley in its natural state would not be a place of choice for a man with latitude in his options. It is an area of pre-Cambrian schists that do not break down into soil under normal conditions of the zone; rather they appear as flakes and chunks of rock, high in potash (12 percent) but with a very small percentage of nitrates, phosphates and organic materials. Calcium is almost completely lacking."

Field grafting is the popular method used up the Douro for attaching the vinifera to the American rootstock. The process involves attaching the vinifera to the rootstock in the vineyards rather than grafting the two first and then planting them together, which is called bench grafting. For field grafting, growers plant their rootstocks in February or March to give them ample time to establish themselves before attaching the vinifera in the late fall.

"The vine must get established first before grafting," said Bruce Guimaraens. "We water them four or five times after planting and then we say, 'Baby, you are on your own.' " The fall grafting in the fields normally has a 90 percent success rate, he said, and there is little difficulty in finding trained vineyard workers to do the job. "When you graft a plant it is like having an operation — a bloody serious operation. The plant must recover," he added.

Key *quinta* owners agree that the day may come when they move to bench grafting. They say there is little reason to convert for the moment, however, with plenty of people to do the job in the vineyards.

BUILDING TERRACES

Perhaps the biggest change in the Douro in the past 20 years has been the introduction of new terracing methods. The best vineyard sites, especially those for vintage Port, were traditionally located on steep slopes with inclines of 20 percent to 60 percent. Many of these vineyards were established well before phylloxera arrived in the region in 1868. These stone terraced vineyards were built entirely by hand by thousands of workers who came from Galicia and other neighboring parts of Spain and Portugal.

The terraces resemble cobblestone steps in an ancient building, scaling the sides of the valley. Their construction was an incredibly tedious and time-consuming project. These terraces are only wide enough for one row of vines, which gives an extremely small crop of grapes and little return on investment.

Today it is difficult to find people to repair the terraces. Tim Bergqvist, owner of Quinta de la Rosa, found a 72-year-old man in Pinhão who came with a young apprentice to mend a small section of stone terracing on his property. All the work was done by hand with no mortar to hold the stone. It took the pair nearly two weeks to build a wall 10 feet high by 20 feet long, working each day from 7:30 a.m. to 5:30 p.m. It is not surprising that such terraces became so difficult to maintain in the 1950s and 1960s that many *quinta* owners either sold their vineyards or stopped growing vines.

"A lot of *quintas* we used in past years for vintage Ports continued to go down and down in production," said Gordon Guimaraens of Cockburn. "The growers started to abandon their *quintas*. It just didn't make financial sense anymore for them."

The introduction of the bulldozer in the early 1970s changed everything. Today, nearly all the new vineyard terraces have been built by bulldozer and a generous quantity of dynamite. The terraces are no longer built of stone, and by carving deeper into the hillside, a bulldozer can make a more gradual slope. Each terrace, or *patamara*, can now support two rows of vines spaced about 6 feet apart to allow for mechanized cultivation.

Building terraces with a bulldozer can be a hazardous occupation. One or two drivers die each year when their machines overturn on the steep slopes. These massive machines have been invaluable for the development of the region. One example of the bulldozer's sheer power was when Fonseca took nearly 60 feet off the top of a mountain to create a vineyard. "I always wanted to have a flat vineyard in the Douro," Guimaraens explained.

The only drawback is that *patamaras* have fewer vines per hectare (2.47 acres) than the old style of terracing. The *patamaras* average about 3,300 vines per hectare, since their terraces take more space. The old, steeper style could manage up to 6,000 vines. "But the old style terraces were like building the pyramids. It is impossible to do now but it was fantastic," said Cockburn's Corte Real Gomes.

Some growers have increased the number of vines per hectare by planting *vinha ao alto,* or up and down. Like many vineyards on the steep slopes in West Germany, the vines are planted in rows perpendicular to the slope. Ramos-Pinto pioneered the method and planted on slopes of up to 45 percent with about 5,000 vines per hectare.

José Antonio Rosas of Ramos-Pinto, said his company has had few problems with erosion and has found this type of cultivation only slightly more difficult — although other growers might question his claims.

"We get more vines per hectare, so we get better quality," he said. "We have used *patamaras* and we prefer it this way. We get better maturation of the grapes. The only larger expense is the maintenance."

CARING FOR THE VINE

Port growers have done little research in pruning and training. The most common style of pruning in the Douro is what the French call the Guyot system, with one or two fruit canes per vine growing along steel wire. This system has been in use for decades, and new thinking on different trellising systems or canopy management is largely overlooked.

The Guyot system makes the vines more resistant to various diseases and pests during the growing season, although there is less of a problem with disease in the Douro than in other European vineyard regions due to its normally dry climate.

There are various diseases and pests that do attack vineyards in the Douro, nonetheless. The most common is oidium. These are usually a problem early in the growing season, and spraying the vineyards properly at set intervals with appropriate chemicals can reduce the effects of these maladies. Spraying usually begins in the early spring.

Rot tends to be more of a problem. It is most serious when it is brought on by rains late in the growing season, when it is too late to spray — spraying this late would risk leaving a residue of chemicals in the wine. Recent wet harvests such as 1986 were particularly bad for gray rot, or *Botrytis cinerea*, which attacks the fruit and can impart "off" flavors to the wine.

Aside from diseases, pests such as grape moths and various spiders are common, as is phylloxera. Most of these pests can be eradicated with various sprayings, with the exception of phylloxera. There are even problems with wild boars in the vineyards eating grapes and tearing down new plantings. Many growers consider it a sport to hunt these wild pigs. A hearty glass of Douro red and a plate of grilled boar would be a prized meal in any *quinta* dining room.

A grower's life up the Douro is one of constant work. After the harvest in September and October, the vineyards are cleared and the soil may be tilled into troughs to catch water during the winter. Fertilizing may also be done during this period. Pruning normally begins in December and carries on for a few months. Everything is done by hand.

In early spring, workers begin turning over the soil between the rows of vines to kill the weeds and aerate the soil. This is usually done by hand with a hoe or by oxen, although some vineyards are set up to use small tractors. When the vines begin to grow, their shoots are trained onto the trellises. Some spraying may also be done to fight oidium and mildew, which primarily attack the foliage and can inhibit photosynthesis.

After the chance of late frost is over, young vines may also be planted. Growers keep their fingers crossed that devastating hail storms or ruinous rains will stay away, and continue spraying and watching over their vines for the rest of the spring and summer. Harvest usually begins in mid-September.

The Douro Valley is constantly changing, both through nature and man. There is always something happening on the terraces, whether it is planting, pruning, spraying or harvesting.

It is a never-ending agricultural cycle in a remote, rugged area. Some people may call it a God-forsaken part of the world, considering its primitive state, arduous climate and forbidding terrain. But many view the Douro Valley as a miracle, since a product as refined as vintage Port originates there.

"I doubt you will find an area that has changed as much in such a short amount of time," said Peter Symington, the head of wine production for his family firm, producers of Graham, Dow and Warre, among others. "But there is a human factor in all of this. A person who has worked certain vineyards for so many years knows what varieties are there. He knows the soil, the climate and other factors. What is more important, he knows what wines are produced from those vineyards."

CHAPTER III

FROM THE HARVEST TO THE WINERY

The harvest is a wild and exciting time in the Douro Valley. It is everything for Port producers. As growers, they spend sleepless nights hoping for good weather during the picking. As winemakers, they try to anticipate how do to get the best out of their people and equipment.

A harvest is when everything should come together. It is a melting pot of tradition, technology, hard work and a bit of luck. In good years, it all culminates in a deeply colored, powerfully rich, young vintage Port. All the time spent each year toiling in the vineyards and preparing equipment in the wineries culminates in late September in a three- to four-week "working holiday." This is a festive time in the Douro Valley. The energy that goes into the harvest fills the air with electricity. Everyone is high from the excitement of the new vintage — not to mention the free-flowing Port for visitors at most of the estates, or *quintas*.

Up and down the Douro River and its tributaries, wineries are operating 24 hours a day. A faint hum can be heard day and night throughout the valley as winemaking equipment is put to the test after laying idle for most of the year. There is a sweet smell of freshly crushed grapes in the air. Roads are crowded with small trucks full of freshly picked grapes. A central town like Pinhão can be as congested as London or New York at rush hour, as trucks laden with grapes try to get through a maze of vehicles and people to their destinations.

THE HARVESTERS

Pickers comb the vineyards all day long. They are as sure-footed as mountain goats as they negotiate the extremely steep terraces. A dozen men, women and children can pick about five or six tons of grapes in a day. Meanwhile, men carry the crop on their backs in 60-kilo wicker baskets, *cestos da vindima*, which they empty into large metal or wooden containers. Sarah Bradford describes the scene well in her book *The Story of Port*: "A piece of sacking draped over the men's head and shoulders prevents the baskets from chafing them, a thong round the forehead stops it from slipping; the basket rests on a pillow covered with grubby rabbit skin and is held in place by a hooked stick or vineyard hoe. The effect is biblical; nothing but the men's old gray trousers and stained check shirts has changed for over a thousand years."

Some houses such as Fonseca have begun using small 25-kilo plastic boxes — a practice followed for many years in the Sherry region — rather than the larger metal containers, to reduce the chance of the grapes starting to ferment before getting to the winery. "I want my grapes to arrive at the winery just as you would find them in the supermarket," said Bruce Guimaraens, estate manager of Taylor and Fonseca.

The grapes are transported by tractor or truck, depending on the distance. A handful of potassium metabisulfite crystals is usually thrown into the grapes to help reduce oxidation and prevent premature fermentation. Some grapes may travel more than an hour by truck along slow, winding roads to reach central wineries. It was not that long ago that the same task was done by ox cart. The sturdy, wooden-wheeled vehicles drawn by a single ox can still occasionally be seen in small villages up the Douro Valley.

Although a few of the harvesters are full-time workers at the *quintas*, most are employed only for the vintage harvest. Some come from local villages; others travel from various parts of northern Portugal. Some may even come from nearby areas of Spain. They generally travel and work in a troupe, or *roga*. The group has a leader, or *rogador*, who negotiates their pay and working conditions with *quinta* owners. The group usually returns every year to the same property. Some have harvested at the same *quinta* for decades, passing on their knowledge and dedication to their children.

The *quinta* becomes their home for these few weeks. It is not uncommon for babies to be born during the harvest, as one was at Fonseca's Quinta do Cruzeiro in 1989. Pickers have simple accommodations; they sleep in steel-frame beds, and cook in kitchens and wash in bathrooms without running water, although this is changing rapidly. An elderly woman usually takes care of the living quarters and meals. Men, women and teenagers work the harvest. All the accommodations are provided by the *quinta*, including food and copious quantities of wine.

One *quinta* owner said it was common for some workers to drink nearly five liters of wine each day. "They say the work is so difficult they need the wine to revitalize them. If they don't get the wine, they won't work," the vintner said. Considering the grueling work, harvesters are paid very little, a meager $10 to $15 a day. In 1989 wages averaged about 2,000 escudos ($13.80) per day for men and about 1,600 ($11.05) for women. A bonus of 1,000 escudos ($6.90) was paid to those who wished to tread in the *lagares* after dinner. By modern standards, this sounds like slave labor; however, shippers say that such pay is good compared to what pickers normally receive during the rest of the year in isolated villages throughout the region. It is also about 50 percent above the national minimum wage.

Despite the low wages and the hard work, the end of vintage is a time for celebration, with each *quinta* hosting a party for its workers. There is joy in completing a harvest. Besides plenty of dancing and general merry-making, there is a tradition for the pickers to write a poem about the harvest, which is read aloud. The *quinta* owner is then given a vine branch, or *ramo*, which represents the last grapes picked during the harvest.

Harvesting as a Shipper

For *quinta* owners and Port shippers, the vintage is a different matter altogether. Besides a heavy work schedule, there is a constant flow of visitors, many of whom are important clients from all over the world. The main houses are well staffed with maids and cooks. An evening usually begins with a cold glass of dry white Port or beer served with freshly roasted almonds from the property's own almond trees. It is a great way to start a relaxing evening, after spending the day in the dusty vineyards and musty wineries of the Douro.

Everyone lets their hair down at these soirées, with conversation usually centering around the day's events. Topics can range from the sugar content of the harvested grapes and the predominance of rot in the vineyards to the birth of a litter of pigs in one of the outlying *quintas*. Dress is extremely casual: open-collar shirts and light trousers for men and light dresses, skirts or trousers for women.

Until quite recently, women were banished from the harvest. Their presence was considered bad luck, the view being that the men might not concentrate as well with women around to distract them. Today the harvest is a family affair. Everyone is involved — grandmothers, mothers and children. There are so many children during the harvest at some *quintas*, such as Noval, that they look like day-care centers instead of wineries. The children are not there to work, of course, but just for the fun.

One does not go up the Douro for a gastronomic experience, especially during the harvest. Good food is hard to find. In butcher shops and markets along the valley, one is lucky to find anything more than an old chicken or a piece of stringy beef or tough goat. Vegetables are scarce, with the exception of onions, tomatoes and the occasional bell pepper.

Quinta cooks do their best, but the standard *quinta* dinner is very British, even in the *quintas* belonging to Portuguese shippers. The meal usually begins with cabbage soup, followed by roasted meat, roasted potatoes and tomatoes or peppers. The wine served is usually a simple Portuguese red from the Dão or Bairrada. Guests at one of Ferreira's *quintas* may have much better luck and enjoy a bottle of Portugal's greatest red wine, Barca Velha, made in the Upper Douro.

It is usually a good idea to sip the table wines slowly at dinner and save oneself for the Port at the end of the meal. This is likely to be a chilled decanter of 20-year-old tawny with a creamy cheese from the region. It is a civilized way to finish off a meal in the Douro, especially during a warm, hectic vintage. Shippers keep very little vintage Port at their *quintas*. The dry, warm weather of the Douro encourages the wines to mature too quickly. Few *quintas* even have proper cellars. Nonetheless, shippers make exceptions for special occasions.

Quinta dos Malvedos is one property with a tradition of serving vintage Port, and it is common to consume three or four vintages in one evening at Malvedos. On one such occasion during the 1989 vintage, James Symington pulled the corks on a 1970 Graham, 1966 Graham in magnum, 1964 Malvedos and 1958 Malvedos. All the wines were served blind and guests were asked for their verdicts. A few of the wines were identified correctly, although no one spotted the 1966 in magnum.

Symington had served the 1966 Graham in two separate decanters and in two separate glasses, and everyone was convinced that there were two completely different wines on the table. "I thought it would be a bit of fun to see how you handled this," he smiled to his guests after revealing his ploy.

A MOVABLE FEAST

One could spend each night of the harvest at a different *quinta*. Each property has its own style and ambiance. Taylor's Quinta de Vargellas is the most polished of the lot. From the moment one arrives at the Vargellas rail station, there is a sensation of opulent luxury. The main house, renovated in 1980, is in immaculate condition, its white façade standing out from the rugged countryside.

Everything is very organized at Vargellas. Cocktails are served at 6:30 p.m. by the tiled pond overlooking the Douro, with guests moving into the sitting room as night sets in. Dinner begins promptly at 7:30 p.m. at a long, elegantly set table where up to 20 guests are seated. A hand bell summons the servants, who carry out their tasks with quiet efficiency. A few glasses of 10-year-old tawny or a mature vintage of Quinta de Vargellas finish the evening. It all seems more like a country house in one of the smart English counties than up the Douro Valley.

Things are not as well planned at Quinta do Tua, in Tua, Cockburn's main estate. It is, nonetheless, equally interesting. Tua is the production center of Cockburn's vintage in the Cima Corgo and Douro Superior, and it acts as a stopover for overworked winemakers and vineyard managers as well as the occasional VIP. The traditional 19th-century whitewashed, stone Portuguese building is at the convergence of the Douro River and the smaller Tua River. Before the road to the *quinta* was enlarged, visitors had to walk across the 50-foot-high rail bridge from Tua on the other side of the river — not an easy task after lunch or dinner.

Quinta do Tua has a warm feeling to it, like a well-used, high-back leather chair. The walls are filled with maps, drawings and photographs of the region and portraits of former owners and employees. Many date back to the last century. It has the feeling of a colonial outpost from the 1930s. "It may be less grand than a lot of *quintas* here but it is very comfortable," said Peter Cobb, a director of Cockburn. "There is a lot of tradition at this *quinta*."

THE WORK OF A SHIPPER

It is not just a nonstop dinner party in the Douro during the harvest. People are here to work, and work they do. Vintners begin to look rather ragged by the end of the harvest. They barely sleep, working all day and entertaining all night. Everyone has his job to do during the harvest. Someone has to check the sugar content of the truckloads of grapes arriving at the winery while someone else carefully monitors the fermentation and fortification.

One person is normally in charge of the entire harvest of a house. For example, Guimaraens, of Taylor and Fonseca, oversees the vintage at Fonseca. He is close to a nervous wreck during this time, much like a father in the waiting room of a hospital expecting his first child.

"You are not going to get much sleep tonight," he said with a grin at the start of an evening during the 1986 harvest. "I try to visit six or seven growers a day, besides our own *quintas*."

Guimaraens relies on the production of numerous growers in the region to meet his company's needs. Some of this production might be good enough to go into his vintage Ports, especially that from properties in good areas near the shipper's own *quintas*. When a shipper contracts to buy a grower's production, he either buys wine, must or grapes.

The grapes are the simplest to manage. They are picked and then transported by truck to the shipper's winery. On arrival, the load of grapes is weighed and checked for quality and ripeness. Most well-equipped wineries use must meters, which quickly read the sugar content of the grapes. Results are recorded so the grower can be paid after the harvest.

Some growers prefer to make the wines themselves. This may be because their *quinta* is too remote to transport grapes. When growers make their own wines, vintners like Guimaraens must make daily visits to check on the winemaking. The shippers may also buy from the various cooperatives in the region, which account for about 40 percent of the Douro's entire production. These cooperatives never make vintage Ports, however.

Even before the harvest begins, shippers send out their people to check the facilities of a contracted grower. Winemaking equipment, from vats to storage tanks, must be in proper condition. One whiff of the interior of a 60-hectoliter wooden vat is enough to tell whether it is in good or poor condition. If there is any sign of spoilage, it is rejected and must be cleaned.

Occasionally, these spot checks find more than spoiled barrels. At Quinta do Vesùvio in 1989, one inspector found a cache of dynamite in a *tonel* — not a good thing to have around a winery full of brandy used for fortification. A *quinta* worker was apparently using it to fish in the river.

Guimaraens and his counterparts remind one of country doctors checking on their patients. Their Gladstone bags are full of basic winemaking instruments. A refractometer checks the sugar content of the grape must. A hydrometer and graduated cylinder verify the progress of the fermentation, and a thermometer takes the temperature of the must.

Nonetheless, Guimaraens does not always rely on such instruments to make decisions. He also takes along a white dinner plate to check the color extraction of the fermentation — a method used for centuries up the Douro. He pours on a small amount of the fermenting, purple grape must to look at its color density.

Henry Vizetelly noted the practice in his 1880 book, *Facts About Port and Madeira*: "One of the treaders lifting up his brawny leg and carefully balancing himself, the saucer is held beneath his dripping foot to receive the *mosto* as it trickles down."

On a *quinta* call, every vat of fermenting wine is evaluated and noted. Port shippers may also give the *quinta* owner advice on how to continue fermentations and when to fortify. Guimaraens records the results of the information from his tests in a small notebook. When he returns to his headquarters in Pinhão, Guimaraens puts the information into a computer. A large printout of all the wines of the vintage is available at the push of a button.

Vintners like Guimaraens can cover hundreds of miles a day in their four-wheel-drive vehicles, crisscrossing the region visiting *quintas*. It is the only way. "We have an agreement to do this," Guimaraens said. "I will stick by a man if he makes 10 pipes of excellent wine. That is what counts."

MAKING WINE IN THE DOURO

Winemaking varies enormously throughout the region. It can be as primitive as men treading grapes in shallow, rectangular stone containers, or *lagares*; or it can be as high-tech as computerized stainless steel vats with temperature control and automated pumping over.

On the whole, the winemaking is simple. Few people are concerned with such notions as hyperoxidation of grape musts or the use of cultured yeasts for fermentations. The grapes are merely delivered with a bit of sulfur to stop oxidation and then fermented. Like any alcoholic fermentation, this consists of the conversion of sugar in the grapes into alcohol, through the work of yeasts, and the resulting production and accumulation of carbon dioxide.

What makes Port different from table wines, however, is fortification. After fermenting for two or three days, the grape must, or half-finished wine, receives a dose of neutral spirit distilled from grapes. The fortification stops the fermentation by killing the active yeasts, which

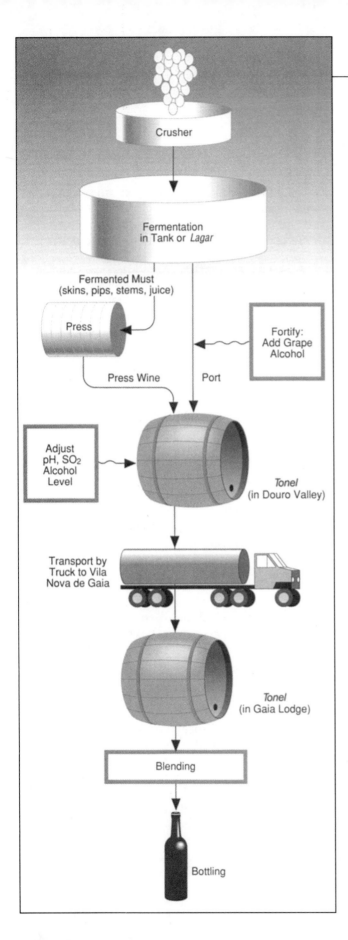

Crusher

Fermentation
in Tank or *Lagar*

Fermented Must
(skins, pips, stems, juice)

Press

Fortify:
Add Grape
Alcohol

Press Wine   Port

Adjust
pH, SO₂
Alcohol
Level

Tonel
(in Douro Valley)

Transport by
Truck to Vila
Nova de Gaia

Tonel
(in Gaia Lodge)

Blending

Bottling

MAKING VINTAGE PORT

This chart illustrates the more common methods currently in use to make top-quality vintage Port. Every option or individual style permutations may not be covered here, but I have tried to indicate the more common differences below.

1. **HARVEST AND CRUSH:** After the picked grapes arrive at the winery, they are dumped into a crusher, where the grapes are lightly punctured to release the juice inside them. Some may remove the stems. The mass of grapes and juice, called must, is then placed in either a *lagar* or fermentation tank.

2. **FERMENTATION:** Whether fermented in *lagar*, autovinification tank or *remontage* (pumping over) vats, the fermentation period takes from two to three days at 82 to 86 degrees Fahrenheit. Once the must reaches between 5 percent and 6 percent alcohol, the juice in the fermentation vessel — now half-made wine — is run off or "racked" into another container, usually a large wooden cask called a *tonel*.

3. **FORTIFICATION:** While the wine is being racked into the *tonel*, 77 percent grape alcohol is added to the juice as it enters the *tonel*, stopping the fermentation while maintaining some of the unfermented sugar content of the liquid.

4. **FINE TUNING:** The remining must in the fermentation vessel is then pressed two or three times. Most producers only add the first pressing back into the young Port. The freshly made Port may then be adjusted for its acidity, sulfur dioxide content and alcohol level.

5. **THE JOURNEY DOWN THE DOURO:** The young Port remains in the casks until the spring following the harvest, when it is moved by tanker truck from the Douro to lodges in Vila Nova de Gaia. Some estate-produced vintage Ports may simply leave their Ports to mature up the Douro.

6. **VILA NOVA DE GAIA LODGES:** Upon arrival in Vila Nova de Gaia, the Ports are again stored in *tonéis* and left to mature for another year, though they are periodically checked.

7. **BLENDING AND BOTTLING:** Blending of vintage lots traditionally begins in February of the second year after the vintage. The final blend is made a few months later and samples are submitted to the Instituto do Vinho do Porto for governmental approval. Once approved, the young vintage Port is bottled without stabilization or filtration.

cannot survive in an environment above 16 percent alcohol. The fortified wine also retains some of the unfermented sugars, making it naturally sweet.

Producers rely on natural yeasts found on the grapes to cause fermentation. There is no need to inoculate the must with cultured yeasts, since wild yeasts perform well at the 5 percent or 6 percent alcohol that the wines reach before being fortified. The fermentation can still be influenced by a number of other factors, such as temperature, cleanliness of the grapes, acidity of the must and strength of the yeasts. Most Port producers fortify with a 77 percent neutral spirit made from grapes. The end result is a Port of about 20 percent alcohol with a sweetness of 3 to 4 degrees Baume.

Used primarily in Europe, Baume describes the sugar content of grapes and wines. One degree Baume equals about 1.8 degrees Brix, a similar American measurement for winemaking. Most vintage Ports have a Brix of about 5.4 to 7.2, or between 5.4 percent and 7.2 percent residual sugar.

This relative sweetness in a Port can distinguish one house from another. Winemakers at Cockburn often try to make a drier Port with a Baume of less than 3.4 degrees, while Ferreira prefers its vintage Ports at 3.8. Some houses may want an even sweeter vintage Port, like Wiese & Krohn, which tries to make its vintage with more than 4 degrees Baume. The ripeness of a particular harvest may also have an effect on sweetness. For example, 1982 was an extremely hot year and produced sweeter Ports, while 1983 had milder weather and produced better balanced, slightly drier Ports.

Fermentation methods vary according to the preference of each producer. There are essentially two types: *lagar* and non-*lagar*. Regardless of the method, the key is to extract plenty of color, fruit and tannin during the short fermentation period. "The problem is that the fermentation process takes only about three days," said John Burnett, managing director of Croft and a biochemist. "Therefore, one has to extract as much as possible in such a short time period. Even the lightest table wines are fermented for at least five or six days. The great red wines of the world are fermented for two to three weeks, sometimes more."

THE *LAGAR*

The most traditional fermentation method is the *lagar*, which has been in use for centuries, and involves a handful of people treading the grapes. The grapes may be crushed before they are put into the *lagares*, which are made of large granite or stone blocks and are usually rectangular in shape. Their dimensions vary, although their walls are usually 3 to 4 feet high. They look a bit like children's swimming pools.

Shippers talk about a *lagar*'s size according to how many pipes it holds, which can be anything from six to nearly 40 pipes. For instance, a 12-pipe *lagar*, a fairly standard size, would be about 9 feet wide by 12 feet long and 4 feet deep. A *lagar* is usually filled to within 6 to 9 inches of the top — some shippers call it a palm's height. This ensures that there is a small blanket of carbon dioxide over the floating mass of crushed grapes, called the cap, during fermentation. The carbon dioxide is produced during the fermentation and keeps the must from oxidizing.

Starting the fermentation normally takes about two to 12 hours. It is started by treading, or cutting, the grapes in the *lagar*. Large amounts of color, fruit and tannin are released at this point. Shippers often say it takes two men per pipe to cut a *lagar*. Thus, a 12-pipe *lagar* needs about two dozen people. It sounds like incredibly tough punishment to tread knee-high in grape juice, skins and stems for hours on end. An older member of the harvest team stands to the side, leading the group and playing an accordion or triangle to keep everyone in time.

For the visitor, however, treading in the *lagar* can be a lot of fun. Guests are often asked to join in after dinner and find themselves locking arms with the pickers and dancing to the music. The owners toast everyone with a glass or two of *bagaceira*, a particularly lethal Portuguese brandy. It is an all-out party.

One British agent for Fonseca at Taylor's Quinta de Vargellas became so overwhelmed at such an event that he dove head first into a *lagar*. "He almost knocked himself out and he didn't come up at first," said Guimaraens. "Bloody hell, we would have lost about £8,000 worth of wine if he hadn't come up."

Not all the *lagares* are sites for outrageous parties. It is more usual to find a handful of men and women quietly producing a few dozen pipes of Port. A typical, small traditional winery would have three or four *lagares* placed about shoulder height above the dirt floor of the building; elevating makes the draining easier. Only one or two are filled at a time.

Treaders work about eight hours at a time and then rest for about four hours. Rather than tread, some estates, such as Quinta do Noval, prefer to use *macacos* — literally, monkeys — after the *lagares* have been cut. They are long wooden poles about the size of a broom with various appendages jutting out. Workers stand on the walls of the *lagar* and periodically push down the cap with the *macacos*. They were introduced about three decades ago when there was an acute shortage of people to tread.

Another labor-saving device for helping fermentations is the *movimosto*, or must mover, devised by Cockburn in the 1970s. A motorized pump is installed in one corner of the *lagar* to extract juice from the must. A worker then sprays the cap with the juice from what looks like a garden hose.

Although Cockburn still uses this method for much of its wine, it is generally considered to be ineffective at pushing down the cap, thus producing very light wines. Sandeman used the process at Quinta de la Rosa from the 1970s until the property's owner, Tim Bergqvist, decided to make his own wines in 1987. Sandeman claims la Rosa's wines were not good enough quality to go into its Robertson's vintage Port, Rebello Valente. But la Rosa's wines from the 1960s, which were all trodden, are outstanding. One can only conclude that the *movimosto* method reduced the quality of la Rosa's wines.

A typical *lagar* takes two to three days to ferment to a level ready for fortification. The potential alcohol is carefully monitored with a hydrometer so that the *lagar* can be emptied and its contents fortified at the right moment. During the fortification, the must is siphoned down from the *lagares* to large wooden casks of 80 to 160 hectoliters in size called *tonéis*. They are usually located on the floor below the *lagares*, allowing gravity to do all the work.

The leftover skins, pips and stems in the *lagar* from the fermentation are then pressed two or three times. Most quality producers only use the first pressing, since the others are too high in aggressive tannins. This may be done with anything from a simple hand press to a large mechanized rotary or screw press. The press wine is then blended back into the finished Port, if the quality is good.

Cockburn and Noval have tried adding alcohol to the must before draining the *lagares* in the hope of extracting more color and fruit from the skins before fortification. Both have dropped the method, however, claiming its benefits were only negligible and it wasted a lot of expensive neutral spirit.

Producers are always looking for ways to improve the performance of their *lagares*. For example, many use the latest crushing and destemming equipment to prepare their grapes for the *lagar*. They also use some form of temperature control. The most common is a heat exchanger, whereby the hot must is pumped out of the *lagar*, cooled and then pumped back. It usually resembles an enlarged version of a refrigerator's cooling system, with its snakelike tubes.

The wine is pumped through pipes that are jacketed and cooled with cold water or some other cooling agent.

The heat-exchanger method is effective but can leave the must slightly oxidized. Some *quintas* have opted instead for metal cooling plates fixed to the bottoms of their *lagares*, which cool the must like an ice cube in a warm drink. Years ago, producers would put bags of ice in their *lagares* in the hope of bringing the temperature down. Since *lagares* are made of stone, they remain relatively cool naturally, generally keeping the fermentation temperatures between 28 and 30 degrees Celsius (82 to 86 degrees Fahrenheit).

Should the must reach a temperature of 31 degrees Celsius (88 degrees Fahrenheit), most producers agree the only thing to do is to empty the *lagar*, regardless of the fermented alcohol level. The risk of blocked fermentation or spoilage is too great at such a high temperature. And if the Port is too sweet, it can be blended with another lot that has been fermented drier than normal.

"The *lagares* still make bloody good wine," said Guimaraens. "It is a mixture of the 20th century and the 18th century in the Douro. It is the best of both worlds here."

Until the early 1960s almost all Port was made in *lagares*. Today, less than 10 percent is made this way. The exception is vintage Port, which many producers still prefer to make in *lagares*. "The foot is the best crusher in the world for making Port. Why should we change?" said Cristiano van Zeller. All of his vintage Port at Quinta do Noval is still trodden. "If the other methods were proved better I would use them, but they have not been."

Added Taylor managing director Alistair Robertson, "If you can go on making wine traditionally, why not? If new methods have proved themselves superior, then it would be stupid to carry on. But they haven't. We wouldn't keep going with *lagares* just because it is jolly good for the tourists."

One of the main drawbacks of a *lagar* is the manpower involved. It is more and more difficult to find people to work the *lagares*. During the revolution, some producers had problems finishing the vintage since there were so few workers in the area. Few people wanted to work the *lagares* because it was seen as degrading.

Some producers still remain optimistic and say it is only a question of raising the salaries of workers. Others disagree. Sophia Bergqvist of Quinta de la Rosa planned to install modern stainless steel fermentation equipment in the early 1990s to be used in conjunction with the property's *lagares*. She foresaw more labor difficulties with the harmonization of the European Economic Community. Not only will producers have to pay more in salaries, but workers will be attracted to other higher-paying European countries.

"We have people on our *quinta* who are waiting for 1992," said Bergqvist, who also works as an international business consultant in London. "They know that there are plenty of higher paying jobs elsewhere. We would prefer to tread but we can't find people to do it. We are always having problems finding people."

AUTOVINIFICATION AND OTHER METHODS

The most common non-*lagar* fermentation method is autovinification, which was introduced in the region during the early 1960s. This method consists of closed-off stainless steel or concrete, epoxy-lined vats with pressure locks. The vats range in size from 50 to 100 hectoliters.

Each tank is filled to within 40 centimeters of the top with must. The tanks' locks open when the pressure of carbon dioxide, a byproduct of fermentation, reaches a certain level. The pressure of the gases pushes the juice up from the bottom of the tank to the top. When the lock opens, the juice filters down onto the mass of grape skins and other debris floating on top of the solution. This pushes down the cap, facilitating the extraction during the fermentation. In other words, it is a self-driven pumping-over system.

Each cycle of pumping over takes about 10 to 20 minutes. The system is said to be difficult to control, although some producers, such as the Symingtons of Dow, Graham and Warre, have installed cooling bars in the vats. This regulates the temperature and, in turn, controls the rate of pumping over.

"Treading is on its way out," said Peter Symington, head of production for his family's houses. The entire production center at Dow's Quinta do Bomfim is autovinified, as is part of Graham and Dow for their vintage Ports. Symington said the autovinification equipment has been upgraded over the years and now has better sprayers to disperse the juice during the pumping over. It can also mechanically pump over before the fermentation begins for additional extraction.

"The difference between a *lagar* and autovinification is the time you have to extract the color," he said. "With the *lagar*, 90 percent is done before the fermentation. Autovinification is during the vinification. Provided you can control the temperature, autovinification is a very efficient system."

Symington also uses stainless steel tanks, which have computerized temperature control and automated pumping over. They can be used for autovinification or programmed to work mechanically. All fermentations at Warre's Quinta da Cavadinha are done in such tanks.

Other houses, such as Taylor, utilize standard stainless steel fermenters that would be at home in any modern winery in California or Australia. Port shippers call this method *remontagem*.

With *remontagem*, the juice is mechanically pumped over at set intervals through a shower-like system of nozzles at the top of the tank during fermentations. Temperature can be accurately controlled, which means the must can be heated or cooled if necessary. The drawback of *remontagem*, according to some winemakers, is that the extraction of color and character may not be as good as with the *lagar* or autovinification during such a short fermentation period.

Other designs of fermentation tanks have been used, such as those with interior screws or paddles that move the cap of grape skins within the tank. Taylor has even investigated the use of horizontal fermentation tanks similar to ones currently being used in Burgundy.

"*Lagares* are really a conservative way to make Port," said Cockburn's Gordon Guimaraens. "Some of our vintages already have been made in stainless, such as 1983 and 1985. I seriously think that we can make a better vintage Port in stainless steel than in *lagares*."

As old-fashioned as *lagares* may be, this process still seems to produce the best vintage Ports. Vintage Ports produced primarily in *lagares* have the greatest concentration of fruit and tannins. Anyone who has tasted a great vintage Port like a Fonseca 1948 or a Graham 1927 can easily understand the magic of the *lagar*. Even Port shippers ask themselves the same question after tasting these wines. "When I taste something like the Graham 1948, I wonder if we can make anything better today," admitted Peter Symington.

FORTIFICATION

Regardless of the method used to make Port, the process of fortification is virtually standard. The time-honored ratio is 110 liters of alcohol to 440 liters of grape must. The total equals 550 liters, the size of a Douro pipe, the traditional elongated cask used for Port.

Recent improvements in winemaking methods have allowed producers to be more accurate.

For instance, Taylor has a fully equipped laboratory at Quinta de Vargellas with a technician who is constantly analyzing fermenting vats during the harvest to find the perfect moment to fortify.

"We know when and how much to fortify this way," said Taylor's Robertson. "We want to analyze everything. If anything is wrong we know it. Before, you didn't know until the wine reached Gaia in the spring after the vintage. You could have had 100 pipes of vinegar."

Producers generally try to inject the alcohol into the must the moment it is being racked from the *lagares* or fermentation vats. This ensures that the fermentation is quickly stopped. The new Port is then mixed for a few hours. Many producers do this by cautiously pumping the Port from the bottom to the top of the tank.

"There is a slight dilution after the fortification," said Croft's Burnett. "But the aldehydes in the spirit ensure that the anthocynanins and polyphenols (the color and tannin components in grapes) are broken down. The wine actually gets darker after the fortification."

Once the Port is well mixed, producers may make adjustments, such as adding tartaric acid to increase the acidity. Others prefer to do this before fermentation. Most producers look for a pH of 3.9 or less, an alcohol content of 19 percent to 20 percent and a total sulfur content of no more than 120 milligrams per liter.

Some producers may also add some enriched grape must to adjust the sweetness and color of their wines. In years past, they may have even used elderberry juice for the same purpose, although this is no longer an accepted practice.

Shippers buy neutral spirit from the government each year before the harvest. The Instituto do Vinho do Porto strictly controls the prices. In 1989 a liter cost about 180 escudos ($1.25) for fortifying during the harvest and 220 escudos ($1.53) after. The clean spirit usually comes from southern France, where there is an overproduction of table wines for distillation.

In years past, the spirit came from Portugal, but the production of grape spirits in Portugal is extremely limited since grape harvests have been short in recent years and the domestic market consumes vast quantities of cheap table wines. Thus, the government often buys grape brandy from France. Some vintners believe it is ludicrous that Port is one-fifth French in some years and criticize the IVP for its highly ineffective buying and supplying methods.

In 1989, for instance, the IVP waited until midsummer to finalize its purchase of grape alcohol for the harvest. The delivery barely arrived in time, since the harvest started much earlier than normal. To make matters worse, the final delivery was contaminated and unusable. If this had been the first delivery, producers might have been forced to make table wine instead of Port. In early 1990 there was discussion in the Port trade of forming its own group to buy the grape alcohol.

For the time being, a few months before the harvest, the IVP gives shippers about a dozen different choices of eaux de vie or neutral spirit. A winemaker looks for the most neutral spirit possible so that it does not impart character to the young Ports.

There have been occasions when non-grape based spirits have been used to fortify vintage Ports. For instance, the excellent 1904 vintage was primarily fortified with German spirits made from potatoes or grains. Shippers have dubbed it the "schnapps vintage," although the nickname is not pejorative. Apparently in the same year one house used unaged grain alcohol from Scotland. Regardless of what it was fortified with, a bottle of 1904 Cockburn I tasted in New York in 1987 was drinkable but fading, with elegant fruit and finesse.

ALCOHOL SCANDAL

More controversial vintages were 1972 and the undeclared 1973 and 1974. Nearly all or part of the production from those years was fortified with an industrial alcohol made from coal in Yugoslavia. It was not harmful. The Port trade was hoodwinked by a middleman somewhere in France. The government had ordered French brandy, but somewhere along the way industrial alcohol was substituted.

It was only in 1974, when the German government was routinely analyzing Port and other wines, that the fraud was discovered. German analysts with a carbon-dating process were extremely surprised to find the Ports made in those years were registering a few thousand years old.

The Ports, some of which were 1972 vintage and other blends, were banned first in Germany and then in various other European countries. The ban was simply a legal question; by regulation, Port had to be produced with grape brandy. No one in the government was ever implicated in the scandal.

"Like other Portuguese government scandals, someone was quickly shown the door and never heard from again," said one shipper. But someone made bundles of money, since industrial alcohol costs a tiny fraction of what grape brandy costs. It was a headache to the entire Port trade. "I had a call in the middle of the night from a London newspaper asking me about the scandal," recalled Croft's Robin Reid. "I didn't know what to say."

Added Robertson of Taylor Fladgate, "It was a nightmare. We bought it in good faith and the government was uninterested. It was a bad time for the trade."

Nonetheless, the synthetic alcohol may have been the cleanest spirit ever used to fortify Port. "These wines were extremely low in aldehydes produced through distillation," said David Sandeman. "A lot of them (aldehydes) can lead to bad hangovers. So one could drink all the 1972 you want and not worry about a hangover."

Jokes aside, the few vintage Ports made in 1972 are still quite good today. They include Rebello Valente, Dow, Offley Forrester and Fonseca-Guimaraens as well as various single-*quinta* wines.

MATURATION AND HANDLING

After being fortified and adjusted for acidity, the new Port rests virtually untouched at the *quintas* until the February or March after the harvest. It remains in vats and casks, occasionally analyzed to ensure all is well. By the early spring, the best wines, especially possible vintage Port lots, are moved down to shippers' lodges in Vila Nova de Gaia.

This is the first time the Port is racked, or moved off its lees, the residue that has fallen out of the wine during the cold months. The lees are made up of organic matter originating in the grapes and yeasts.

Large tanker trucks transport the wines on their three- to four-hour journey down slow, winding roads to Gaia. Some wine also may be sent by rail. The vehicles can range from a proper tanker truck to a flatbed truck with a couple of large metal tanks strapped to the bed.

Before the late 1950s, when the Douro River was blocked by a series of dams, the same journey was made by river. The wine was put into wooden casks and loaded onto *barcos rabelos*, distinctive flat-bottomed riverboats that resemble the double-prowed ships of the Vikings. They could be as long as 60 feet or as small as 25. Some *barcos rabelos* held as many as 80 pipes, while others carried only a few pipes.

José Joaquim da Costa Lima described the scene in his 1939 leaflet, *A Few Words About Port*: "Casks are taken by ox cart to the river, where they are transshipped into the typical Douro boat or *barco rabelo* which is especially suitable for navigating the river Douro. Flat bottomed, they cast off easily, without risk of capsizing on the innumerable rapids, or falls, which have to be negotiated all the way down the river. In order to make steering easier, these boats have a long wooden rudder of a peculiar shape, which is fixed in the stern and, acting like a powerful lever, makes it extremely efficacious. It is the rudder which in conjunction with the shape of the sails, that makes the boat so characteristic."

Their single-sail rigging was only good for going upriver when the wind was coming up the valley. Otherwise, it made the crafts extremely tipsy. Casks were normally only partially full so that they would float if the boat capsized. This was also a good excuse for the boatmen to have a few liters of Port on the journey downriver.

Normally, boatmen would ride the current and navigate the rapids to get downriver. They would then use their sails and oxen along the river to pull their boats upstream. The trip would take a day or so downriver and two or three to get up — if things went well. Many parts of the river were treacherous. Capsizings and drownings were common.

The most famous riverboat death was that of the legendary Baron J.J. Forrester in 1862. Forrester was the founder of the house of Offley Forrester and a leader in the Port trade at the time. According to legend, he drowned after his *barco rabelo* capsized because of the weight of the gold-laden money belt he was wearing to pay Douro farmers.

Aging and Shipping in the Douro

Although top-quality new wines are traditionally moved from the Douro in early spring, some Port shippers leave their wines in the valley for a longer period — even vintage lots. Some are even bottled there.

This practice is partly due to a change in Port shipping laws in 1986. Before, Port shippers had to keep their stocks in Vila Nova de Gaia, the city across the river from Oporto. Under the new law, shippers are allowed to bottle and ship their wines from the Douro as long as they continue to have a minimum stock of 300 pipes of Port. Also, under the rule change, growers who wish to make, bottle and ship their own wines may do so without having a minimum of 300 pipes, although they still may ship only one-third of their inventory each year. This applies only to *engarrafadores*, or those producers with estate-bottled Ports.

The change in the regulations has lead to an increase in small growers bottling and shipping their own wines, and there are more and more independent *quintas* shipping a few thousand cases a year. The trend is comparable to the increase in domaine-bottled Burgundies in the 1970s and 1980s, when small vintners began bottling their wines themselves instead of selling them in bulk to négociants. *Quintas* such as la Rosa, Romaneira, Infantado and Crasto are now making and shipping their own wines rather than selling them to large Vila Nova de Gaia-based shippers.

Quinta do Noval is the only major house moving its operation up the Douro. Noval's van Zeller began moving all of his stocks up the Douro in 1989. His uncle built a modern, insulated lodge on the property in 1982, and van Zeller believed it made little sense to maintain two lodges. Noval will retain its Gaia lodges for bottling and shipping, as well as aging its vintage Ports in cask and bottle.

Besides the current problems with communication and transportation in the Douro, most shippers are against aging wines in the Douro because of the hot, dry weather. They say the wines age too quickly. Some producers also believe wines develop a "Douro bake," which can be described as a spicy character with a high amount of volatile acidity. It can add complexity to a wine in small quantities but can be viewed only as a flaw if too strong.

Van Zeller agreed there can be problems with this, but he said, "If you take care of your wine you don't get the bake. Some farmers have dirty barrels, old *lagares* or whatever. They just don't take care of their wines. It is simply a question of that, and nothing more."

It may be decades before the Douro is dotted with dozens of small *quintas* bottling and shipping their own wines. Most small growers do not have the time, resources or knowledge to sell their wines in Portugal and abroad.

"Producers up the Douro are like what we were perhaps 30 years ago," said Manuel Angelo Barros, whose family shipping firm controls a handful of houses, including Barros and Kopke. "They don't look around. When they give you their wine, they say here it is and it is the best wine in the Douro."

Nonetheless, small growers in Burgundy and Beaujolais not long ago had similar views of the world and relied heavily on négociants' business. Things have changed there; perhaps the Douro will be next.

With the harvest completed and their wines on the way down to Gaia, shippers can begin to reflect on the quality of the vintage. They may have already tasted a few wines and will go over their records, covering everything from the weather and soil conditions to the fermentation and fortification at particular *quintas*. It is time for the shippers to get to know their wines better.

Asking a shipper his opinion on the quality of a vintage a few months after the harvest often attracts a terse response: "It is too bloody early to talk about it." Still, there are exceptional vintages when Port shippers seem to know they are onto something good.

"Very occasionally you can tell a wine will be a vintage at a very young stage," said Guimaraens. "The smell from the *lagar* with the young wine, you know that it will be great. It was like that in 1985. It was great from the word go. The bouquet was stunning from the *lagar*. Everything was great."

CHAPTER IV

VILA NOVA DE GAIA AND THE PORT LODGES

Although born in the rugged Douro Valley, vintage Port is raised in Vila Nova de Gaia, an 18th-century city across the Douro River from Oporto. The lodges, or warehouses, of all the major Port houses dwell on a maze of narrow, bumpy cobblestone roads running up the hillside from the riverbank. This is the nerve center of the Port trade. Shippers hold their stocks of Port here, blend and bottle here, market and entertain here. More importantly, Gaia is where shippers make their decisions to declare a vintage — a resolution made about three times a decade.

"Gaia is a fundamental part of the Port trade," said Cristiano van Zeller, managing director of Quinta do Noval. "Gaia is the past. It is the bedrock of the trade. There is a homelike feeling to the place."

Gaia is connected to Oporto by two bridges — an elegant iron bridge, Ponte Luiz I, finished in 1886, and the modern concrete bridge of Ponte de Arrabia, built in 1963. Ponte Luiz is the most direct link to Gaia from Oporto. The state declared Vila Nova de Gaia the exclusive *entreposto* (market center) for Port wine in 1777, but there were other reasons for building Port shippers' lodges there. According to *A Portuguese in London*, a selection of early 19th-century business correspondence published by A.A. Ferreira, "Wine stores (lodges) have always existed in Vila Nova, and in Gaia for the simple reason that many gentlemen and merchants with wine estates in the Douro had their residence there." Moreover, the city of Oporto imposed a tax equal to 1 percent of the value of goods exported at the end of the 1800s, which prompted more wine merchants to move their Port stocks to Vila Nova. The towns of Vila Nova and Gaia were merged into a municipality in 1832.

Today, as one crosses to Gaia, one is overwhelmed with advertisements for the various Port houses. Signs in French, German, English and Portuguese invite visitors to stop at various houses. The days when workers along the waterfront rolled casks full of Port off the decks of *barcos rabelos* are finished, even though a dozen of the wooden riverboats are moored along the wharf for sightseers. Nonetheless, time moves slowly in Gaia. The somber ambiance seems conducive to aging Ports.

As one walks through a shipper's damp, dirt-floored lodges lined with hundreds of weathered wooden casks stacked neatly in rows, it seems little has changed in the past century. The main sign of the 20th century is the traffic. Tanker trucks lumber by loaded with Port. Flatbed trucks squeeze into delivery bays with loads of empty bottles. Other trucks pick up palates stacked with cases of Port to be shipped to various cities throughout the world. Taxis, cars and dirty, green and orange buses motor by with businesspeople and visitors. It can take more than half an hour to travel a mile to the center of Oporto from Gaia on a Friday evening. "It is easier to park your car on the other side and walk across the bridge," said Henrique Burmester Silva, an owner of the small Port house J.W. Burmester. "The traffic here is a nightmare."

The massive Port lodges, with their clay-tiled roofs, start at the riverbank and line the steep hillsides. They come in various shapes and colors, from white and pink to bare, dusty concrete. They are large buildings and may house thousands of barrels and millions of bottles of Port. Some could easily shelter a 747 jetliner, while others would fit only a small twin-engine airplane. Most shippers have maintained their lodges in the same condition as they were 100 years ago, although a few houses such as Poças Junior and Messias have built new concrete buildings. The traditional lodges maintain a fairly constant temperature of about 65 degrees Fahrenheit and a humidity of 85 percent.

Many of the lodges are decorated with large signs proudly displaying the names of their firms. Other signs along the main waterfront road, Avenida Ramos-Pinto, indicate the location of lodges. They read: "Croft 300 meters to left," "Barros 200 meters away," "Visit the lodges" or "Visitez les caves." It can be extremely confusing. At each turn one encounters another lodge. One might find oneself under the massive black figure of Sandeman's Don overlooking the river, while down the road to the left one finds the ornate orange and yellow lodges of Adriano Ramos-Pinto. Moving up one street, one passes the small lodges of Wiese & Krohn and Kopke. On the other side of the road, one stumbles into the unmarked, green, corrugated metal doors of the tiny cellars of Niepoort. Up a street perpendicular to Niepoort and around the corner lie the lodges of Silva & Cosens, producers of Dow Ports and the headquarters of the Symington Port empire. Next door is the pristine white lodge of Burmester.

ENTERTAINING IN GAIA

Port houses are always welcoming someone, whether an agent, wine merchant, restaurateur, journalist or fellow shipper. Most houses have boardrooms for lunches and dinners. The meals usually consist of several courses, with plenty of Portuguese fish and meat, as well as vegetables and salad. Friday lunches are traditionally dried salted cod — the infamous *bacalhau*. One is likely to be served a vintage Port at a shippers' lunch, and a good 10- or 20-year-old tawny is always offered at the end of a meal — even after a vintage. It is traditional to try to guess the vintage as the decanter is passed around the table. All the houses also have a lunch room for workers, who are given a hot meal and wine during their hour-and-a-half lunch break. They normally put in an eight- to nine-hour day, finishing at 6 p.m.

It wouldn't be right describing lunch in Gaia without mentioning the Factory House, in Oporto just by the Ponte Luiz. The large gray stone Georgian building has been part of the Port trade since 1790, when it was completed with financial contributions from the British Port shippers. The Factory House is still a British-only organization (see Chapter I for more information). Offley Forrester and other once-British shippers are no longer members, since they are owned by Portuguese or non-British nationals. The Factory House is used for official engagements for the British Port trade and for its members. In addition, there is a lunch held every Wednesday for members. Such functions are usually for men only.

A few years ago, an American journalist was invited to the Wednesday lunch — and because of her name, no one suspected that she was a woman. She was politely asked to leave upon her arrival, while a few of the factory members sheepishly hid behind chairs. In another episode with an American journalist, members almost came to blows when they were asked if they had been declaring too many vintages during the 1980s. James Symington slammed his fist on the table and said, "It enrages me when people in London say we have declared too many vintages. We only declare a wine because it is bloody good!"

Aside from such rare events, the Factory remains a civilized antidote to the hustle and bustle of Oporto and the Port trade. It is comparable to a London gentlemen's club. Moreover, it is one of the best places to enjoy a good bottle of vintage Port in Oporto, since each member house donates five cases of vintage a year to the Factory House's cellar. Members also give 14 cases of wine when they join, which may be Port. In recent years, a few new members have given claret.

The Port lodges in Gaia are also a popular stop for tourists during the summer, mostly in July and August. Most of the leading houses have tasting and sales rooms open to the public. It all adds to the confusion as masses of people take to the streets, stopping in at each house to visit and taste Ports. Many are expatriate Portuguese visiting family and friends during their holidays. Ferreira, for example, may get as many as 1,000 people a day during August. No one leaves without buying a bottle or two of Port. Ferreira sells thousands of cases of wine to visitors each year — although very little is vintage Port.

"It is very important business," said Pedro Silva Reis, whose family owns part of Real Vinicola. "We say the farther the lodges are up the hillside, the better the quality of visitors, since there is parking for buses down by the waterfront."

VINTAGE PORT STOCKS

Vintage Port represents a tiny percentage of a shipper's inventory in Vila Nova de Gaia. The majority of wooden vats and casks, concrete tanks, and stainless steel and fiberglass containers hold stocks for a shipper's bread-and-butter rubies and tawnies. Some houses also may have a large percentage of slightly higher quality wines to go into their vintage character or late-bottled vintage Ports. These have little to do with genuine vintage Port; they are simply glorified rubies. They are constantly being handled, blended and treated and do not improve with age in the bottle like a vintage Port. The only exceptions are a few traditional late-bottled vintage Ports, crusted Ports and vintage tawnies.

A quality Port house prides itself on the expert care of its various wines. In a lodge, workers carry out a seemingly endless series of winemaking processes, including fining, racking, filtering and stabilization as well as sensory and chemical analyses. Just as a sculptor shapes a piece of marble, these coarse young Ports must be tamed into something pleasantly drinkable and salable in just a few years.

By comparison, vintage Port is left to itself. It is handled very little and never manipulated by fining or filtering. A Port maker's goal for a vintage is the opposite of that of most other wines. A vintage Port must be as pure and powerful as possible so it slowly evolves over decades in the bottle. "If anything goes wrong with our vintage lots in the cellar, we should all be shot," said Jeremy Bull, a consulting winemaker for Cálem who worked for nearly three decades for Taylor and Fonseca as a blender and taster. "Vintage is the easiest wine to make. There should be no problems, unless some idiot does something stupid."

It is surprising how few vintage Ports have gone bad considering that until recently, quality control was almost nonexistent. Some producers have had problems with acetic bacteria in their lodges, which can increase a wine's volatile acidity. One producer even pasteurized his 1985 vintage Port to ensure against spoilage. Others have damaged wines through improper cellar procedures such as poor racking or using unclean vats and cellar equipment. These problems arise infrequently with the best producers of vintage Port.

YOUNG VINTAGES FROM THE DOURO

The process of making a vintage Port begins when the young wines arrive from the Douro Valley in February or March after the harvest. Shippers already have made a preliminary selection in the Douro of wines that could potentially go into the vintage blend. "We know quite well the areas and the farmers that produce the best wines for vintage," said Eduardo Seixas, the head blender for Sandeman. "We collect the best wines from those *quintas* to be shipped down to Gaia."

When they arrive in Gaia, the wines are analyzed and tasted again. The potential vintage wines are usually aged separately until the blending begins. Some producers may leave their young Ports in small, wooden 534-liter casks. Others use large 50- to 100-hectoliter wooden vats. A few even leave them in stainless steel containers in hopes of conserving more fruit in the wines — although it doesn't seem to work. Quinta do Noval and Fonseca have conducted studies on keeping wines in stainless steel containers instead of wooden ones. They found no benefit; in fact the wines were too rough and raw. The tiny amount of oxidation and evaporation that occurs during the year spent in wooden casks or vats seems to soften the wines' rough edges.

A lodge loses about 2 percent of its Port per year through evaporation. This varies according to the size and type of casks a shipper uses. For instance, Niepoort uses small lodge pipes, 534 liters, while Taylor Fladgate keeps its wines in large wooden vats with a capacity of a few thousand liters. Neither container gives a woody character to the wines since they are not made of new wood; however, in the smaller casks wines mature slightly more quickly.

Equally important is the length of time the wines spend maturing. Niepoort keeps its vintage wines in lodge casks for about a year, then moves them into large vats four or five months before bottling. Until recently, Kopke used to leave its vintage wines in small casks for nearly two years. "We lost too much of the fruit in the wine," said Emanuel Rodrigues, the young winemaker of Kopke, who began reducing the time spent in wood with the 1982 vintage. "We now bottle about six months earlier to conserve the fruit."

Some shippers also believe wines mature differently according to the location of their lodge on the hillside. "Our winemaker recently looked at a lodge for sale but it was located too far up the hillside of Gaia," said Dirk van der Niepoort. "The wines would have matured more quickly there compared to our current lodge, which is much closer to the river. It is a question of evaporation." The same concept applies to the location of the wines within the lodge itself. Those placed in casks at the top of a stack of three or four barrels will mature slightly faster than those at the bottom.

There is also a question of how often the wines are moved or racked from one vat to another. Most shippers keep their racking to a minimum to limit oxidation. "We want to maintain as much of the fruit as possible so we never rack the wines once they arrive from the Douro Valley," said Arnold Gilbert, part-owner and winemaker of Burmester. "The only other time the wine is racked is just before bottling."

To reduce oxidation, the wines are racked directly from one cask or vat to another. "The key is to try to move the wines around the lodges with as little oxidation as possible," said Andrew Burkes, an enology professor from Australia's Riverina Enology School who took a year's sabbatical working at Taylor Fladgate in 1989 and 1990. "Racking is not necessarily a bad thing as long as it is done well."

Producers may use inert gases such as nitrogen to protect their wines from the air when racking from one vat to another. Most shippers simply fill their casks and vats from the bottom up. This racking of vintage Ports, and of other wines sensitive to oxidation, is slightly different from the traditional method used for more commercial wines, like standard tawnies. Those are run off in the open air from one container into a vat and then pumped into another container, which accelerates their aging.

BLENDING A VINTAGE PORT

With a range of vintage-quality wines at their disposal, shippers spend long hours evaluating and blending wines in their tasting rooms during the early spring, about one and a half years after the harvest. For example, most shippers began seriously blending their 1985s in early 1987. They work with anything from five to 15 different lots of wine to come up with a final blend. Normally, there is a small panel of tasters to do this, which supposedly ensures a consistent quality and house style. For example, Taylor and Fonseca have a panel of five tasters that includes principals Alistair Robertson, Huyshe Bower and Bruce Guimaraens, as well as two enologists who are full-time members of the staff. They taste independently over a few days and then compare their findings.

"It is winemaking by consensus," said Robertson. "It is extremely important not to know the volumes of the wines. And the tasting must be blind. Nonetheless, you have expectations and it is like Bordeaux in a sense, they follow certain patterns. Certain vineyards always seem to go in."

Many of these tastings occur in rooms with magnificent views looking across the Douro River to the densely populated hillsides of Oporto. Other tasting rooms are less grand, overlooking a courtyard or an adjoining building's rooftop. A drearier view may make for better blending, since concentration is essential to bring together various lots of wines to produce the flagship Port.

Standing in a white-tiled tasting room in one of the lodges can be a daunting experience. Usually, hundreds of bottles line the walls. Each represents different barrel samples of wines. Some may be from specific *quintas*; others may be certain blends of tawnies and rubies. Samples of various finished wines and bottlings are also stored for reference, together with a few bottles of competitors' wines for comparative tastings. For instance, Sandeman's tasting room houses about 600 different bottles.

A tasting room is in constant use, with technicians monitoring the evolution of each wine in the cellar. A bottle may represent a single 534-liter pipe or a few hundred thousand liters of finished wine. A few may represent wines that will go into the vintage blend. "The tasting room makes or breaks your business," said Robertson. "It is truly the creation point of a house."

Each house has its own methods of tasting and blending, but they follow a general pattern. The various lots of wines available for the blend are evaluated for their depth of color, tannin content, concentration of fruit and overall balance. The minimum requirement for a good-quality vintage is color. Potential vintage Ports must be extremely dark and opaque to ensure a long life in the bottle. The darker the wine, the more phenolic compounds it contains, which account for the color and tannins in a wine, as well as some of its flavor components. "The very worst thing is if it does not have any color," said consulting blender Jeremy Bull. "If it doesn't have color, it is not worth arguing about. Color is everything in this game."

Of course, young Ports must not have obvious flaws in their smell or taste. Wines with detectable amounts of volatile acidity or other winemaking defects cannot be used in a blend. The style of a young Port may also come into play. A wine overly harsh or tannic could throw a blend out of balance, as could one with too much of a particular taste or character. Even young wines with great suppleness and delicacy may not be right for a house's particular vintage blend. It is always a balance, and totally subjective. The decision is the shipper's.

With agreement on the quality of their various lots, shippers begin making potential blends. All the various components are first blended together, and then a few of the lots are eliminated. One lot may have an inferior nose, while another may lack depth of fruit on the palate. It is up to the discretion of the taster, like any other critical tasting. "You might make a blend and say that is not that much different from the first. You might then say, I wonder what would happen if we only use those three there. It is up to you," added Bull.

Some shippers apparently even go to the extreme of blending in young Ports from another vintage to boost the power and color of their vintage blends. For instance, some deeply colored and harder 1986 might help a blend of a fleshy, fruity and fat 1985. This practice is neither legal nor ethical, but rumors of such blending methods underline how serious some houses take their vintage blends.

When possible vintage blends become available, other members of the house may be asked for their opinions. For the multinationals, this may mean sending samples to their overseas headquarters or waiting for a superior to visit Gaia. For instance, David Sandeman, the London-based chairman of Sandeman, always flies out to Oporto to supervise the final blends of a new vintage. Some houses may even exchange samples with neighbors to get feedback.

But the final responsibility rests within each house. Years later the decision may be considered a stroke of genius or a tactical error. "Your name is there on that wine for decades, not just for one or two years," said Bull. "And all the time, if you made a bad one, people are going to be saying over and over, 'Oh my God, this is awful.' It will affect the reputation of your other vintages. So it had better be bloody good."

GOVERNMENTAL APPROVAL

Once a final blend is decided upon, the alcoholic strength of the Port is brought up to a level of 20 percent to 21 percent, since the wines may have dropped in strength slightly through evaporation. The same neutral spirit is used as in the initial fortification up the Douro. Normally less than 0.5 percent is added. The proposed vintage blend is then sent to the state-run Instituto do Vinho do Porto, which chemically analyzes the wines and evaluates them in tastings with a panel of judges. If approved by the IVP, the wine will receive the black and white paper seal — *selo de garantia* — which is seen on the neck of all Port bottles. Regulations state that a vintage Port should be "a Port of one harvest produced in a year of recognized quality with exceptional organoleptic characteristics, dark and full-bodied with very fine aroma and palate and which is recognized by the IVP as having the right to the description 'vintage.' "

Although the IVP passes almost all the vintage samples submitted, there have been some inconsistencies in the procedure. Leading vintage Port shippers have had samples refused, while upstarts with no reputation for vintage have had their wines passed. Some producers have even sent in a rejected wine saying that it is a different sample, and have had the wine passed on the second go. It is amazing what the IVP has certified as vintage in past years. Some of the vintage Ports passed from companies like Real Companhia Velha in the 1970s and 1980s are not even up to the standard of a decent ruby. Such wines are light colored and insipid, lacking any structure for bottle aging. They are clearly not within the boundaries of the IVP's own regulations.

Standard Ports such as simple tawnies and rubies are even worse. There are Ports available on the domestic market for about $3 a bottle that taste like synthetic cough syrup and have nothing to do with Port. It is difficult to understand such discrepancies. Officials from the IVP claim that their approval method is thorough and meticulous, but this is hard to believe. One answer could be that samples sent for approval are different from those actually bottled. Or there may be political reasons that emerge behind closed doors.

DECLARING A VINTAGE

Shippers traditionally make their vintage declarations in March or April, after receiving IVP approval. This is about 18 months after the harvest. When shippers declare a vintage, they are simply publicly announcing their intent to bottle and market a particular vintage Port. Single-*quinta* or second-label wines are also vintage Ports, although they do not receive the marketing support of a true declared year. Regardless, there is always much debate over declarations. Shippers discuss the quality of their wines with other houses and try to get an indication if others will follow. James Symington of the Symington group echoes the view of most shippers: "Making a declaration is a purely independent decision. A shipper only makes a declaration when he has top-quality wine. It is as simple as that."

The fact that Quinta do Noval and Cockburn passed on declaring the highly regarded 1977 vintage underlines the individuality of declarations. Both houses, however, now agree that not declaring 1977 was a major error. For Cockburn, it meant that the company would not declare another vintage until 1983, effectively putting them out of the vintage Port game for nearly a decade. Noval, on the other hand, declared the 1978 vintage, which is extremely light and forward compared to the superb 1977s. Both houses lost face in the vintage race and only now have begun to gain back their reputations. "It is all a matter of prestige," said David Bain, financial director of Taylor. "It is very serious business, making a declaration. It is a little like choosing the Pope."

Today, very few of the leading vintage Port shippers would dare to declare a vintage on their own — unless the quality of the young Port was absolutely extraordinary. Highly regarded vintages are made on the reputations of a handful of leading houses such as Taylor, Fonseca and Graham. If these houses declare, other houses will usually follow. For instance, nearly all Port houses declared a 1985 vintage. "One had to have a 1985," said J.F. Falcão Carneiro of the small house of Wiese & Krohn. "The British houses declared the 1985 vintage and they are the ones that have a reputation for making vintage Ports."

Not so long ago, houses were much more secretive about the vintage business. Few knew what the others were doing regarding their declarations. Now, houses openly confer with one another about their intentions. "It is not healthy for the market to have split declarations anymore," said Noval's van Zeller. "It confuses the market." The most recent example of a split vintage was the declaration of 1983 and 1982. Houses like Croft and Noval declared the 1982

THE MANY FACETS OF PORT

The vintage Port industry is characterized by a unique blend of old-world tradition and modern technological innovation. The following pages provide a glimpse of some of the people and places that combine to produce the world's finest vintage Ports. All photos were taken by James Suckling unless otherwise noted.

Above left, Cristiano van Zeller crouches next to an ungrafted Nacional vine at Quinta do Noval. *Above right*, David Sandeman, chairman of Sandeman, rides in a small boat on the Douro River with his Quinta do Vau in the background. *Left*, *cestos da vindima*, or traditional harvest baskets, pile up at Cockburn's Quinta do Tua

Above, Peter Cobb, left, John Smithes and Gordon Guimaraens during the 1989 vintage at Tua

Right, the small town of Pinhão in the heart of the Douro Valley. Taylor-Fonseca runs a storage lodge on the riverbank. A *barco rebelo* is moored on the river

Above left,
Robin Reid and John
Burnett discuss and
sample proposed lots
for the 1987 Quinta da
Roêda in the Croft
tasting room in Vila
Nova de Gaia. *Left*,
Taylor-Fonseca's Alistair
Robertson, foreground,
and Bruce Guimaraens
taste various
samples of their wines
at Fonseca's
headquarters in Vila
Nova de Gaia

Right, John Burnett of Croft evaluates some freshly made Ports during the 1989 harvest at Quinta da Roêda. *Below*, a young sample of deeply colored 1989 Port from one of Fonseca's *quintas*

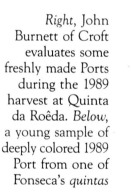

A view of the two river cities, Oporto on the left and Vila Nova de Gaia on the right. An elegant iron bridge links the cities

Above left, Fernando Nicolau de Almeida, of Ferreira, discusses the virtues of his vintage Ports and his legendary table wine, Barca Velha. *Below left*, Paul Symington in Graham's lodge in Vila Nova de Gaia in 1985

Right, James
Symington and a
worker at Quinta
do Vesùvio, once
owned by the
famous Dona
Antónia Ferreira.
The Symingtons
bought the
massive property
in 1989. *Below*,
the steeply terraced
vineyards of the
Douro Valley.
Below right,
ancient terraces
contrast with
more modern
ones on the left.
Wider terraces
without
stoneworks are
more popular
today

DANA LYON

Terraced
vineyards and
quintas are literally
carved out of the
rugged terrain of
the Douro Valley

ANDREW QUADY

Above, workers tread grapes for Port in a *lagar* during harvest. *Below left*, Bruce Guimaraens, of Taylor-Fonseca, checks the progress of the fermentation in a *lagar* during the 1989 harvest

The extensive terraces and buildings of Quinta do Noval
tower above the town of Pinhão. Noval produces the most collectible
vintage Port in the world, Quinta do Noval Nacional

vintage, while other top shippers like Taylor, Fonseca, Graham and Dow produced 1983s.

Many houses prefer to make a single-*quinta* or second-label vintage Port in good but undeclared years. These are vintage Ports in their own right, made from a single vintage, bottled after two years and approved by the IVP. Many shippers sell these wines eight to 10 years after bottling, so that they are drinkable on release. Single-*quinta* Ports come from one property, while second-label vintage Ports are blends like a regular vintage, but made in much smaller quantities. The best known single-*quinta* wine is Taylor's Quinta de Vargellas, while second-label wines include the likes of Fonseca-Guimaraens and Graham's Malvedos. These wines can be better than many declared vintage Ports. The 1964 Fonseca-Guimaraens and 1962 Malvedos are packed with concentrated, ripe fruit flavors and firm backbones; they are better than many 1963s.

Some Port shippers often say that single-*quinta* and second-label Ports are made in "off" years, which gives an unjustified negative connotation to the wines. There are a few Port producers who say the opposite and believe that such limited-production Ports should be the very best vintage Ports made, rather like a reserve wine. Vintage declarations are, in a way, a contrived marketing scheme for many Port houses, since most could produce excellent vintage Ports nearly every vintage. It could be more like Bordeaux, where each château makes its *grand vin* nearly every vintage, although the quantity depends on the quality of the overall vintage. "Even in the most ghastly years, I dare say someone probably makes some very good wines," said Robertson after a tasting of three decades' worth of Vargellas, Malvedos and Fonseca-Guimaraens — most of which were very good. "If the area makes 140,000 pipes of Port, it would be peculiar if one shipper or two couldn't make a few pipes of exceptional wines."

The 1987 vintage is a good example of the vintage declaration puzzle. Some houses such as Niepoort, Offley and Martinez declared 1987, but with the exception of Ferreira, most of the leading vintage Port shippers passed, instead deciding to make single-*quinta* or second-label wines. To make the whole thing even more confusing, some houses made a 1987, but did not declare it as a vintage. For instance, Quinta do Noval made about 1,200 cases of 1987. There is a traditional practice of bottling a few pipes of vintage Port even in undeclared years, according to Symington. "We used to always bottle a couple of pipes," he said. "We had a Dow 1965 which was a wonderful wine. But it really wasn't for selling."

One factor is that, although most shippers may not admit it, declaring a vintage depends heavily on having enough excellent wine. "We did not have a sufficient amount of wine to declare 1987," said Bull, who made a single-*quinta* 1987 Quinta do Foz at Cálem rather than a full-fledged vintage. "The wine itself was vintage quality. I can't tell exactly how much is sufficient, but you obviously can't declare 12 pipes of a wine for the worldwide demand. You cannot declare a year which you cannot supply your customers."

Other factors come into play in declaring a vintage, such as the proximity to the last declaration or the state of the economy in general. Many houses passed on the 1931 and 1958 vintages because they still had plenty of stocks to sell of 1927 and 1955. "The 1931 was my first vintage," recalled John Smithes, a former managing director of Cockburn. "It was a wonderful year. But we didn't declare because we had too much of the 1927. The market was in a slump and no one had money in those days. The 1958 vintage was the same. The 1955 was a large vintage and we had 1960 on the way. We couldn't declare." Cockburn was in such poor financial shape during the war that it couldn't buy the wines to declare the legendary 1945 vintage.

Social and political upheavals also have an effect. For instance, some shippers believe that the weak 1975 vintage was declared as a direct result of the 1974 revolution in Portugal. It took four or five years for the country to recover. Vintners clearly remember stories in British newspapers proclaiming the Port trade's last vintage. Only one of the houses, Real Companhia Velha (Royal Oporto), was actually nationalized during the revolution. Borges & Irmão was also taken over by the state; it was part of a bank that was nationalized. At the time there were threats of other houses going the same way.

"The main reason we declared the 1975 vintage was because we had the quality wines, but you have to remember it was right after the revolution," said Cockburn's Peter Cobb. "There were those people who thought they must put a stamp on something that could be the last vintage they made." Even the British wine trade was uneasy about the situation. "We were really under pressure from the British wine trade to ship the 1975 vintage," said James Symington. "They wanted to know that the Port trade still existed."

Oporto Bottling

The 1975 vintage was revolutionary in another sense — it was the first general declaration completely bottled in Portugal. In 1974 the Portuguese government passed a law that made it mandatory for all vintage Port to be bottled in Vila Nova de Gaia. The decision sent shock waves through the trade, especially to wine merchants in the United Kingdom. "We say 1970 was the last vintage bottled in England and 1975 was the first year declared in England," said Manual Angelo Barros of the Portuguese house of Barros, Almeida.

For centuries, most Port had been shipped in bulk and bottled by clients abroad. The British wine trade took great pride in its vintage Port bottlings. A few months after a vintage declaration, the wooden casks of Port would be shipped to merchants throughout the United Kingdom. They were normally sent in 534-liter casks, although some producers used hogsheads (267 liters) and quarter casks (134 liters).

Most houses employed their own coopers to make and repair these casks. Today Cockburn is the only house to do this, although other houses retain workers to repair and maintain their wooden vats and barrels. On arrival in Britain, the casks would be laid down in cellars until bottling in late fall or early winter. The quality of the bottles, corks and labels usually was left to the discretion of the clients, although many Port shippers supplied customers with labels and branded corks.

Exceptions to the practice were the vintages of 1942 and 1945, which were entirely bottled in Portugal due to import restrictions associated with World War II that were intended to reduce the purchase of foreign products. Until 1949, four years after the war had ended, the British imposed import quotas on wine merchants; few were interested in using their allocations to buy vintage Port, which might take years to sell. Instead, they bought tawnies and rubies along with table wines, which gave them a quick turnover. Arguably, this exercise in what the British wine trade calls "Oporto bottling" planted a seed. Some houses such as Cockburn began to reduce their bulk shipments of vintage Ports, because bottling meant more revenue for them.

"We tried to sell only Oporto-bottled with the 1960 and 1963 vintages under the initiation of Wyndham Fletcher, but it didn't work," said Cobb. "There were too many longtime clients in Great Britain who wanted to carry on the tradition of British bottling. They wouldn't accept the change." Pressure from the United Kingdom trade kept the practice alive for another three decades.

Before 1974, much of the bulk shipments of vintage Port ended up in cellars along the Thames River near London Bridge. Key wine merchants had their warehouses in the area, since it was close to the London docks. Besides vintage Port, they stored and bottled Sherry, Madeira and table wine such as white and red Bordeaux. Vintners now in their 60s and 70s vividly remember these Dickensian years in London cellars. The warehouses, many built in the early 19th century, were dark, dusty and dingy. Casks of wine would be unloaded from ships and rolled along the quay cellars or lifted onto flatbed trucks and moved to nearby warehouses. Both maintaining inventories and bottling were labor-intensive jobs carried out in sometimes extremely confined and damp conditions.

Most of the bottling equipment was primitive. Some was done completely by hand. There was little control over when or how the bottling took place. It was common to hear of casks of vintage Port getting lost and turning up years later. For instance, David Sandeman received a telephone call in 1984 from a merchant who found a cask of 1958 Sandeman in his cellar, which apparently had been overlooked. "Anybody in those days that could afford to buy a cask could do so and then bottle it themselves," said Robin Scott-Martin of Bristol wine merchant John Harvey & Sons.

But Scott-Martin, like many other British wine merchants, believes British-bottled vintage Port was always better quality than Portuguese-bottled, if a reputable merchant did the bottling. Companies such as John Harvey & Sons, Berry Brothers & Rudd, Justerini & Brooks, and Avery's of Bristol bottled both table and fortified wines. They were very well equipped. "It was a question of experience in bottling," he said. "We were bottling all the time."

Most of the Port houses had extremely poor bottling lines even in the 1970s. "When I joined Taylor, the bottling situation was three or four old women sitting on boxes of Port and using one of these little 'milking-the-cows,' three- or four-spout fillers," said Bull, who started at Taylor in the early 1960s. "Then a chap would bang in the cork with a hammer, and then another chap would attach the capsule with a string."

Few Port houses at the time had the money to invest in a bottling line. It was simply easier and more profitable to ship in bulk. "I have never heard many complaints from the Port shippers about the quality of the bottling in the United Kingdom," added John Avery of Avery's of Bristol. "They mostly went along with the idea that British bottling was better than Oporto's."

Mandatory Portuguese bottling has improved the overall quality of vintage Port, since it can be better controlled at the source. A better consistency of house style is more likely if the wine is bottled by the shippers themselves. The United Kingdom wine trade is full of stories of improper bottling methods, some of which were actually illegal, such as adding cheap ruby Ports to increase quantities of vintage. Such impropriety was discovered only decades later. For instance, a bottle of 1927 Graham opened for a tasting for this book was completely undrinkable due to what appeared to be poor bottling. The Port came in an almost clear, Scotch-style bottle without a branded cork. "United Kingdom bottling was always a problem in a way," said James Symington. "You never knew whether it was bottled at the right time or if it had been fined before the bottling. There was no way of telling."

MODERN BOTTLING AND SHIPPING

Today all the leading vintage Port shippers have modern bottling lines. Some can bottle as many as 10,000 bottles an hour, as well as automatically label, box and put the cases on palates. There is also a broad range of various plate and membrane filters to facilitate proper bottling, although these are not used for vintage Ports. The bottling equipment can insert the corks under a vacuum or extract any oxygen left in the bottle. Sometimes a tiny amount of sulfur dioxide may be added.

For vintage and other limited-production Ports, a visit to a small, quality shipper like Niepoort will convince anyone that a simple bottling line is more than adequate for vintage Port. Niepoort uses a tiny 600-bottle-an-hour line. The neck foils are put on by hand and the bottles are placed in boxes by two or three workers.

Regardless of their bottling line capacity, most shippers use extremely high-quality, thick, black bottles for their vintages and opt for the best corks, measuring in length from 45 to 52 centimeters — the size used for château-bottled Bordeaux or premium California wines. A limited amount of half bottles and magnums are usually bottled each vintage, as well as a few double magnums, jeroboams and imperials. Half bottles are an excellent size for vintage Port, since the wine matures more quickly and three or four people can comfortably enjoy a half bottle of vintage after a meal. Wine merchants, however, say it is difficult to sell half bottles of young vintage Port, though mature wines in smaller bottles sell for a premium.

The shape of the traditional vintage Port bottle has been evolving since the broad-shouldered, slightly tapered black bottles came into use. In recent years, many shippers have been modifying their bottles so that the corks fit in the necks perfectly straight. In the past, the necks were slightly wider at the bottom than at the top. This caused corks to fan out like Champagne corks after years in the bottle, making them difficult to extract. In fact, it is nearly impossible to pull a cork unbroken on a 30- or 40-year-old vintage Port. Today's new designs should make things easier.

After bottling, vintage Ports are capsuled, labeled and placed directly into their wooden cases. The IVP's black-and-white paper *selo de garantia* is also attached on each bottle's neck. They may be stored in producers' cellars for a few months before shipping. Part of the bottling will be held back in inventory and stored as unlabeled bottles, which are traditionally stacked on their sides, one on top of the other, in large bins holding a few thousand bottles each. Most houses place foil caps on each bottle to protect the corks. The entire process may be done on a bottling line or by hand. The cases are assembled just before shipping and loaded onto trucks to be taken to the nearby port of Leixoes, about 6 miles north of Oporto. The cases go into metal containers holding either 800 or 1,200 cases. The containers are then placed on large ships to be sent to customers around the world.

Most Port houses claim that they only ship in the fall or spring, when the weather is mild. They also ask for the containers to be placed within the hold of the ship to protect them from the elements. Nevertheless, there are plenty of cases still arriving in the United States with Port seeping from their corks — an indication of poor storage conditions. More houses should insist on using temperature-controlled containers for their vintage Port shipments to help ensure that the wine arrives in good condition. This only adds about 50 cents a bottle to the overall cost of the Port.

Since Oporto bottling became compulsory, most houses have shipped only about 60 percent to 70 percent of their entire production of a vintage. The rest is held back in reserve in their lodges. Before, they shipped nearly all the wine to Britain and held back only a few cases for their personal consumption. As a result, most houses have very limited stocks of old vintages in Oporto. Some shippers may have only a few cases of pre-1955 vintage Ports, and only a few bottles of the very rare years like 1927 or 1908. "It is amazing how few old vintages shippers have in Oporto," said Ben Howkins, author of the Port book *Rich, Rare and Red* and the United Kingdom representative of Taylor Fladgate. "People just didn't hold back stocks."

The situation has been much better since 1977. Most leading houses have kept a few thousand cases of their most recent vintages. The wines are periodically released on the market or used for special promotional events. Croft is a good example of how some houses are holding back young vintages. "We didn't really start holding back stocks until 1978," said managing director John Burnett. "Now, we sell a small amount *en primeur* (as futures) and hold back the rest. We want to have a sufficient amount of old vintages to supply our market for 20 years. This is a part of the patrimony of the company. It is very important to us."

Vintage Port is the flagship of any house. Its quality can make or break the reputation of a Port shipper. Making, blending and bottling a vintage is a highly individual matter. Maybe this is why Port shippers can spend hours discussing the virtues of particular vintages and certain wines — and not always their own. Vintage Port is their passion. It is the best they have to offer. "A house may make great aged tawnies or *colheitas*," said Rolf van der Niepoort, who owns the tiny house bearing his name, "but vintage Port is king."

CHAPTER V

THE VINTAGES: 1900-1987

Discussing the merits of one vintage compared to another is one of the favorite pastimes of Port lovers. This chapter explores the differences among many vintages of the 20th century. It is based on my tastings of vintage Ports since 1985. In addition, I have reviewed various books, such as Ernest Cockburn's *Port Wine and Oporto*, Wyndham Fletcher's *Port* and Sarah Bradford's *The Story of Port*. I have also discussed the vintages with veteran Port tasters.

The adage that vintage Port is made only about three times a decade is not true. Vintage Port may be *declared* on average three times per decade, but surely "non-declared" vintage Port is made much more often than that. For instance, vintage Port was made nearly every year in the 1980s and 1970s. Of course, not all were declared vintages, and for one reason or another Port houses may have made only a small amount of Port, whether single *quinta*, second label or undeclared.

Vintage Port can be made nearly every vintage. While some Port shippers and specialists argue that this is false, the results of my tastings support the claim. Alistair Robertson of Taylor Fladgate and Fonseca admitted, like many of his colleagues, that it would be surprising if someone could not make good wines in any given vintage, considering the massive size of the Douro Valley. Like any other wine region, there are microclimates and soils unique to certain areas, and in some years particular regions or vineyards in the Douro do better than others. Declaring a vintage, rather than simply making some vintage-quality wines, is more a question of quantity and marketing. Just taste vintage Port like the 1982 Malvedos or 1964 Fonseca-Guimaraens, and you will discover the truth. They may have been undeclared vintages but they are 100 percent vintage Ports all the same.

The vintages are rated on their overall quality, and their evolution is taken into account. A year like 1950 may have been good from the beginning, even though the wines are now getting over the hill. The ageworthiness of younger vintages, on the other hand, is a serious factor in their scoring. In years of which I have no personal experience, I have used reliable outside sources. In addition, I did not taste any of the vintages before 1977 in their very early stages, so I relied on other references to rate them.

The vintages in this chapter were rated on *The Wine Spectator* 100-point scale:

95-100 Classic
90-94 Outstanding
80-89 Good to Very Good
70-79 Average
60-69 Below Average
50-59 Poor

I have included general information about the style of each vintage and the wines' current drinkability, when possible. The best wines of the years are also noted, as well as pertinent information on weather conditions and market factors. Bottle variation is always a factor in tasting old vintage Ports, so this is also taken into consideration. Estimated average current U.S. and United Kingdom auction and retail prices are also included, written as: US auction/retail, UK auction/retail; those prices that are unavailable are noted as NA.

1987: VERY GOOD (88)
BALANCED, ELEGANT, GOOD FINESSE

The 1987 vintage is very good, and most Port shippers agree that the year could easily have been declared generally if there had been more wine to go around. Most of the leading names in Port decided to make single-*quinta* or second-label vintage Ports. Quite a few houses did declare, however, including Niepoort, Ferreira, Martinez, Offley and various single *quintas*.

The majority of vintage Ports I have tasted from 1987 have a wonderful balance of fine tannins and elegant fruit. Although I never tasted the 1967 vintage when it was young, there seems to be a harmonious structure similar to the 1987. They may not be the longest-lived wines, but the 1987s will provide extremely good drinking 10 to 15 years after the harvest date.

The vintage was one of low yields; the weather was dry through most of the winter and spring, with rainfall around half the norm. Grapes were slow to develop, but the dry, hot summer weather, with temperatures often reaching over 100 degrees Fahrenheit, put the grapes back on schedule. Growers in the Douro Valley realized the harvest would be one of the earliest in memory; most started in early September. There were a few days of rain during the harvest, but for the most part grapes were picked in extremely good condition. Yields were slightly below average, as was the overall quantity of the vintage.

Some of the stars of the vintage are Quinta do Noval Nacional, Quinta de Vargellas, Malvedos, Niepoort, Fonseca-Guimaraens, Quinta do Noval and Ferreira. 1987 has not been well received by the trade, even though the Niepoort, Quinta do Noval and Ferreira are very good quality, perhaps better than their 1985s. Collectors who missed out on these houses' 1985s would do well buying their 1987s. Some of the other Ports, such as the Vargellas, Malvedos and Fonseca-Guimaraens, will probably not be released on the market until mid-1990. Their excellent quality will be worth the wait.

Current prices: US $26/NA UK £15/NA

1986: GOOD (80)
FIRM, GUTSY, A LITTLE SIMPLE

The 1986 vintage will not go down in history books as an exceptional vintage. No one declared it, although some very fine single-*quinta* and second-label vintage Ports were made. The wines in general are slightly softer and rounder than the 1987s. They lack the breeding of the 1987s or 1985s. Nonetheless, the best of the vintage, like Vargellas and Fonseca-Guimaraens, are pretty wines that should be drinkable about a decade after the harvest.

Current prices: US $35/NA UK £14/NA

1985: CLASSIC (96)
OPULENT, INTENSE, SOLID BACKBONE

Producers found the 1985 vintage stupendous from the start. These Ports are filled with rich fruit and firm tannins. This was a year when nearly everybody made good wines, and it was the first time a unanimous declaration was made since 1975. There are dozens of very good to outstanding wines in this vintage. Some critics say that 1985 lacks the backbone or grip of a truly great vintage, but every time I taste a range of 1985s, I am bowled over by their huge amounts of luscious fruit and round tannins. The best 1985s have the structure to compare with the 1966s, 1955s, 1935s and 1934s. I recommend drinking the best 1985s starting in the late 1990s. I have heard of people drinking 1985s just five years after the vintage, and though it is difficult to resist all that sweet fruit, those who do will surely be rewarded.

The 1985 vintage was a classic in every way. The year started with a normal cold winter, although the months of February and March were slightly warmer than usual. With some rain in the spring, temperatures remained normal until summer. In June it became extremely warm and the rest of the summer was perfect. The grapes were picked in near-perfect condition. With a large, healthy harvest, fermentations went well. Many Port producers said they could tell from the moment the grapes were fermented that they had a winner.

The best wines of the vintage come as no surprise. Fonseca, Graham, Nacional, Taylor, Dow and Cockburn are sublime. There are a few dark horse wines in 1985, however, that could finish in front of some of the better known houses in years to come. They include Burmester, Kopke, Niepoort and Smith Woodhouse. All three houses represent extraordinary quality for the money. The best wines should not be opened until the turn of the century — they will carry on for another two or three decades.

Current prices: US $31/$28 UK £19/£13

1984: GOOD (81)
LEAN, LINEAR, ONE-DIMENSIONAL

I may be slightly overcritical of 1984. The vintage made some very attractive wines, but it is not surprising to me that none of the major houses declared 1984. The wines are rather lean and one-dimensional. Still, they show very appealing, straightforward fruit flavors and silky tannins. The most successful wines are Quinta de Vargellas, Dow Quinta do Bomfim, Burmester and Graham's Malvedos. All of the 1984s will be delicious by the mid-1990s.

Current prices: US $17/NA UK £12/NA

1983: OUTSTANDING (92)
POWERFUL, TANNIC, AGEWORTHY

The more I taste 1983s, the better I like them. They are muscular, and underline what Port shippers mean when they say a young Port has grip. The best 1983s were still very tannic and almost raw at six years old. The top wines, like Graham and Cockburn, will age as well as any of the 1985s, and should not be drunk until the turn of the century. I still do not understand why the vintage was not declared generally. 1983 was what the Port trade calls a split vintage, since some houses opted to declare 1982. Those who chose 1982 clearly made a mistake. The 1983 is similar in style and structure to 1966, which is another tannic, powerful year that is drinking extremely well after nearly 25 years of bottle age.

The weather during 1983 was variable, but in the end, these variations seemed to moderate the sometimes severe weather during the growing season in the Douro Valley. The winter was very cold and dry, while most of the spring was exceedingly wet. These conditions led to poor flowering in some vineyards. The summer did not help the situation; it was rather moderate in temperature with some rain. In early September nature turned on the afterburners, and what some growers had first thought would be a disastrous vintage turned into a glorious harvest. With an average-size crop, growers picked healthy grapes under clear skies.

Most well-known houses that declared 1983 made very good to outstanding wines. Some of the surprises of the vintage include Offley Boa Vista, Smith Woodhouse, Ferreira, Quinta do Seixo and Quarles Harris. Powerful, burly wines with an abundance of fruit and tannins, they are as good as the big names of the vintage such as Taylor and Fonseca. Another interesting facet to the vintage is that Cockburn re-entered the vintage Port game after standing on the sidelines since 1975. The hard-hitting 1983 Cockburn puts this house firmly back with the top vintage Port producers.

Current prices: US $30/$28 UK £17/£10

1982: GOOD (84)
SWEET, RAISINY, UNBALANCED

There are some very good 1982 vintage Ports, but few truly outstanding ones. Croft and Quinta do Noval led the field in declaring the vintage, and both were apparently extremely keen on the year. Noval has since agreed that the vintage has not evolved as well as first expected. Croft remains positive about the year, though its 1982 is very weak. Clearly, there are some delicious wines from 1982, and those like Graham's Malvedos, Niepoort and Warre Quinta da Cavadinha would honor anyone's decanter. They are sweet, velvety wines with a round and fruity mouth-feel.

My one major complaint with 1982, however, is that many wines seemed to have been made with grapes that were much too ripe. Many of the 1982s are too sweet and raisiny on the palate and are slightly unbalanced, lacking the class of 1983 or 1980. The vintage is in the same league as the very sweet 1978 or perhaps the 1950. It will not be a long-lived vintage but should drink well until 2000 to 2005.

There was little rain in 1982. The Douro Valley was in near-drought conditions for most of the year. The winter was cold, and precipitation was almost nonexistent. The spring was also dry and the vines flowered under excellent conditions. The summer was blistering hot and rain never fell. By the time the harvest started in the second week of September, many of the grapes already had begun to shrivel like raisins. Nonetheless, the harvest was completed with little difficulty, and although the fermentations were hot and hard to control in some areas due to the high sugar levels, most Port producers were happy with the quality of their wines.

I have only found two wines from this vintage that are outstanding — Graham's Malvedos and Niepoort. Malvedos is beefy, thick and fruity on the palate, with luscious fruit flavors. Niepoort was a close second, also showing plenty of opulent, sweet fruit and firm tannins. Most of the other 1982s are very close in quality and I rated most of them as very good. One vintage Port in 1982 that was of particular interest came from Montex Champalimaud. It is a single-*quinta* wine made near the town of Regua in the lower part of the Douro, where most of the more common Ports originate. With a deep color and extremely sweet fruit, the 1982 Champalimaud shows that good wines are not found just in the Cima Corgo.

Current prices: US $25/$14 UK £15/£8

1980: VERY GOOD (87)
SOLID, WELL STRUCTURED, FOCUSED FRUIT

The 1980 vintage has been overlooked since it was first sold in 1982 as futures. Its very good quality was never in question; however, the wine trade, mostly in the United Kingdom, believed it was too expensive. The 1980s have remained in the shadow of the amazingly good 1977s, 1983s and 1985s. The wines themselves are very typical vintage Ports, with firm, well-focused fruit and plenty of backbone. Most will be drinking well in the early 1990s, and will continue to improve for another decade or two.

The growing season was variable in 1980. After a wet winter, the spring began with plenty of rain, and the weather warmed by the start of the summer. There was a poor flowering, which reduced the number of berries on the vines. The months of June, July and August were dry and hot, which helped what appeared to be a difficult year. Some rain fell before the harvest in late September, but the picking of the grapes was done under mostly clear skies, although scattered showers occasionally fell.

The Symington group made the stars of the vintage — Dow, Graham, Warre and Smith Woodhouse. Taylor Fladgate also made a successful vintage Port. Not all the big names had success. For instance, the 1980 is Fonseca's worse vintage Port this century. Even the legendary Noval Nacional was rather weak. Some major houses such as Croft, Noval and Cockburn decided not to declare the year. Those shippers who did made much smaller quantities than normal.

Current prices: US $30/$27 UK £16/£11

1979: AVERAGE (74)
LIGHT, SWEET, INSIPID

No one should have declared 1979, considering its dull quality overall. Calling the year "average" is very generous. Even Graham's Malvedos is a dud compared to other recent vintages. On the other hand, Quinta da Cavadinha and Quinta do Bomfim made some respectable vintage Ports. Although they are not wines to cellar for any length of time, they are simple, with clean fruit flavors and soft tannins, and are enjoyable to drink.

Current prices: US $29/NA UK £14/NA

1978: Good (84)
FRUITY, SOFT, READY

There were no outstanding wines made in 1978, but the year produced some attractive and delicious vintage Ports. Nearly all were extremely drinkable in 1990, with layers of sweet, ripe fruit and soft, round tannins. Many producers commented on the high residual sugar levels in their wines. Some of the 1978s are extremely sugary.

Nevertheless, wines like the Ferreira, Bomfim, Eira Velha and Vargellas are fragrant and delicious, with a caressing mouth-feel. They are ready to drink now and should continue to maintain their fruit for another decade or so. The major disappointment of the vintage is Quinta do Noval, which strangely decided to declare the 1978 instead of the grand 1977. The Noval 1978 is one of the weakest wines of the vintage. The good 1978s can be deceiving due to their soft structure. They should evolve quickly; however, it could turn out to be a year like 1960, which some critics thought would have passed away long ago but has still kept going in many cases.

Current prices: US $27/$17 UK £16/£8

1977: Classic (97)
TOUGH, TANNIC, COMPLEX, AGELESS

The 1977 is the best vintage since the glorious 1963. It has a monumental combination of concentrated rich fruit, iron-clad tannins and firm acidity. Many of 1977s may have the potential to age for 100 years, offering the Port lover decades of enjoyment. They are wines to be cellared for future generations, if one can be patient enough.

To taste the 1977 Fonseca is to experience perfection in vintage Port. The wine is so complete in every way it is hard to describe, and the Taylor is nearly the same. Those two wines and the Dow are clearly the stars of the vintage. In fact, all of the 1977 vintage Ports I tasted that scored 80 points or more will easily improve well into the 21st century.

The weather in 1977 was quite severe in many ways. It rained heavily for much of the winter and the spring was unseasonably cold. There were isolated instances of frost. This cold weather slightly delayed the flowering and continued mild temperatures for most of the summer slowed the development of the fruit. September, however, was extremely hot and threw the vines into high gear. The harvest began at the end of the month, and healthy grapes were picked under good weather conditions. The harvest was slightly smaller than average.

There was some idea that 1977s were starting to be ready to drink in 1990, but I believe most of these vintage Ports need a minimum of 15 years of bottle age. Only in 1990 were they beginning to come out of their dormant period, and some, such as Graham, were tasting slightly dumb still, not giving as much fruit and depth as one would expect. Graham, however, like so many of the 1977s, is truly spellbinding. These are great vintage Ports, showing an abundance of wonderful fruit while maintaining a superb structure.

Surprisingly, some producers did not make a 1977, including Cockburn and Noval. Both houses have already publicly admitted their embarrassment for not declaring a 1977. Perhaps they did not have the quality.

There were some poor vintage Ports made in 1977. Houses like Feuerheerd, Kopke, Cálem and Messias made flawed wines that were extremely high in vinegarlike volatile acidity. It only adds credence to the adage that great grapes can be ruined by poor winemaking.

Current prices: US $50/$40 UK £27/£17

1976: AVERAGE (76)
SIMPLE, VARIABLE, SHORT

Few houses made vintage Ports in 1976, so I can conclude only that the overall quality of the year was not very good. The 1976 Fonseca-Guimaraens must be a fluke, since it is a massively rich and structured wine — much better than its weakling sister, 1975. It still needed five more years of bottle age in 1990. Quinta de Vargellas is also good, with fresh fruit flavors and well-knit tannins, though it is completely ready to drink. Another second-label wine from a major house, Graham's Malvedos, is very weak and clumsy.

It might be better to buy Smith Woodhouse's late-bottled vintage if one is interested in drinking a wine from the 1976 vintage. Bottled after four years in cask, it is a traditional late-bottled vintage and is not cold-stabilized, fined or filtered. It throws a crust like a vintage. The 1976 Smith Woodhouse late-bottled vintage is very good, with rich flavors and balanced fruit.

Current prices: US $32/NA UK £18/NA

1975: GOOD (80)
LIGHT, ONE-DIMENSIONAL, FRUITY

The 1975 vintage has received more hype than it ever has deserved. Some Port shippers admit that it was a child of the Portuguese revolution in 1974, when many producers thought 1975 was going to be their last vintage before being nationalized. Others say that politics had nothing to do with declaring 1975 and that their wines from the vintage looked very good when they declared. They merely did not evolve as well as expected. I only rated the 1975 as "good," since most of the wines are no longer improving and are starting to become very alcoholic. I am sure that even when 1975 was young it was never more than good.

It is difficult to say why 1975 is rather light compared to other vintage Ports at the 15-year stage. The weather was relatively good. There was a lot of rain during the winter, although most of the spring passed without precipitation. The summer was warm and sunny for the most part. The only problem may have been the rain just before the harvest, which occurred in the first week of October. This may have diluted the grapes slightly. The picking was done under clear skies, however.

1975 may be the only generally declared vintage that produced no outstanding wines. Even the legendary Quinta do Noval Nacional was not that great in 1975, although it was good and will improve with some bottle age. Cálem, Kopke, Ferreira and Noval are also very attractive.

Current prices: US $42/28 UK £19£12

1974: AVERAGE (74)
AROMATIC, ANGULAR, SMALL PRODUCTION

I do not have many notes for 1974, and only lesser-known houses like Barros and Kopke declared the vintage. Those wines are very light and simple. The Quinta de Vargellas was drinkable in 1990 but did not appear to be improving much. I would recommend staying away from this vintage, although Smith Woodhouse and Warre made some very good traditional late-bottled vintage Ports. Indeed, the Smith Woodhouse was still deliciously impressive in 1990.

Current prices: US $38/NA UK £19/NA

1972: AVERAGE (79)
LIGHT, FRAGRANT, EASY TO DRINK

Only Dow, Rebello Valente and Offley Forrester declared 1972. Taylor also made a good Quinta de Vargellas. These few vintage Ports are good quality, with fresh fruit flavors and light tannins. They were still very drinkable in 1990, but did not seem to be improving.

Quantities were very small, since the weather was difficult for most of the year. The winter and spring were without incident, and the summer started out very well, with a hot June and July, but it rained intermittently through the rest of the summer. Another difficulty with the vintage was that the wines were fortified with synthetic alcohol. Perhaps that is why the few vintage Ports made in 1972 have an unusual canned fruit aroma.

Current prices: US $36/$27 UK £18/£12

1970: CLASSIC (95)
HARMONIOUS, WELL STRUCTURED, INTENSE FRUIT

Many of the 1970 vintage Ports are magnificent wines with an abundance of rich, ripe berry flavors, firm tannins and a long finish. It is difficult to find better wines than the 1970 Taylor, 1970 Quinta do Noval Nacional and 1970 Fonseca. All three of these wines were not completely ready to drink in 1990 and needed another two or three years of bottle age. Most of the 1970s are very drinkable now but will continue to improve for another two decades. They are classic vintage Ports with the concentration of fruit and tannin to ensure excellent longevity.

The weather was nearly perfect throughout the year, with just enough cold weather and rain in the winter to stress the vines, and sufficiently warm temperatures and clear skies to ensure proper flowering. The summer was hot and mostly clear. September had a few showers during the first half, but by the third week the weather was warm and sunny again to start the harvest. The good weather continued through the picking. Fermentation and fortification went well just about everywhere.

The uniform quality of the vintage is amazing. Out of the 35 vintage Ports I have tasted over the years from the 1970 vintage, 28 were good to outstanding. Moreover, 20 scored 85 points or more on *The Wine Spectator* 100-point tasting scale. Any of the well-known houses' vintage Ports will please even the most finicky Port drinker. This is also a vintage to try some of the lesser-known houses like Niepoort, Quarles Harris, Rebello Valente, Martinez, Gould Campbell, Delaforce, Morgan Brothers and Burmester. This generally declared vintage is truly excellent.

Current prices: US $60/$42 UK £28/£18

1969: AVERAGE (72)
LIGHT, SIMPLE, TINY PRODUCTION

I have only tasted one 1969 vintage Port, Quinta de Vargellas, and it was very impressive, with aromatic violet and fruit on the nose and sweet berries on the palate. I do not believe any other houses made a 1969, except for those who made a little for their employees and owners, so the overall quality probably did not add up to much.

Current prices: US $50/NA UK £20/£19

1968: AVERAGE (77)
ONE-DIMENSIONAL, FRUITY, SMALL CROP

There were a few more 1968s made than 1969s, although no houses declared either vintage. I have tasted the Fonseca-Guimaraens, Quinta de Vargellas and Malvedos. The Fonseca and Vargellas were still good in 1990, though the Malvedos was fading.

Current prices: US $52/NA UK £19/NA

1967: VERY GOOD (88)
FOCUSED FRUIT, ANGULAR, ELEGANT

When Cockburn decided to declare the 1967 vintage instead of the excellent 1966, some of its employees claimed it would prove to be as great as the legendary 1927. The handful of other houses that declared also were very keen on the vintage. While Cockburn 1967, certainly a very good wine, will never live up to the quality of its superb 1927, some of the other 1967s may. What strikes one about a good 1967 is its firm structure and elegant fruit. It reminds me of a fine claret.

All of the 1967s I have tasted over the years were drinking very well, and most will easily improve into the next century. The weather was difficult for much of the growing season. The winter was extremely cold, with temperatures often dropping below zero. A cool and sometimes wet spring led to a poor flowering, and growers expected a small harvest. The summer was hot and there were many thunderstorms, notably near the beginning of the harvest. The picking, however, proceeded under good conditions.

Besides Noval's Nacional, the best wines of the vintage are not very popular in most other years. Rebello Valente and Martinez are both impressive, powerful wines with plenty of fruit and tannins. Other great wines such as Sandeman and Fonseca-Guimaraens were very tannic and could have used a few more years of bottle age when I tasted them in 1990. In fact, these two wines are nearly as good as their 1966s — and generally less expensive.

Current prices: US $62/$37 UK £28/£13

1966: OUTSTANDING (93)
IRON BACKBONE, GOOD CONCENTRATION, FRESH FLAVORS

There has always been a debate among Port aficionados as to whether 1963 or 1966 is better. Some believe 1966 is superior, though this may have more do to with the fact that 1966s sell for about half the price of 1963s. Although most 1966s are wonderful, I prefer the 1963 with little hesitation. Nonetheless it is easy to understand why some people are so impressed with the 1966s. They are solid and well built, with superb proportions of tannins, fruit and acidity. The best are classic vintage Ports.

The growing season was very good in one sense — there was very little rain. The winter was normal, with some showers, but there was no rain from April to September, and drought conditions arose during the summer, reducing yields. Some of the vines could not nourish their fruit properly, and most of the key vineyards had vines with very small berries. Some of the fruit was burned and shriveled by the sun. The harvest started in the third week of September. Rain finally arrived a few days after the harvest started, but it had little effect on the quality of the grapes. The overall harvest was small, and the berries were small and rich in tannins.

The best wines from 1966 are those from the highly reputed houses, though Niepoort and Offley also made excellent wines. The stars are clearly Noval Nacional and Fonseca. They are massive wines with a bounty of ripe fruit and hard tannins. For maximum enjoyment, I thought they needed another five years of bottle age when I tasted them in late 1989. They will age for many more decades. The Graham, Sandeman, Cockburn, Noval and Croft are also outstanding. Especially noteworthy in this group is the 1966 Quinta do Noval, which is much better than the Noval 1963, and probably the best Noval since 1955.

Current prices: US $76/$55 UK £34/£22

1965: GOOD (80)
RICH, FOCUSED FRUIT, TINY PRODUCTION

I know of only one house that declared 1965, Wiese & Krohn, and it made a very good wine. Fonseca-Guimaraens made the wine of the vintage, however. The 1965s have a surprising amount of delectable fruit and a silky mouth-feel. Few shippers discuss the 1965 vintage, however, apparently because quantities of very good wines were limited; possibly only one or two dozen pipes were available.

Current prices: US $21/$35 UK NA/£26

1964: GOOD (81)
APPEALING FRUIT, STYLISH, SOFT, ROUND

The 1964 vintage made some useful, good-quality Ports, although no major houses declared. Most of the 1964s, like Quinta de Vargellas and Malvedos, are at or past their peaks, including the Noval Nacional. The Fonseca-Guimaraens, however, was still quite youthful in 1990, and should drink well through the decade.

Current prices: US $55/37 UK £21/£15

1963: CLASSIC (98)
COPIOUS FRUIT, FORCEFUL, EXTREMELY AGEWORTHY

The 1963 vintage needs no introduction. It lives up to its superlative reputation in every way. A nearly complete failure in most European wines regions, 1963 produced vintage Ports with monumental concentrations of ripe fruit and perfectly integrated tannins. The best are Rubenesque — rich, round, luscious creatures that are irresistibly ageless. At nearly 30 years old, almost all of the 1963s I tasted in 1990 were still in perfect drinking condition and showed few signs of decline.

The winter was average, with cold spells and rain. Spring was much cooler and wetter than normal, though the weather during the flowering was good and ensured a proper berry set. The summer was mostly dry, with long warm days. September was perfect for harvesting, with hot days and cool nights. It is difficult to pinpoint just what made 1963 great, but why question nature when the results are so stupendous?

There are truly some astounding Ports in this vintage. The Quinta do Noval Nacional is out of this world, with layers of ripe grapy flavors and tons of tannins. I once tasted it with a Port shipper who thought it was a barrel sample of a wine nearly 30 years younger. The Fonseca, Graham, Taylor and Sandeman are almost as impressive, but are more earthly in their rich, ripe fruit flavors and perfectly knit tannins. With the exception of Noval's regular bottling, almost all the major shippers made beguiling wines. The Noval 1963 is good but slightly disappointing, since it had already reached its peak in the mid-1980s. One does not have to stick to the big names, however, to find success. Houses like Delaforce, Niepoort, Smith Woodhouse and many others made excellent wines in 1963. Reviewing 26 different 1963s, I gave at least 80 points to all but one. Five scored more than 95 points.

Current prices: US $116/$90 UK £47/£34

1962: Good (82)
PLEASANT, FRUITY, SOFT

Only Offley Forrester declared 1962. Although I have never tasted the Offley, the other three vintage Ports I have tasted are very good indeed. They are well-structured wines with rich fruit and ripe tannins and should offer very good drinking during the 1990s. Noval's Nacional was made in this vintage and is very good.

Current prices: US $68/NA UK £20/£11

1961: Good (80)
VERY RIPE, ROASTED FLAVORS, SWEET

Portugal, like most of Europe, was very dry and hot for most of the year, so the vintage produced some very ripe, sweet wines with plenty of fruit and tannin. Quantities were small, and almost none of the houses wanted to declare, since there was a general declaration in 1960. Wiese & Krohn declared about 10 pipes' worth, while other houses made single-*quinta* or second-label wines. The few 1961s I tasted in 1990 were drinking very well. Some, such as the Fonseca-Guimaraens, should improve for another four or five years before reaching their peak. Quinta de Vargellas, however, is extremely disappointing in this vintage, with very high levels of volatile acidity.

Current prices: US $76/NA UK £35/NA

1960: Very Good (87)
BALANCED, SWEET, ELEGANT, PEAKED

Years ago, many vintage Port experts said that 1960 vintage Ports were light and quick-maturing, but many are still excellent to drink. Many reached their peak in the early 1980s and have remained on a plateau ever since. It would be wise, however, to drink them at this point because it is doubtful any will improve with age. The best of the 1960s, such as Croft, Dow and Wiese & Krohn, are excellent examples of the delicacy and richness a fine vintage Port offers at the peak of its evolution. They are a joy to drink.

Some of the 1960s evolved slightly more quickly due to rain halfway through the harvest.

The growing season was average by all accounts until the late summer, when it became exceedingly hot. The heat carried through to late September, but then rain and cold weather arrived. Some growers did not get all of their crop in before the rains, though most made good vintage Ports.

Current prices: US $83/$54 UK £33/£22

1958: GOOD (84)
FRAGRANT, FRAGILE, FRUITY

Apparently 1958 was a mild and sometimes wet year, as in most of Europe; nonetheless, some very useful vintage Ports were made. More than a dozen houses declared the vintage, and those that did not would have if not for the vintage's proximity to the generally declared 1955. All the 1958s I tasted in late 1989 were on a slow decline, even though they were very enjoyable wines. They should be drunk as soon as possible, although some, such as the Fonseca-Guimaraens and Wiese & Krohn, should hold on for a few years. The leading vintage Port shippers who declared 1958 include Noval, Sandeman and Warre. Cockburn made two or three pipes for the private consumption of its owners.

Current prices: US $94/$47 UK £32/£17

1957: VERY GOOD (85)
ANGULAR, TANNIC, LIVELY, TINY PRODUCTION

Although I have only tasted three 1957 vintage Ports, I have been impressed with their quality. Only Mackenzie, Wiese & Krohn and Butler & Nephew declared. I have tasted the Wiese & Krohn and was impressed by its firm structure and fresh fruit. Although they did not declare the vintage, Dow and Sandeman made a few pipes of 1957, which were sold to a selected number of United Kingdom merchants; the Sandeman was excellent when I drank it in late 1988. Any of the 1957s will be hard to find due to their very limited production.

Current prices: US $140/$38 UK £32/£17

1955: OUTSTANDING (94)
HARMONIOUS, REFINED, FRUITY, SOLID

The 1955s are complete vintage Ports with wonderfully balanced proportions of mature, rich fruit flavors and mellow, firm tannins. They are superbly balanced. When the vintage was declared in 1957, the Port trade was in the doldrums. Shippers could not give their wines away. This difficulty was the result of a generally depressed wine market in the United Kingdom, and had nothing to do with the quality of the vintage. Most 1955s were drinking beautifully in 1989, and they seemed to have long lives ahead of them. They were on a plateau in their evolution, and I estimate they should remain there into the next century.

The 1955 growing season was apparently an excellent year in nearly every way, although the temperatures were slightly above average for most of the spring and late summer — two crucial periods for the vines. The clear, warm weather held out for the harvest. The four best wines of the vintage are Niepoort, Fonseca, Graham and Sandeman. Niepoort is the great surprise in the group, and is truly a blockbuster. It showed masses of fruit when I tasted it in early 1990, and seemed almost ageless. The other three leaders were not far behind.

Current prices: US $160/$135 UK £65/£47

1954: VERY GOOD (85)
FRAGRANT, BALANCED, FRESH, FRUITY

I have tasted only one 1954, the Graham, so it is hard to generalize, but the vintage has a good reputation among shippers. Burmester, Mackenzie and Offley Forrester declared small lots of vintage wines. The Graham is impressive, with a wonderful balance of fresh fruit and medium tannin. Apparently Graham sold part of its vintage declaration to the Bristol, England, wine merchant John Harvey & Sons, which bottled and sold it as Harveys 1954. This wine also has a very good reputation among Port collectors in Britain.

Current prices: US $155/NA UK £46/NA

1952: GOOD (80)
FRUITY, SIMPLE, SWEET, TINY PRODUCTION

There are few 1952s available. I have tasted only Graham's Malvedos, and in 1989 it was still holding on, with lovely, silky, mature fruit flavors. Kopke and Mackenzie also declared the vintage.

Current prices: US $125/NA UK £35/NA

1950: VERY GOOD (86)
SUBTLE, SWEET, SOFT

Most of the 1950s have seen better days. When I tasted a few of them with a Port shipper in late 1989, he said that they were no longer vintage Ports but more like aged tawnies. Most would have been better in the early 1980s, though some, such as the Sandeman, Dow and Quinta do Noval, were still lovely in 1990. They may not impress one with gobs of fresh fruit and firm tannins, but they are pleasantly fruity, with a soft, caressing mouth-feel. The Noval Nacional, on the other hand, is still a vigorous, full-bodied vintage Port with plenty of fresh, sweet plum flavors and a long finish. Nacional is the exception in 1950, but the year more than lives up to its reputation as a light and useful vintage.

Current prices: US $150/$112 UK £56/£25

1949: AVERAGE (70)

This vintage has no reputation, and I have never tasted a 1949. Warre shipped a few pipes to British customers in need of vintage Port after World War II.

Current prices: Not available.

1948: CLASSIC (99)
MASSIVE, SUPER RIPE, POWERFUL

There has always been a debate over which vintage is better, 1948 or 1947. I have always favored the 1948s. They are massively proportioned wines with layers of ripe berry flavors and iron backbones. These wines are easily on their way to aging 100 years or more. I have tasted only three wines from the vintage: Fonseca, Taylor and Graham. But they scored 100, 99 and 98, respectively. They were all magical. Their concentration of ripe fruit was due to an extremely hot growing season, leaving the grapes bulging with natural sugars when picked. It was so hot during the harvest that some producers had problems controlling their fermentations. Those who managed, however, made stunning wines.

Current prices: US $295/$245 UK £125/£95

1947: OUTSTANDING (93)
BALANCED, INTEGRATED, ATTRACTIVE

The 1947s have always been described as light and delicate. Many British wine merchants in the early 1950s said that the 1947s would not last — they were very wrong. I tasted four 1947s in late 1989, and they were drinking beautifully. They were pretty, with the elegance and exquisite craftsmanship of a fine antique Swiss watch. There was no indication of declining quality in their evolution. The 1947 Cockburn underlines the quality of the vintage, showing delicious, round cassis flavors and fine, silky tannins. These are truly fine vintage Ports.

Current prices: US $225/$180 UK £75/£45

1946: AVERAGE (70)

I recently discovered bottles of 1946 Sandeman in a London auction but have never tasted a wine from this vintage.

Current prices: Not available.

1945: CLASSIC (98)
YOUTHFUL, CONCENTRATED, SUPERLATIVE QUALITY

The Douro Valley made magnificent wines in 1945, as did most other vineyard areas in Europe. Shippers spoke of the vintage as a small one, but many houses produced average-size declarations. The aftermath of World War II created difficulties for the vintage. Many shippers had little money to buy wine; one such house, Cockburn, did not declare the 1945. An added burden was created by import restrictions in Britain, which forced houses to bottle in Portugal. Thus, shippers had to bear the costly investment of holding their stocks. All that aside, the wines were superb. Nearly all the 1945s are packed to the brim with concentrated sweet fruit flavors and firm tannins. In late 1989, I tasted eight 1945s and was speechless before so many great wines. The best wines of the vintage are Croft, Niepoort, Taylor and Sandeman.

Current prices: US $380/$315 UK £160/£105

1944 AVERAGE (70)

I have never tasted a 1944, although I have seen bottles of Dow in Britain.

Current prices: Not available.

1943: AVERAGE (70)

Apparently Barros, Guimaraens and Sandeman, among others, shipped some vintage Port in this year, though 1943 never had a very good reputation.

Current prices: Not available.

1942: VERY GOOD (86)
PLEASANT, ELEGANT, FRUITY

Few people ever took the 1942s seriously, but many were still very good to drink in early 1990. I have tasted six 1942s and four were very good to outstanding. They do not have the huge concentration of the 1945s but are more in the style of the 1947s — soft, delicate and delicious. The 1942 Sandeman, Graham and Niepoort are all outstanding.

Current prices: US $225/$210 UK £88/£65

1941: AVERAGE (70)

I have only tasted Noval 1941, and in 1985 it was already completely over the hill.

Current prices: US $70/NA UK £25/NA

1940: AVERAGE (70)

I have no notes, although some houses shipped a few pipes.

Current prices: Not available.

1938: GOOD (80)
USEFUL, LIGHT, PLEASANT

Only a handful of shippers declared the vintage. I have tasted Noval and Taylor; the latter was still good in early 1990, but it faded quickly in the glass. It was probably better 20 years before.

Current prices: US $185/NA UK £95/£80

1937: AVERAGE (70)

A few pipes were shipped. Allegedly, a bottle of A.J. da Silva (Noval) has surfaced in a cellar in the United States. What 1937s are left probably should have been consumed years ago.

Current prices: US $110/$80 UK NA

1935: CLASSIC (95)
AROMATIC, REFINED, FIRMLY STRUCTURED

This was another split vintage, and although the 1935s may not have the power of the 1934s, they possess a striking harmony. Their fruit and tannins are well integrated, and they are truly pleasing to drink. I tasted seven 1935s in early 1990, and almost all the wines were outstanding. The star of the vintage is Graham, which has amazingly fresh cherry flavors and a superb backbone of ripe tannins.

I have also tasted a 1935 Quinta da Romaneira, a property now making its own vintage Ports, and it was outstanding. The bottle came from the private cellar of the family that owns Taylor Fladgate, the Yeatmans. Taylor used to buy the wines of the property in the 1930s, and a few pipes were bottled for the family. Strangely, Taylor, which has a great reputation for the vintage, had the lowest score in the group — although it still managed an 88. I tasted two bottles of the Taylor 1935 on the same night, and each had been bottled and stored differently. They were exactly the same: very delicate and balanced. It is almost surprising how balanced the 1935s are, since it was a difficult growing season — a dry winter, cold spring with some frost and a variable summer. Nonetheless, some splendid wines were made.

Current prices: US $330/$250 UK £125/£115

1934: OUTSTANDING (93)
RIPE, POWERFUL, CONCENTRATED

It is difficult to say which I like better, the 1934 or the 1935. Sandeman and Dow may have had the best solution in declaring both years. The best 1934s are riper, fuller wines than the 1935s. They impress one with their power and flavor instead of their balance and delicacy. Some 1934s are fading a bit now, however, which is why I rank the year slightly below 1935.

The Quinta do Noval was the most impressive 1934 I have tasted. It was a giant wine with an immense concentration of fruit and tannin. It came as a surprise during an early 1990 tasting, since I had reviewed the wine in 1985 and it was over the hill. It must have been a question of different bottlings. The Sandeman, Fonseca and Warre also showed well in the same tasting, but the Dow 1934 was starting to fade. I have tasted it four or five times since 1986, and it is evolving into a nice old tawny.

1934 was a year of excesses. There was a drought in the winter, the spring was slightly wet and there was a summer heat wave for most of July. The harvest started late, in early October. Despite such variable weather, excellent wines were made.

Current prices: US $310/$250 UK £105/£78

1931: CLASSIC (95)
LUSCIOUS, RICH, COMPLETE

Tears come to Port shippers' eyes when they think of the 1931 vintage. Most made some excellent lots of vintage wine, but the market was so difficult after the stock-market crash in 1929 that few houses declared. The only major shipper to declare was Noval, which made its reputation on the vintage. In late 1989, the 1931 Noval was extremely rich and round, with an abundance of ripe cherry and chocolate flavors and a long finish. It is extremely scarce, however, since about 6,000 cases were made. I have also tasted a bottle of 1931 Cockburn, which was not sold but kept for the private consumption of the shareholders. The wine was not as concentrated as the Noval but had a wonderful elegance and balance to it.

Current prices: US $1000/$700 UK £430/£330

1929: GOOD (80)

I have never tasted a bottle; however, records indicate that the growing season was very good. Apparently Offley Forrester declared.

Current prices: Not available

1927: CLASSIC (100)
SUPERB CONCENTRATION, BALANCE, BREEDING, LARGE PRODUCTION

The 1927 vintage was phenomenal. It was called light and early-maturing by some when it was first sold, and houses made two or three times the quantity of their normal declaration — some made more than 40,000 cases. The 1927s are stupendous across the board. Vintages like this come only once a century. To have such large quantities of such great wines is unbelievable. There was so much 1927 vintage Port for sale that some London wine merchants used it for their ordinary ruby blends.

I tasted 11 1927s in late 1989 and a few more in early 1990, and all of them were superb. All but three scored 90 or above. They are classy, superbly balanced wines with wonderful, concentrated fruit flavors. They are aging incredibly well and should easily make their 100th birthday next century. Every house was a star in this vintage, although there is bottle variation due to storage conditions and other factors.

Current prices: US $380/$280 UK £165/£135

1926: AVERAGE (70)

Kopke and Ramos-Pinto produced some vintage Port.

Current prices: US $85/$40 UK NA

1925: AVERAGE (70)

Offley Forrester was the only house to declare.

Current prices: US $80/$40 UK NA

1924: VERY GOOD (85)

I have never tasted a bottle, but suspect they will be fading by now. Nearly all the major houses declared.

Current prices: US $275/$225 UK £160/£100

1923: AVERAGE (70)

Noval (A.J. da Silva) is said to have shipped a few pipes. It is over the hill now.

Current prices: Not available.

1922: VERY GOOD (85)

Most of the leading houses declared. They were said to be delicate and well made, though I have never tasted a bottle.

Current prices: US $240/$200 UK £135/£75

1920: VERY GOOD (85)
ELEGANT, BALANCED, FRUITY

Almost all the major Port houses made a 1920. I have tasted only the Sandeman, and in early 1990 it had evolved into a delicious tawny.

Current prices: US $300/$165 UK £135/£75

1919: AVERAGE (75)

A few houses declared, though I have no notes.

Current prices: Not available.

1917: Very Good (88)
RIPE, RICH, FLAVORFUL

The wines of 1917 always have had a reputation for being overripe and concentrated. Some thought they lacked breeding. The summer was extremely hot and dry, causing the grapes to shrivel in many vineyards. Although there was a little rain in September, the harvest started in early October and the weather held for the picking. I only have tasted the Sandeman and it was excellent — sweet, soft and succulent. If this is any indication, they could still be drinkable.

Current prices: US $300/$130 UK £160/£65

1912: Classic (98)
CONCENTRATED, POWERFUL, SUPERBLY STRUCTURED

1912 is unquestionably a great vintage. Some Port aficionados have called it the greatest of this century. I have only tasted the Cockburn, and it was fabulous in late 1987. It was still youthful, with rich, peppery fruit flavors and a long, earthy finish. The 1912s should be very drinkable through the 1990s.

Current prices: US $350/$275 UK £180/£77

1911: Good (80)
ATTRACTIVE, FRUITY, RIPE

Sandeman may have been the only major house to ship, and it was done primarily as a celebration of the crowning of King George V. I tasted it twice in 1990, and one bottle was completely gone, but a half bottle was delicious.

Current prices: US $275/$250 UK £125/£90

1908: Outstanding (94)
FINE, BALANCED, FLAVORFUL

The 1908s were said to be slightly stalky and green in their infancy, which can be a good sign for a young vintage Port. Some of the 1977s share this characteristic. The weather was nearly perfect for much of the growing season. In fact, it was so hot and clear during the harvest that some producers found it difficult to control their fermentations. Those who declared the vintage made excellent wines. I have tasted Cockburn and Sandeman. The Cockburn was starting to fade a little in 1985, but it still had the fruit character of a vintage Port. The Sandeman was more like a good tawny when tasted in early 1990.

Current prices: US $370/$325 UK £165/£120

1904: OUTSTANDING (90)
DELICATE, BALANCED, FRUITY

The 1904 harvest was a big crop. The grapes were extremely ripe, and the vines were apparently overloaded with grapes. This may have lead to a slight lack of concentration in the wines, but the vintage has always had an excellent reputation. I have tasted both the Sandeman and Cockburn 1904s. The Cockburn had already reached the tawny stage in its evolution when I tasted it in late 1987. The Sandeman was still very fine in early 1990, with sweet fruit flavors and silky tannins.

Current prices: US $400/$350 UK NA

1900: OUTSTANDING (90)
CLASSY, BALANCED, DELICATE

I only have tasted the Warre 1900, and in late 1989 it was starting to fade into a tawny. Apparently a few years before it was still in superb condition. The 1900 vintage has an excellent reputation, even though the wines lacked color at an early stage. They were always balanced and fruity.

Current prices: US $425/$300 UK £140/£100

C H A P T E R VI

THE MAJOR PORT GROUPS

The vintage Port trade has been dominated for more than a century by a handful of wine companies. These firms have built the image and the style connoisseurs have come to expect in the highest quality vintage Ports.

These companies, several owning more than one premium Port house, are the Port Groups — the movers, shakers and market makers in the world of Port.

The groups that own Port houses that remain the leaders are well known to anyone with even the slightest interest in Port. They are the handful of shippers that can sell their new vintages months before they are bottled in the same way a classified-growth Bordeaux wine estate sells its wines *en primeur*, as futures. These firms also fetch the highest prices for their older vintages in wine shops, restaurants and wine auctions around the world. These seven Port "giants," in alphabetical order, are Cockburn, Croft, Ferreira, Quinta do Noval, Sandeman, The Symington Port Shippers (Dow, Graham and Warre) and Taylor, Fladgate-Fonseca (Taylor and Fonseca).

With the exception of Ferreira and Quinta do Noval, the houses making up these Port groups were founded by British merchants who traveled to Oporto in the late 1700s and early 1800s to trade in wine, textiles and other Portuguese goods. Quinta do Noval, although entirely Portuguese owned, was a latecomer to the trade, and only built its reputation as a quality Port producer in the 1930s through its close business relationships with London wine merchants. Ferreira, another staunchly Portuguese house, has yet to make a reputation in the British or American market as one of the top vintage Port producers, but it is still a highly respected name in the Port trade itself.

It is not mere coincidence that most of these companies have British origins. Great Britain has always been the focal point of the Port trade and is where these companies made their reputations. As Sarah Bradford wrote in *The Story of Port*, "It has been called 'the Englishman's wine'; Englishmen discovered Port wine, English shippers made and make it, and for centuries, only Englishmen drank it."

But British heritage is not what makes these firms great. The people behind these groups — those who make the day-to-day decisions and bear the ultimate responsibility for the success of their wines and the image of their houses — are equally important to the production of great vintage Port. This chapter is about those people and the firms they founded or built.

COCKBURN SMITHES
(Cockburn, Martinez Gassiot)

Peter Cobb and Gordon Guimaraens cannot forget their mistake with Cockburn's 1977 vintage Port. Their company, Cockburn Smithes, sat on the sidelines while nearly all the other major houses declared what was the greatest vintage since 1963. It took Cockburn nearly a decade to regain its stature as a major player in the vintage Port game, after making two excellent wines in 1983 and 1985.

"It was really a great shame we did not declare the 1977," said Guimaraens, 52, production director for the house. "We went to Bristol and tried to persuade them that they had the wine. But it was up to the board. They said no. They didn't think we had the market for the wine. It really hurt."

Added Cobb, 51, the commercial director, "It was a commercial error. Think in the last eight or 10 years how much money we lost. It was a complete mess. Some people thought that we had completely dropped out of the vintage Port market."

But John Smithes, the former managing director of Cockburn and a legendary figure in the Port trade, to this day believes it was the right decision. He had retired from the board by the time the 1977 declaration was being discussed, but he apparently had an influence over the final decision. "I thought 1977 lacked something," said Smithes in 1989 during the harvest at Cockburn's *quinta* in Tua. "I thought 1975 was much better. It was a faster-maturing wine and much better to drink. I even like 1978 better than 1977. I don't understand why people prefer 1977. Maybe it is simply the color."

It was nothing new for Cockburn to pass on an outstanding vintage. The same thing happened in 1966, when Cockburn preferred to declare 1967, and in 1945, when the firm decided to wait until the elegant 1947 vintage for its next declaration. But the 1977 debacle still stung. "After that, we had a revolution," Cobb said. "We (in Gaia) made the vintage decision from then on. We won't be caught out again."

What happened with the 1977 vintage was really a question of image. It meant little in terms of revenues for what has been long considered the best-run company in the Port business. The 6,000 cases of vintage 1977 were blended back into the house's ruby Port brand, Special Reserve. But the experience probably brought everyone in Cockburn closer together, adding to the strong team spirit there.

"There is a Cockburn spirit here," said António Vasconcelos, 45, Cockburn's managing director since 1989. "Although we are part of a multinational, people on the management level react as if it were their own company. They almost don't feel they work for a multinational. We say what we think. We have a lot of freedom."

Vasconcelos believes part of this feeling of independence comes from Cockburn's having had offices in London and Oporto before it was taken over in 1962 by wine merchant John Harvey & Sons of Bristol. The Portuguese side of the business was sold about three years before the London side. "At one time Harveys had to come to Cockburn London to buy their own wines," said Cobb, who joined the company in 1960 and whose family was the major shareholder before the sale. A year before, in 1961, Harveys bought another Port house, Martinez Gassiot, which was a publicly traded company. Both houses became part of the Allied Lyons drinks empire when it bought Harveys in 1971.

Now Hiram Walker-Allied Vintners, it has an excellent reputation in the wine business for maintaining quality operations, such as Château Latour in Bordeaux, John Harvey Sherries in Jerez, Spain, and the Clos du Bois and Callaway wineries in California. None of its wine operations is treated simply as a production unit.

"This Cockburn spirit is something amazing," Vasconcelos said. "It comes from something long ago." Cockburn was founded in 1815 by Robert Cockburn and George Wauchope. The company became Cockburn, Wauchope & Greig in 1828. About 16 years later it became Cockburn Smithes, after Henry Smithes joined the firm. Henry soon introduced his brother John to the company and moved back to London to work in the sales office there. About that time, C.D. Cobb arrived on the scene and became a partner. The basic structure of the two companies remained the same until the early 1960s, when the various members of the Cockburn, Smithes and Cobb families sold their shares.

Today Cockburn ships about 600,000 cases of Port a year, including wine sold through its sister house Martinez Gassiot. About two-thirds of the total is Cockburn. Its biggest market is the United Kingdom, which accounts for about two-thirds of Cockburn's total shipments. Its fine ruby and Special Reserve are the largest selling Port brands there, with about 150,000 cases in annual sales. The company spends millions of dollars each year promoting the brand in the United Kingdom, largely in television advertising.

The success of Cockburn's Special Reserve has been great for the company financially, but may have negatively affected its image among connoisseurs. "That has had an effect on the way many people view our vintage Port," said Cobb. "It is a question of image. We cannot be all things to all men."

On the other hand, being well known for ruby Ports is an incentive for Cockburn to make the best possible vintage Ports. While other major premium vintage Port producers declare between 10,000 and 25,000 cases in a specific year, Cockburn has kept recent declarations well under 10,000 cases. "We could sell twice as much vintage Port," said Cobb. "But it has to be the best from the best year. We have to have something really good,"

Peter Cobb is all marketing man. Silver haired, medium height, with a slim build, he is a straight talker with a sense of humor. While visiting Cockburn's vast vineyards at Vilarica, he answered a question about grape varieties: "Don't ask me that stuff. I don't even know the grapes' names."

Gordon Guimaraens is the man behind Cockburn's production. Guimaraens is extremely shy and quiet, standing about 6 feet 4 inches tall and as thin as a rail. He is a brilliant taster and blender and began his career with Martinez in 1952. His storklike figure is the complete opposite of his rotund brother Bruce, head of production for Taylor and Fonseca.

Traveling down the Douro during the 1989 vintage in a small wooden riverboat with an outboard motor, Gordon Guimaraens seemed to know every vineyard along the river between Vale de Figueira and Tua. With each bend in the river, he knew the name of the *quinta*, the owner and the quality of the wine. He passed Quinta do Cadina and then Telhada.

"These are all vintage material," said Guimaraens, who added that the Cockburn vintages come from a handful of *quintas* along this part of the river. "When I started in the Port trade, I was first told to get to know the vineyards. But it was really a question of getting to know the wines from a particular vineyard. We didn't know the grape varieties or anything else. But now you have to know what you have behind the product."

One way to know what is behind the product, Guimaraens said, is to own your key vineyards. Cockburn's most recent *quinta* acquisition was Quinta dos Canais, across and slightly downriver from Vargellas. Cockburn bought the 740-acre property in 1989 for $2.6 million. By 1994 it should produce about 300 pipes of Port from 170 acres of vineyards. A winery may also be built there.

"We bought it because we had problems finding enough top-quality wine for our top-quality Ports," said Guimaraens. Canais was already a small component in Cockburn's vintage. "But it is going to take a lot of work" to bring the property up to speed.

Cockburn is accustomed to making major investments in vineyards. In 1979 it made a bold move, buying nearly 4,000 acres of land in the valley of Vilarica, one of the most north-eastern sections of the Douro Superior. It was a slight gamble to buy the property because it had no authorization from the government to make Port, although authorities gave assurances that new plantings would be legal in a few years.

The gamble paid off when Vilarica received an authorization. Until then, the wine from Vilarica could be used only under production authorizations for vineyards in the Baixo Corgo. It was a perfectly legal switch but limiting in terms of the amount of Port that could be produced. The Vilarica property is much flatter than most of the other good areas in the Douro, making its vines easier to maintain and harvest.

Cockburn can produce a pipe of Port from Vilarica for about one-quarter the cost of its competitors, or about 25,000 escudos ($175) a pipe. Guimaraens believes he can produce vintage-quality wine from Vilarica even though it only has a C rating from the Casa do Douro. Otherwise, it ensures a good supply of quality wines for Cockburn's Special Reserve ruby.

A large percentage of Cockburn's annual production is made at its winery in Tua, about 10 miles east of Pinhão. The rest of the wine is bought from either growers or cooperatives. Most of the Port is made in stainless steel temperature-controlled tanks, but a small percentage is still made through a method called *movimosto*. It was devised in the 1970s by Trevor Heath, then managing director, to alleviate the shortage of labor for the *lagares*.

The *movimosto* system is adequate, but hardly a replacement for treading. It tends to make lightweight wines — good for bread-and-butter rubies but not for vintage Port. In fact, Guimaraens said that 90 percent of their vintage wines are still trodden in *lagares*. There is little that can duplicate a well-worked *lagar*, although John Smithes once had a mechanical leg built to be hoisted into a bubbling *lagar*. It was not a great success.

Cockburn has a long tradition of marching to its own drummer, and it has occasionally tripped along the way. For instance, Reggie Cobb refused to buy any 1945, even though it was one of the greatest vintages this century. "I asked my uncle why he didn't buy the 1945," said Peter Cobb in late 1989 during lunch at the Cockburn lodges in Gaia. "With some sign that the war was coming to an end, my dear uncle bought the 1944. It was a bloody awful year, but he didn't have any money to buy the 1945."

It has always been a question of timing. For instance, John Smithes' first harvest, 1931, was one of the best of his career. "It was wonderful but we didn't declare," Smithes said. "We had too much 1927 to sell. No one would buy the 1931." The only major house to declare the 1931 was Quinta do Noval.

Even when Cockburn bottled a superior vintage, there were no assurances that it would sell. Some of the 1935 Cockburn, which is still superb today, ended up in blends of cheaper wood Ports because it could not be sold. The London office told cellar workers to pull the corks on bottles of 1935 and empty them into wooden casks.

Luckily for Cockburn, it no longer has such difficulty selling its vintages. In fact, one can seldom find current vintages of Cockburn, especially the 1983. "We will never have a problem in declaring a vintage again," said Vasconcelos. "It has been argued out and written down.

We make the decisions about when to declare…Cockburn is a special company, and it has a special culture to it. It is sometimes hard to describe."

CROFT
(Croft; Delaforce, Sons & Co.; Morgan Brothers)

It is difficult to imagine the Port trade without Robin Reid, who spent more than four decades promoting and managing the Port house of Croft before retiring in late 1990. Reid epitomized the trade. A sturdy, gray-haired Briton, he always has a jolly anecdote or two up his sleeve. Some say he has Port in his veins.

None of that seems to matter in today's corporate-drinks world, however. What counts in the 1990s is marketing and meeting sales targets. The old-boy network is of little use to a multinational company like International Distillers & Vintners, a division of Grand Metropolitan and the owner of Croft since 1972. IDV also controls Croft's Sherry operations, as well as the Port houses of Delaforce, Sons & Co. and Morgan Brothers.

"There is no room for people like me anymore, really," said Reid, 65, pacing back and forth in his office in early 1990. In his dark blue pinstriped suit without the jacket, well-tailored shirt, bright tie and suspenders, he could have easily fit into London's City or New York's Wall Street as a senior partner in an investment banking firm or law office. His long, silver-gray hair was combed back and his round face had a determined look to it. "The future is young professional men. I have fulfilled my charter. Now we have a new era of marketing and products."

Reid started working at Croft in 1948 as what he describes as "the most junior clerk in the company." He had grown up in Oporto, where his family had been general traders to the United Kingdom since the early 1800s. He speaks fluent Portuguese.

"It was a family inclination. We traded anything we could get our hands on," Reid said. "Trading and selling is in my blood."

Reid said that when he started, it was considered an honor to work for a Port shipper, and only after 30 or 40 years of service might one finally reach a managerial position. Reid made the move in just 14 years, when he was named managing director of the firm.

"It was a beautiful old company when I took over, but an absolute relic," he said. "I brought the house up to speed…The heyday of the company was when you were given the business to run yourself, provided you produced the goodies (meaning profits). People today have no memory of it. Maybe it is a shame, but perhaps modern times need modern methods."

Reid could see the writing on the wall in 1986 when he stepped down as managing director of Croft. He saw that there was a solid man to take over, John Burnett, a seasoned member of the Port trade with a doctorate in microbiology from Cambridge. "The men of the future are the John Burnetts and not the Robin Reids," Reid said. "They are the modern managers of today."

Burnett is a no-nonsense, intense professional who takes the trade extremely seriously. His career is his life. "I am 100 percent Croft," he said. "We are almost in the 21st century. We have corporate systems. We have better labor. We have more quality control. A general manager has to be a jack of all trades and a master of none. It is more difficult nowadays having such a position."

Burnett began his wine-trade career in 1960 with Harveys of Bristol. After working closely with Harveys' Port house, Cockburn, for six years, he took the next six years off to work on a first degree at Cardiff University and a Ph.D. at Cambridge. For his Ph.D., he studied extra-molecular DNA in tryparisomes, which cause sleeping sickness in man and animals.

"It was a training really more than anything else," Burnett said, adding that the experience has helped him in managing Croft today. "It is asking the questions and getting the right answers. It gives you objectivity to think clearly." After leaving the university, he joined Cockburn as production manager and worked there until 1978. He enjoyed working at Cockburn, which was research-oriented and quality-control minded, but there was apparently little room for advancement. When Croft offered him a similar position, he took a chance on a faster track to the top of the company.

Now managing director, Burnett is in constant communication with IDV in London, whether talking on the telephone, sending faxes or flying at the last moment to destinations in Britain, Europe or America to meet with superiors. On the day of an interview for this book, Burnett had arrived in Oporto at 1 a.m. after a 12-hour car journey from Spain's Sherry region. He had attended a meeting in Jerez, the center of IDV's Sherry operation, to go over budgets with the head of operations in Spain and Portugal. "I am quite tired but still functioning," said a sleepy-looking Burnett.

Burnett, 46, always seems to be in a rush. He is built like a rugby player, 6 feet 2 inches tall and about 210 pounds. His slightly aggressive demeanor matches his build. Dark haired, with round features, he is extremely intelligent and dedicated. "I tend to do far too much rushing around," he said as he strolled through the premises of Croft in Vila Nova de Gaia. "It will kill me sooner or later. It has been like this ever since I was made managing director. One hopes it will get better but large groups want more and more information."

IDV runs Croft with the precision of a small, elite military unit. There is not an ounce of fat here. "We are a well-trimmed company," said Burnett. "Every moment, you have to work very hard." Every expenditure must be justified. A healthy profit is essential as well as a solid return on any investments.

"John and his small team are run ragged here because of the central information question," said Reid. "You spend more time answering questions than really developing your business. The policy for the future is that Croft is a production unit per se and nothing else…It is a very tightly controlled ship. There is no fat on the meat. That is the hallmark of the IDV group."

Most Port trade members find IDV's philosophy too severe. "Burnett is nothing but a factory manager," said one Port shipper. "His hands are completely cut off."

IDV's philosophy has proved detrimental for making the best Ports, especially vintage Port. For example, the head office made a decision without the agreement of Burnett or Reid to double the production of Croft's 1982 vintage. Apparently, the two men had made an average quantity of the 1982, about 15,000 to 25,000 cases. Their superiors told them it was too small a quantity to justify such a commercial exercise as declaring a vintage. The quantities were doubled, and Croft made what is probably its worst declared vintage ever.

Burnett vehemently denies the whole affair and maintains the 1982 Croft's quality is good. "If you can have a wine that is ready in 12 instead of 24 years that can't be all bad," he said. Reid simply shrugs his shoulders. But the 1982 Croft can be described only as light and insipid, having nothing to do with the grandeur of past Croft vintages.

Croft has shipped Port since 1678. It was originally the merchant house of Phayre and Bradley, which traded wine from Oporto and Monção in the Minho, today's *vinho verde* table-wine region. The Croft family began making frequent trips to Oporto from northern England in the 1730s, seeking sturdy and reasonably priced wines to ship back to a prosperous wine merchant business in York. The most famous of the family was John Croft, who in 1788 wrote his *Treatise on the Wines of Portugal Since the Establishment of the English Factory at Oporto*. His son John was made a baronet by the crown for his activities during the Peninsula War (Napoleon's war against Spain and Portugal). He reported to Wellington on French troop movements in the region.

Over the years, many great characters have worked for Croft. One manager, J.R. Wright, is infamous for his decision not to make any wine in 1868. He had traveled up the Douro in late summer just before the harvest to assess the quality of the grapes. It was an extremely hot year and much of the fruit was shriveled and dry. A few days later he returned to Oporto and told the trade that Croft would not be making any 1868. Rain arrived shortly after he left, reviving the vines. Proudly keeping to his word, Croft passed on the 1868 while the rest of the houses made superb wines — some of which are still good today.

Croft has belonged to a United Kingdom drinks company for nearly a century. Gilbey, then a family-run drinks merchant, took control of Croft in 1910. The company produced gin, ran a profitable wine merchant business and owned a property in Bordeaux, Château Loudenne. In 1962 Gilbey merged with United Wine Traders and became International Distillers & Vintners. In 1972 Grand Metropolitan bought IDV.

Today the Croft Port group sells about 450,000 cases a year, which includes brandy sales in Portugal. About two-thirds is sold under the Croft label, and most of the remainder under Delaforce. Croft is well distributed worldwide and is not reliant on any particular market, although the United Kingdom accounts for about 20 percent of its total shipments. It is also strong in the Netherlands, where both Croft and Delaforce are brand leaders.

The majority of Croft's Port is made at its production facility at Quinta da Roêda, on the outskirts of Pinhão in the center of the Cima Corgo. Croft has owned Roêda since 1895. The current production facilities were completed in 1971, and have a capacity of about 10,000 pipes of Port. Most of the nearly 400 growers under contract to Croft transport their grapes to Roêda to be processed, though a small percentage make the wines themselves. For instance, Quinta da Corte, now an important element of Delaforce's vintages, still makes its own wine. In addition, a single-*quinta* Corte Port is made in undeclared years. Some *quintas* under contract to Croft still use *lagares*, although Roêda uses only automated pumping-over tanks.

Roêda itself has about 250 acres of vineyards. There has been some replanting under the World Bank program. Production should reach about 24,000 cases of Port by the mid-1990s.

Roêda also has a small parcel of ungrafted vines from which Croft hopes to produce something similar to Quinta do Noval's rare Nacional vintage Ports. Reid planted about 4,000 vines for Croft's tricentennial celebration. The first vintage was 1985, and all the wine was made in *lagares*. Reports on the early wines from these plantings have not been encouraging, but there should be potential for producing something very good.

The Nacional-type planting was just one of Reid's promotional ideas. He also has been active in promoting the entire Port trade through the Confraria do Vinho do Porto, a promotional group similar to organizations in Burgundy and Bordeaux. Reid and others in the trade realize that there is more to making and selling Port than studying the balance sheet. Reid believes it all helps the prestige of Port, however insignificant such ideas may seem to corporate people.

No one knows that better than John Burnett. Not only does he have to maintain the company's heritage, but he also has to keep everyone happy back in England at IDV's headquarters. "There is a lot of faith and confidence put in us here," Burnett said. "I am responsible to make sure the business plan works."

A.A. Ferreira

Francisco Javier de Olazabal's family is the closest thing the Port trade has to true blue blood. Not only does it have direct ties to past Portuguese kings and aristocratic families throughout Europe, but it also encompasses a highly respected name in the Port trade, Ferreira.

The house is best known for one of Port's greatest characters, Dona Antónia Adelaide Ferreira. During most of last century, this formidable woman amassed half of the Douro Valley as her private domaine and as a source for the growing wealth of her firm. Her vast land holdings in the Douro at the time led some people to compare her to the prime minister of a small nation. Her massive stocks of Ports made Ferreira the envy of all other shippers. At her death in 1896, her estate was valued at more than £3.3 million.

"We are the only major shipper that truly started in the vineyard," said Olazabal, 51. As Antónia Adelaide's great-great-grandson, Olazabal is the eighth generation to work in the Port trade, maintaining the distinguished reputation of his house. A.A. Ferreira was founded in 1751 by Manuel Ferreira, a well-established Douro grower. It was not until his grandsons José Bernardo and António Bernardo took over in the beginning of the 19th century that the firm began to grow quickly. With the marriage of their descendant António Bernardo and his cousin Antónia Adelaide, the company's massive holdings were consolidated and enlarged.

Olazabal remains the president of A.A. Ferreira — the first two initials were added to the company's name after the death of Dona Antónia Adelaide — even though his family no longer owns the company. In 1986, Sogrape, producers of Mateus Rosé and many other Portuguese table wines, bought the company for an estimated $23 million. Olazabal and two other former directors, also family members, retained their positions and are still bullish on the future of Ferreira. They are confident the company will continue to maintain its place on the world market and produce outstanding Port. The key shareholder of Sogrape, Fernando Guedes, is their distant cousin and Ferreira complements Sogrape's long-term goals, they said.

"With my experience over the last two years, I don't think the company's quality will be affected," said Olazabal, a relaxed and well-spoken gentleman who would be at home in any corporate boardroom. "I think in some fields we will be more efficient. Sogrape has made it very clear that Ferreira will operate as an independent company. We have brought something new to Sogrape and they have brought something new to us."

Sogrape dominates the Portuguese table-wine trade, shipping nearly 2.6 million cases of wine a year. Its Mateus Rosé is synonymous with Portuguese table wine in most of the world, although the slightly fizzy, off-dry wine has a rather lowly image. Sogrape also makes a range of wines from various regions, including Dão, Bairrada and the Douro. Many of these more upscale wines suggest that one day Sogrape could do for Portugal what Spain's Torres, America's Mondavi and Italy's Antinori did for their respective countries.

"It is difficult to promote quality wine from Portugal," said Salvador Guedes, 31, Sogrape's marketing director and a shareholder in the company. "Mateus is one of our main assets, but we are going sideways to develop a quality line. We will always be associated with Mateus, but we want to re-create the image of Sogrape."

Obtaining a quality Port house was an important part of revamping Sogrape's somewhat pedestrian image. In the mid-1980s, Sogrape openly sought various options in the Port trade. Many in Oporto thought Quinta do Noval would be an obvious candidate for some sort of merger or buy-out, considering the Guedes family ties as cousins of Noval's owners, the van Zellers. However, when Ferreira came onto the market, Sogrape spared nothing to buy the house. The other main bidders in the running were already in the Port game: Allied Lyons, owner of Cockburn, and Seagram, owner of Sandeman.

Olazabal and other Ferreira family members still in the business gave a sigh of relief when Sogrape became the successful buyer. "It was quite a surprise for me," said Olazabal, who had been sure the company would go to a large multinational. "I have nothing against the other companies but there are a few things we could do with Sogrape which we couldn't do with the others. First, we maintained the character of the house, and second, we had no problems with redundancies."

Ferreira sold for a time-honored reason familiar to many family businesses: too many shareholders. There were more than 150 shareholders forming a family tree of ownership like the maze of roots under an ancient oak, and many were unhappy with their return on investment. It made more sense to sell than to watch such a highly regarded company slowly disintegrate.

Since the sale, the only major change has been the addition of two new members to the board, both from Sogrape. "It is amazing that the whole thing has remained totally intact," Olazabal said. "The result is that we produce more Port and better Port."

Ferreira produces about 375,000 cases a year of Port, as well as 10,000 cases of table wines. It also ships Ports under the Tuke Holdsworth, Hunt Roope and Constantino labels, although Constantino is now better known as a brandy producer.

For decades, Ferreira had been considered the Port the Portuguese drink, although Offley Forrester has made inroads in the domestic market in recent years. Ferreira had a leading position in 1989 while selling at prices 15 percent higher than competitors. Ferreira's advertising slogan — "Was it you who asked for Ferreira?" — is a household phrase in Portugal. In many other markets, such as France, the company specifically targets expatriate Portuguese.

Ferreira has always made consistently good Port, from its simple rubies and tawnies to its 10- and 20-year-old wood and vintage Ports. A large part of Ferreira's success is due to Fernando Nicolau de Almeida, the father-in-law of Olazabal and a legendary figure in the Port trade. The small, soft-spoken, 76-year-old winemaker has been making and blending Ports on his own at Ferreira since the 1945 vintage, after working under his father for a few years. "I follow very much my father's style," he said. His father joined the company in 1908, after working with a British Port shipper, Robert Atkinson. "My father always taught me to give more color and a little more sweetness each time you blend. If you have to hesitate, you should give it up…The British say we make our wines in a very Portuguese style. That is not true. We make as good a Port as they do."

Not only does he make Ports as good as many of the British houses, but Nicolau de Almeida also produces what is considered Portugal's greatest table wine, Barca Velha. First made in 1953, Barca Velha is a gutsy yet classy red produced from various grapes grown in the Douro, half from vineyards over 600 feet high and the remainder from low-lying areas. The grapes from the elevated sites give the wine its finesse and class, while the lower areas offer power and richness. More than 60 percent of the grapes used in Barca Velha are Tinta Roriz, also known as Tempranillo in Spain, grown at Ferreira's Quinta do Vale de Meão, in the Douro Superior. "Normally we sacrifice our best Port grapes from Meão and put them in the Barca Velha," Nicolau de Almeida said proudly.

The wine is produced at Meão and then transported down to Gaia. Before bottling, the young wines spend one to two years in new 275-liter Portuguese oak barrels called hogsheads. Production never reaches more than 8,000 cases. The 1982 and 1985 are exceptionally good. They are massive, powerful wines similar to a top Châteauneuf-du-Pape. They usually are ready to drink after six to seven years of bottle age, but can continue to improve for decades. Vintages deemed not up to par, such as the 1977 and 1980, are sold under a different label, Ferreirinha Reserva Especiale.

Why don't more Port shippers make great table wines? "Most people don't care about table wines here," said Olazabal. "More important, it is the man behind the wine. Fernando has been making Barca Velha for more than 30 years."

Another reason for Ferreira's consistent quality in both table wine and Port is its large holdings of vineyards. It owns about 350 acres of vineyards, and continues to buy the production of numerous farms owned by former shareholders and Ferreira family members. This covers some 30 percent of the company's annual production. Five of the well-known *quintas* are in prime Port growing areas, all capable of producing vintage lots. The properties include Quinta do Porto, Quinta do Seixo, Quinta do Leda, Caedo and Quinta do Vale de Meão. Only the latter is not owned by the firm, but remains under the ownership of the Olazabal family. All the properties are extremely well kept, and at Quinta do Seixo a large portion of the vineyards are planted using the up-and-down method instead of traditional terraces.

Nearly 60 percent of Ferreira's Port is made at Quinta do Seixo, about 2 miles downriver from Pinhão. This is a relatively recent acquisition for Ferreira, which bought it from vintner Sousa Guedes in 1979. Some locals consider its massive, open-air, stainless steel tanks to be a real eyesore. But what it lacks in aesthetics it makes up for in efficiency. It is one of the region's most modern wineries, with stainless steel, temperature-controlled, automated pumping-over tanks. Besides Port, Ferreira also produces Esteva, a good quality, inexpensive Douro red table wine. In addition, Seixo has about 185 acres of vineyards of its own, producing about 20,000 cases of Port. Seixo is a key element in Ferreira's vintage Ports, and on rare occasions, such as 1983, it makes a single-*quinta* vintage Port.

Quinta do Porto has been under Ferreira's control since 1863. Located just across the river from Seixo, it is Ferreira's showpiece, complete with lavish accommodations for guests and a large swimming pool on a nearby terrace. It includes about 60 acres of vines. Most of its grapes are transported to Seixo to be processed, although a small amount of wine is still made in the four *lagares* on the property. The *quinta's* production is used primarily for Ferreira's 10-year-old tawny, although in recent years some lots have been used for vintage Ports.

Quinta do Vale de Meão and Quinta do Leda are two of the most easterly properties in the Douro Valley, situated more than 50 miles upriver from Pinhão in the Douro Superior region. Meão is the best known of the two. The Ferreira family acquired it in 1877. It has about 125 acres of vines. Leda is a comparatively new property, planted in 1979, and consists of about 100 acres of vines.

For more than a century, Ferreira also controlled Quinta do Vesùvio, the showpiece of the Douro, but in early 1989, its 180 shareholders — all members of the Ferreira family — decided to sell the property to the Symington family for about $2.5 million. Encompassing nearly 1,000 acres, it includes a 40-room mansion, a small chapel, an olive oil factory, and a massive old winery with eight 40-pipe *lagares*. It was a favorite property of Dona Antónia Adelaide Ferreira and during her reign was described by a French writer as "a gracious image of the Douro and even more, the prototype to all wine estates."

Would Dona Antónia be disappointed to see her beloved company and estates no longer in the hands of her family? Olazabal doesn't think so. "The style and tradition of the house remain first of all Portuguese," he said. "I don't know if that makes us better or worse but it makes us different from any of the multinationals or other outsiders. The decisions concerning the company are taken here in Portugal and not in some boardroom in London or New York."

QUINTA DO NOVAL
(Quinta do Noval, Quinta do Noval Nacional, Van Zeller)

Cristiano and Teresa van Zeller know all about starting at the top. In 1982 they took control of their family Port house, Quinta do Noval, at the impressionable ages of 23 and 22, with little prior experience in the wine trade. The brother-and-sister team had little choice after a family feud left no one else to run the company.

"We were the only ones to do it," said Teresa, now 30. "No one was available. Everyone else was too young. The older generation was gone." Teresa and her brother began rebuilding Noval's once stellar reputation as a leading producer of vintage Port with the help of friends in the trade and by learning on the job. Today, Noval is on its way to regaining a solid position in the Port world, making better vintage Ports with each declaration.

Nearly a decade of family squabbles had taken their toll on the company. Even more damaging, Noval had tarnished its reputation as a serious vintage Port producer when it passed on the heralded 1977 and produced an extremely light 1978. Its 1982 was only a slight improvement.

Prior to that judgment error, Noval had been considered one of the very best producers of vintage Port, making excellent wines in such years as 1966, 1955, 1945, 1934 and 1927. For decades it was the only Portuguese-owned Port house to be considered in the same class as such well-known British firms as Taylor, Graham and Cockburn. Its real claim to fame, however, was being the only major house to declare the 1931 vintage — a move that put Noval on the map. The 1931 Noval is still considered one of this century's greatest vintage Ports.

Noval's excellent image has been strengthened further still by its production of a few hundred cases of the world's most collectible vintage Port, Quinta do Noval Nacional, which comes from 2.5 acres of old, ungrafted vines at the house's property up the Pinhão Valley in the heart of the Cima Corgo. Nacional is usually the most darkly colored, intensely concentrated vintage Port produced each vintage. Even today, the 1931 Nacional resembles a wine 50 years its junior, and fetches the highest auction prices for a vintage Port — nearly $2,000 a bottle at auction.

A house with such an illustrious reputation was an awesome burden for the young pair to take on. "I didn't have time to think about it," said Teresa, a tall, slender women whose looks and intelligence enchant many a wine merchant. "If I had thought about it, we might not have succeeded." Added her brother, Cristiano, 31, a towering, black-bearded man who stands 6 feet 4 inches and weighs nearly 280 pounds, "It was not easy. I had an idea about the difficulty of the task, but I really didn't know how bad it was."

The van Zellers do not like to discuss the family feud that erupted in the early 1980s. Fernando van Zeller, 59, the uncle of Cristiano and Teresa, was at the center of the feud. He still flinches when asked about it. "It was very difficult at the time," he said in early 1990. "I spent 19 years of my life there. It was like an unfinished symphony, leaving there in 1982."

Like most family feuds, this one involved money and power. At the time, Fernando had been running the company since 1963. The company was divided among Fernando, his two brothers, Cristiano, father of Teresa and Cristiano, and Luiz, father of Rita and Maria José (two of four sisters who work for the company) and his sister, Isabel, who sold her shares to the children of Cristiano and Luiz. Cristiano died in 1979 and Luiz followed in 1982; their shares passed on to their children. Today, Noval is owned by three branches of the family: Fernando has 36 percent, Cristiano, Pedro and Teresa have 32 percent, and Rita and Maria José with their two other sisters have 32 percent. The latter two groups of shareholders vote as a block and control the house with 64 percent of the shares.

When his brothers died, Fernando wanted a controlling interest in the company. He was tired of not being able to run the company on his own, since shareholders had to approve all major decisions. When his bid to take control of the company failed, Fernando left and his nephew and niece took over. "I have nothing to do with running the company now," said Fernando, a tall, jovial man with gray-streaked hair and a Vandyke beard. He owns a Lisbon-based company that produces plastic goods. "I am not really sad now. Wine for me now is only for drinking and nothing else."

Fernando's children, however, are now actively involved in Noval. Fernando, 31, and Alvaro, 30, both work on the production side of Noval. Alvaro, an enologist trained at the University of Bordeaux, primarily looks after Noval's Port production, while Fernando oversees the firm's *vinho verde* estate, Solar das Bouças. Noval is run entirely by family members in their late 20s or early 30s. Rita, 29, takes care of the administration, while her sister, Maria José, 27, is in charge of shipping. Teresa is in charge of world sales and Cristiano is team leader, the managing director. "We are a company full of yuppies," said Cristiano, a warmhearted yet serious fellow. "We are all young and enthusiastic about what we do."

There is a lot to be enthusiastic about. The Quinta do Noval estate, from which the company derives its name, is one of the finest properties in the Douro Valley. Located in the heart of the Pinhão Valley, its white terraced vineyards cover nearly 300 acres and dominate the area. The property is on the east side of the valley and includes a large Portuguese country house, a chapel and a traditional winery with *lagares* on one level and wooden vats on the lower floor. All the vintage wines are made here. The *quinta* also has a modern winery a few hundred yards below the house with temperature-controlled, pumping-over fermentation tanks. There is also a massive insulated warehouse — sometimes called the white elephant of the region — where Noval is moving most of its stocks.

The Douro lodge was completed in 1983. Construction began after a fire destroyed Noval's headquarters in Vila Nova de Gaia in late 1981, causing Ł1 million ($1.85 million) in damage, including the loss of about 1,000 pipes of wine and nearly all the company's records. When Fernando decided to build the lodge up the Douro, other shippers thought he was mad. They said his wines would mature too quickly, giving them a "Douro burn," and that communication and transport were too difficult to make such a move worthwhile.

In 1986 the Portuguese government changed the Port-shipping rules, making it legal to export from the Douro. Van Zeller's gamble has paid off, although the effect on the quality of the wines remains to be seen. Cristiano is very positive about the move: "I didn't make the decision to move up here but it could be useful in the end. There should not be a problem with Douro burn here. The lodge is very well insulated. Besides, Douro burn has a lot to do with wines which have not been properly handled. They pick up volatile acidity." He said Noval Ports will be transported down to Gaia to be bottled, and that vintage Ports will continue to be aged and bottled at Noval's lodges there.

The enthusiasm does not stop in the Douro. The company of Quinta do Noval is small and manageable, selling about 80,000 cases a year worldwide. In addition, it bottles the Ports of Rozès, a major brand in France owned by Moët-Hennessy. Most of Noval's sales are in a premium ruby called LB, which was created by Noval's British agent, Rutherford, Osborne & Perkin in the late 1940s. LB was first sold as a late-bottled vintage and then changed to a non-vintage blend. Noval also has a good reputation for producing well-made, good quality aged tawnies. It has always emphasized the premium end of the market.

"My idea was to concentrate on the high end of the market when I took over," said Fernando, who by the late 1970s had increased sales of Noval's bottled Ports to nearly 90 percent from 15 percent in the 1960s. Inventory grew from about 170,000 cases of wine to about

370,000 cases. Sales spread into other markets. Shipments to Great Britain and Belgium were reduced from 90 percent of the total to 40 percent. "I didn't want to be so reliant on two markets," he recalled.

Fernando also changed the name of the house to Quinta do Noval Vinhos. Before 1973, the Port firm has been called A.J. da Silva. He made the change because there were two or three other houses with the same last name, and consumers were confused. Da Silva is one of Portugal's most common surnames. Old bottles of Noval vintage Ports can still be found labeled A.J. da Silva's Quinta do Noval.

The firm of A.J. da Silva was founded in 1813. António José da Silva began his business selling fertilizers and chemicals to the Port growers. He often took wine for payment and soon began shipping Port. He initially sold most of his wine to Fonseca, according to Fernando, but by the 1850s, da Silva was shipping Ports to merchants in Britain. In 1894 da Silva's grandson, also António José, bought the property of Quinta do Noval.

Quinta do Noval's name first appears in land registries in the mid-1710s. The *quinta* was first owned for more than a century by the Rebello Valente family, which originally received the property from the Marquês de Pombal. In the early 1800s, the Viscount Vilar d'Allen took control after marrying a Rebello Valente. The viscount was a true bon vivant. There are stories of him transporting dancing girls from Paris for long weekends at Noval. The phylloxera epidemic, however, changed the viscount's fortunes and, like many other growers in the area, he was looking for a buyer by the 1890s.

When António José da Silva bought Noval, it was slightly run down. He embarked on replanting the property and renovating the existing buildings at the estate. His son-in-law Luiz Vasconcelos Porto continued to improve the *quinta* and expand the wealth and reputation of the house of A.J. da Silva. Vasconcelos Porto had been a junior secretary in the Portuguese Embassy in London in the late 1910s and met da Silva and his only daughter there. He was asked to entertain the da Silvas during their stay in London, and shortly thereafter he married Teresa da Silva. They had two children, Rita and António. Rita married Cristiano van Zeller, and the van Zellers had three sons and a daughter before his death in 1937 of heart disease. António remained a bachelor.

Vasconcelos Porto ran the company for more than five decades, retiring in 1963. He is credited with building the wide, white terraced vineyards at Noval and making various other improvements to the estate. He also built the brand's image in the United Kingdom, which until then had been dominated by a handful of British houses. "He didn't know much about the Port trade," said David Rutherford, 76, of Rutherford, Osborne & Perkin, agent for Noval from 1925 to 1984. "But he would have succeeded in anything he did. He was a gentleman with a capital 'G.' "

Rutherford's father, Jack, worked closely with Vasconcelos Porto. They focused their marketing efforts on private clubs and universities such as Oxford and Cambridge. "My grandfather did nothing without Jack," recalled Fernando. "Not only did they work as a team selling Noval's Ports in Britain, they also tasted and agreed on the final blends of many of the wines together." The true blending talents at Noval, however, came from Vasconcelos Porto's cousin Frederico van Zeller, who blended Noval's wine from 1927 to 1975. Afterward, Frederico worked as a consultant and taster for various houses including Noval until his death in 1988 at the age of 84.

As the oldest, Fernando was the first of his generation to join Noval, but only worked there from 1949 to 1951. "It was too difficult, since I couldn't change anything," he said. "My grandfather was too set in his ways. He stayed too long in the company." Fernando went off and made his own fortune in business but returned in 1963, after his grandfather asked him back so he could retire.

When Fernando rejoined the firm, his brother Luiz was already in charge of the vineyards. Fernando took care of everything else. His other brother Cristiano worked as an engineer for the hydroelectric company that built the series of dams up the Douro Valley. Fernando turned the company around financially, building the brand in a selected number of markets, though still emphasizing Britain and Belgium.

The transition was not smooth, however. Noval's 1963 was not up to scratch compared with the other leading houses. Although it is still a nice glass of Port, it is much more mature than other top 1963s, which are still incredibly rich and fruity. Fernando said that his brother had tried a new fertilizer in the vineyards and the property slightly overproduced that year, diluting some of the concentration in the grapes. This may also account for the lightness of the 1964 Quinta do Noval Nacional; the 1963 was not affected.

There were no other major problems with quality at Noval until 1977, when Luiz apparently tried another product in the vineyards that caused the vines to underproduce. "I don't know what happened," said Fernando. "But we simply did not have good enough quality wines to declare that year."

Noval's commercial success continued under Fernando, who began thinking about asking his son and nephew to come into the business in 1979 on a part-time basis. His son Fernando Jr. was studying economics at the university in Oporto and his nephew Cristiano was studying engineering. The two young men worked at Noval during holidays and occasionally during the school year.

Meanwhile, shareholders began to complain to Fernando about how he was running the company. A strong-willed, outspoken man, he made a doomed attempt to take control. "I hate family feuds, but it was one of those things," said Rutherford. "Fernando played his cards very poorly."

Fernando said he has not visited Noval since 1983, but still hears about the business through his sons. "Let the young people running the company make their mistakes," he said, reflecting on the situation. "As long as they make good wines it doesn't matter."

SANDEMAN
(Sandeman, Robertson's Rebello Valente)

In late summer of 1989, David Sandeman crisscrossed the Iberian Peninsula in a corporate jet showing the host and camera crew of a popular American television program the Sandeman operations in Sherry and Port. The Sandeman empire is impressive. Even the jet bears the famous Sandeman logo, a black figure of the Don, stenciled on its side.

Sandeman said he never bothered telling the Americans that both the jet and the Port house bearing his family name are owned by Seagram. The Canadian drinks giant took over Sandeman in 1980, acquiring both its Portuguese and Spanish operations for £17 million ($30.6 million). The deal included the tiny Port shipper Robertson Brothers, producers of Rebello Valente vintage Ports. Since the sale, Sandeman has become the leading Port brand in the world, selling nearly 1 million cases through one of the strongest and most sophisticated drinks distribution networks on the globe.

David Sandeman, 60, has remained the chairman of the company bearing his name, but his role seems more that of a consultant than a decision maker. "I am totally involved," he said in his office in London after being asked if he was simply in marketing and public relations. "I am involved in the marketing, but I am also very active in the blending and quality control. I have been involved in the blending back to 1955."

Sandeman still approves many of the final blends of the firm's best Ports, from its premium ruby, Founders Reserve, to vintages and old tawnies. There is a constant flow of samples between his London offices and Vila Nova de Gaia, almost as it was before shipments in cask to Britain virtually stopped in the mid-1970s.

"In addition, I am out in Gaia three or four times a year," said Sandeman, who always makes a special trip to Gaia to taste vintage samples. "I am always looking at what is coming up. People in the trade do not know when I am there visiting. I am there to work."

Whatever the energetic Englishman's involvement in the winemaking, the quality of Sandeman's Ports during the 1980s has not been up to the standards of some of the extraordinary vintages the house made in 1963, 1945, 1935 and 1934. Ports like the 1985 and 1982 Sandeman are very good but not outstanding. Even the Founders Reserve, which Sandeman himself created and introduced to the United States, is no longer the darkly colored, rich Port it used to be. The sales and marketing people at Seagram were perhaps overly ambitious with its sales plans during the 1980s, and it was difficult to maintain the quality. In 1989, after a short crop in 1988, the company even had to buy the stocks from another shipper, Vasconcelos, to meet anticipated sales forecasts in the 1990s. The purchase included 3,000 pipes of Port, and a portion of the wine was apparently mediocre and could not be used in the Sandeman blends.

Sandeman, however, may make a complete about-face in the 1990s and re-emphasize quality rather than quantity. At the beginning of 1990, Seagram had already mandated a decrease in annual sales volumes and an increase in price. "Someone in Seagram finally figured out that it was more profitable to sell less quantity and better quality. You get better margins," said one of Sandeman's neighboring shippers.

Moreover, David's energetic son George, 36, who spent nearly a decade in New York working for Seagram Chateau & Estate Wines Co., a quality importer, has been named general manager of Sandeman in Vila Nova de Gaia. It is the first time a member of the Sandeman family has lived in Oporto and worked in the Port trade since 1868.

"There is an element of stability that I hope I can bring to the company," said George Sandeman in early May 1990, just before moving to Oporto. "It is an awesome responsibility, but I thought I had to do it. I could feel my ancestors looking down at me and saying I had to do it."

According to Ed McDonnell, chairman of Seagram International, which controls the House of Sandeman, placing George Sandeman in charge of the Port house was a major move back toward quality. "Already, it is a new culture for us," he said in early 1990. "We are selling half the volume in Portugal now and we are making more. It was not the right product philosophy before, which was 'Make it and let it go.' We were not doing what we should with Sandeman."

McDonnell said Seagram became "religious" about quality after buying the Cognac house of Martell for close to $1 billion in 1989. The company realized the only way to recoup such a massive investment was to sell only the very best quality, a philosophy that has trickled down to other parts of the Seagram group. Seagram has proved it can oversee premium wine producers, considering its excellent track records with Champagne Perrier-Jouët and Sterling Vineyards in California. "Thank God we had David on the whole thing," McDonnell said. "Sandeman (the company) will not take much to reorganize. It is very underrated."

Since the mid-1980s, the Port trade has viewed Sandeman as being run on corporate autopilot. The Gaia operations seemed primarily a production operation for Seagram. That may change. "The philosophy of the 1980s for many companies was to have the sales and marketing as one arm and the production as the other," said George. "We are going back to the old, traditional form of business. You do everything together and you concentrate on quality."

It is not completely fair, however, to say Seagram waited until 1990 to begin investing in quality at Sandeman. The company bought Quinta do Vau for $3.5 million in July 1988, the first large, high-quality vineyard Sandeman has owned in its 200-year history. Located about 2 miles east of Pinhão, the property covers 195 acres. About 15 percent was planted to vineyards in 1989, producing a mere 80 pipes of top-quality Port. Production should increase to nearly 500 pipes by the mid-1990s. "This is a real base for us," said David Sandeman on a visit to Vau during the 1989 harvest. "It is like Vargellas or any other key *quinta*. We can improve the quality and improve the capacity to produce more vintage wines."

Most of Sandeman's best wines are made at its installation at the village of Celéiros at the top of the Pinhão Valley. It produces about 4,500 to 5,000 pipes of Port during the harvest. All of the wine is made through autovinification and *remontagem*. There is another winery at Canbres near Regua, which is used to make Sandeman's standard rubies and tawnies. Cooperatives are also contracted to produce wines under the firm's supervision.

Sandeman also buys wines from small growers throughout the Cima Corgo to augment its supply of best-quality wines. The vintage lots are always sent down to Sandeman's lodges in Gaia during the winter after the harvest, but a large part of Sandeman's regular production goes to its massive lodge in Regua, the central town of the Baixo Corgo region. The storage capacity is about 13,000 pipes and there is also a large winery for processing grapes from the area.

Tasting Sandeman's vintages reveals a drop in quality in the 1970s. Sandeman attributes this decline to a loss of key *quintas* during that time. According to Sandeman, the company cut back on buying Port from growers in the Cima Corgo in the mid-1970s, from about 17,000 pipes in 1973 to about 14,000 in 1975. "It is always a problem of losing some *quintas* and getting others," he said. "And we lost some key ones in the mid-1970s...It was for a combination of reasons. We slightly overstocked one year and since we didn't need to buy the next, someone stepped in and took control."

Ian Sinclair, who was managing director of Sandeman Port from 1978 to 1980, doesn't remember losing any key *quintas* in the 1970s and called the whole idea "a load of rubbish." The proof, nonetheless, is in the bottle. The vintage wines are very good, but they have not been up to the stellar quality of the 1940s, 1950s and 1960s since that period. Some of the decline in quality also could have been a result of changing over to autovinification for the vintage production, which if not used properly can make fairly mediocre wines. Today, about 75 percent of Sandeman's vintage is made in autovinification tanks.

Sandeman began importing Port to the United Kingdom after George Sandeman created a wine merchant business in 1790 in the City of London with a £300 loan from his father and brother. The company sold Sherry from James Duff of Cádiz as well as Port. Sandeman claims that the 1790 Sandeman Port was one of the first true vintage Ports.

The company slowly grew during the 1800s, diversifying into insurance and trading in textiles. Sandeman even had its own schooner, the Hoopoe, to carry wine and textiles between Britain and Iberia. The wealth of Sandeman continued to grow and in 1868 Albert George Sandeman took control of the company. The governor of the Bank of England for two years, he strengthened the firm's business and made it a private, limited company in 1902.

His son Walter Albert Sandeman became chairman of the company in 1923. He is credited with acquiring one of Sandeman's greatest assets — the silhouetted figure of the Don that has become the Sandeman logo. This is a shadowed black profile of a man in a cape wearing a wide-brimmed hat commonly seen on *caballeros* in the Sherry district. The figure is holding a glass of wine, either Port or Sherry, depending on the occasion. Sandeman paid 50 guineas for the painting of the Don in 1928.

Walter Albert's two sons took turns as chairman of the company. Henry ran Sandeman from 1937 to 1953 and Patrick took over from 1953 to 1959. Sandeman became a publicly traded company in 1952 and acquired Robertson in 1953. At his retirement, Patrick Walter's eldest son, Timothy, succeed him as chairman, and David, his other son, joined the company. "I started writing out railway consignments at our offices in the city," recalled David Sandeman, who became chairman in 1982 after the Seagram takeover.

Initially, David spent much of his time overseeing the Sherry operation, since his first marriage was to a member of the Valdespino family, another of the great Sherry families. He also handled sales and marketing for most of the world, other than Scandinavia and Britain, while his brother Tim ran the rest of the operation.

Sandeman bought Offley Forrester in 1962, selling 50 percent in 1966 to the French apéritif company St. Raphael, which was controlled by Martini & Rossi and was distributing Offley Ports in Europe. Seagram decided to sell Sandeman's interest in Offley a few years after it took control.

David often regrets selling the family business, but he said they had no choice. Going public was the beginning of the end. The family quickly lost controlling interest in the company after the death of a few shareholders. For a while, Allied Brewers and Watneys became large shareholders. Their shares passed to Hiram Walker. "The shares became too spread out," he said. "Soon, the family shareholders could only rely on 20 percent of the company."

Sandeman continued to expand, however, until the late 1970s, when the Sherry giant Rumasa began a campaign to take control of the company. Under the guidance of José Maria Ruiz Mateos, Rumasa already had built a small empire in the Sherry business. The empire crumbled in the early 1980s, when the Spanish government nationalized Rumasa, claiming Mateos had built his business through illegal banking practices.

"We couldn't let Rumasa do the same to us as it had done to the rest of Sherry," said Sandeman. "They succeeded in destroying the Sherry trade and we didn't want to let them have their foot in the door to destroy the Port trade. They proposed to accept any percentage of our company they could get. Rather than being left in an untenable position, we sold out to Seagram."

Buying the entire operation of Sandeman for about £17 million, Seagram made one of the wine trade's all-time best buys. Today, most well-known wine estates in Bordeaux or California sell for more.

It was the end of a long family tradition in the Port and Sherry trade, but many Port shippers simply shrugged their shoulders. They saw little change in Portugal, since Sandeman had always been viewed as an absentee member of the Port trade.

David Sandeman saw it another way: "I would say it worked to our advantage, remaining London-based and not being part of the trade in Gaia. It is only really in recent years that the Port shippers have started to travel. For many years, they just sat there and shipped and never went out into the market. Our family has always traveled all over the world promoting our Ports."

Now, with George Sandeman in charge based in Oporto with the endless resources of Seagram — jets, marketing and money — Sandeman should be a Port shipper to be reckoned with. "I want to use the weight of Seagram to make the best quality Ports at Sandeman," said George. "If historically I was going to contribute something to Sandeman, I would like to help the house have a renaissance in quality."

SYMINGTON PORT SHIPPERS
(Dow, Graham, Gould Campbell, Quarles Harris, Smith Woodhouse, Warre)

Peter Symington knows there is a lot riding on his shoulders when he blends vintage Ports. No other house relies so much on vintage Port for its reputation as Symington Port Shippers, producers of Graham, Dow, Warre, Smith Woodhouse, Gould Campbell and Quarles Harris.

It is not that the Symington group relies heavily on vintage Port for its revenues. Vintage Port represents a small fraction of the 1.4 million cases of Symington Ports sold each year. Making up about 15 percent of the world Port market, Symington Ports are drunk in just about every corner of the globe. Besides the famous names, Symington sells such brand leaders as Cintra in France, supplies private-label Ports throughout Europe, and runs a lucrative business in bulk Port. But all this revolves around Symington's reputation for making excellent vintage Ports. Vintage Graham, Dow and Warre must push the company's standard rubies and tawnies in much the same way that first-growth Bordeaux Mouton-Rothschild promotes the sales of simple Bordeaux Mouton-Cadet.

"We know the importance of our vintage wines," said Symington, 46, production manager of the group. A tall, stocky man with a reserved personality, he has the perfectionism of a Swiss watchmaker. "We are not prepared to bottle something unless it is very, very good."

This has been the case since the Symington family almost went broke in the late 1950s. The Port market was severely depressed then, and the Symingtons were in debt after borrowing money to expand their business and later to buy out the Warre family's shares in their business. Moreover, the shipping laws changed, requiring all Port shippers to have in stock at least three times their annual shipments. "There were a variety of times we almost went to the wall then," said Ian Symington, 61, Peter's brother and a member of the board. "It was a matter of survival."

When the shipping laws changed, the Symingtons negotiated with a few established growers to buy large stocks of wine on credit. They also sold a 20 percent interest in their company to Dubonnet, the French apéritif company, which was then selling Cintra Port. Pernod Ricard later bought Dubonnet, and still retains a small interest in the Symington business.

More important to the Symington recovery, however, was the decision to sell Warre's 1958 vintage. Only two other major houses, Sandeman and Noval, declared the vintage, and the 1958 Warre had little competition. It sold very well, providing the family with immediate cash flow. The Symingtons learned how profitable a declaration can be, and the 1960 and 1963 vintages also contributed to the company's financial health. "In those days, it was very much hand to mouth," said Ian, a quiet, thoughtful man whom friends fondly call "the computer." "In the 1950s, times were so bad that even the Symingtons would not join the company. There just wasn't enough business. It was very haphazard then but we always chose very good wines."

Business always has been slightly haphazard for the Symingtons, though they always land on their feet. In 1970 they bought W. & J. Graham, which included the Port firm Smith Woodhouse and the Quinta dos Malvedos estate. The estate was touted over the years as the backbone of Graham's vintage, although until recently it only made about 15 pipes of Port a year. Malvedos was in such a bad state that the Symingtons realized they couldn't afford to renovate it after buying Graham. Moreover, the Port trade was going through a down period. So they sold the property to a local Portuguese merchant. Ten years later they bought Malvedos back, even though it still needed a substantial investment in the house and vineyards.

Even today, some people remain skeptical of the Symingtons' business judgment. In the late 1980s, the Symingtons went on a spending spree, investing millions in the purchase and renovation of *quintas* and building a new bottling hall and buying shares in The Madeira Wine Co. "If bad times come to the Port trade, one wonders what will happen to the Symingtons," said one neighboring Port shipper. "They seem to have really overextended themselves." Even Paul Symington, 36, a member of the board and a representative of the new generation in the firm, admits the company has a lot on its plate at the moment. "The problem now is keeping it all manageable," he said.

Chances are that the investments will benefit the company — when the Symingtons gamble, it usually pays off. "It is difficult (for an outsider) to understand the speciality of the way we do business," said Ian. "It is such a personal thing. It does not follow any classical pattern...We always have done what we thought was good for the company. What has been good for the company has been good for the family."

When people speak of the Symingtons, it is usually in the plural form. Today there are seven members of the family working in the firm. They do everything from blending and bottling to administration and sales. James Symington, 55, one of two managing directors, often jokes that there always seems to be a Symington on an airplane going somewhere to sell Port. It is often said that airlines operating between Oporto and London would lose a lot of money if the Symingtons no longer took their regular trips. "People joke about our traveling, but we run this entire damned business from here and it's an awful lot of work," said James, an energetic and humorous man.

Most members of the family still retain their British passports and are educated at either the British School in Oporto or a public school in England. They tend to keep to themselves, and most of their friends are British. Many of them speak poor Portuguese. "I am the fourth generation here, but I would never give up my British passport," said Paul, a handsome man who spent time working in Paris and London before joining the company. "I love it here in Portugal, but we have a very British tradition also."

This mixture of the various generations working together creates a dynamism where everyone benefits. "They are teaching me more than I am teaching them now," said Ian of the younger members of his family. While the older generation has worked for years in the Port trade, much of the younger generation has tried jobs outside the family business, whether it be banking, selling or marketing. "It is better not to get involved in the family business right away," said Paul. "You might get kicked around. You need to be able to say, 'Well, at my other business we did it this way.' "

The history of the Symington family in Portugal began in 1882, when Andrew James Symington came to Oporto to trade in paper and cotton. He joined the Port firm of W. & J. Graham five years later, and worked for various Port shippers including the now defunct Southard. He acquired equity in a Port company in 1905 when he joined Warre & Co. He soon acquired the small but well-established house of Quarles Harris. By 1914, Symington owned 100 percent of Warre and asked members of the Warre family to become shareholders, since the family had long ago sold its shares in the house. The Warres then owned Silva & Cosens, shippers of Dow. The two companies joined forces through an exchange of shares. Symington received one-third interest in Silva & Cosens and the Warres got the same in Warre & Co.

The three sons of A.J. Symington, Maurce and twins John and Ronald, took over the business in the 1920s. The brothers continued to run the company through difficult periods during the Great Depression and World War II. In 1947 Maurice's son Michael, now 65, joined the company. He was followed two years later by his cousin Ian, son of John, and Ronald's son James joined in 1960. This continued a tradition that someone from each of the original three brothers' families has a voting seat on the company's board of directors.

With so many relatives working together, it sounds like a perfect formula for major family fights, but the Symingtons say that they all get along. "We are all so very different that we seem to get along well," said Paul. "Besides, we have a tradition to maintain." Johnny has a more pragmatic view: "We get on and do the work and don't worry about such things. We all have confidence in one another."

Probably the greatest vote of confidence goes to Peter, who has been making and blending Symington Ports for nearly three decades. Said Ben Howkins, the United Kingdom representative of Taylor Fladgate and author of the book *Rich, Rare and Red*: "Someone should give Peter a Nobel Prize for blending. He is really great." His standard wines are very good, as are his aged tawnies, but Peter truly excels at making traditional late-bottled vintage Ports, single-*quinta* vintages and regular vintages.

Peter attributes his success to working under his father for many years learning the time-honored techniques of blending. He also spent a year in Burgundy in 1964 with the house of Joseph Drouhin, and in Bordeaux with négociant Louis Eschenauer. His true blending genius shines through in the vintage Ports from what the Symingtons call their second-tier houses: Smith Woodhouse, Gould Campbell and Quarles Harris. Peter says these vintage Ports are "more an exercise in winemaking" than anything else. They are not tied to particular *quintas*, like Dow with Quinta do Bomfim or Warre with Quinta da Cavadinha. Nonetheless, vintage Ports like the Smith Woodhouse 1985 and Gould Campbell 1977 can be compared to the best wines in those years. "There is a lot of satisfaction when you get a good result with those wines," he said. "It is interesting because they are not as well known as our other houses. People can be very surprised after tasting them."

Peter may work with as many as 3,000 different growers in a harvest. One of the few in the family who speaks fluent Portuguese, he knows which growers have the best grapes and who makes the top-quality wines. "Peter knows the Pinhão Valley and other top areas like no one else," said Paul. Since 1985 Peter has been working with Australian David Baverstock, a Roseworthy-trained enologist who oversees quality control. "One has to experiment," said Peter. "I am satisfied with what we have, but we should try other things. It is not good to be complacent and say that I make bloody good wine. It is a good thing to have new blood. You need to have new ideas."

About 40 percent of all the Symingtons' Port is made at Quinta do Bomfim. During the vintage, the winery can pump out more than 10,000 pipes of Port, nearly 700,000 cases. It looks like a small refinery, with its massive vinification center complete with huge autovinification tanks. Some of the Symington vintage Ports are made here, although according to Peter, much of their best wine is made elsewhere in *lagares* or small, automated stainless steel tanks. Bomfim also includes about 170 acres of vineyards, producing about 180 pipes of Port. The production should reach about 300 pipes by 1995 through new plantings. The best Ports from the Bomfim vineyards traditionally go into the vintages of Dow, though a single-*quinta* vintage is also made.

Quinta da Cavadinha is the Symingtons' showplace winery in the Douro. It is a small property, with 87 acres of vineyards producing about 180 pipes of Port. The secret of Cavadinha lies inside the main building, which houses five hybrid fermentation vats. The 12-pipe stainless steel tanks utilize both the autovinification method and automated pumping over. They are temperature controlled and rather squat in shape to increase the skin-to-liquid ratio, therefore extracting more color during fermentation.

The two other *quintas* under Symington ownership are Quinta dos Malvedos and Quinta do Vesùvio. Quinta dos Malvedos includes about 300 acres of vines and should produce about 500 pipes of Port by the turn of the century. Quinta do Vesùvio (see Ferreira) currently produces about 180 pipes of Port from its 210 acres of vineyards, although there is plenty of room for expansion since the property consists of about 1,000 acres. New plantings should push the production up to 350 pipes by the mid-1990s and 600 by the turn of the century. The Symingtons plan to make a single-*quinta* wine from Vesùvio and could even make the *quinta* into a proprietary shipper — a Château Lafite or Latour of the Douro.

"The quality of our vintage wines is a question of the tradition in owning our own top *quintas*," said Peter. "We only own the top estates. It is important to own the key *quintas* to ensure the style of your vintage Ports."

Other houses own their own vineyards, so there must be more to the Symingtons' success. "It is like everything else we do; the continuity has a lot to do with it," said Peter. "It is a question of passing on information from father to son. It is something to build on."

Taylor, Fladgate & Fonseca
(Fonseca, Fonseca-Guimaraens, Taylor)

It's uncanny how Alistair Robertson and Bruce Guimaraens embody the style of their vintage Ports. Robertson is as sleek and polished as a mature vintage Taylor, while Guimaraens is as big and impressive as a similar glass of Fonseca.

The two men are shareholders in Taylor, Fladgate & Yeatman and Fonseca-Guimaraens. Their two companies are to Port what Rolls Royce and Bentley are to automobiles. Fonseca consistently makes some of the very best wines in each declared vintage, while Taylor continues to attract premium prices in wine shops and auctions around the world.

"I am equally proud of both," said Robertson after the 1934 Fonseca outshone the 1935 Taylor in a tasting of 1934s and 1935s. Fonseca often finishes ahead of the rest in blind tastings. "It doesn't matter that Fonseca often does better in tastings than Taylor, not at all. I am very happy with both."

The two houses have been kept separate since Guimaraens & Co. sold to the shareholders of Taylor Fladgate in 1948. Their wines originate from different properties. They are matured and blended in different lodges in Vila Nova de Gaia. The final say in their production comes from two different people — Guimaraens for Fonseca and Robertson for Taylor. They share only the same administration and bottling facilities.

"They compete against one another," said Huyshe Bower, Robertson's distant cousin and the commercial director as well as a small shareholder in the two companies. "We have done our very best to try to keep differences between the two houses. They are both tops in their field."

The group as a whole annually sells about 300,000 cases of Port. Taylor's shipments account for about 230,000 of the total, with the remainder being Fonseca. Taylor is clearly the workhorse of the group, while Fonseca simply adds to revenues. Fonseca concentrates on its premium ruby, Bin 27, and other Ports, while Taylor sells an array of Ports from inexpensive tawnies and rubies to vintage. Its biggest seller is the Taylor late-bottled vintage, a good vintage-dated ruby. It accounts for about half of Taylor's total sales. Robertson and his associates are increasing the sales of the late-bottled vintage, which means better prices and margins. "We have been continually trying to upgrade," said Bower. "Our reliance on LBV takes a lot of planning."

Taylor took this quality route in the mid-1980s. It reorganized its stocks of Ports in the lodge at Gaia and took on a financial controller, David Bain, a chartered accountant who had worked for the giant accounting firm Coopers & Lybrand. Prior to that, the company had been in a weak position. It had been loosely managed and had been making little, if any, profit. Trying to sell more late-bottled vintage meant increasing stocks, cutting back sales and slowly pushing up prices. The upgrade worked.

Nonetheless, Taylor lost a key member of the company in the process: Jeremy Bull. As Taylor's head taster and blender, Bull had been with the company since the early 1960s. He had been long considered one of the most competent tasters in the trade. Such great vintages as Taylor 1963, 1970 and 1977 underline his excellent ability as a taster. The change in the structure of the company was apparently too much for Bull, not to mention personality conflicts with new members of the company. Bull doesn't speak about why he left, but his talents for blending are not going to waste. Since his departure, he has been working as a consulting taster and blender at Cálem. The Portuguese house's vintages, notably the 1985 and single-*quinta* 1987, are immense improvements over previous years.

Guimaraens has taken on some of Bull's duties. Just over 6 feet 3 inches and 280 pounds, he is like a bear with a pot of honey when he is up the Douro tasting Port. The 54-year-old vintner spends a large amount of his time in the growing region discussing and negotiating with the more than 300 growers who supply his company with grapes and wine. With his thick English accent and polished Portuguese grammar, Guimaraens loves chatting with the locals and is extremely inquisitive. He works hard for his growers, and acts as if they were part of his own special team — with himself as the head coach. He is always on the lookout for new talent, much to the dismay of other shippers. "Bruce is a very good person but slightly dangerous," said one neighboring shipper. "He is always trying to get some of our suppliers."

Guimaraens is obsessed with the Douro and its Ports. There are always surprises and new experiences as he travels the region. Every vintage and every wine is different. "I have been here for 33 vintages," he said during the 1989 harvest. "And I am always looking for a common factor in what makes a great vintage. It could be pH or it could be the weather. I really have not found it. The only common thing I have is that it shouldn't rain during the harvest to have a great vintage. But that is no secret."

According to Guimaraens, there are some years that he can tell right from the beginning will produce something great. "Very occasionally, you can tell a great year from the start," he said, tasting a few samples of freshly made 1989s at the company's small lodge in Pinhão. He closed his eyes as if trying to remember the aromas from the *lagares* during such great years as 1977 and 1985. He then turned to the sample of 1989. "These wines are very nice, but I doubt they will be vintage quality," he said. "1989 is not a balanced year. When you get the maturation of the grapes with a temperature of 43 degrees Celsius, it can't be balanced."

Nonetheless, 1989 was a memorable vintage for Guimaraens. During the end of the harvest festival at Fonseca's Quinta do Cruzeiro, Guimaraens seemed almost tearful. The party marked the end of the vintage and also the retirement of the longtime caretaker of the property. There was much dancing, hugging and handshaking. The three dozen pickers and workers seemed to glow with admiration for Guimaraens. He has a special rapport with the Portuguese up the Douro.

Alistair Robertson plays his role as the managing director of Taylor and majority shareholder of the two Port houses with equal aplomb. He controls about three-fourths of the shares of the firm. Robertson speaks softly but in an authoritative tone. A slim 6 feet 4 inches tall, he is a handsome, clever man. During the vintage, Robertson, 52, entertains guests at the lavish Quinta de Vargellas, which has been part of Taylor since 1893. Not only does it have a modern winery with both temperature-controlled fermentation tanks and *lagares*, but its accommodations are like a charming country hotel. The company's other *quintas* are simply functional. They include Quinta do Panascal, Quinta do Santo António, Quinta do Cruzeiro and Quinta de Terra Feita. Wines from Vargellas and Terra Feita are used for Taylor while the other three produce for Fonseca.

Robertson and his wife, Gillyanne, are among the wine trade's most gracious hosts. They are amusing and friendly, and understand the importance of public relations to the image of

Taylor. When, during the 1989 harvest, an inebriated guest made snide remarks about another member at the party, Gillyanne simply told him that they took what they did very seriously and people who were not genuinely interested in the product really had no business being at Vargellas. Since there were no trains until the following morning, the guest had no option but to keep quiet during the rest of the evening. With the Robertsons, most meals are less eventful but they are always amusing. During one dinner in 1987, Robertson got into a friendly argument with Guimaraens over who had the most Portuguese blood. Guimaraens joked that Robertson didn't have any. "Now hold on," Robertson said, smiling and passing a decanter of 20-year-old Taylor tawny to his dinner partner. "You know I am not all British. I am a kind of blend."

Robertson can trace his ancestry in the Port trade back to Job Bearsley, who came from England to northern Portugal to trade cotton and salted cod for wine in the 1670s. He founded the firm in 1692 and began using the numeral 4 with two "xx's" as his trademark, to be branded into bales of cotton and barrels of wine. His son Peter was the first Englishman to buy property up the Douro with the purchase in 1744 of Casa dos Alambiques, at Salgueiral near Regua. Today the property contains a large vinification center that Taylor uses to produce its lesser quality Ports from the Baixo Corgo.

The company frequently changed its name and ownership until the mid-1800s, when Joseph Taylor, John Fladgate and Morgan Yeatman were firmly in place as shareholders. From 1808 to 1813, the company even had an American partner, Joseph Cano, who continued the business through most of the Peninsula War. There were no major changes in company ownership until the turn of the century. It was a small concern shipping a few hundred casks a year of Port, mostly to Britain.

In 1921, Frank Yeatman became the sole owner of the firm after the death of his brother Harry and another partner. Yeatman was a colorful character, and there are plenty of stories about him. According to one in George Robertson's book *Port*, when a young doctor in England gave the 80-year-old Yeatman a check-up, he asked how much alcohol the Port shipper normally consumed. Yeatman replied, "Just a normal amount," and "obviously Port." When the doctor pressed as to how much Port Yeatman drank in an average year, he replied, "About a pipe, or in layman's language, 720 bottles approximately."

There are also plenty of stories about Frank Yeatman's son Dick, who took over from his father and ran the company with his cousin Stanley. "My uncle was a delightful old boy," said Alistair Robertson of Dick. "But he never really bothered with commercializing. I don't think he really liked the idea of sending his Port away." Dick spent much of his time experimenting with various plantings up the Douro at Vargellas or in the tasting room at their lodges in Gaia. One of his creations was Taylor's Chip Dry, probably the best dry white Port then and now. It was all rather Dickensian, according to Robertson. "Dick ran it as a hobby," he said. "We had high chairs for the record keeper, and we had only one telephone. It was next to the loo (lavatory). If there was someone in it, they were told not to make any noise if the phone rang. It was like a small domaine in France."

Dick Yeatman bought Fonseca just after World War II, when, like many other companies, the Port house had run into financial difficulties. It had been established in the late 1700s as Fonseca, Monteiro & Co. Manuel Pedro Guimaraens bought the company in 1822 and was the first to build the reputation of the Guimaraens family. He had an English wife and spent much of his time away from Portugal.

Nephew Robertson gained control of Taylor, Fladgate and Fonseca more through a process of elimination than anything else. He was born in Oporto but was educated in England. He occasionally spent his holidays with his Uncle Dick, but his first real trip to the Douro for the harvest was in 1957. "I came with friends during the vintage," he said. "But we really played around more than anything else. I thought at the time that the last thing I would do was live and work in Oporto."

After finishing his national military service with the Scots Guards, he began working in the wine trade with B. Grant & Co. He then moved over to Buskins Watford, which later became part of Grants & St. James. By 1964 he was the wine and spirits sales manager for Scotland. "I was not much of a Port buff then," he said. "It was more of a habit of life from being in Oporto." He continued working in Scotland for three years, until Beryl Yeatman, his aunt, asked him to come back and help her run the business; his uncle had died in 1966. "I was 29 at the time," he said. "It was a tiny operation, and times were very tough in the trade. We said we would give it two years and try to turn it around. Otherwise, my aunt would sell out."

More than 20 years later, Robertson has no regrets. Beryl Yeatman died in 1989 at 82, and she was president of the group until a few years before her death. Robertson was like a son to her, and she was extremely proud of the guidance and prosperity he brought to the company. Taylor, Fladgate and Fonseca has grown from a tiny concern to one of the top Port groups and has clearly maintained its stature among vintage Port producers. With Guimaraens keeping a sharp eye on the production, both Fonseca and Taylor vintage Ports continue to be some of the best wines produced in each declaration. "We inherited great names in vintage Port," said Robertson. "So we haven't put our money into developing brands with simply more volume. We have put our money in the premium end."

CHAPTER VII

VINTAGE PORT: A CLASSIFICATION

Why classify vintage Port? One might argue that each vintage Port comes from several *quintas,* or wine estates, rather than from a single vineyard, as do most of the wines of Bordeaux, and so Ports do not lend themselves to classification.

But a classification of vintage Port is useful to better understand the differences in quality among similar wines. Vintage Port producers make some of the greatest wine in the world, and they deserve to have their wines ranked in an order that reflects each house's achievements. Bordeaux has its 1855 classification, ranking 61 châteaux into five classes, and although it is rather outdated, it remains a barometer of quality for the region. It was based on the perceptions of a handful of Bordeaux wine merchants. The primary criterion was price, although the prejudices of the merchants must have had an effect.

The main consideration in classification of the various Port houses was their track records in producing quality vintage Ports. Tasting more that 500 different vintage Ports has given me the opportunity to make comparisons among the houses, and in some cases among the vintage Ports produced by a single house. Most of the wines mentioned in this book were evaluated in blind tastings.

While the tradition of a producer had a bearing on my classification, I felt that its more recent track record was more important. Some houses may have made stunning wines 15 or 20 years ago, but if they did not make excellent vintage Ports in the 1980s, it weighed heavily against them, unless obvious improvements were evident in most recent years. Other houses were unranked because they make mediocre vintage Ports, scoring in the 70s or below. These houses are to vintage Port what the *crus bourgeois* or *petites châteaux* are to classified-growth claret. Moreover, a few producers, such as single-*quinta* shippers, were not classified because they did not have long enough track records for serious consideration.

As in the Bordeaux classification, a house's price record at auction and in wine shops was also taken into consideration. There is a group of vintage Ports that always bring top prices in both Great Britain and America, primarily at auction. Quinta do Noval Nacional consistently fetches the highest prices, often setting records. Taylor, Graham and Fonseca also attract higher prices than other houses. There are some producers, such as Niepoort and Ferreira, that appear grossly undervalued, especially at auction, in view of their superlative quality. The lack of interest in these wines at auction did not negatively affect their ranking.

I considered using the same terminology as the Bordeaux classification by ranking the wines as first growths, second growths and so on, but with few exceptions, vintage Port is still primarily a blend, so the term "growth" seems inappropriate. Therefore, I have chosen to classify the wines in five "tiers." Each tier represents vintage Ports that are similar in quality. The first tier includes outstanding vintage Ports that are consistently great in nearly every vintage. Second-tier vintage Ports are almost as good as the first, but they do not have the track records for reaching that pinnacle of superb quality. Each subsequent tier represents a slight decline in overall excellence, although I would be more than happy to drink or cellar most of the vintage Ports from any of the producers included in my classification.

The first tier should come as no surprise to most vintage Port drinkers. Noval Nacional, Taylor, Fonseca and Graham have longstanding reputations for their outstanding quality. Nacional was the only one in the first group that had a few questionable vintages, such as the 1980, 1978 and 1964, but this rare vintage Port is usually the best of every declared year, and it is without a doubt the most collectible vintage Port made.

Quinta do Noval's inclusion in the second group was also questionable, since it made relatively weak wines in 1978, 1982 and 1963. Noval has shown improvement in 1985 and 1987, however, and soon the house should be making first-class wines as it did in 1966, 1947 and 1934. Cockburn would not have been included in the second tier if it had not produced two extremely good wines in 1983 and 1985. It had a slightly weak period in the 1960s and 1970s.

It may come as a surprise to see Niepoort in the second tier, but this small, family-run house consistently makes vintage Ports packed to the brim with fruit and tannins, giving them extraordinarily long lives. Tasting the 1970 or 1955 Niepoort should make a believer out of anyone. Dow and Warre are indisputably members of the second tier, and if Dow continues to produces such great vintage Ports as it has since the 1960s, it could very well make it into the first tier one day.

The third tier has two houses that come as slight disappointments. Croft and Sandeman have made some stunning vintage Ports in this century, and they would have been ranked in the second tier years ago; however, both have fallen off in quality in recent vintages, especially Croft. The 1982 Croft is an extremely weak effort for such a respected house, while the 1985 does not seem to be evolving well. When one compares the 1963 or 1945 Croft with its most recent vintages, it is difficult to understand why the wines are not as good. By comparison, Ferreira is a solid member of the third tier, producing consistently good, well-made vintage Ports. Martinez and Smith Woodhouse also make very good, reliable vintage Ports. Smith Woodhouse in particular has produced show-stopping wines in the 1980s.

Burmester, in the fourth tier, has been making excellent vintage Ports for decades. Delaforce has made some stunning vintage Ports in past years, although recent vintages like 1982 have been rather mediocre. Rebello Valente has suffered the same fate since its superlative 1977. Gould-Campbell, Quarles Harris and Offley Forrester have been much more consistent in making very good vintages, and they all have good track records for the 1980s. Fonseca-Guimaraens, Malvedos and Quinta de Vargellas may be considered second-label vintage Ports, made in undeclared years; however, in years like 1987, 1984 or 1967 these three names can be as good as many full-fledged vintage Ports from 1985, 1983 or 1966.

The last category includes a range of single-*quinta* wines as well as major houses. Cálem, Kopke and Ramos-Pinto are the rising stars of the group and could give some of their competitors in higher tiers a run for their money in future years. All the single *quintas* in this group are extremely close to one another in quality, and offer exceedingly good value.

It will be interesting to see which other vineyard-designated vintage Ports and Port houses become popular over the next decade. A classification in 10 years might include the likes of Churchill, Champalimaud, Quinta de la Rosa, Quinta da Romaneira and even Royal Oporto, if their quality improves.

My vintage Port classification is a photograph of the performance of vintage Port producers until the 1987 vintage. It is not written in stone, and some houses will inevitably improve while others might stagnate or decline.

For those people who remain skeptical of the merits of this or any other classification, the eminent British wine writer Edmund Penning-Rowsell shed some light on the importance of the 1855 Bordeaux classification in his book *The Wine of Bordeaux*: "…while there are many who say that the classification is irrelevant, meaningless or outdated, it is still a factor to be taken into consideration in any survey of Bordeaux. That the grading remains a subject of controversy is the best demonstration that it still counts for something."

For a more detailed look at the producers listed below, see the profiles in Chapter X.

A CLASSIFICATION OF VINTAGE PORTS

FIRST TIER

Fonseca
W. & J. Graham

Quinta do Noval Nacional
Taylor Fladgate

SECOND TIER

Cockburn Smithes
Dow
Niepoort

Quinta do Noval
Warre

THIRD TIER

Croft
A.A. Ferreira
Martinez Gassiot

Smith Woodhouse
Sandeman

FOURTH TIER

Burmester
Delaforce, Sons & Co.
Fonseca-Guimaraens
Graham's Malvedos
Gould Campbell

Offley Forrester
Quarles Harris
Quinta de Vargellas
Robertson's Rebello Valente

FIFTH TIER

A.A. Cálem & Filho
C.N. Kopke
Morgan Brothers
Manoel D. Poças Junior
Quinta do Bomfim
Quinta da Cavadinha

Quinta da Corte
Quinta da Eira Velha
Quinta da Roêda
Adriano Ramos-Pinto
Wiese & Krohn

CHAPTER VIII

BUYING AND INVESTING IN VINTAGE PORT

With the exception of a few great Bordeaux, no other fine wine is bought and sold like vintage Port. It is a commodity when young, and is traded as if it were pork bellies or grain. Once it reaches 20 to 30 years old, vintage Port becomes more of a collectible and is bought and sold like art or antiques. Perhaps this is why vintage Port is the most talked-about but least often consumed fine wine.

Christie's auction house described this well in its *Price Index of Vintage Wine, 1989 Edition:* "Purely from the point of view of the auction room one can forget all wood Ports, whether young ruby or old tawny. Vintage Port is the marketable commodity, for it needs time in bottle to mature fully and during this time — 15 to 25 years — someone, somewhere, has to invest and cellar the wine. Meantime it can be, and often is, traded."

Vintage Port is extremely popular with wine collectors and investors, whether from a New York wine shop or a London auction house. Investors may be private individuals who are interested in buying cases of vintage Port and selling them years later at auction, or wine merchants who buy and cellar Port for sale to clients at a healthy profit years later. Collectors have less mercenary reasons for buying vintage Port. They merely wish to buy it for its intrinsic quality as one of the world's great dessert wines, although buying it at the best possible price admittedly adds to the enjoyment.

For the collector and investor alike, one of the main attractions of vintage Port is its simplicity. It is much easier to understand than wines from other European fine-wine regions like Bordeaux or Burgundy. There is no need to learn numerous foreign names for appellations and wine producers, not to mention the pros and cons of each vintage. With vintage Port, there are only a dozen or so producers of investment-quality wines, and only a few vintages are declared each decade.

The phrase "investment quality" may raise a few eyebrows, but it is the best way to describe the handful of vintage Ports that have traditionally been bought and sold actively by the wine trade and consumers in both the United States and Great Britain. Even Port shippers acknowledge that only a few houses have had a corner on the vintage Port market for more than a century. Said Portuguese shipper José Falcão Caneiro, whose family makes good quality vintage Ports at Wiese & Krohn, "Before, vintage Port was really something for the English houses and a few others. We never had the demand before. We had to sell our vintage Ports very, very cheaply." These sought-after vintage Port producers include Cockburn, Croft, Dow, Fonseca, Graham, Quinta do Noval, Sandeman, Taylor and Warre. They are to vintage Port what blue-chip stocks are to Wall Street.

WHERE TO BUY

Vintage Ports can be found in just about any fine-wine retail outlet in the world. A selection of fine wines in a wine shop would not be complete without a few vintage Ports. Restaurants with good wine lists usually offer vintage Port by the glass or bottle along with their other dessert wines. Wine auctions, regardless of their venue, nearly always include a few lots of vintage Port.

London, however, remains the vintage Port capital of the world. While Americans have been buying more and more vintage Port each year, the British have been buying vintage Port consistently for the past two centuries. There is no other place in the world offering the selection of vintage Ports found in London, and that includes Portugal. Dozens of fine wine merchants in London offer a range of vintages from young 1985s, 1983s and 1977s to mature 1963s, 1960s and 1955s. The number of different producers is almost as numerous; from Taylor to Churchill, they are all in London. Here a restaurant would not be considered a serious establishment without one or two decanters of vintage Port readily available for customers at the end of their meals. Private clubs such as Boodles, Brooks or the Savile have good stocks of vintage Ports, which are always available for members. Even wine bars such as the Davys group and El Vinos have dozens of vintage Ports on their lists — Davys' Skinkers wine bar near London Bridge may have one of the greatest Port lists in the world.

This abundance of vintage Port in London makes it the least expensive place to buy the wines. Prices can be from 20 percent to 40 percent less than elsewhere. For instance, the London *en primeur* (pre-arrival) prices for 1985 vintage Ports in mid-1987 were 20 percent to 25 percent less than in the United States. Most of the top names such as Taylor, Graham and Dow were sold for $225 to $250 a case. The same wines started at $300 in most U.S. wine shops. Older vintages also sell for substantially less in United Kingdom wine shops, and are usually better cared for, due to the the mild temperatures and good cellaring conditions available. Well-respected London wine merchants with good vintage Port lists include Berry Bros. & Rudd, Justerini & Brooks, Corney & Barrow, La Vigneronne, Stones of Belgravia, Farr Vintners, Bibendum, Thos. Peatling Ltd., Harrods and Selfridges. Outside London, try Adnams, Southwold (Suffolk); Whitwhams, Altrincham (Cheshire); and Reid Wines, Averys, and John Harvey & Sons, in Bristol. Many of these merchants will also store cases of young vintage Ports in their cellars for a nominal annual fee. Some merchants, such as Berry Bros. & Rudd, will even decant their clients' vintage Port for them. "It enables our client to drink it that day," said Nicholas Wright of Berry Bros. "We don't charge for the service. It is a question of getting the last drop out of the bottle."

Wine auctions, however, are what make London special for the Port buyer. There are dozens of sales each year that almost always offer vintage Ports. The key London houses are

Christie's, Sotheby's and International Wine Auctions. Auctions are held in other countries as well, including the Netherlands, France, Belgium, Italy, Switzerland, Japan and the United States, but few of the sales held in these countries offer the breadth of vintage Ports of a London auction. The only auctions similar to those in London are held in Illinois and California. The Illinois sales are conducted in Chicago by Christie's and Chicago Wine Auctions. The California auctions take place in San Francisco by Butterfield & Butterfield and Los Angeles by Christie's. It is not necessary to attend an auction to buy vintage Port; bidding can be done by mail, telephone or in person. Contact the above auction houses to obtain more information and catalogs.

The major disadvantage of buying at auction is having to deal with the shipping and taxes after the sale. It all can be rather confusing and time consuming. Most auctions charge a 10 percent buyer's premium on everything purchased and a 10 percent seller's premium on everything sold. Thus a case of 1977 Graham bought for £240 ($434) in a London Christie's auction actually costs £264 ($478) plus 15 percent sales tax, if applicable. Those people selling their Port must subtract 10 percent from the sale price. It is important to know exactly what the premiums and taxes are before bidding at an auction. Many people pay over the odds at auction due to improper preparation. In addition, foreign buyers at European auctions usually are entitled to a refund on the sales tax once the wine is exported.

Shipping wine bought at auction is less straightforward, especially if the auction occurred abroad. None of the houses, with the exception of Chicago Wine Auctions and International Vintage Wines, will arrange shipping after the sale; though most will give buyers the names of various shipping companies. One of the best in London is Seabrook Export Services. American buyers may not find it worth their while buying at auction in London because of the added hassle and costs. For example, it costs about $70 to ship a case of wine air freight to Los Angeles from London. This includes handling and packing. Costs on arrival include a $200 handling fee for the customs clearance broker, plus duties. Freight costs to anywhere in the United States are about the same, although each state has different rules and duties on importing wines. Some prohibit personal wine exports. With all the trouble, it is usually not worth buying at auction abroad unless you buy in quantity. Shipping at least 15 cases reduces the overall expense. In addition, shippers may consolidate several small consignments.

An alternative for small-lot purchases is to transport the wine yourself. A case or a few bottles of old Port bought in London are easy to carry or check through on a flight to America, as long as the wine is properly packed. On a flight from London to San Francisco, I once checked a mixed 12-bottle case of 1985 vintage Port in a specially designed, styrofoam wine carton. Nothing was broken on arrival in California, and there were no extra baggage fees or duties. Some United Kingdom merchants, such as Berry Bros., will pack wine for personal export in special styrofoam cases with handles.

All this said, it is probably easier for most people to walk down to their trusted wine merchant and buy a bottle or case of vintage Port. The slightly higher price is usually worth the savings in time and money.

BUYING FOR COLLECTING AND INVESTING

Some people cringe at the thought of collecting or investing in vintage Port, and I have to agree to some extent. Wine is made to be drunk, not to be horded or bought and sold like stocks in IBM or Xerox. But as mentioned above, vintage Port is one of the most trade-oriented fine wines.

PRICE PERFORMANCE FOR COCKBURN AT LONDON AUCTION

Vintage	1980	1981	1982	1983	1984	1985	1986	1987	1988	1989	1990
1927	£350	£350	£420	£1,260	£1,221	£1,150	£1,012	£1,496	£1,188	£1,760	£NA
	350	350	400	540	807	890	858	1,144	1,188	1,318	NA
1955	180	205	220	360	370	460	462	495	462	550	536
	130	155	150	240	330	370	363	396	363	374	484
1960	100	120	120	210	220	230	286	264	242	253	286
	78	98	110	135	165	175	198	198	214	231	242
1963	92	135	135	195	270	360	418	462	385	408	429
	82	105	100	135	190	310	325	298	330	330	275
1970	74	85	68	115	145	185	242	220	231	275	266
	60	58	52	75	95	140	176	176	187	187	204
1983	NA	NA	NA	NA	NA	NA	NA	123	98	121	155
	NA	NA	NA	NA	NA	NA	NA	116	98	121	128
1985	NA	NA	NA	NA	NA	143	NA	NA	154	148	NA
	NA	NA	NA	NA	NA	143	NA	NA	154	148	NA

PRICE PERFORMANCE FOR CROFT AT LONDON AUCTION

Vintage	1980	1981	1982	1983	1984	1985	1986	1987	1988	1989	1990
1927	£260	£NA	£NA	£NA	£1,232	£1,100	£1,265	£NA	£1,320	£1,150	£NA
	260	NA	NA	NA	1,232	928	1,144	NA	948	1,150	NA
1945	280	270	370	720	850	1,150	1,210	1,155	1,430	1,290	NA
	230	230	300	500	720	920	968	1,155	1,430	1,100	NA
1955	160	180	240	320	380	528	550	484	440	627	NA
	135	165	180	260	300	300	385	440	363	484	NA
1960	110	135	135	220	230	280	231	264	253	264	330
	80	100	105	145	170	180	186	209	187	198	238
1963	105	130	155	210	280	480	484	396	418	429	432
	105	96	110	145	210	310	341	319	308	330	352
1966	90	82	105	155	192	264	253	264	275	275	264
	70	74	85	110	170	145	165	214	214	231	241
1970	68	74	72	110	140	240	214	203	214	253	253
	58	60	60	78	100	150	170	181	192	209	214
1977	NA	NA	NA	92	110	NA	214	209	220	220	176
	NA	NA	NA	72	110	NA	143	181	170	159	176
1985	NA	NA	NA	NA	NA	NA	NA	NA	NA	130	164
	NA	NA	NA	NA	NA	NA	NA	NA	NA	130	164

Prices are pounds per case at London auction. High and low prices for each year are shown. Prices include 10% seller's premium where charged. NA — not available.

A large percentage of young vintage Port is bought by people who never intend to pull the cork. Five or 10 years later, it is sold at auction for a profit. I know one man who made so much money selling hundreds of cases of 1977 Dow at auction that he made a down payment on a châteaux in Bordeaux. Stories of English gentlemen selling their cases of mature vintage Port to finance private-school fees for their children are more common.

Collectors are less motivated by financial gain and more interested in owning particular old vintages or obscure wines. They are like book collectors trying to have a complete set of first editions of Charles Dickens or James Joyce. Neither uses their collections, but owning the complete works of Dickens or every vintage of Quinta do Noval Nacional gives them a thrill. That such complete collections are incredibly valuable must enhance their enjoyment.

The most sought-after vintage Ports have good track records at wine auctions. They consistently fetch the highest bids from both investors and collectors. I have applied a collectibility rating for these vintage Ports, which are all reviewed individually in this book, using designations similar to ratings used for bonds in the financial world. There are three levels of collectibility ratings — AAA, AA and A. The highest rating is AAA and the lowest A, with the only exception being Quinta do Noval Nacional. I gave this wine a rating of AAAA to emphasize its incredible value as a collectible — far and away better in this respect than the AAA category. Any rating, however, is still very good, since nearly 40 percent of the vintage Port producers in this book received no rating. A house or particular vintage Port had to be sold at auction on a regular basis — at least two or three times year — to be given a collectibility rating. Moreover it had to show a reasonable appreciation in value over 10 to 20 years. (See price performance graphs for a handful of houses in this chapter.)

COLLECTIBILITY RATINGS FOR VINTAGE PORT

AAAA

Quinta do Noval Nacional

AAA

Fonseca	Taylor Fladgate
W. & J. Graham	

AA

Cockburn Smithes	Quinta do Noval
Croft	Sandeman
Dow	Warre

A

Delaforce & Sons	Offley Forrester
A.A. Ferreira	Quinta de Vargellas
Fonseca-Guimaraens	Quarles Harris
Graham's Malvedos	Rebello Valente
Gould Campbell	Smith Woodhouse
Martinez Gassiot	

PRICE PERFORMANCE FOR DOW AT LONDON AUCTION

Vintage	1980	1981	1982	1983	1984	1985	1986	1987	1988	1989	1990
1927	£370	£NA	£390	£560	£774	£960	£816	£1,248	£528	£NA	£1,978
	370	NA	390	560	774	741	816	1,248	528	NA	1,978
1945	310	280	370	760	760	1,450	1,012	1,155	1,097	1,338	1,429
	250	245	290	504	720	750	902	1,056	934	1,338	1,429
1955	155	180	200	310	440	480	506	528	506	858	923
	135	158	190	290	360	350	462	484	396	550	748
1960	100	120	135	180	252	250	253	275	275	297	311
	78	60	110	135	180	155	198	220	220	253	253
1963	110	125	130	200	264	374	440	459	462	485	528
	85	96	110	145	200	320	330	330	352	350	418
1966	90	90	105	160	190	264	275	264	297	291	297
	62	74	90	115	160	175	203	253	231	242	264
1970	70	70	78	120	132	220	220	242	253	263	275
	48	58	60	78	88	105	170	187	160	220	233
1977	NA	NA	NA	82	210	210	220	242	230	231	253
	NA	NA	NA	80	70	160	167	181	165	176	142
1983	NA	NA	NA	NA	NA	NA	NA	NA	121	135	154
	NA	NA	NA	NA	NA	NA	NA	NA	99	109	110
1985	NA	NA	NA	NA	NA	NA	NA	NA	143	NA	132
	NA	NA	NA	NA	NA	NA	NA	NA	143	NA	130

PRICE PERFORMANCE FOR FONSECA AT LONDON AUCTION

Vintage	1980	1981	1982	1983	1984	1985	1986	1987	1988	1989	1990
1927	£316	£NA	£NA	£720	£960	£1,116	£1,080	£1,188	£1,155	£NA	£2,310
	272	NA	NA	600	800	960	1,080	1,188	1,155	NA	2,310
1945	305	NA	NA	NA	NA	1,100	NA	NA	NA	NA	2,044
	240	NA	NA	NA	NA	1,050	NA	NA	NA	NA	2,044
1955	160	190	240	360	420	480	506	462	594	594	NA
	145	170	200	252	360	370	506	462	465	594	NA
1960	98	115	120	200	210	230	231	275	264	291	396
	90	96	110	140	180	185	231	231	220	231	275
1963	105	130	130	240	260	540	462	528	462	660	682
	86	94	115	145	196	340	341	352	385	495	592
1966	98	110	120	180	198	270	275	286	275	331	308
	68	72	82	125	160	185	198	231	242	209	283
1970	68	76	85	105	135	250	253	242	231	264	319
	60	54	60	76	88	155	198	192	209	220	242
1977	NA	NA	68	NA	140	220	231	253	297	263	300
	NA	NA	60	NA	110	171	187	187	198	223	209
1983	NA	NA	NA	NA	NA	NA	NA	NA	NA	154	141
	NA	NA	NA	NA	NA	NA	NA	NA	NA	115	110
1985	NA	NA	NA	NA	NA	NA	NA	NA	NA	184	182
	NA	NA	NA	NA	NA	NA	NA	NA	NA	126	182

Prices are pounds per case at London auction. High and low prices for each year are shown. Prices include 10% seller's premium where charged. NA — not available.

Quinta do Noval Nacional, the only wine to receive the "off-the-scale" AAAA rating, is clearly the most collectible vintage Port. At auctions throughout the world, it sells for three to four times the price that other vintage Ports bring. For example, the 1970 Nacional sold for about £1,000 ($1,800) a case in London auctions in 1989, while a case of 1970 Taylor fetched about £300 ($555). Nacional also holds the world-record auction price for a vintage Port. A bottle of the 1931 Nacional sold for about $1,500 in a London auction in 1988. The next record is held by Taylor 1945 at about $700 a bottle. Although its quality is superb, Nacional's stellar price is due primarily to its rarity, since only 200 to 250 cases are produced in a vintage. It is the Romanée-Conti of vintage Port.

After Nacional, Taylor historically has attracted premium prices higher than other vintage Port houses, regardless of the vintage. When young vintages are sold, Taylor always sells for 10 percent to 15 percent more than the others. Mature vintages are the same. Taylor in the cellar can be like money in the bank, as the graph indicates on page 125. Fonseca and Graham have improved their price performance in recent years, however, and have competed well in certain vintages with Taylor. Considering their superlative quality, they offer solid investments.

The houses included in the AA ratings will not increase in value as rapidly as Taylor, Fonseca or Graham; however, they show good growth in price over the years, and are good investments. For instance, those who paid £100 ($185) a case for the Cockburn 1983 in 1985 could have sold it for almost £140 ($259) at United Kingdom auctions four years later. The price escalation is more dramatic with older vintages. The Dow 1963 sold for about £3 ($5) a case wholesale to wine merchants in 1965. Today it sells regularly at auction for £475 ($878). A case of the 1970 Dow sold for £11 ($20) in 1972 and fetched £240 ($444) at 1990 auctions. Those vintage Ports with an A rating show similar but less sensational increases.

Regardless of the ranking or producer, all collectors and investors purchase by vintage. The most sought-after vintages are 1985, 1977, 1970, 1963, 1955, 1948, 1947, 1945, 1935, 1934, 1931 and 1927. Anything pre-1927 also sells for high prices, especially 1912, 1908, 1904 and any 19th-century vintages. All vintage Ports from 1963 or before have shown large price increases since the late 1980s. For example, a case of 1963 Graham could have been bought for as little as £350 ($648) in 1986. Four years later, the highest bid was £600 ($1,080). Increases in prices of the 1955s have been less substantial, though wines from 1948 and before have continued to rise in price.

It is difficult to say what vintage will be the next to post large increases in price after the 1963s. Some say 1970 is the most obvious candidate, since the 1966 has always been overshadowed by 1963 and the large quantities of 1966 exhausted long ago. The 1970 vintage as a whole is excellent, and still easily attainable in the market. Only Nacional and AAA-rated vintage Ports have shown substantial price increases since 1988, however. The 1970 Taylor sold at London auctions for between £190 ($351) and £270 ($499) in 1988, while in 1990 it reached £240 ($444) to £310 ($573). These prices do not include premiums and taxes. Fonseca and Graham showed similar increases over the same period. These three 1970s, along with Nacional, are likely to continue to appreciate during the 1990s as older stocks of vintage Port diminish. The AA vintage Ports should also increase in value.

While there may be some doubt regarding the price appreciation of the 1970 vintage, it is almost certain that 1977 will increase in value through the 1990s. Prices for the 1977s have remained stable on both sides of the Atlantic since 1988, and Port buyers have been anticipating increases for some time due to the vintage's superlative quality. Some auction buyers believe 1977 may be the next great vintage for investment, and that buyers will overlook the 1970s. Comparing the 1977 and 1970 on a purely financial basis, 1977 is probably a better investment

PRICE PERFORMANCE FOR GRAHAM AT LONDON AUCTION

Vintage	1980	1981	1982	1983	1984	1985	1986	1987	1988	1989	1990
1927	£310	£350	£440	£NA	£1,260	£1,620	£1,045	£NA	£NA	£NA	£1,650
	300	300	440	NA	930	1,082	1,045	NA	NA	NA	1,650
1945	280	280	380	1,150	1,140	1,350	1,320	1,375	1,636	1,815	NA
	230	280	370	540	880	850	1,032	1,210	1,078	1,078	NA
1955	185	185	250	380	560	660	770	616	770	715	794
	145	160	190	260	380	420	439	484	528	577	715
1960	100	140	180	170	280	297	275	264	264	275	341
	78	84	110	145	159	175	176	231	231	207	275
1963	110	125	165	220	275	380	418	440	462	638	660
	82	92	115	140	220	300	341	385	385	380	594
1966	85	100	125	180	209	280	286	297	308	308	352
	72	72	84	110	145	195	220	242	242	270	320
1970	85	78	84	125	140	240	242	242	264	330	341
	60	52	66	76	95	154	181	187	187	220	242
1977	NA	66	58	92	145	220	253	275	253	275	287
	NA	43	58	75	75	154	176	165	173	198	210
1983	NA	NA	NA	NA	NA	NA	NA	126	143	170	185
	NA	NA	NA	NA	NA	NA	NA	126	101	111	127
1985	NA	NA	NA	NA	NA	NA	NA	NA	NA	170	198
	NA	NA	NA	NA	NA	NA	NA	NA	NA	170	182

PRICE PERFORMANCE FOR QUINTA DO NOVAL AT LONDON AUCTION

Vintage	1980	1981	1982	1983	1984	1985	1986	1987	1988	1989	1990
1927	£460	£490	£420	£NA	£1,056	£NA	£NA	£NA	£NA	£NA	£1,143
	344	324	420	NA	1,056	NA	NA	NA	NA	NA	1,143
1945	250	260	310	620	850	740	660	1,056	1,020	NA	NA
	250	260	310	620	850	740	660	1,056	1,020	NA	NA
1955	150	160	210	320	420	462	429	447	447	407	484
	135	160	180	216	320	364	396	396	385	330	473
1960	105	120	120	175	220	250	264	231	214	261	264
	82	95	90	130	175	175	159	220	198	214	238
1963	110	130	150	220	253	340	374	352	308	440	396
	85	105	110	140	195	300	319	319	209	341	281
1966	78	87	115	150	295	220	231	253	253	315	241
	66	70	80	90	150	165	181	192	209	214	231
1970	72	72	85	92	126	220	209	203	220	220	231
	56	58	54	78	90	145	165	170	176	200	200
1985	NA	NA	NA	NA	NA	NA	NA	NA	147	160	133
	NA	NA	NA	NA	NA	NA	NA	NA	147	160	132

Prices are pounds per case at London auction. High and low prices for each year are shown. Prices include 10% seller's premium where charged. NA — not available.

due to its lower prices and higher profile among auction buyers. Any of the 1977 vintage Ports I have rated, especially those with an AA or higher ranking, should be sound investments in the 1990s.

The 1985s and some of the 1983s with AAA ratings should also appreciate in value during the 1990s. Although there are some good wines from 1978, 1980, 1982 and 1987, it is doubtful they will increase much in value. A few of the single-*quinta* Ports or second-label blends produced in the less popular vintages, like Taylor's Quinta de Vargellas or Graham's Malvedos, may be interesting to buy, but they will show only slight increases in value over the next decade.

BUYING FOR DRINKING

For most people, buying vintage Port is not an investment — much to my relief. It would be a shame if vintage Port was bought only as a commodity and never drunk and enjoyed. It is also more difficult today to make money investing in vintage Port due to high interest and exchange rates. Those people interested in buying vintage Port purely for investment reasons might do better to put their money in an interest-bearing bank account.

Purchasing vintage Port without the worry of return on investment can be a lot of fun. There is an array to choose from, and many are relatively good values. To start, there are a few houses that are virtually unknown to investors, yet produce excellent vintage Ports. To these Port shippers I gave no collectibility rating, but included them in my classification. The best example is Niepoort, a second-tier producer. Others include Burmester, Cálem and Wiese & Krohn. Any wines with an A collectibility rating are good values compared to the big-name vintage Ports.

Single-*quinta* and second-label vintage Ports are also usually good buys for people interested only in pure drinking pleasure. Wines such as Quinta de Vargellas, Quinta da Corte and Fonseca-Guimaraens are released about eight to 10 years after the vintage date. They are sold when they are ready to drink, and can improve for another decade or two in the bottle. For current drinking, they usually offer much better value than similar wines from the leading houses in declared vintages. For example, the 1964 Fonseca-Guimaraens sold for about £20 ($37) a bottle in London wine shops in 1990 while the 1966 Fonseca was £38 ($70).

As for declared vintages, it should come as no surprise that the years of little interest to investors and collectors are the best buys. These include 1987, 1983, 1980, 1978, 1967, 1966 and 1960. The 1966 is probably the most underrated vintage of the group, with Taylor, Graham and Fonseca 1966 selling for half to two-thirds the price of their 1963. The 1966s are nearly as good as the 1963s, and in some cases, such as Quinta do Noval, they are better. The only drawback is that they are hard to find. The 1967s are even better buys than the 1966s; for example, the Cockburn 1967 sells for about £165 ($305) a case. The 1960s are also about half the price of the 1963s, though some are starting to fade in quality. Buyers should be prudent with this vintage, as with other mature years like 1958 and 1950.

For a young vintage that is just beginning to drink well in the 1990s, 1980 is an exceptionally good value. There are some very good wines that should offer solid drinking through 2000, and they are priced lower than any other drinkable vintage, with the exception of the 1978s. On the other hand, 1975 is the most overrated vintage. Most of the wines are simple, light and rather uninteresting, yet they sell for almost the same prices as the 1970 and at higher prices than the 1980. I do not recommend buying 1975. In contrast, 1983 is a very good vintage for laying away in one's cellar, and even the best wines of the vintage, like Graham and Taylor, are priced lower than the 1985s, even though there is not much difference in quality. The very good 1987s may also offer good value; however, I would not buy 1987s that are priced at the same level as the 1985s.

PRICE PERFORMANCE FOR SANDEMAN AT LONDON AUCTION

Vintage	1980	1981	1982	1983	1984	1985	1986	1987	1988	1989	1990
1927	£383	£360	£260	£660	£880	£966	£898	£1,320	£2,040	£1,455	£NA
	370	360	230	620	440	966	898	1,079	1,815	1,438	NA
1945	NA	260	NA	820	780	860	770	NA	1,056	1,047	1,390
	NA	260	NA	350	780	860	770	NA	888	902	1,390
1955	145	155	120	310	340	440	NA	NA	363	418	NA
	135	150	110	300	330	290	NA	NA	363	330	NA
1960	96	105	140	350	220	220	220	242	231	253	283
	80	84	100	150	160	110	203	208	198	220	221
1963	92	100	125	190	260	320	363	363	429	417	418
	76	84	94	130	250	250	298	319	308	352	352
1966	68	82	98	155	155	200	242	253	253	277	275
	54	74	58	110	135	180	187	209	209	220	275
1970	60	76	75	96	126	170	198	203	220	220	219
	49	54	40	88	98	135	148	203	176	198	205
1977	62	56	NA	NA	125	176	200	203	187	231	165
	58	54	NA	NA	110	153	137	181	162	148	165
1985	NA	NA	NA	NA	NA	NA	NA	NA	NA	110	NA
	NA	NA	NA	NA	NA	NA	NA	NA	NA	110	NA

PRICE PERFORMANCE FOR TAYLOR FLADGATE AT LONDON AUCTION

Vintage	1980	1981	1982	1983	1984	1985	1986	1987	1988	1989	1990
1927	£492	£480	£720	£1,280	£1,260	£2,076	£1,716	£1,320	£2,420	£1,320	£NA
	352	350	420	960	1,060	1,260	1,320	1,320	1,140	980	NA
1945	490	360	480	1,550	1,300	1,750	1,815	1,870	2,090	2,530	3,305
	290	324	340	640	1,070	1,200	1,320	1,188	1,375	1,925	2,424
1955	220	240	340	620	680	680	726	825	770	1,100	1,264
	165	180	225	280	435	540	572	594	528	594	792
1960	120	155	150	220	270	310	308	319	308	414	396
	98	120	115	150	185	210	242	253	247	264	297
1963	150	155	170	310	341	520	506	572	572	660	682
	94	115	120	190	250	360	374	385	418	484	572
1966	95	115	135	190	242	290	309	309	330	330	333
	76	82	86	120	160	185	209	242	242	269	294
1970	90	91	105	140	190	224	253	264	297	297	330
	66	64	60	85	110	157	187	174	209	240	242
1977	NA	NA	NA	82	165	290	319	375	319	341	352
	NA	NA	NA	82	90	200	231	320	264	235	264
1983	NA	NA	NA	NA	NA	NA	NA	NA	NA	176	176
	NA	NA	NA	NA	NA	NA	NA	NA	NA	92	154
1985	NA	NA	NA	NA	NA	NA	NA	NA	NA	209	215
	NA	NA	NA	NA	NA	NA	NA	NA	NA	169	171

Prices are pounds per case at London auction. High and low prices for each year are shown. Prices include 10% seller's premium where charged. NA — not available.

PRICE PERFORMANCE FOR WARRE AT LONDON AUCTION

Vintage	1980	1981	1982	1983	1984	1985	1986	1987	1988	1989	1990
1927	£360	£276	£456	£732	£NA	£356	£832	£NA	£NA	£NA	£1,452
	360	276	456	430	NA	142	832	NA	NA	NA	1,052
1945	300	260	386	420	840	880	1,210	990	NA	NA	NA
	240	245	386	420	740	820	935	990	NA	NA	NA
1955	150	185	210	360	390	500	484	484	495	528	NA
	135	160	180	220	340	500	352	429	418	528	NA
1960	115	130	145	210	220	240	275	286	264	300	275
	85	92	110	140	170	170	198	209	209	220	242
1963	100	135	140	230	280	380	429	440	440	605	484
	85	100	110	125	195	300	308	352	330	389	397
1966	88	82	110	180	198	240	242	275	275	284	300
	72	70	86	120	155	185	198	220	231	220	242
1970	74	76	84	100	140	210	231	214	242	254	297
	60	58	60	76	92	145	176	176	181	143	209
1977	NA	60	62	NA	126	200	209	209	242	231	245
	NA	56	62	NA	72	145	170	176	187	176	178
1983	NA	NA	NA	NA	NA	NA	NA	NA	NA	135	154
	NA	NA	NA	NA	NA	NA	NA	NA	NA	110	118
1985	NA	NA	NA	NA	NA	NA	NA	NA	NA	NA	176
	NA	NA	NA	NA	NA	NA	NA	NA	NA	NA	132

Prices are pounds per case at London auction. High and low prices for each year are shown. Prices include 10% seller's premium where charged. NA — not available.

SOURCE: *THE WINE SPECTATOR*, SOTHEBY'S AND CHRISTIE'S

BUYER BEWARE

Proper storage, which will be more thoroughly covered in Chapter IX, is a subject that should be taken seriously when buying vintage Port or any other fine wine. Although vintage Port can be surprisingly durable, it can be spoiled by poor storage. I recommend buying vintage Ports only from wine merchants who properly store their wine. Stay away from establishments that keep their Ports standing straight up or under lights. I once entered a well-known New York wine shop in late October to buy a bottle of wine, but it was so hot inside from the central heating that I could barely breathe. The corks were pushing out of double magnums of wine on display. Needless to say, I left the premises without buying anything.

Another point to consider is where the vintage Port you are buying was bottled. This has no bearing on vintages after 1972, since mandatory Oporto bottling of vintage Port came into effect in 1974; however, as indicated elsewhere in this book, most vintage Ports were not bottled by producers until the 1970s. I always try to buy the pre-1970 vintage Ports that were bottled either in Portugal or by well-regarded British wine merchants such as Berry Bros., John Harvey & Sons, or Averys. If it is impossible to find out who did the bottling, don't worry about it. Most pre-1960 vintage Ports are still sold unlabeled. The only way to tell the wine's indentity is by an embossed capsule or a branded cork. It is interesting to note, however, that some Port experts claim British-bottled vintage Ports are always superior to those bottled in Portugal. To me, this is obviously not true, since the entire 1945 vintage was Oporto-bottled and I have yet to come across a poor bottle.

Recently, some older vintage Ports have been re-corked by wine merchants and auction houses. It is standard practice for many first-class Bordeaux and Burgundy estates to re-cork their wines after 20 to 30 years. Château Lafite, for instance, provides this service free, and annually sends representatives to America to re-cork collectors' bottles. A new cork is used and the level of the wine in the bottle is checked. Those that are not completely full are "topped up" with the same or a similar wine.

None of the Port houses offers this service. I have heard that some merchants are re-corking vintage Ports themselves and topping up with different vintages. A recorked 1908 Taylor may have been topped up with some 1963. Some may argue that a tiny amount of 1963 or some other vintage in a 1908 makes little difference, but to my mind it is no longer 100 percent 1908. I would stay away from re-corked vintage Port unless someone can guarantee it has been topped up with the same wine.

CHAPTER IX

ENJOYING VINTAGE PORT

There is never enough said about the storage and service of vintage Port. Like other fine wines of the world, too many bottles of vintage Port are ruined by improper handling, whether from being stored in a dry, hot place or from being served undecanted in a tiny, unattractive glass.

One of the beauties of vintage Port is its ability to improve with age. Since most need eight to 15 years of bottle age, it is essential to store them under the best possible conditions. Why pay \$35 or £20 for a bottle of vintage Port, and then store it in a dry, warm place where the cork may dry out or the wine may spoil? The older the Port the more disastrous the effects of poor handling for the wine gets more fragile with age.

Proper service is equally important. Some people find decanting tedious, even pretentious, but it is the only practical way to serve vintage Port. There are numerous stories of people serving vintage Port undecanted or leaving a bottle opened for three or four weeks. Restaurants appear to be the worst offenders, selling their customers glasses of spoiled vintage Port. I have been served glasses of murky vintage Port in well-regarded restaurants in both America and Britain; the decanting was done incorrectly or not at all. Port shippers traveling in America always return with stories about a waiter or bartender who complained about their vintage Port having "all those particles in it."

All this said, the inherent durability of vintage Port can be impressive. I have tasted mature vintage Ports from bottles less than three-quarters full, and the wines were still excellent. I remember a bottle of 1945 Rebello Valente that was upright for nearly six months and was only about three-quarters full. When first decanted it had a slightly musty nose, but it evolved into a luscious nectar in about 20 minutes and continued to improve for more than an hour. If a great claret had been treated the same way, it probably would have been undrinkable.

George Robertson was partly right when he wrote in his book *Port*, "There is no need to cosset Port, as it is a naturally strong wine and has been 'brought up' to withstand many varied climates and conditions in various corners of the world. Its very birth is a difficult one because of the schistous soil and the extreme climatic conditions in the Douro Valley, so it will not object too strongly to some rough treatment in its life, so long as this is not too prolonged."

STORAGE

According to J.C. Valente-Perfeito in his book *Let's Talk About Port*, a popular saying among wine collectors in the 1940s was "A wine cellar too hot or too cold murders a wine before it is old." The saying still holds true. The optimum temperature for storing vintage Port, as with other fine wines, is between 55 and 60 degrees Fahrenheit. Temperatures up to 68 or 70 degrees can be tolerated for short periods. What is perhaps more important is that the temperature remain fairly constant, with only gradual and slight fluctuations — perhaps not more than two or three degrees per day. For example, my personal cellar in London ranges in temperature from about 50 degrees in the middle of the winter to about 65 in the summer.

Humidity is another significant factor in storage, although it is often overlooked. The humidity should never drop below 50 percent; otherwise, corks may dry out and lose their elasticity. In damp London, my cellar almost never dips below 55 percent humidity. When I lived in California, it was much drier, so I tried to keep my wines in a relatively humid part of the house. Some friends even kept theirs in a bathroom, which I do not recommend. It might be wiser to use a humidifier or even place a small container of water with your wines, especially if you have an air conditioner. While an air conditioner maintains a cellar at the right temperature, it also takes much of the humidity out of the air.

All this might sound rather impractical, since most American homes do not have well-insulated underground cellars. Although a cellar unit, which resembles a refrigeration cabinet, may be a good option, they cost thousands of dollars and can take up quite a lot of space. One simply has to make do. I have found storing a few cases of wine or Port in an interior closet of the house is fairly efficient, as long as it is dark and relatively cool. If one plans to lay down a few cases of young vintage Port to drink in 10 or 15 years, however, it may be advisable to store them elsewhere, either with a wine merchant or in rented storage. Annual storage fees, which range from $5 to $15 a case, are inexpensive compared to the initial investment and the long-term rewards of good storage.

Regardless of where they are stored, bottles of vintage Port should be kept on their sides to ensure that the cork does not dry out. This also helps the development of a solid crust. Bottle size, whether it be half bottle, regular bottle or magnum, is unimportant. Most vintage Port bottles have a white paint mark on their sides that can help you to keep the bottle in the same position, so that the crust develops in a uniform fashion. The paint mark should always face upward. If a bottle is moved and replaced for some reason, it should be placed back in the same position with the mark facing upward. This is particularly useful for people buying vintage Port by the bottle. If one buys by the dozen, it is best to leave the vintage Port in its original wooden case to age, since the bottles are already neatly packed on their sides.

WHEN TO DRINK?

The biggest decision one has to make with vintage Port is when to pull the cork and drink it. There are no steadfast rules. Some people like the sweet coarseness of a young vintage Port with three or four years of bottle age. Others prefer their Ports to be mellower, with some of the rough edges rounded by a decade or more of aging. Some vintage Ports develop more quickly than others, because of house style or the quality of a vintage. For example, the 1983 Borges vintage Port is much more mature today than the Graham from the same vintage. While the best 1980s are quite drinkable now, the same wines from the 1977 vintage are still closed and need further aging. Bottle size may play a role in a Port's development. I remember drinking a half bottle of 1955 Sandeman that seemed about five to six years more forward than the same wine in a regular bottle. Larger bottles such as magnums develop more slowly.

I find that most vintage Ports begin to be drinkable eight to 15 years from the vintage date. Thus a 1980 Graham or 1980 Niepoort began to be enjoyable in 1988. Like other good 1980s, they should improve for decades longer, but at eight years old they had lost some of their harshness and baby fat. Nevertheless, I find it slightly disappointing to drink a powerful, well-structured vintage Port before it has reached its 15th birthday. The wine needs time to develop and grow into itself.

Americans are often criticized for drinking their vintage Ports too young. According to Bartholomew Broadbent, the son of Christie's British auctioneer Michael Broadbent and the U.S. representative for Symington Ports, in late 1989 the 1977 vintage was the "standard pour" vintage Port in most fashionable restaurants on the West Coast. It also was apparently not out of the ordinary to see bottles of 1983 and 1985 vintage Port opened and consumed. "Who are we to say it is wrong?" he said. "If people like it, why not let them drink their vintage Ports young? At least they are drinking it."

In fact, Wyndham Fletcher said in his book *Port* in the 1910s and 1920s the British tended to drink their vintage Ports younger than they do today. Recalling a discussion on when to drink vintage Port with the late Fred Cockburn, a Port shipper, Fletcher wrote: "Fred said, 'I do remember when I first came to London in 1919, I used to lunch with my old father (who had been senior partner in the firm) at the Union Club, and the tap vintage was Cockburn's 1912.' The wine was then only seven years old, and the 1912 was, and for that matter still is, no lightweight."

It is easy to understand the attraction of a young, well-balanced vintage Port. A glass of 1977 Fonseca or 1983 Graham explodes with fruit on the palate. Nonetheless, it seems a shame to drink vintage Port at such an early stage of its development. One of the main reasons for paying a premium price for vintage Port is its ability to improve for decades in the bottle. This is the primary difference between a great wine and an ordinary one.

OPENING AND DECANTING

Opening and decanting a mature bottle of vintage Port can be difficult. The necks of the bottles are often coated with wax and difficult to handle. The corks are nearly impossible to pull intact, and the sediment, or crust, is easy to mix in with the wine. Despite these difficulties, drinking it without decanting is like drinking a fine cup of coffee with its grounds.

It is best to stand a bottle of vintage Port upright for at least 24 hours before serving. This ensures that the sediment has had time to fall to the bottom of the bottle. Standing a bottle upright a week before serving is even better, particularly with 30- or 40-year-old vintage Ports or bottles recently purchased. When handled properly, these old bottles often decant perfectly clear to the last drop. If necessary, it is possible to take a bottle of vintage Port straight from the cellar and decant it on the spot. As long as one has a steady hand and a good eye for sediment, one can do a competent job of decanting.

There is no mystique about how far in advance vintage Port should be decanted. The older the vintage Port, the more quickly it should be drunk after decanting. Generally speaking, vintage Ports less than 20 years old should be decanted at least two hours before service to allow them to breathe. Those 10 or less years old could use three or four hours, depending on the particular wine. It is more difficult to judge with older vintages, but opening them about one hour before drinking is usually adequate. Lighter, more mature vintages 40 or more years old are best decanted moments before drinking. Some of these old bottles are nothing more than ghosts of vintage Port, and it is important to catch a glimpse of them in your glass.

The temperature of the Port is also important. It is best served near cellar temperature, between 65 and 68 degrees Fahrenheit. Serving vintage Port warm can make it more volatile and difficult to taste, while colder Port tends to be too tannic and closed. Most people tend to serve their red wines, especially Port, too warm, since their houses are centrally heated to more than 70 degrees.

Pulling the cork is the most difficult task. First, if a wax seal covers the cork, it can be tough to remove; a few solid taps to the wax with the end of the corkscrew, a hammer or some other blunt instrument should suffice. Opening bottles 30 or more years old is even more difficult. Their corks will inevitably break at about three-quarters their length. The size or shape of the corkscrew does not seem to matter. The problem is that the cork fans out like a Champagne cork in the neck of the bottle and becomes too brittle to pull in its entirety. Many vintage Port producers have been using bottles with straighter necks since the late 1980s, and this may improve the situation. For the moment, opening a bottle of mature vintage Port often results in cork pieces falling into the wine. A funnel with a wire screen or a piece of muslin is a useful tool to decant a bottle cleanly. I have even used my wife's nylons (well washed and soaked in ruby Port). Never use a coffee filter or other paper filter, since they can impart flavors to the Port.

Port tongs are an alternative to pulling the cork, and they can work extremely well. The key is to get the iron tongs nearly red-hot before using them. Next open the tongs and firmly grip the neck of the bottle where it meets the shoulder and remove it after a minute or two. Then apply a small wet towel to the same spot. The rapid temperature change should break the glass neatly. Some people reportedly use a wet feather instead of a towel with good results. Unfortunately, my experiences with Port tongs have not been very successful. I find them clumsy and difficult to use. I once spent nearly two hours with Alistair Robertson and Bruce Guimaraens trying to use tongs to open a bottle of 1963 Taylor. After numerous failures, we returned to the corkscrew and funnel.

Pulling the cork out at least partially intact is often a must to verify the authenticity of a vintage Port. Many older bottles do not have labels or embossed seals around the cork, and the only way to identify them is by their branded corks. I once bought a bottle of 1935 Dow at a Christie's auction, and when I removed the cork, it turned out to be a 1955 Cockburn — apparently the wrong bottle was sent to me. The 1935 was sent a few days later after I contacted Christie's about the mix-up. In another instance, a friend opened a bottle of Rebello Valente that he was sure was pre-1900, but when the cork was removed the stamp "1945" was faintly visible on the side.

Once the bottle is open, be sure that the decanter is clean before staring to pour. Rinse it out with fresh water, as well as a bit of ruby or tawny Port, if available. Some people make a fuss about the type of decanter used, insisting on a triangular, cut-glass ship's decanter or some other type, but the shape makes little difference. A glass water jug can be just as efficient. Some people like to decant a bottle of Port, rinse out the bottle and then pour the Port back into the original bottle, finding it is interesting to see the original bottle while drinking the vintage Port.

Decanting efficiently merely takes a steady hand and a sure eye. It should be done in one movement; slowly moving the bottle in one hand from a 12 o'clock position to 9 or 8 o'clock. The moment any sediment begins to enter the decanter, stop pouring. As mentioned above, I find a funnel extremely useful, since the crust can easily be seen on its sides, though some people prefer to use a candle or flashlight under the neck of the bottle to illuminate the sediment. Others even use specially designed decanting cradles, though they seem to be more for show than anything else.

GLASSES, PASSING THE PORT AND OTHER TRADITIONS

The type of glass used to serve vintage Port is relatively unimportant. One wine producer once boasted that his wine was so good it could be drunk from an old boot — though it probably is not a good idea to go to such extremes. Drinking a fine Port from a well-crafted crystal glass is like listening to Beethoven's Fifth Symphony on a first-class stereo system. Using the right equipment enhances one's enjoyment, whether of classical music or vintage Port. The worst glasses to use are the small, cut-crystal type designed for liqueurs, not wine. They are too small to smell or "nose" the wine properly. A regular white-wine tasting glass is preferable.

The traditional vintage Port glass is slightly smaller than a standard tulip-shaped, white wine glass and has a U-shaped bowl with a 5- to 6-ounce capacity. They are good, all-around glasses, and should be filled only half full for proper tasting and appreciation of the wine. Premium crystal glassware producers such as Riedel and Baccarat make elegant and efficient wine glasses, however, they have yet to make an outstanding Port glass. Until they do, I think Port is better served in larger, well-designed white-wine glasses than in smaller ones.

There already have been reams written about the tradition of "passing the Port." It is difficult to establish exactly when the tradition began, but it almost certainly originated with the British sometime during the last century. Traditionally, the decanter of Port, which may or may not be vintage, is placed in front of the host, who serves the guest to his right and passes the decanter to the guest on the left. The Port continues clockwise around the table. There are various theories as to why it is passed clockwise. Sarah Bradford wrote in *The Story of Port* that "learned writers have traced its origins back to the Greeks, the Romans, the Celtic 'lucky turn.' " George Robertson, in his book *Port*, suggested that the tradition started with the Royal Navy, when members insisted that the Port be passed to the left, or port, side. It seems more likely, as noted by Ben Howkins in *Rich, Rare and Red*, that passing the Port to the left is the most natural way "as most people are right-handed it is easier to lift the decanter with the right hand and pass it across the body to the left."

Another British custom ensures that the decanter makes its way back to the host. It is considered poor manners to ask for the decanter, and a host well versed in his or her Port etiquette may ask the person nearest to the decanter if he knows the bishop or doctor of Norwich or some other village in England. Such a question should not be answered except by passing the decanter to the left. Ernest Cockburn described the process well in his book: "One of the more heinous villainies which can be perpetrated at dinner is not to pass the Port decanter, and it is by no means uncommon to hear the misdemeanant asked some questions as 'Do you know the Bishop of Winchester?' If the reply should be 'No,' he is told that 'he is an awfully good fellow — but he never passes the Port!' "

Perhaps the most amusing ritual in serving vintage Port is playing "name the vintage." It goes by many other names, such as "mystery decanter" or "vintage blunder," and is not unique to Port since it can be played with any wine. The host places the decanter full of Port on the table. After it is poured around the table, guests are asked to guess the vintage and name of the shipper. A little bit of luck goes a long way in guessing the right vintage, and even more so in identifying the shipper. Vintage Port aficionados relish telling their "war stories" about guessing the right vintage. Of course, no one likes to talk about his failures.

Sherry Red Bordeaux Champagne Red Burgundy White Wine Port

The right glass for the right wine

Another tradition is to serve vintage Port with Stilton cheese for dessert or at the end of a meal. There are stories of vintage Port being served chilled as an apéritif in France and Belgium, but it is doubtful this happens often. Vintage Port is well complemented by cheese and perhaps some roasted walnuts and apple slices. The spicy, creamy flavors of Stilton and other blue cheeses go well with vintage Port, although hard, flavorful cheeses such as Cheddar or Gloucester are also good. Allegedly some people believe in taking a large piece of Stilton, scooping out the center of the cheese and pouring in a small amount of vintage Port — thus ruining both the Port and the cheese.

The perfect marriage of cheese and vintage Port, however, can be found only in Portugal. The creamy, rich flavors of the cheese from ewe's milk, Queijo da Serra, made in the Serra da Estrela mountain area, is sublime with a silky, sweet, mature vintage Port. In Portugal I also have drunk young vintage Port with pepper steak, which works extremely well. The fiery peppered cream sauce is neutralized by the sweet, robust fruit of the infant Port.

Vintage Port also often finds itself in the company of cigars and cigarettes at the end of a meal, and although I love a fine cigar, a smoke-filled room is hardly the best place to enjoy the nuances of a fine vintage Port. It is generally a good idea to refrain from smoking until the second passage of the decanter, which gives everyone an opportunity to appreciate the vintage Port without smoke.

Ernest Cockburn had the right idea about smoking cigars with Port: "…the 'Man who smokes with Port' can smoke — but he cannot smoke with Port. But I dislike him most when he comes to my house and seeks to indulge his habits just as I am settling down to enjoy perhaps my finest 1896 vintage Port, and it is in the position that I see endless ground for argument… To many such as myself smoke prevents the careful study, appreciation and personal pleasure derived from a glass of fine Port wine, as it stultifies the bouquet of the wine and vitiates the atmosphere in which fine wine should be consumed."

CHAPTER X

THE PORT HOUSES: PROFILES AND TASTING NOTES

T his chapter reviews a range of vintage Ports from 58 different producers. There is a descriptive tasting note and score based on *The Wine Spectator* 100-point scale for each wine. A profile for each producer includes pertinent historical and technical information. In each entry, producers are classified from first tier to not rated, reflecting their overall quality and track record in making vintage Ports. In addition, a collectibility rating is given: AAA, AA, A or not rated. Best vintages are underlined and a short entry highlighting the vital facts of each producer is provided, including producers' addresses, telephone numbers, owners, founding dates and average vintage Port production in declared years. Advice on when to drink the wines and current U.S. and United Kingdom auction and retail prices are also listed. All United Kingdom prices include a 15 percent value-added tax, and auction prices incorporate the 10 percent buyer's premium. For more information on how the wines were evaluated, please see the "Introduction" chapter of the book.

Barros, Almeida
CLASSIFICATION: *Not rated*
COLLECTIBILITY RATING: *Not rated*

At a Glance

BARROS, ALMEIDA
Rua da Leonor de Freitas 182,
C.P. 39
4400 Vila Nova de Gaia,
Portugal
02-30.23.20

Owners: Barros family

Founded: 1913

Average production: 4,000-
5,000 cases

With all its different houses, one might expect Barros, Almeida to produce very high quality vintage Port, but only recently have some of the vintage Ports from Barros been better than merely acceptable.

Founded in 1913 by the Barros family, the Barros, Almeida group now includes seven different houses: Barros, Vieira de Sousa, Hutcheson, The Douro Wine Shippers & Growers Association, Feuerheerd Brothers, H. & C.J. Feist, and C.N. Kopke. The group also ships Port under the name A. Pinto dos Santos, as well as under various other brands for clients throughout Europe. The Barros, Almeida group sells about 450,000 cases of Port annually, mostly in France, Holland, West Germany and Belgium, and is better known for its old tawnies than for vintage Ports or premium rubies. The Barros and Kopke 20-year-old tawnies are outstanding.

With the exception of Kopke, the vintage Ports sold under the Barros label are the best in the group. "We always select the best wines for Barros," said Manuel Angelo Barros. Kopke has its own lodge to mature and blend its Port. The rest of the Barros, Almeida Ports are aged and bottled under the same roof at Barros' lodges in Vila Nova de Gaia.

Barros emphasized that each house's Ports, especially the vintage, are kept separate in their lodges, although I find the various vintage Ports from the Barros, Almeida group extremely similar in character and style. Kopke is the only one that is clearly different.

The vintage Port blending at Barros seems rather haphazard, with the exception of the Kopke. When I asked Barros how they maintained a house style for each firm's vintage Ports, he replied, "It is not easy to say. It just depends. We simply put different Port aside for the different houses."

Most Barros, Almeida vintage Ports bottled under Barros' label (the others have separate entries in the book) are clean, fruity, light and simple. They can be consumed six years after the vintage date, since they do not have the complexity, depth of fruit or structure for further aging. The 1985 and 1987 Barros are the closest the firm has come to making exciting vintage Ports. Both wines showed a better concentration of fruit and tannins than any of the preceding years, with the exception of the 1970.

The 1970 shows that Barros has the ability to produce ageworthy, interesting vintage Port. I have had the 1970 twice, and it always shows more than enough chocolate and cherry notes on the nose and palate to keep your attention. It is perfect to drink now and compares favorably with many other 1970s.

Relatively small amounts of vintage Port are made at Barros. For example, about 4,800 cases of the 1985 Barros were produced. All the wines are bought from various growers in the Rio Torto Valley and near the village of São João da Pesqueria. The company owns about 230 acres of vineyards in the Douro, including such *quintas* as Santa Luiz, Dona Matilde, Lobata, Don Pedro, Mesquita and Alegria. Barros has a large winery at Quinta da Santa Luiz.

Barros is the first to admit his vintages are on the light side, and he says they are doing as much as they can to make better Ports. "We try to make the best we can but the British houses and a few Portuguese have the best vineyard sites up the Douro. It is a question of positioning. It is difficult to get good enough grapes for vintage."

PORTO BARROS 1985 VINTAGE PORT. BOTTLED AND SHIPPED BY: BARROS, ALMEIDA & CA.-VINHOS, S. A. R. L. VILA NOVA DE GAIA. PRODUCE OF PORTUGAL. 26 2/3 FL. OZ. ALCOHOL 20% – 75 CL.

TASTING NOTES

1987 BARROS: Marks a return to the major leagues for Barros. Good purple color, with a very fresh, grapy, aromatic nose, medium- to full-bodied, with medium tannins and a balance of elegant fruit. No show-stopper, but has some class. Last tasted: 1/90. Drink 1995-1996. Release: $28 (£14). Current retail: $28 (£14). Current auction: NA. **81**

1985 BARROS: This is an early-drinking 1985 but it is nicely crafted all the same. Medium purple with a ruby hue, a very fresh and grapy nose, medium-bodied, with clean, fresh fruit flavors, medium tannins and a long finish. Last tasted: 1/90. Drink 1994-1996. Release: $24 (£10). Current retail: $29 (£14). Current auction: NA. **80**

1983 BARROS: A decent early-drinking wine showing simple, fresh fruit flavors but not a lot of complexity or structure. Medium ruby, with a fresh, simple, fruity nose, medium-bodied, with clean fruit flavors, good balance and a medium finish. Last tasted: 1/90. Drink 1990-1993. Release: $8 (£7). Current retail: $29 (£15). Current auction: NA. **76**

1978 BARROS: Another sweet and simple Port. Medium to light ruby, with fresh, floral grape and licorice aromas, light-bodied, with light tannins, quite sweet, short finish. Last tasted: 1/90. Drink 1990. Release: $7 (£5). Current retail: $30 (£13). Current auction: NA. **75**

1974 BARROS: Medium ruby with a garnet edge, a pleasant violet and chocolate nose, medium-bodied, with light, sweet, velvety fruit flavors, decent tannins and a light finish. Last tasted: 1/90. Drink 1990. Release: £3. Current retail: $40 (£20). Current auction: NA. **74**

1970 BARROS: Very sweet, but quite good. Medium red with a garnet hue, chocolate and cherry aromas, medium-bodied, with good depth of fruit and clean flavors. Last tasted: 1/90. Drink 1990. Release: £2. Current retail: $60 (£30). Current auction: £11. **82**

BORGES & IRMAO
CLASSIFICATION: *Not rated*

COLLECTIBILITY RATING: *Not rated*

Sociedade dos Vinhos Borges Irmão is part of the nationalized bank group Banco Borges & Irmão, so the company understands the concept of holding back reserves. Borges has vintage Ports dating to 1870 in its cellars, and apparently has available commercial stocks of wines back to the 1970s.

But this heritage appears to have done very little to better Borges' understanding of the style and quality of true vintage Port. With the exception of the 1982, all of the firm's recent vintages are barely acceptable. For the most part they are clean, with pretty fruit flavors, but they are so light in body that anyone with any knowledge of vintage Port would be shocked to taste them.

Laying these wines away in one's cellar would be a major disappointment. They lack the fruit concentration and tannin structure for long-term aging. The 1970 Borges I tasted in 1990 was well past its prime. I recommend drinking Borges Ports about four or five years from their vintage date.

The best Borges vintage Port, the 1982, still only scored 79 points out of 100 in my tasting. It showed interesting roasted nut, chocolate and fruit character but still seemed too simple. Nonetheless, it was a perfectly drinkable example of the 1982 vintage.

Most of the vintage wines come from Borges' own properties. Quinta do Juncão is located in the Pinhão Valley, with about 134 acres of vineyards. It produces about 220 pipes of Port per harvest, mostly made through autovinification. Quinta da Soalheira encompasses about 100 acres, producing about 90 pipes of Port. Production of Borges vintage Ports is no more than 10,000 cases a year.

Borges is better known for its table wines, which come from nearly all the key regions of Portugal. Its white *vinho verde*, Gatão, with its distinctive glass jug and its label depicting a cat in black boots, is one of the most popular table wines in Portugal. The quality is also good. Borges' sales of table wines and Port total about 1 million cases a year.

The company dates back to 1884, when António Nunes Borges and his brother Francisco began a merchant company trading primarily in foreign currency, tobacco and matches. A few years later the brothers began trading in table wine and Port. Vinhos Borges & Irmão was formed after the company established Banco Borges & Irmão. In 1907, the brothers decided to run the two companies separately, but under the same holding company. The bank was nationalized after the Portuguese revolution in 1974, which also put the wine business under state ownership.

"We are not acting as a nationalized company," said Mário Saravia Pinto, export director for Borges. "We have always acted as an independent company."

Rumors of Vinhos Borges' sale to a multinational group have been circulating for years, and it may eventually happen. Borges certainly has the potential to produce good vintage Ports with all of its resources.

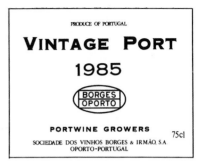

TASTING NOTES

1985 BORGES: This is so light and ready to drink that it is more like a ruby or a late-bottled vintage. Medium to light red, with simple aromas of cherries and chocolate, light-bodied and clean, with sweet cherry flavors and light tannins on the finish. Last tasted: 5/90. Drink 1990. Release: $15 (£10). Current retail: $15 (£14). Current auction: NA. **70**

1983 BORGES: Amazingly sugary; most 1983s are relatively dry. Medium red, with a redwood and mature cherry nose, medium-bodied, with simple, syrupy cherry flavors, medium tannins and a long finish. Too sweet for me but drinkable nonetheless. Last tasted: 5/90. Drink 1990-1992. Release: $12 (£7). Current retail: $29 (£15). Current auction: NA. **70**

1982 BORGES: The best Borges vintage I have tasted. It is not overly roasted and raisiny like many other 1982s and it shows some interesting fruit. Medium deep ruby, with a chocolate and roasted nut nose, medium-bodied, with sweet, ripe fruit flavors, medium tannins and a silky finish. Last tasted: 5/90. Drink 1991-1993. Release: $12 (£6). Current retail: $30 (£13). Current auction: NA. **79**

1980 BORGES: Another lightweight vintage that is much more like a ruby or late-bottled vintage. Red with a light ruby center, spicy black cherry aromas, medium- to light-bodied, with light tannins and a sweet fruit finish. Last tasted: 5/90. Drink 1990. Release: $12 (£6). Current retail: $23 (£13). Current auction: NA. **70**

1979 BORGES: Remarkably light and forward. The alcohol is showing now, indicating that it is on its way down. Light red with an almost garnet hue, aromas of cherries and nuts, light-bodied, with simple, sweet cherry flavors and a hot, unbalanced finish. Fading. Last tasted: 5/90. Best to avoid. Release: $11 (£6). Current retail: $22 (£12). Current auction: NA. **65**

1970 BORGES: Rustic, tired and stinky. This is over the hill. Medium red-garnet, with musty varnish aromas, medium-bodied, with thick varnish flavors. Last tasted: 5/90. Best to avoid. Release: £2. Current retail: $60 (£28). Current auction: £11. **59**

J.W. BURMESTER

CLASSIFICATION: *FOURTH TIER*

COLLECTIBILITY RATING: *Not rated*

BEST VINTAGES: *1985, 1980*

The owners of J.W. Burmester downplay their vintage Ports, even though their house often makes wines as good as the most reputable names in the business.

"We don't make much publicity about our vintage Ports," said Arnold Burmester Gilbert, owner and winemaker at Burmester. Added Henrique Burmester S. Silva, a director of the firm, "The markets we have emphasized, they don't like vintages that much. Places like France, Belgium and West Germany just don't like it."

They could have vintage Port lovers lining up to buy their wines when the word gets out. Burmester's vintage Ports can be superb. The 1985 Burmester is on the same level as the vintage's best, including Taylor and Graham. It is a deeply colored, massively proportioned wine with a bounty of fruit and tannin and a finish that seems to go on and on. This is a serious wine to lay away for the next century.

More mature vintages, such as the 1963 and 1970, are not as fantastic but are very good nonetheless. They are drier wines — like many of the British houses' vintage Ports — with an attractive silky, fruity mouth-feel. I have never drunk Burmester vintages older than the 1963, but I have heard that the 1927 is breathtaking.

"Years ago, we only made four or five pipes of a vintage Port," said Gilbert, who also sells a vintage under his surname, although it is the same wine as Burmester. "Our name is not known because we shipped mostly in bulk to northern countries like Norway and Sweden. About 40 years ago we were the suppliers of the Swedish royal family."

Today Burmester sells about 70,000 cases of Port each year. Two thirds are sold in bottle and the rest in bulk. Gilbert said that the wines they bottle themselves have always been premium Ports, while the cheap rubies and tawnies were sold in bulk to agents in France and Belgium.

As for its quality Ports, Burmester makes superb vintage-dated and mature tawnies, such as the Burmester 20-year-old. In addition, it makes some outstanding late-bottled vintage wines, which are not fined or filtered like most other LBVs, and improve with age in the bottle like a vintage Port. The 1964 Burmester Late Bottled Vintage is still an excellent mature Port.

Burmester produces between 2,000 and 6,000 cases of vintage Port a year. It made about 5,800 cases of the 1985 and 2,500 of the

1984. "It is impossible to make a good wine in a weak vintage in large quantities," said Silva. "That is why we made a small amount of the 1984. We had the wine, so why not declare?"

The house owns no vineyards, although it has been looking to buy a *quinta* in the Douro Valley. The vintage wines are made both in *lagares* and by autovinification. Burmester Silva would not say exactly where he buys his vintage wines, although he said most of it comes from east of the village of Pinhão, near Graham's Quinta dos Malvedos. Maybe this is why he likes to say that the style of his vintage Ports is somewhere between Graham's and Croft's.

There is some confusion over when Burmester was founded. According to Gilbert, the company was trading as Burmester & Nash in the 18th century. The original shareholders were English, even though Burmester is a German surname. The owners left Portugal after the invasion of Napoleon's troops. Gilbert's great-grandfather Johan Wilheim Burmester took over the firm in 1834. Today, the company has four shareholders: Fernando Formigal, Fatima Burmester Pimenta, Gilbert and Silva. They are all family members. "It is not a big enterprise," said Silva. "It's just a very small family enterprise."

While tasting a few of their vintages in their small lodges in Vila Nova de Gaia, Gilbert and Burmester Silva reflected on the quality of their recent vintages, particularly the 1985. They seemed surprised while tasting the young vintage Port and shook their heads as they sniffed and took small sips of the wine. Said Gilbert, "This 1985 is so rich and fresh still. I am surprised. I thought it would be older." Burmester Silva agreed and the two men shook their heads. They seemed almost disappointed. No one else in the tasting room understood the humor. The wine was outstanding.

TASTING NOTES

1985 BURMESTER: This is a great achievement for a 1985, perhaps one of the best wines of the vintage. Inky color, with berry and grape must aromas, full-bodied, with tons of fruit and tannin, very concentrated. Finish is extremely long. Outstanding. Last tasted: 1/90. Drink 1996-1998. Release: $25 (£12). Current retail: $25 (£16). Current auction: NA. **93**

1984 BURMESTER: Very good for an unheralded vintage, if a little lean. Deep ruby, with a concentrated earthy, grapy nose, medium-bodied, with very good fruit flavors, medium tannins and a simple, youthful, fruity finish. Last tasted: 1/90. Drink 1993-1995. Release: £11. Current retail: £14. Current auction: NA. **84**

1980 BURMESTER: This is an enchanting, stylish wine with plenty of exotic, ripe fruit flavors. Deep ruby, with an excellent, earthy, black truffle nose, full-bodied, with ripe fruit flavors and well-integrated tan-

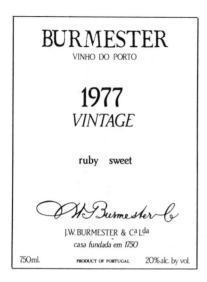

BURMESTER

VINHO DO PORTO

1977
VINTAGE

ruby   sweet

J.W. BURMESTER & Cª Lᵈᵃ
casa fundada em 1750

750ml.   PRODUCT OF PORTUGAL   20% alc. by vol.

nins. Last tasted: 1/90. Drink 1993. Release: $18 (£7). Current retail: $33 (£15). Current auction: NA. **88**

1977 BURMESTER: Starts out rather slow on the palate, but it opens into a classy glass of Port. Medium to deep ruby, with a perfumed floral and currant nose, medium-bodied, with medium tannins and a very balanced, clean fruit finish. Not a blockbuster, but very good. Last tasted: 1/90. Drink 1991-1993. Release: $11 (£5). Current retail: $37 (£28). Current auction: NA. **82**

1970 BURMESTER: This is a racy wine with superb balance. Deep ruby, with perfumed black currant aromas, full-bodied, with an excellent balance of ripe currant flavors and silky tannins on the finish. Last tasted: 1/90. Drink 1990. Release: £2. Current retail: $55 (£32). Current auction: NA. **86**

1963 BURMESTER: This is a very elegant and tightly knit wine that needs to open, but it quickly evolves in the glass. Medium ruby with a garnet edge, a nose of black currants, truffles and tea, medium-bodied, with lovely, delicious fruit flavors and a balance of tannins. It has a silky mouth-feel on the finish. Last tasted: 1/90. Drink 1990. Release: £.90. Current retail: $110 (£42). Current auction: NA. **83**

A.A. CÁLEM & FILHO

CLASSIFICATION: *FIFTH TIER*

COLLECTIBILITY RATING: *Not rated*

BEST VINTAGES: *1985, 1975*

The recent vintage Ports of A.A. Cálem & Filho are racy, elegant wines with focused fruit and silky tannins that seduce a taster. This flashy style seems to fit the proud, outspoken owner of Cálem, Joaquim Manuel Cálem, who also is Portugal's agent for Ferrari automobiles. "My vintage Ports are made in a style I like," said Cálem, a small, energetic man used to having things his way. "I want them to be sweet but elegant." His house sells about 350,000 cases of Port a year. Cálem is best know for its simple rubies and tawnies, which are exceptionally good for the price. Cálem is a market leader in Portugal and also produces table wines from the Douro and Dão.

Cálem's recent claim to fame was when its 1985 vintage Port finished first in a blind tasting of 1985s held by the London *Times*. It apparently finished above all the top names. My own view is that the 1985 Cálem is clearly not on the same level as the best of the vintage, although it is a very good Port. It shows a wonderful harmony of anise and fruit flavors and silky tannins, with medium grip on the finish. It has plenty of stuffing for aging, but it doesn't have the concentration of major-league Ports like Graham or Taylor.

The 1985 Cálem marked the beginning of a working relationship with Jeremy Bull, one of the most talented taster-blenders in the Port trade. Bull had worked three decades for Taylor Fladgate, blending the legendary Taylors of the 1960s and 1970s. After a falling-out with the owners of Taylor, he left and set up shop as a consultant. He soon took a position with Cálem.

Bull was not directly involved in the production of the Cálem 1985, but he arrived just in time to make the final blend of the 1985 during the spring of 1987. "I had to work with what we had," said Bull, a soft-spoken man who is passionate about Port. "But there were some very good things to choose from."

The 1987 Cálem, a single-*quinta* wine made from Cálem's Quinta da Foz near Pinhão, was made entirely by Bull. It maintains the attractive style of the 1985, with plenty of ripe fruit and silky tannins. It merely lacks the extra complexity of the 1985, which was a blend of wines from various *quintas* near the village of Pinhão.

Cálem had a policy of putting "Quinta da Foz" on the labels of Ports from declared vintages, although the firm no longer does this,

---

AT A GLANCE

A. A. CÁLEM & FILHO
Avenida Diogo Leite 26
4400 Vila Nova de Gaia,
 Portugal
02-39.40.41

Owner: Joaquim Manuel Cálem

Founded: 1859

Average production: 4,000-
 6,000 cases

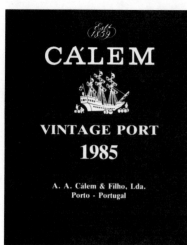

except in a year like 1987 when the entire production of vintage Port was from this *quinta*.

Cálem's Quinta da Foz is the backbone of all of the house's vintage Ports, which total 4,000 to 6,000 cases a year. Foz, which is at the west end of the village of Pinhão, includes about 27 acres of vineyards, producing about 60 pipes of Port. All the wines at Foz are still made in *lagares*. "Quinta da Foz will produce everything from a vintage Port to a good quality tawny," said Bull in late 1989. "You watch the various wines from the *quinta* and then decide which go into your vintage blends."

Foz also features a large, traditional house and a winery, as well as a guest house that is rented out part of the year. The train from Oporto runs right next to the dining room, which can add to the liveliness of an evening at the property. Mornings can be difficult, however, for those who sample the Port a little too often the night before. Wines from the adjacent properties of Quinta do Sagrado and Quinta da Sangra may also go into Cálem vintage lots. They are both made at Foz. Sagrado now includes about 25 acres of vineyards and should produce about 85 pipes of Port when new plantings come into production. Sangra has 5 acres of vines and makes about 15 pipes of Port. Sagrado may one day make its own single-*quinta* Ports.

For its vintage wines Cálem can also use the wines from some of its other *quintas*: Santo António in the Pinhão Valley, and Carvalheira and Rio de Moinhos, both in the Rio Torto Valley. The properties have vineyards ranging in size from 6 to 30 acres. There are also 45 acres of recent plantings at Quinta do Vedial, in the Pinhão region, and Cálem hopes to produce vintage-quality wines there.

Cálem was founded in 1859. The Cálem family's original business was shipping Portuguese table wines to Brazil. The company's ships would bring wood back on their homeward voyages, which led to the establishment of a cooperage. The Cálems later started trading in Port.

Cálem seems to have taken vintage Port production much more seriously in the 1980s, although its 1975 had already proved it could make a serious wine. The 1975 Cálem is arguably the best vintage Port produced in that mediocre year. If the trend continues into the 1990s, with the help of Jeremy Bull, Cálem will be a house to watch in the vintage Port game.

TASTING NOTES

1987 CALEM QUINTA DA FOZ: Made entirely from Cálem's Quinta da Foz, this young Port shows lots of fruit, with a rich and velvety mouth-feel. It will be an earlier drinker than the 1985. Purple, with ripe fruit and orange peel aromas, full-bodied, with lots of fruit flavors and a velvety finish. Last tasted: 6/90. Drink 1995-1996. Release: $28. Current retail: $28. Current auction: NA. **84**

1985 CALEM: The first vintage that brought Cálem attention. Deep purple, with an intense floral and licorice nose, full-bodied, good grip, a medium concentration of fruit flavors and a long finish. Very good potential. Last tasted: 6/90. Drink 1995-1997. Release: $25 (£10). Current retail: $36 (£21). Current auction: NA. **88**

1983 CALEM: A racy Port with very good structure. It puts Cálem back in the driver's seat for quality. Purple-ruby, with a ripe blackberry nose, full-bodied, with a good concentration of sweet fruit flavors, full tannins and a balanced finish. Last tasted: 6/90. Drink 1994-1996. Release: $18 (£9). Current retail: $38 (£18). Current auction: £7. **84**

1982 CALEM QUINTA DA FOZ: A sweet and simple vintage Port with plenty of attractive flavors. Medium ruby, with a plum and roasted nut nose, full-bodied with velvety ripe fruit and a medium finish. Last tasted: 6/90. Drink 1993-1995. Release: $16 (£8). Current retail: $34 (£18). Current auction: NA. **82**

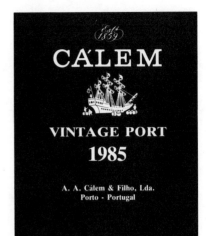

1980 CALEM: Extremely sweet and short on body and backbone. Medium ruby, chocolate, cherry and spice on the nose, medium-bodied, with sweet cherry and tomato flavors, medium tannins and a short finish. Last tasted: 6/90. Drink 1990. Release: $14 (£7). Current retail: $34 (£17). Current auction: £6. **78**

1977 CALEM: It is hard to say what happened here but this is very forward and weak for a 1977. Medium ruby with a garnet edge and slightly burnt vanilla aromas, medium-bodied, with burnt vanilla and fruit flavors, light tannins and a short finish. Last tasted: 11/89. Best to avoid. Release: $11 (£5). Current retail: $55 (£20). Current auction: $23 (£12). **69**

1975 CALEM: This is perhaps the best 1975 I have ever tasted. Most are weak, insipid and fading fast but this isn't. Medium ruby, lovely boysenberry aromas, medium-bodied, with round tannins and lots of velvety, sweet cherry flavors. Last tasted: 2/90. Drink 1990. Release: £4.50. Current retail: $50 (£25). Current auction: £13. **86**

1970 CALEM: Lacks a little gusto but a very nice Port. Medium ruby, with a perfumed, ripe raspberry nose, medium-bodied, with ripe cherry flavors and medium tannins. Last tasted: 11/89. Drink 1990-1994. Release: £2. Current retail: $50 (£32). Current auction: £13. **80**

1966 CALEM: Sweet and silky, showing more elegance than many 1966s, but needs more weight. Medium ruby-red, with a fruity blueberry nose, medium-bodied, with silky, sweet fruit flavors, light tannins and a medium finish. Last tasted: 11/89. Drink 1990. Release: £1.25. Current retail: $65 (£40). Current auction: $40 (£16). **82**

1963 CALEM: Very sweet, and still has a bounty of red berry flavors. Medium ruby with a garnet edge, very sweet, perfumed, grapy nose, full-bodied, with thick, rich and sweet berry flavors and a long finish. The alcohol is starting to surface. Last tasted: 12/89. Drink 1990. Release: £.90. Current retail: $85 (£42). Current auction: NA. **82**

CHAMPALIMAUD

CLASSIFICATION: *Not rated*

COLLECTIBILITY RATING: *Not rated*

Mention the name Champalimaud in the Port trade and there is always a reaction. Perhaps better know for its very good red table wines from the Douro Valley, Champalimaud also produces vintage Ports from its 110 acres of vineyards at Quinta do Cotto, about 9 miles west of the town of Regua.

Some Port shippers are probably upset by Champalimaud's ability to make good vintage Ports from its vineyards in the Baixo Corgo, an area that usually produces light, fairly characterless Ports that are used for other shippers' rubies and tawnies. Others have more of an aversion to the man who oversees the *quinta* and wine production, Manuel Champalimaud.

Champalimaud has a reputation for making outrageous remarks about the Port trade, from his goal of declaring a vintage every year to calling traditional shippers of vintage Port "liquor people." The plain-looking, dark-haired man can ruffle some feathers, but he also knows how to make good wines, both Port and table.

His 1982 and 1985 Quinta do Cotto Grande Eschola red table wines are good by anyone's standards. They are full-bodied wines with rich, ripe berry flavors, reminiscent of a good Gigondas or other southern Rhône wine. If more table-wine producers in Portugal made wines like his, the country would have a reputation for making fine wines rather than plonk. He produces about 2,000 cases of Grande Eschola per year.

As for his vintage Ports, I have only tasted his 1982, and it showed well in a blind tasting of Ports from the same vintage. It was completely different in style from the others. Slightly lower in alcohol, it was extremely jammy, with tons of sweet fruit. It was almost cloying, but still in balance. If it had a little more tannin, it would have been outstanding.

His competitors claim Champalimaud manipulates his wines by mixing in elderberry juice to get a darker color and a greater intensity of fruit. But Champalimaud denies such accusations. "The basic difference between me and all those other shippers is that I make my vintage Port conforming to the new and modern rules of winemaking," he said. "I treat them just like I treat my red table wines. I keep the oxidation down to a minimum."

Champalimaud has bottled and sold only the 1982 on his own. Other harvests have been sold in bulk. All of his Ports are made on the *quinta* in autovinification tanks. Champalimaud produced about 700 cases of the 1982, and a few were shipped to America, although it is more widely available in Great Britain. He may bottle some 1989 vintage, but he was still not sure in early 1990.

Although very different in style from typical vintage Ports, the 1982 Champalimaud is an interesting wine. Its extremely dark, inky color and jammy nose are rather unique for a 1982. Most other 1982s are more developed, with lighter colors and more mature aromas and flavors. When I evaluated the 1982 at a blind tasting, some Port shippers in attendance said they didn't like it, finding the wine atypical for the vintage. These negative remarks were probably more due to their prejudice against the shipper than to the quality of the wine. Once you have tasted Champalimaud vintage Port, it is easy to pick out in a blind tasting.

"The style of my Ports is not a question of equipment," said Champalimaud. "It is a question of mentality. The way I make my Ports, they will have a longer life than all the other vintage Ports but they will be drinkable sooner." Whether Champalimaud can have it both ways remains to be seen.

TASTING NOTES

1982 CHAMPALIMAUD: For a 1982, this has tons of sweet, almost cloying fruit. Its black color is impressive and its extremely fruity nose stands out. Lacks the class to be considered truly outstanding. Dark purple-ruby, with a jammy nose, full-bodied, with very sweet fruit flavors, medium tannins and a lingering finish. Last tasted: 2/90. Drink 1992-1994. Release: $20 (£7). Current retail: $20 (£15). Current auction: NA. **86**

CHURCHILL (CHURCHILL GRAHAM)

CLASSIFICATION: *Not rated*

COLLECTIBILITY RATING: *Not rated*

AT A GLANCE

CHURCHILL GRAHAM
Rua do Golgota 63
4100 Uporto, Portugal
02-69.66.95

Owners: Graham family

Founded: 1981

Average production: 4,000-
4,500 cases

It took a lot of nerve for Johnny Graham to launch his tiny Port house, Churchill Graham, in the early 1980s. It had been decades since anyone set up on his own, but Graham has always been an assertive, hard-working man in the Port trade. "I had this idea of creating something different — something not big but jolly good in quality," he said.

In most instances, his Ports, shipped under the Churchill label, are good. His Churchill vintage character, crusted and vintage Ports are all interesting wines. Churchill's annual sales are 8,000 to 10,000 cases. Owned by Graham and his two brothers, Churchill is tiny compared to other houses, and could one day become to Port what Maison Leroy is to négociant Burgundies. Both are small enterprises seeking out the best wines in their respective regions.

"In the Port trade, you cannot exaggerate things," said Graham, who began his career in 1973 with Cockburn Smithes and trained under John Smithes, a legendary Port blender. "You cannot expand too quickly. You have to try to maintain quality."

The quality of Churchill's vintage Ports has been heralded in Great Britain since the firm's first declaration, 1982. Young Churchill vintage Ports always show well in blind tastings. They are formidable wines with extremely dark colors and raw, concentrated aromas. They have masses of chewy fruit on the palate.

The evolution of some of Churchill vintages remains questionable, however. I evaluated all of the Churchill vintage Ports at least three times in early 1990 in blind tastings, and they all exhibited a slight varnish note and an almost acetic character. Some, such as the 1983, are flawed with this character. It is difficult to say where the character comes from. Perhaps it is a result of overly hot fermentations or barrels infected with acetic bacteria. Laboratory analyses of some wines show slightly higher levels than normal of volatile acidity. As the wines age, this varnish character may become more pronounced as the fruit declines. I would recommend drinking these wines earlier than others, perhaps about eight years after the vintage date. Watch their evolution closely.

I drank the 1982 Churchill with Graham in early 1990, and its rich, round, ripe fruit flavors caressed the palate. It was a very good glass of vintage, but I don't think it is a Port to lay away for decades due to the slightly "off" component on the nose. The 1987 Churchill Agua Alta would be one of the most impressive wines from the vintage if not for the same thing. It is good nonetheless, and should be drinking well by 1995.

All Churchill vintages come from the Douro grower Jorges Borges de Sousa, who owns six *quintas* in prime areas in the Cima Corgo. Quinta do Roncão is a few miles east of Pinhão, while the *quintas* of Manuela, Fojo, Agua Alta, Tapada and Celeiros are in different locations in the Pinhão Valley. Graham has used Agua Alta and Fojo to make single-*quinta* wines. Everything is produced in *lagares*.

Borges has helped Graham establish his house from the beginning. He sold him stocks on credit, and Graham admits he could never have started without him. As a sidelight to the story, when Graham started the company, he first shipped under the name Churchill Graham, but the Symington family, which owns the house of W. & J. Graham, sued for trademark infringement. The whole affair was settled out of court a few months and a few thousand pounds later and Graham began shipping under the Churchill brand.

After the harvest, the young vintage Ports stay at the Borges' *quintas* until early spring, when they are moved down to Churchill's lodges in Vila Nova de Gaia. Churchill's stocks are between 400 and 500 pipes. Graham began renting a small lodge from Taylor, Fladgate, for whom he worked as a consultant between 1981 and 1983, but moved to a larger one in 1990. Graham sells 2,000 to 3,000 cases of his vintage each year.

Graham comes from the Port clan that started the house of Graham in the last century. W. & J. Graham was bought by the Symington family in 1970. His godfather, the late Dick Yeatman, owner of Taylor, Fladgate, was a great Port shipper.

With such an illustrious bloodline and solid experience in the Port trade, one would expect Graham to succeed with Churchill. He already has in many ways. His Ports should only continue to improve in quality.

TASTING NOTES

1987 CHURCHILL AGUA ALTA: I have tasted this in three blind tastings, and it has always been impressive except for a slight varnish character on the nose. Many people won't notice it, but it could get worse with age as the fruit dissipates, so drink this while it is still young and fruity. Great inky color, with ripe raspberry and chocolate notes, slight varnish aromas, extremely full-bodied, with layers of rich raspberry flavors, full tannins and a long finish. Last tasted: 5/90. Drink 1995-1997. Release: $37. Current retail: $37. Current auction: NA. **83**

1986 CHURCHILL FOJO: There are some attractive floral fruit flavors, but the nose has a slightly odd component. Medium purple, with a floral, perfumed, slight varnish nose, medium-bodied, with floral, earthy

flavors, medium tannins and a good finish. Last tasted: 2/90. Drink 1994. Release: £14. Current retail: £14. Current auction: NA. **78**

1985 CHURCHILL: This is an impressive wine on the palate, but I tasted it blind four times in early 1990 and a slightly odd, acetic nose showed three times. It doesn't seem to be getting any worse, however. Deep ruby-purple color, with earthy berry and slightly volatile aromas, full-bodied, with lovely, velvety fruit flavors, medium tannins and a sweet, round finish. Last tasted: 6/90. Drink 1993-1995. Release: $22 (£12). Current retail: $32 (£17). Current auction: £8. **81**

1984 CHURCHILL FOJO: For the rather lean 1984 vintage, this is very ripe, with an abundance of attractive, roasted, ripe fruit flavors. When I tasted this wine blind, some other tasters found it slightly acetic on the nose, but I didn't. Medium ruby-purple, with perfumed black currant aromas, full-bodied, with rich, sweet fruit flavors and medium tannins that firmly hold the wine together. Last tasted: 2/90. Drink 1992-1993. Release: £12. Current retail: £14. Current auction: NA. **79**

1983 CHURCHILL AGUA ALTA: The strange acetic character of this wine overpowers everything else. Medium ruby with a red edge, intense nail polish aroma, medium-bodied, with grapy, varnish flavors and a short hard finish. Last tasted: 7/90. Best to avoid. Release: $22 (£9). Current retail: $27 (£15). Current auction: £6. **69**

1982 CHURCHILL: Delicious, sweet and opulent, but an acetic, varnish aroma detracts from the overall quality. Some people may not mind this "off" characteristic but it will probably get worse with time. Medium ruby with a purple center, a grapy, earthy, slightly "off" nose, medium-bodied, with silky, well-integrated tannins and a sweet, long finish. Last tasted: 6/90. Drink 1990-1992. Release: £10. Current retail: £14. Current auction: £10. **78**

COCKBURN SMITHES

CLASSIFICATION: *SECOND TIER*

COLLECTIBILITY RATING: *AA*

BEST VINTAGES: *1983, 1935, 1927, 1912*

Until the mid-1980s, many people thought Cockburn Smithes was out of the vintage Port market, but its 1985 and 1983 vintage Ports proved that the house was back as a top-notch producer.

The 1985 and 1983 Cockburn are tough, concentrated vintage Ports with steely tannic backbones and more than enough fleshy cherry flavors to complement their excellent structure. While rather rough and austere when young, they still maintain good finesse and balance. They will require at least 15 years of aging.

David Orr, a former managing director of Cockburn and now overseeing Bordeaux first-growth Château Latour, echoed the view of almost everyone closely associated with the Port shipper. "Cockburn had been out of the vintage Port market for so long that we knew that the 1983 had to be very, very good," he said. "We had to show everyone that we were serious about vintage Port again."

Cockburn has always put a lot of importance on its vintage Port, although the company has been extremely individualistic. It has a record of not declaring outstanding vintages; it passed on 1977, 1966 and 1945. Nevertheless, what has been declared has been very good.

The Cockburn vintage Ports are known for their elegance and great balance. Some people say that Cockburn vintage Ports are drier than others, although I have always found them to have plenty of sweet fruit when young. Perhaps when they mature they show more dried fruit character, particularly dried cherries. They may be drinkable earlier than vintage Ports from some of the other leading houses, but they remain on a quality plateau for many decades.

For instance, many British wine merchants believed the 1927 Cockburn was extremely light and not worth laying down in their cellars. Wyndham Fletcher, a former director of Cockburn and the author of the book *Port*, wrote about a London wine merchant who telephoned Ernest Cockburn to complain about the 1927's quality. The merchant said, "That 1927 of yours is so light, my boy, it tastes like breakfast wine. Will you take it back?"

The 1927 is still a wonderful vintage Port to drink today. It shows how well an excellent vintage of Cockburn reaches a harmony of delicate fruit and silky tannins. Apparently, the 1927 has been at this level for two or three decades. It may last forever at this rate.

The Cockburn vintages between 1963 and 1975 are not quite up to the quality of the great wines of the 1920s, 1930s, 1940s and 1950s. It is difficult to say why there was a slight decline in quality, although it could be linked to Cockburn's changeover to using *movimosto* for fermenting in *lagares*.

Gordon Guimaraens, Cockburn's production director, said that *movimosto* had nothing to do with it. "Quite a bit of our 1983 was made by *movimosto*, like Canais," he said. "So you can make good wines with the system. You have to know how to use it. People tread before the fermentation and then use the *movimosto* to keep the cap down during the fermentation."

He did say that production of top-quality wines declined in volume in the 1960s and 1970s, however. Quinta dos Canais, a top property now owned by Cockburn, went from producing 240 pipes of Port to 30. Due to the depressed state of the Port business at the time, growers in the Douro Valley did not invest in their vineyards. Some stopped growing completely. Cockburn's investment in its giant vineyard site near Vilarica was partly in reaction to these *quinta* losses. Guimaraens believes that Cockburn can produce vintage quality wines there, but I have my doubts. The vineyard is only rated C by the Casa do Douro, and nearly all the other best vintage Port vineyards are classed A or B.

In addition, the Vilarica vineyards are planted on gentle slopes, more like vineyards in California's Napa Valley than in the Douro, where the best Ports traditionally come from steeply terraced vineyards. Cockburn, however, may prove me wrong.

Until the early 1990s, Cockburn was still using eight primary *quintas* for its vintage blends. Nearly all are located in the region just east of the village of Tua. The eight *quintas* include Canais, Arnozelo, Gricha, Perdiz, Coalheira, Alegria, Tua and Eira Velha. Cockburn made a single-*quinta* vintage Port from Tua in 1987 and Eira Velha in 1978 and 1982.

Cockburn bought Canais in 1989. Only a tiny part of the *quinta's* 740 acres is planted to vines. Production is now about 96 pipes of Port, although it will increase to about 240 in a few years. In addition, Cockburn uses wines from Quinta da Eira Velha, which is situated at the beginning of the Pinhão Valley. Eira Velha makes a single-*quinta* wine in undeclared years, which is now shipped by Martinez Gassiot, the sister house of Cockburn.

"You always have to remember that a great vintage Port is a blended commodity," said Guimaraens. "Few single *quintas* can make as great a wine as a blend." He proved his point in September 1989 by serving a bottle of 1958 Cockburn and one of 1958 Quinta dos Canais, neither of which was an officially declared vintage for Cockburn. The blend had much more structure and depth of fruit. It was rich and fruity and still in wonderful condition. The Canais was quite good at first but it quickly dissipated in the glass.

Guimaraens said a large part of Cockburn's vintage wines are fermented in stainless steel *remontagem* tanks at its production facilities in Tua. The grapes from various nearby *quintas* are transported to Tua by truck or rail. A few of the *quintas*, such as Canais and Arnozelo, make their own wines in *lagares* and then send them to Cockburn's lodges in Vila Nova de Gaia the winter after the vintage.

The excellent 1983 and 1985 Cockburn vintage Ports were made in very small quantities, about 6,000 to 7,000 cases of each. This is about one half to one third of the vintage production of other leading houses. Cockburn hopes to increase the volume of its declarations in the future, but slowly. It has not been easy gaining back its reputation for making excellent vintage Ports and no one at Cockburn wants to jeopardize it now.

TASTING NOTES

1985 COCKBURN: Shows an abundance of thick, rich fruit and plenty of backbone. Very inky, dense color, a rich, floral nose of berries and cherries, full-bodied, medium sweet, with massive anise and cherry flavors and extremely well-integrated tannins and acidity. Last tasted: 6/90. Drink 1996-1998. Release: $33 (£13). Current retail: $37 (£20). Current auction: $28 (£12). **90**

1983 COCKBURN: A big, tough Port for long-term aging. It underlines what people mean when they say a great young vintage Port should overpower one's palate with fruit and tannin. Inky color, with perfumed cherry and berry aromas, full-bodied, with tons of tannins, intense cherry and berry flavors and a lingering finish. Last tasted: 6/90. Drink 1998-2000. Release: $22 (£10). Current retail: $45 (£18). Current auction: $28 (£12). **97**

1975 COCKBURN: A pleasing wine, but lacks intensity, like many 1975s. Light ruby-red, perfumed cherry aromas, light-bodied, with fresh fruit flavors and light tannins, slightly dry on the finish. Last tasted: 1/90. Drink 1990. Release: £5. Current retail: $44 (£18). Current auction: $28 (£13). **77**

1970 COCKBURN: This is ripe and ready to drink. It is slightly more forward than many of the 1970s from the other top houses. Medium ruby-red, with rich aromas of cherry and marzipan, medium-bodied, with ripe cherry flavors, balanced tannins and a solid finish. Last tasted: 12/89. Drink 1990. Release: £2.30. Current retail: $78 (£28). Current auction: $68 (£20). **86**

1967 COCKBURN: This was the center of the debate on whether 1967 or 1966 was the best vintage. Unfortunately, this wine, although it is very good, is no match for the best 1966s. Medium ruby with a garnet edge, intense plum and blackberry nose, medium-bodied, with plenty of berry flavors, tightly knit tannins and a medium finish. It will continue to improve. Last tasted: 12/89. Drink 1990. Release: £1.50. Current retail: $55 (£32). Current auction: $45 (£15). **85**

COCKBURN'S.
1985
VINTAGE PORT

Produced and Bottled by
Cockburn Smithes & Cia Lda Oporto, Portugal
Produce of Portugal/Vinho do Porto

75cl e   20%vol

1963 COCKBURN: This is a very attractive, mature and subtle wine. Medium ruby with a garnet edge, leafy vanilla and cherry aromas, medium-bodied, with a very good concentration of clean fruit flavors and a medium finish. A bit one-dimensional. Last tasted: 12/89. Drink 1990. Release: £1.15. Current retail: $110 (£40). Current auction: $85 (£34). **88**

1960 COCKBURN: Aromatic and silky, but it is peaking now. Medium red with a slight brown hue, a nose of berries and leather, light-bodied, with leathery brown sugar and berry flavors, light tannins and a hot finish. Last tasted: 8/88. Drink 1990. Release: £.90. Current retail: $85 (£30). Current auction: $51 (£24). **80**

1958 COCKBURN: It is unfortunate that this wine was not declared, since it is better than most that were. It is medium ruby-garnet, showing a rich cherry-candy nose, medium-bodied, with rich, lovely, quite dry fruit flavors, good backbone and a silky finish. Slightly one-dimensional. Last tasted: 11/89. Drink 1990. Not available. **84**

1955 COCKBURN: A classy Port, showing all the elegance and wonderful fruit a top 1955 has to offer. Medium red with a light rim, cherry and spice on the nose, medium-bodied, with elegant cassis, tomato and fruit flavors and silky tannins on the finish. Defines finesse. Last tasted: 11/89. Drink 1990. Release: £1. Current retail: $155. Current auction: $110 (£41). **90**

1950 COCKBURN: Like a very good glass of 20-year-old tawny. Medium garnet, with a light, nutty plum and vanilla nose, light-bodied, with sweet vanilla, nut and fruit flavors and an elegant finish. Perhaps past its prime. Last tasted: 11/89. Drink 1990. Release: £.60. Current retail: $110 (£65). Current auction: $90 (£38). **76**

1947 COCKBURN: This is an extremely smooth and velvety wine that embraces the palate with rich, delicious cassis flavors. Medium garnet-ruby, with chocolate, earth and tomato on the nose, medium-bodied, with a rich, round mouth-feel and a very fruity, long finish. On a plateau of quality. Last tasted: 11/89. Drink 1990. Release: £.45. Current retail: $185 (£75). Current auction: $150 (£45). **90**

1935 COCKBURN: Superlative finesse in a bottle. Light red, with a claret-like black currant nose, medium-bodied, with superbly balanced plum and cherry flavors, medium soft tannins and a long finish. It is truly wonderful now. One of Cockburn's greatest wines. Last tasted: 2/90. Drink 1990. Release: £.30. Current retail: $320 (£145). Current auction: $200 (£79). **92**

1931 COCKBURN: This vintage was not declared by Cockburn but a few cases were bottled. Not as great as the legendary Noval 1931, but very distinctive in its own right. Light ruby, with a dried cherry and sugar cane nose, medium-bodied, with sweet cherry flavors, but still quite dry and very elegant on the finish. Improves immensely after two hours in a decanter. Last tasted: 1/90. Drink 1990. Not available. **89**

1927 COCKBURN: This wine has a legendary reputation as one of the greatest vintage Ports ever produced. It is clearly outstanding, although I am not sure it is Cockburn's greatest. It is a sexy, elegant wine and drinking extremely well now. Medium garnet with a red center, very aromatic plum nose, medium-bodied, with delicious plum flavors and an elegant balance of silky tannins. Last tasted: 12/89. Drink 1990. Release: £.30. Current retail: $300 (£145). Current auction: $200 (£146). **91**

1912 COCKBURN: This is amazing for its youthfulness. It is an unusually deep red for such an old wine, and is still showing a lot of life, with rich cherry aromas, plenty of spicy, peppery fruit flavors and a long, earthy finish. Last tasted: 10/87. Drink 1990. Release: £.40. Current retail: $350 (£180). Current auction: $275 (£77). **91**

1908 COCKBURN: Starting to fade a bit but still shows the classic Cockburn elegance and strength. Just slightly weaker than the 1927. Deep garnet-red, with aromas of cherry and earth, light-bodied, with a lovely balance of delicate, soft cherry flavors and an elegant finish. Last tasted: 10/87. Drink 1990. Release: £.20. Current retail: $395 (£185). Current auction: $325 (£143). **89**

1904 COCKBURN: This is starting to resemble a tawny, but it is still a novelty to drink. Light garnet-red, light-bodied, with musty cherry and nut aromas and flavors and a rather dry finish. Fading fast. Last tasted: 10/87. Drink 1990. Release: £.20. Current retail: $330 (£120). Current auction: $240 (£94). **75**

1896 COCKBURN: Tastes like a 20- or 30-year-old tawny; not bad for a wine nearly 100 years old. It is extremely delicious for its age. Light red with a garnet edge, a nose of coffee and earth, medium-bodied, with woody coffee flavors, light tannins and a balanced finish. Very delicate and faint. Last tasted: 2/90. Drink 1990. Release: £.15. Current retail: $400 (£130). Current auction: $240 (£100). **82**

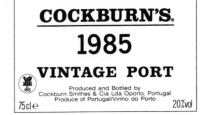

CROFT

CLASSIFICATION: *THIRD TIER*

COLLECTIBILITY RATING: *AA*

BEST VINTAGES: *1945, 1935, 1963*

The vintage Ports of Croft are some of the most deceptive produced. When young, they seem slightly lighter in color and more delicate than many of the other wines from leading producers, but with 15 or 20 years of bottle age, they can impress a taster with an array of elegant fruit flavors and great finesse.

Robin Reid, the former managing director of Croft who joined the company well before it became part of drinks giant International Distillers & Vintners in 1972, often says that Croft vintages gain power in the bottle. "I would rather judge our vintage wines at 20 years of age than at two," he said.

Wines like the 1960 Croft give credence to Reid's claim. The wine was considered very light when young, and many people thought it would peak years ago. Today it is a wonderful example of an extremely well-balanced, mature Port and is still not showing any signs of decline. It is a near-perfect glass of vintage Port.

I have no idea what the 1945 Croft was like when it was young, but it probably was never in the typically graceful Croft mold. It remains a blockbuster of a wine, with copious amounts of coffee, chocolate and fruit flavors. In a blind tasting of the 1945s from the leading houses, the Croft finished ahead of the pack. It is truly a great wine.

Recent vintages of Croft, however, have not been up to the house's past standards. The 1985 is a good wine, and may fall into the category of a lighter wine that will build itself up in the bottle. I have been watching its evolution, however, and it appears to be losing some of its grip.

The 1982, on the other hand, is a complete washout. It is lighter than many standard rubies and falling apart. John Burnett, Croft's current managing director, stands up for the wine and says that it will improve with age. From my tastings, I can only conclude that the wine will lose even more fruit with time.

Croft makes an estimated 13,000 to 18,000 cases of vintage. Burnett and others at Croft refuse to divulge how much the house actually makes. The 1982, according to various sources in the Port trade, was double Croft's normal production, which may account for its lightness. But large production doesn't necessarily mean a flawed vintage. According to Reid, Croft produced about 36,000 cases of the 1963, and that wine is infinitely better than the 1982. Some Port houses made more than 40,000 cases of the legendary 1927 vintage.

The heart of Croft vintages comes from Quinta da Roêda, located just north of the center of Pinhão. Roêda includes about 250 acres of vineyards and produces about 400 pipes of Port each vintage. Croft will not say what percentage of its vintages comes from Roêda, but it must be a large part. The rest comes from growers under contract.

"Some wines come from Ribalonga," said Burnett. "We have bought from there for 200 years. It has always been a Croft stronghold." He also said that some wines come from Rio Torto, Pinhão Valley and Roncão Valley.

Some of the wines Croft buys are still made in *lagares*, and the rest is produced at Quinta da Roêda, where Croft's main production center is situated. Croft uses autovinification at Roêda. The temperatures are strictly controlled during the fermentation. The wines remain at Roêda until after the first winter and then are transported down to Croft's lodges in Vila Nova de Gaia.

TASTING NOTES

1985 CROFT: This is evolving more quickly than I expected, but there are still some clean cherry notes on the nose and palate. Medium to deep ruby, with a slightly roasted nut, cherry nose, medium-bodied, with a well-defined backbone, medium tannins and a sweet finish. Last tasted: 6/90. Drink 1995-1997. Release: $30 (£13). Current retail: $37 (£18). Current auction: $29 (£14). **81**

1982 CROFT: I tasted this at least six times in 1990, and I am amazed by its poor quality. It is light, forward and diluted and has nothing in common with the excellent Ports of this house. Light ruby, with roasted coffee, spice, vanilla and plum on the nose, light-bodied, with light tannins and a dry finish. The alcohol is showing. Last tasted: 6/90. Best to avoid. Release: $22 (£10). Current retail: $37 (£16). Current auction: £8. **69**

1977 CROFT: When I tasted this in 1988, I thought it was extremely well structured, but the wine has lost some of its body. Deep ruby, with a raisin and chocolate nose, medium-bodied, with medium-hard tannins and a rather austere finish. Slightly out of balance. Perhaps it needs more time. Last tasted: 4/90. Drink 1992-1994. Release: $14 (£6.50). Current retail: $50 (£28). Current auction: $44 (£16). **85**

1975 CROFT: Like many 1975s, it is starting to break up, though it is still decent for current drinking. Medium ruby, with light cherry and earth aromas, medium- to light-bodied, with sweet anise and cherry flavors and light tannins. Last tasted: 8/88. Drink 1990. Release: £5. Current retail: $40 (£18). Current auction: $28 (£13). **76**

1970 CROFT: Refined, supple and fresh. Medium ruby, with a nose of plums and black pepper, medium-bodied, with medium to fine tannins and sweet black pepper and fruit flavors. A lovely glass of Port. Will improve for many years. Last tasted: 12/89. Drink 1990. Release: £2.30. Current retail: $70 (£25). Current auction: $55 (£18). **89**

1966 CROFT: Very elegant in the classic, understated Croft style. Medium red with a ruby center and an earthy, roasted, cherry nose, medium-bodied, with firm tannins and an abundance of licorice and berry flavors. Last tasted: 12/89. Drink 1990. Release: £1.50. Current retail: $68 (£30). Current auction: $60 (£21). **90**

1963 CROFT: Has great elegance and harmony, and should continue to improve for many years. Medium ruby-red, with very fresh plum aromas, medium-bodied, with very delicate fresh fruit flavors, lively acidity and a delicate finish. Last tasted: 12/89. Drink 1990. Release: £1.15. Current retail: $110 (£59). Current auction: $85 (£33). **91**

1960 CROFT: Impressively complex, with lots of character for a 1960. Deep garnet with a ruby center, chocolate, cherry and plum aromas, medium-bodied, with vanilla and cherry flavors, a silky mouth-feel and a long finish. Last tasted: 9/89. Drink 1990. Release: £.90. Current retail: $88 (£30). Current auction: $57 (£20). **90**

1955 CROFT: In a blind tasting of the top 1955s this came out near the bottom. Nevertheless, it is perfect to drink now. Medium garnet with a ruby center, fresh plum aromas, medium-bodied, with elegant cherry flavors and a long finish. Last tasted: 11/89. Drink 1990. Release: £1. Current retail: $145 (£45). Current auction: $100 (£33). **84**

1950 CROFT: Light-bodied and very sweet. Medium garnet, aromas of roasted nuts and plum, soft and silky on the palate, with sweet, nutty plum flavors. An interesting glass of 40-year-old vintage, but it would have been better a decade ago. Last tasted: 4/90. Drink 1990. Release: £.60. Current retail: $170 (£70). Current auction: $125 (£35). **77**

1945 CROFT: A truly hedonistic glass of Port, incredibly rich and delicious. Deep ruby with a garnet rim, rich coffee and chocolate aromas, full-bodied, with a rich, round texture, tons of chocolate and ripe fruit flavors and a long, long finish. Last tasted: 11/89. Drink 1990. Release: £.40. Current retail: $375 (£135). Current auction: $220 (£94). **99**

1935 CROFT: This is a very chewy and velvety wine with stunningly rich flavors. Medium red with a garnet edge, a rich, perfumed plum nose, medium-bodied, with sweet plum flavors, soft round tannins and a superbly long finish. Last tasted: 2/90. Drink 1990. Release: £.30. Current retail: 285 (£95). Current auction: $240 (£73). **93**

1927 CROFT: An exotic, stylish wine that is still enchanting. Medium garnet with a ruby center, ripe licorice nose, medium-bodied, with coconut, vanilla and plum flavors. It is a little hot on the finish. Last tasted: 12/89. Drink 1990. Release: £.20. Current retail: $350 (£150). Current auction: $195 (£105). **87**

C. DA SILVA

CLASSIFICATION: *Not rated*

COLLECTIBILITY RATING: *Not rated*

C da Silva is relatively new to vintage Port, with 1963 being its first declaration. Though three decades seems a long time, the firm appears still to be trying to establish a style for itself.

Out of five vintages of da Silva, I could only get excited about the 1987. It shows some interesting earth, tar and fruit character and ample tannins. The rest of the Ports were sweet, round and simple, with little to keep a taster coming back to the glass. All of the da Silva vintage Ports were clean and fresh, but they lacked the depth of fruit and backbone to be considered anything more than fairly pedestrian.

C. da Silva sells about 200,000 cases of Port a year worldwide. Vintage accounts for about 3 percent of its sales. The firm specializes in tawnies; France and West Germany are its main markets. Some of the company's vintage Port — also sold under the brands of Presidential and Dalva — have been shipped to the United States, although Holland remains its biggest vintage Port market.

All of da Silva's Ports are made at its modern winery, Quinta de Avidagos located in Alvacoes do Corgo, about 4 miles northeast of Regua. The company has contracts with about 250 growers, who sell grapes rather than wine. Vintage wines are made in *lagares* and average about 5,000 to 6,000 cases in a declaration.

The ownership of C. da Silva is kept secret, and employees only say it has been under the control of a Dutch foundation, Stitching AMFO, since 1988. Before, it was owned by a subsidiary of the now-defunct Rumasa Sherry giant. Prior to 1982, it was a family-run company. C. da Silva should not be confused with A.J. da Silva, which was changed to Quinta do Noval in 1973.

C. da Silva has invested more than $2.7 million in a new lodge and equipment in Vila Nova de Gaia since 1987, and claims to have one of the most modern bottling lines available. Whether the investment improves the quality of its vintage Port remains to be seen.

AT A GLANCE

C. DA SILVA
(PRESIDENTIAL)
Rua Felizardo de Lima 247
4400 Vila Nova de Gaia,
Portugal
02-39.41.28

Owner: Stitching AMFO

Founded: 1862

Average production: 5,000-6,000 cases

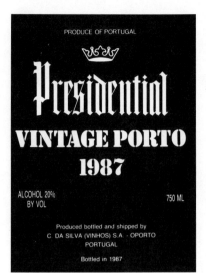

PRODUCE OF PORTUGAL

Presidential

VINTAGE PORTO
1987

ALCOHOL 20%
BY VOL

750 ML

Produced bottled and shipped by
C. DA SILVA (VINHOS) S.A. - OPORTO
PORTUGAL

Bottled in 1987

TASTING NOTES

1987 PRESIDENTIAL: This is a solid 1987 with ample fruit and tannin to give it longevity. Medium purple, with a ripe raisin and tar nose, full-bodied, with full tannins and ripe fruit flavors. A little one-dimensional. Last tasted: 2/90. Drink 1996-1998. Not released. **80**

1985 PRESIDENTIAL: Seems short on grip and flesh for a 1985, but it's nonetheless a pleasant wine. Medium purple, with a perfumed cranberry nose, medium-bodied, with medium fruit flavors, rather delicate tannins and a light finish. Last tasted: 2/90. Drink 1992-1993. Release: $30 (£10). Current retail: $30 (£10). Current auction: NA. **78**

1978 PRESIDENTIAL: Simple, with clean fruit flavors, but it lacks guts. Medium ruby-purple, with aromas of fresh plums and grapes, medium-bodied, with black cherry flavors and a light finish. Very drinkable, yet simple. Release: £5. Current retail: $34 (£15). Current auction: NA. **77**

1977 PRESIDENTIAL: This is not up to the standards of a good 1977. It is too forward and light. Medium red, with fresh plum aromas, medium-bodied, with simple plum flavors and a round tannic structure. Last tasted: 2/90. Drink 1991-1993. Release: £5. Current retail: $42 (£20). Current auction: NA. **72**

1970 PRESIDENTIAL: Enjoyable but very simple on the palate. Medium ruby with a garnet edge, chocolate and plum on the nose, medium-bodied, with plum and spice flavors and a light finish. Last tasted: 2/90. Drink 1990. Release: £2. Current retail: $50 (£29). Current auction: $18. **75**

DELAFORCE, SONS & CO.

CLASSIFICATION: *FOURTH TIER*

COLLECTIBILITY RATING: A

BEST VINTAGES: *1963, 1970*

A bottle of 1834 Delaforce lies in the wine library in Vila Nova de Gaia, commemorating the arrival of founder John Delaforce. Strangely, it is 34 years older than the house of Delaforce, which he officially founded in 1868. The vintage was apparently purchased in bottle from another producer by Delaforce and marketed as his own.

Such an anomaly, like the occasional lapse in quality of Delaforce vintage Ports, is not easy to understand. Wines like the 1963 and 1970 Delaforce are comparable to the very best from Taylor, Graham and Fonseca. They are thick, rich and powerful, with plenty of blackberry flavor and a hard backbone of tannins that makes them long-lived, classic vintage Ports.

The 1982 Delaforce, however, is much lighter and more forward than similar vintages from well-respected houses. It is difficult to say why the 1982 Delaforce is so weak, but the tendency toward a lighter style seems to run through the International Distillers & Vintners Port group, which includes Delaforce and Croft. Croft's recent vintages are also disappointing. The exception is Delaforce's excellent single-*quinta* vintage, Quinta da Corte.

This change to a lighter style may be intentional. "We are here to react to the market," said Robin Reid, a director of Croft, in an interview in early 1990. "We have changed because the demand has changed. Who wants wines that are not ready to drink for 15 or 20 years?"

The vintage Ports of Delaforce come from *quintas* primarily in the Roncão Valley and parts of the Rio Torto. Some of the wines are still produced in *lagares*, although the majority are produced in auto-vinification tanks. "We don't change the farmer who wants to make wines with *lagares*," said David Delaforce, managing director of the London branch of the company.

Delaforce said that his house remains very selective about its vintage declaration, and production ranges from 6,000 to 9,000 cases. The vintages are blended by the same committee that makes Croft Ports.

The firm was founded by George Henry Delaforce in 1868. He was 24 years old and his father, John Delaforce, had been manager for Port shipper Martinez Gassiot. The younger Delaforce established markets in the United Kingdom, Norway, Denmark, Germany and Russia. Delaforce was also the supplier to the Portuguese royal family

---

AT A GLANCE

DELAFORCE, SONS & CO.
Largo Joaquim Magalhães 23, Apartado 6
4401 Vila Nova de Gaia, Portugal
02-30.22.12/30.36.65

Owner: IDV (Grand Metropolitan)

Founded: 1868

Average production: 6,000-9,000 cases

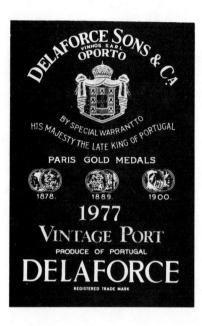

in the 1890s. George's two sons, Henry and Reginald, changed the company to a partnership in 1903, Delaforce, Sons & Co. The house remained in the family's hands, usually with various Delaforce sons in charge, until IDV took over in 1968, Delaforce's centenary year.

John David Delaforce admits that some recent vintages, such as the 1977, appear light, but he remains optimistic about their longevity. "The 1977 is not a blockbuster in color but we think it is elegant and will last a long time," he said. "It will continue to confound people."

TASTING NOTES

1985 DELAFORCE: A ripe and roasted style of Port. Medium ruby, with a raisiny, slightly burnt nose, medium-bodied, with silky, sweet fruit flavors and medium tannins. Last tasted: 6/90. Drink 1995-1996. Release: $24 (£11). Current retail: $27 (£20). Current auction: NA. **81**

1982 DELAFORCE: Surprisingly forward and light, like a poor ruby. Medium red-ruby, with a burnt chocolate and coffee nose, light-bodied, with coffee and fruit flavors, light tannins and a hot, dry finish; unbalanced. Lasted tasted: 6/90. Best to avoid. Release: $20 (£10). Current retail: $27 (£15). Current auction: NA. **69**

1977 DELAFORCE: More forward than many wines from this vintage. Medium red-ruby, with coffee and roasted nut aromas, medium-bodied, with medium tannins and a silky, roasted character. Sweet finish. Last tasted: 2/90. Drink 1990-1993. Release: $11 (£5). Current retail: $44 (£25). Current auction: $28 (£12). **80**

1975 DELAFORCE: Pleasant and simple. Medium to light red, light cherry and spice nose, light-bodied, with spicy fruit flavors and a light, tannic finish. Last tasted: 2/90. Drink 1990. Release: £4.50. Current retail: $33 (£17). Current auction: $22 (£11). **76**

1970 DELAFORCE: This is the last excellent Delaforce. It is a big, rich, ripe wine, still a little clumsy. Red with a deep ruby center, with an intense, roasted, earthy berry nose, medium-bodied, with hard tannins and silky, sweet, ripe fruit flavors. Last tasted: 2/90. Drink 1990. Release: £2. Current retail: $40 (£24). Current auction: $30 (£16). **89**

1966 DELAFORCE: Very enjoyable; lacks some of the hardness of many other 1966s. Medium red, with a vanilla, cinnamon and spice nose, medium-bodied, with rich raisin, vanilla and fruit flavors and a medium tannic finish. Last tasted: 2/90. Drink 1990. Release: £1.30. Current retail: $65 (£26). Current auction: $45 (£19). **85**

1963 DELAFORCE: The best Delaforce in three decades. It is a massive monster. Deep red-ruby color, with a wonderfully rich blackberry nose, full-bodied, with enough tannins to hold together tons of superb fruit. Will continue to improve. Last tasted: 2/90. Drink 1990. Release: £.90. Current retail: $100 (£29). Current auction: $70 (£19). **93**

DIEZ HERMANOS
CLASSIFICATION: *Not rated*
COLLECTIBILITY RATING: *Not rated*

The company of Diez Hermanos no longer exists, however, Offley Forrester, which bought the house in 1968, still uses the name and hopes to develop a market for the brand in the 1990s.

Until 1982, Diez vintage Ports were made from the wines of Offley's Boa Vista. Presumably, the best lots were kept for Offley and the others went to Diez. I have only tasted the 1977 Diez, which is very attractive, and extremely accessible for a 1977. It shares the ripe fruit flavors and sweetness of the 1977 Offley, but lacks the complexity.

Diez declared vintages in 1940, 1942, 1960, 1963, 1970, 1975, 1977, 1980, 1982 and 1987. Production equals a few thousand cases. The vintage Ports of Diez were made in *lagares* until 1977 and since have been produced in stainless steel *remontagem* tanks at Offley's Boa Vista. The most recent vintage, 1987, was made in *lagares* again, since the wines no longer come from Boa Vista but from small properties in the Pinhão Valley.

The house of Diez Hermanos was founded in 1875 as a Sherry shipper in Jerez by Don Salvador Diez and his four brothers. The family originated from Soria, Spain, where the brothers' antecedents date back to 1482. Business quickly grew and the Diez brothers soon opened a trading office in Paris, and also started selling in Madeira. It was not long before they were buying and selling Port, and near the turn of the century they bought Port shipper Manuel Misa and changed its name to Diez Hermanos Ltd.

In 1929, Pablo Diez Ivison married Maria Diez and moved to Oporto, setting up a new office for the Diez group. The Portuguese company imported Sherry and produced brandies as well as Port. Diez Ivison ran the firm until his death in 1966, and two years later Offley bought the company.

Diez is a brand to watch, since Offley intends to give it a push in the 1990s. The clout of its parent company, Martini & Rossi, ensures that one will hear more about the firm in the future. In addition, Offley has been making good Ports under Martini & Rossi, and there is no reason why Diez should not do the same.

AT A GLANCE
DIEZ HERMANOS
Rua Guilherme Braga 38, Apartado 61
4401 Vila Nova de Gaia, Portugal
02-30.27.11
Owner: Martini & Rossi
Founded: 1875
Average production: 2,000-3,000 cases

TASTING NOTES

1977 DIEZ HERMANOS: This is a good all-around 1977, although slightly more forward and ready to drink than the very best. Medium brick red, with a very ripe fruit, toffee and chocolate nose, medium- to full-bodied, with medium sweet toffee and fruit flavors, medium tannins and a ripe finish. Slightly simple but very enjoyable. Last tasted: 4/90. Drink 1990-1992. Release: £4. Current retail: £20. Current auction: NA. **82**

DOW

CLASSIFICATION: *SECOND TIER*

COLLECTIBILITY RATING: *AA*

BEST VINTAGES: *1966, 1970, 1977, 1983*

T he vintage Ports of Silva & Cosens, better known as Dow, are some of the most consistently well-made Ports available. They are firm wines with exuberant sweet berry flavors and a hard backbone of tannins, yet they maintain an incredible amount of subtlety and class.

Michael Symington, the former managing director of the Symington group, which controls Silva & Cosens, boasted in an interview in 1986 about the quality of Dow: "We promise you if you invest your money in vintage Port (from Dow) that you will have a damn good drink in the end."

This is a promise he can easily keep. Nearly all the vintages of Dow I have encountered have been outstanding. If Dow continues to make such superb wines as the 1985 and 1983, it will surely become a solid member of the first tier of vintage Ports.

The 1983 is particularly first-class, and clearly one of the best of the vintage. It is a powerful young Port with a profusion of complex fruit flavors wrapped around a strong tannin backbone. The 1985 is almost as good, but seems slightly more fleshy without the attractive style of the 1983.

Silva & Cosens seems to have a knack for making great wines in the slightly less great years. It not only made a slightly better wine in 1983 than in 1985 — which is the best vintage of the 1980s — it also made better wine in 1966 than in 1963. The 1966 Dow is one of my favorites. It is a classy, racy wine with a dry hardness that seems to focus its layers of violet and cherry flavors. It is a truly fine wine.

But my tastings of older vintages of Dow indicate that its wines may lack the staying power of the first tier. The wonderful Dow 1945, 1934 and 1927 are now past their peaks. Perhaps it is best to drink Dow Ports between 15 and 35 years after the vintage date.

"The Dow vintage Ports are not like those beefy ones," said William Warre, a Master of Wine who represented Dow in the United Kingdom in the 1950s, 1960s and 1970s. He now works for John E. Fells & Sons, the United Kingdom agent of Dow and Warre. "They are rather more delicate, feminine wines. They seldom let anyone down in quality."

Silva & Cosens was founded in 1862 by the Portuguese family of Silva, which had a wine merchant business in London. The house

AT A GLANCE

DOW
Travessa Barão de Forrester, Apartado 14
4401 Vila Nova de Gaia, Portugal
02-39.60.63

Owner: Symington Port Shippers

Founded: 1798

Average production: 13,000-16,000 cases

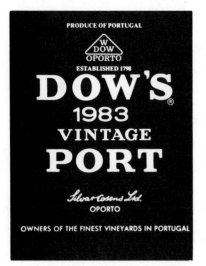

did not begin shipping Ports under the Dow brand until James Ramsey Dow became a partner in 1877 and adopted the brand name of Dow. His firm, Dow & Co., had been shipping Port since 1798. One of the most famous owners of Silva & Cosens was George Warre, who became a shareholder in Silva & Cosens in 1868. After his death in 1913, Silva & Cosens exchanged shares with Warre & Co. A.J. Symington was a major shareholder of Warre at the time. His family took complete ownership of the two houses by 1960.

The backbone of Dow vintages has traditionally come from Quinta do Bomfim, on the north bank of the Douro River just east of Pinhão, near Croft's Quinta da Roêda. George Warre built Bomfim in the mid-1890s. Today, Quinta do Bomfim is the main production site of the Symington group. All the wines there are made through autovinification. Grapes from Bomfim and just about everywhere else in the Douro Valley are vinified there, although Bomfim has about 170 acres of vineyards of its own.

The vintage lots of Dow, however, still contain a large amount of *lagar*-made wines, since the best wines from Bomfim's vineyards still only account for 35 percent to 55 percent of the final Dow vintage blend. Wines from a handful of *quintas* up the Rio Torto and near Tua are also used. They are mostly produced in *lagares*. Dow produces between 13,000 and 16,000 cases of vintage.

With a strong view toward tradition and quality, the Symingtons have maintained Silva & Cosens' tradition for making racy, stylish vintage Ports.

Tasting Notes

1985 DOW: Fleshy and raw, bursting with fruit on the palate but starting to close up. Deep, dark ruby-purple, with intense tar and berry aromas, full-bodied, with ripe berry flavors, full tannins and a long finish. Last tasted: 6/90. Drink 1996-1998. Release: $30 (£13). Current retail: $35 (£22). Current auction: $27 (£12). **89**

1983 DOW: Very stylish and big, with a classy balance of fruit and tannin. Deep ruby-purple, with a multidimensional nose of perfume and grapes, full-bodied, tannic and tightly knit. Last tasted: 6/90. Drink 1996-1998. Release: $20 (£10). Current retail: $34 (£19). Current auction: $25 (£12). **94**

1980 DOW: A good example of Dow's attractively dry Ports. Medium to deep ruby, with a nose of tar and fresh grapes, full-bodied, with peppery fruit flavors, medium tannins and a silky finish. Will improve with age. Last tasted: 6/90. Drink 1991-1993. Release: $15 (£9). Current retail: $32 (£12). Current auction: $25 (£10). **90**

1977 DOW: Impressively hard and powerful, but very closed for the moment. It should age for many decades. Dark ruby, with rich raspberry and earth aromas, full-bodied, with an excellent balance of full tannins and generous berry flavors. Last tasted: 4/90. Drink 1995-1997. Release: $12 (£6.50). Current retail: $60 (£28). Current auction: $57 (£16). **94**

1975 DOW: Shows silky, fresh cherry flavors and a light, caressing finish. It is not a heavyweight but one of the more enjoyable 1975s. Last tasted: 4/89. Drink 1990. Release: £5. Current retail: $45 (£18). Current auction: $30 (£15). **80**

1972 DOW: Very light and fruity, with extremely simple but fresh flavors, even though the alcohol dominates a bit. Medium ruby with a garnet edge, a slightly hot boysenberry nose, medium-bodied, with rather dry cherry flavors and a short finish. Last tasted: 1/90. Drink 1990. Release: £2. Current retail: $39 (£20). Current auction: $32 (£18). **79**

1970 DOW: A classic vintage Port, both fleshy and firm on the palate. Medium to deep ruby, with a fresh strawberry nose, full-bodied, with focused fruit flavors, medium tannins and a long finish. Still needs time. Last tasted: 12/89. Drink 1990-1993. Release: £2.30. Current retail: $66 (£29). Current auction: $49 (£20). **94**

1966 DOW: An extremely sound wine with focused fruit flavors and great class and breeding. Deep ruby, with floral, grapy aromas, full-bodied, with rather hard tannins, well-knit cherry and berry flavors and a long finish. Last tasted: 12/89 Drink 1990-1992. Release: £1.50. Current retail: $90 (£38). Current auction: $80 (£25). **94**

1963 DOW: Incredibly youthful and powerful, slightly raw still. Medium ruby with a red edge, concentrated black cherry and earth aromas, full-bodied, with intense berry flavors, full hard tannins and an excellent finish. Last tasted: 2/90. Drink 1990-1992. Release: £1.15. Current retail: $125 (£42). Current auction: $108 (£42). **92**

1960 DOW: Superbly balanced and at its peak. Light ruby with a garnet edge, a rich coffee and chocolate nose, medium-bodied, with lovely balanced fruit and coffee flavors and a long, silky finish. A joy to drink. Last tasted: 2/89. Drink 1990. Release: £.95. Current retail: $88 (£32). Current auction: $50 (£26). **88**

1955 DOW: Plenty of fruit and a solid backbone. Brilliant ruby-garnet, with a rich tomato and cassis nose, full-bodied, with tons of fruit flavors, medium tannins and a rich finish. Will still improve with age. Last tasted: 4/90. Drink 1990. Release: £1. Current retail: $190 (£85). Current auction: $170 (£66). **91**

1950 DOW: Sexy, silky and delicious. Deep garnet with a ruby center, cassis and plum aromas, medium-bodied, with delicious, delicate plum flavors, a silky texture and a super finish. Last tasted: 11/89. Drink 1990. Release: £.60. Current retail: $80 (£60). Current auction: £13. **86**

1947 DOW: A supreme, rich Port that beckons to be drunk. Medium garnet-ruby, with a light cassis and tomato nose, medium- to light-

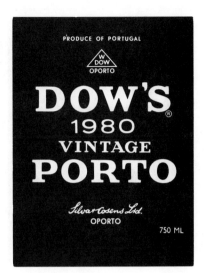

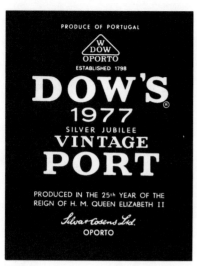

bodied, with very delicate cherry flavors and a silky mouth-feel on the finish. Last tasted: 11/89. Drink 1990. Release: £.45. Current retail: $230 (£80). Current auction: $209 (£47). **88**

1945 DOW: Massive, but still a little clumsy and coarse. Deep ruby with a garnet hue, a raisin and licorice nose, full-bodied, with raisin and licorice flavors. Slightly hot on the finish. Last tasted: 11/89. Drink 1990. Release: £.40. Current retail: $370 (£195). Current auction: $280 (£116). **89**

1935 DOW: It is very difficult to find 1935 Dow, and the one bottle I have tasted had a lower mid-shoulder fill. It showed a faint cherry, nutty nose and light, ripe silky fruit on the palate. It quickly faded away in the glass. Other bottles may be better. Last tasted: 6/90. Drink 1990. Release: £.30. Current retail: $300 (£100). Current auction: $250 (£106). **79**

1934 DOW: I have tasted this five or six times, and good bottles are delicious. Light red, with a garnet edge, with slightly roasted nut and ripe berry aromas, medium-bodied, with very ripe, roasted fruit flavors that open up after an hour or so in the glass. A bit hot. Last tasted: 6/90. Drink 1990. Release: £.30. Current retail: $350 (£100). Current auction: $285 (£75). **84**

1927 DOW: This was the second bottle I tasted within a span of four months. The first was more like a 20-year-old tawny. Medium red with a garnet rim, cherry and blackberry aromas, medium- to light-bodied, with a lovely, delicate mouth-feel, quite dry, with elegant cherry flavors and a medium finish. Last tasted: 4/90. Drink 1990. Release: £.20. Current retail: $425 (£150). Current auction: $300 (£150). **87**

H. & C.J. Feist

CLASSIFICATION: *Not rated*

COLLECTIBILITY RATING: *Not rated*

The vintage Ports of H. & C.J. Feist are cleanly made but are in need of more body and grip. They are simply too light and easy to drink when young.

Feist is part of the Barros, Almeida group, which until recently has been making light wines at all of its houses, with the exception of Kopke. "The problem is getting enough top-quality grapes," said António Oliveira, the Barros winemaker who also blends the wines for Feist. "Most of the best places have been with the English for hundreds of years. They got there first."

Overproduction does not seem to be the problem. Oliveira said he always keeps the quantities down. He made about 4,000 cases of the 1985. But perhaps this is too much considering the quality grapes he has. Nearly all the wine is made at the Barros production facility in the Douro, Quinta da Santa Luiz.

The company was created in 1836 in London by two German cousins, H. Feist and C.J. Feist, who were wine merchants specializing in Port. They opened an office in Oporto in 1870. Feist's London office lost large amounts of money during World War II, and during the Blitz its offices were completely destroyed. The London office was closed after the war but the Portuguese operation continued. By the early 1950s, it was looking for a buyer, and Barros, Almeida came to the rescue in 1953.

Vintage Port is not a priority for Feist, a major brand in France that sells more than 120,000 cases of simple rubies and tawnies.

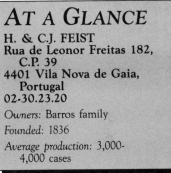

AT A GLANCE

H. & C.J. FEIST
Rua de Leonor Freitas 182,
  C.P. 39
4401 Vila Nova de Gaia,
  Portugal
02-30.23.20

Owners: Barros family

Founded: 1836

Average production: 3,000-
  4,000 cases

TASTING NOTES

1985 H. & C.J. FEIST: Light for a 1985, but the fruit is clean and pleasant on the palate. Light purple with some ruby, a nose of grapes and spices, medium-bodied, with sweet grape and watermelon flavors, light tannins and finish. Last tasted: 1/90. Drink 1992. Release: $20 (£10). Current retail: $24 (£14). Current auction: NA. **72**

1982 H. & C.J. FEIST: A well-made wine that lacks concentration of fruit. Medium ruby, with a clean grape and black cherry nose, medium-bodied, with good fruit flavors, medium tannins and a long

PORTO
FEIST
1982 VINTAGE PORT

TRADE MARK

Est. 1836
PRODUCED & BOTTLED BY:
H. & C. J. FEIST-VINHOS, S. A.
OPORTO — PORTUGAL
750 ML   ALC. 20% BY VOL.
CONTAINS SULFITES

PRODUCED IN THE DOURO DEMARCATED REGION
PORT WINE
PRODUCE OF PORTUGAL

It is a natural characteristic of Port Wine to become cloudy and show a deposit or "Crust" after being for a short period in bottle. Therefore in order to ensure the Wine being in a brilliant and perfect condition, the bottle should be stood upright in an even temperature for about twenty four hours and then carefully decanted before serving.

IMPORTERS FOR THE UNITED STATES
THE CARLTON COMPANY
BALTIMORE, MD.

finish. Last tasted: 1/90. Drink 1990-1992. Release: £6.50. Current retail: £13. Current auction: NA. **78**

1978 H. & C.J. FEIST: A good, clean, peppery wine for short-term drinking. Light brilliant ruby, with an extremely fresh cherry nose, medium-bodied, with peppery fruit flavors, light tannins and a medium finish. One-dimensional. Last tasted: 1/90. Drink 1990. Release: £5. Current retail: £13. Current auction: NA. **78**

A.A. Ferreira

CLASSIFICATION: *THIRD TIER*

COLLECTIBILITY RATING: *A*

BEST VINTAGES: *1935, 1983, 1978*

A.A. Ferreira has always had a special style of vintage Port. "Our vintages are sweeter than most others," said Francisco Javier de Olazabal, president of Ferreira. "It is that sweetness that makes our wines age better."

Ferreira's sweeter style certainly makes the wines more drinkable at an early age. Ferreira never makes a blockbuster vintage Port, but its wines are always very good. I have never been disappointed by a Ferreira vintage Port.

Nearly all the vintage wines of Ferreira are produced in modern *remontagem* stainless steel fermentation tanks at its property Quinta do Seixo, about two miles downriver from Pinhão. Seixo has only been a main part of the Ferreira vintage blend since 1979, when Ferreira bought the property.

Quinta do Vale de Meão traditionally has been a much more important component in the Ferreira vintage blends. Owned by members of the Ferreira family since 1877, the *quinta* is one of the easternmost in the Douro Valley. It is about 50 miles upriver from Pinhão, and includes about 125 acres of vineyards. Wines from Quinta do Vesùvio were also used in the Ferreira blend, but that estate was sold in 1989 to the Symingtons.

Ferreira has had a string of good vintage Ports in the 1980s. Nearly all the wines are extremely well balanced, with an abundance of sweet velvety fruit and a firm backbone to hold everything together. Oddly, Ferreira's best wine of the 1980s, the 1983, is the only single-*quinta* vintage Port it has ever produced.

Shippers usually say that single-*quinta* Ports are not as good as blends, but the 1983 Ferreira Quinta do Seixo should prove them wrong. It is the driest Port the company has ever made, with a sensational grip and backbone. This vintage was excellent in the Seixo area; both the Dow and the Offley Boa Vista, from nearby properties on the Pinhão River, were exceptionally good wines that year.

The most recent Ferreira vintage, the 1987, is an impressive wine with a balance of sweet, velvety fruit flavors and sugar-coated tannins. The company's guru-like winemaker, Fernando Nicolau de Almeida, believes the 1987 may be one of the greatest vintage Ports ever made at Ferreira. The elderly vintner loves to emphasize the elegance and

AT A GLANCE

FERREIRA
Rua da Carvalhosa 19-103
4400 Vila Nova de Gaia,
   Portugal
02-30.08.66

Owner: Sogrape

Founded: 1751

Average production: 4,000-
   12,000 cases

finesse of a vintage, but I would have liked the 1987 to have just a little more punch of fruit and tannin, although it is very good.

Ferreira normally makes between 10,000 and 12,000 cases of vintage in a declared year, and the wines are ready to drink after about 10 years of bottle age. They then remain on a plateau for another decade or two, depending on the overall quality of the vintage. Some wines, such as the 1935, are still great today.

Despite its steady hand at producing quality vintage Ports, Ferreira goes relatively unnoticed among vintage Port aficionados — a situation that may change with time, especially in the United States.

"We make as good vintage Ports as many of the leading British houses," said Olazabal. "The problem is that the vintage Port scene in England is very closed. Perhaps the States will be more willing to try something different."

TASTING NOTES

1987 FERREIRA: Well balanced, with delicious sweet fruit and a firm backbone. Inky color, with a very ripe raisin and grape nose, full-bodied, with sweet fruit flavors, medium tannins and a long finish. Last tasted: 11/89. Drink 1997-1999. Release: £14. Current retail: £14. Current auction: NA. **88**

1985 FERREIRA: A rich, sweet Port that grows in intensity on the palate. Medium to deep purple, with perfumed, earthy raspberry aromas, full-bodied, with very sweet, syrupy fruit flavors and medium tannins. Very round and luscious. Last tasted: 11/89. Drink 1996-1998. Release: $20 (£11). Current retail: $26 (£20). Current auction: NA. **87**

1983 FERREIRA QUINTA DO SEIXO: This is one of the best Ferreira vintage Ports ever. It was made entirely from a single property, Quinta do Seixo. It is much drier than most Ferreira vintages, with more punch and stuffing than the 1982. Deep ruby-purple, showing a perfumed, ripe raspberry nose, full-bodied, with lovely raspberry flavors, full tannins and a medium finish. Last tasted: 11/89. Drink 1996-1998. Release: $14 (£10). Current retail: $22 (£16). Current auction: NA. **91**

1982 FERREIRA: Very ripe and sweet. Deep ruby, with a nose of berries, anise and black pepper, full-bodied, with very ripe fruit flavors, full tannins and a rather short finish. It needs time but will be drinking well soon. Last tasted: 11/89. Drink 1992-1994. Release: $14 (£8). Current retail: $25 (£15). Current auction: NA. **81**

1980 FERREIRA: A soft, round and deliciously drinkable vintage Port. Medium red, with mature spicy fruit aromas, medium-bodied, with sweet plum flavors, round tannins and a long, fruity finish. Well balanced. Last tasted: 11/89. Drink 1991-1992. Release: $13 (£7). Current retail: $21 (£16). Current auction: NA. **80**

1978 FERREIRA: There were not many excellent 1978s, but this is one of them. Deep ruby, with a very rich raspberry and black cherry nose, full-bodied, with an excellent concentration of berry flavors and medium tannins. Lovely ripe fruit on the finish. Last tasted: 11/89. Drink 1993-1996. Release: $11 (£5). Current retail: $28 (£16). Current auction: NA. **89**

1977 FERREIRA: Not a blockbuster for a truly great vintage, but enjoyable all the same. Medium ruby, with rich raspberry aromas, full-bodied, with plenty of grape and plum flavors, medium tannins and a ripe, long finish. Last tasted: 11/89. Drink 1992-1995. Release: $11 (£5). Current retail: $35 (£20). Current auction: £22. **86**

1975 FERREIRA: This is one of the few 1975s that is holding on well. It must be due to the wine's very high sugar content. Medium ruby, with a fresh, perfumed cherry nose, medium-bodied, with soft fruit and delicious plum flavors. Great for drinking now. Last tasted: 11/89. Drink 1990. Release: £4.50. Current retail: $40 (£23). Current auction: NA. **81**

1970 FERREIRA: A very sweet, fruity and enticing wine. It has sweet, woody aromas that open to a palate of very sweet, soft fruit. Medium ruby, with a plum, cherry and vanilla nose, medium-bodied, with berry and vanilla flavors and a balanced finish. Last tasted: 4/89. Drink 1990-1992. Release: £2. Current retail: $40 (£23). Current auction: $25 (£12). **86**

1966 FERREIRA: This is wonderful to drink now, with lovely mature fruit flavors. Medium red with a garnet rim, chocolate and plum aromas, medium-bodied, with sweet, silky fruit flavors, medium tannins and a crisp finish. Last tasted: 11/89. Drink 1990. Release: £1.30. Current retail: $81 (£25). Current auction: $38 (£12). **85**

1963 FERREIRA: A sweet, mature and satisfying 1963 that doesn't need any more cellaring. Medium red with a garnet rim, ripe plum and tobacco aromas, medium-bodied, with plenty of fruit flavors, medium tannins and a long finish. Will improve. Last tasted: 8/88. Drink 1990. Release: £.90. Current retail: $110 (£30). Current auction: $50 (£24). **85**

1960 FERREIRA: Deliciously mature and lovely for current drinking. Medium red with a garnet hue, earthy, fruity aromas, medium-bodied, with sweet, silky fruit flavors and a balanced finish. Last tasted: 8/88. Drink 1990. Release: £.90. Current retail: $100 (£20). Current auction: $35 (£15). **80**

1955 FERREIRA: A rather hard wine but it still shows attractive fruit flavors and a firm tannic structure. Medium ruby-garnet, with earthy, spicy, nutty aromas, full-bodied, with plenty of chocolate, spice and fruit flavors, solid tannins and a rich finish. Last tasted: 11/89. Drink 1990. Release: £1. Current retail: $110 (£48). Current auction: $97 (£23). **85**

FERREIRA
1985
VINTAGE PORT

BOTTLED BY
20% vol.   A.A. FERREIRA, SUCESSURES PORTO   e 75 CL
PRODUCED AND BOTTLED IN PORTUGAL

1950 FERREIRA: Fading fast but still showing delicate cedar and fruit flavors and a caressing finish. Medium to light garnet, with a light, perfumed vanilla and tobacco nose, light-bodied, with tobacco and plum flavors and a light finish. Drink before it fades into a tawny. Last tasted: 11/89. Drink 1990. Release: £.60. Current retail: $90 (£45). Current auction: NA. **79**

1945 FERREIRA: This is rather simple but wonderfully fruity. It fades away quickly in the glass. Medium garnet, with a light coffee and berry nose with a touch of volatile acidity, medium-bodied, with an elegant balance of sweet fruit flavors and light tannins. This is more of a novelty than a great wine. Last tasted: 11/89. Drink 1990. Release: £.40. Current retail: $205 (£75). Current auction: $150 (£44). **81**

1935 FERREIRA: This is truly a great wine. Shows great finesse, with lovely, sweet fruit flavors. Deep red with a garnet edge, ripe plum aromas, medium-bodied, with fresh apricot and plum flavors and a dry finish. A joy to drink. Last tasted: 2/90. Drink 1990. Release: £.30. Current retail: $200 (£65). Current auction: £66. **93**

FEUERHEERD BROTHERS

CLASSIFICATION: *Not rated*
COLLECTIBILITY RATING: *Not rated*

Feuerheerd Brothers is barely in the minor league of vintage Port houses, since it makes such weak and one-dimensional vintage Ports. Some other house's premium rubies are more interesting than Feuerheerd vintages.

Nonetheless, the 1970 Feuerheerd gives some indication that good vintage Ports were once bottled under the house's label. It is a lovely, delicate wine with a good balance of cherry flavors and firm tannins. I have also tasted a 1927 Quinta de la Rosa vintage Port, made when that *quinta* was part of Feuerheerd, and the mature vintage held its own with all the big-name Ports from the same year.

The Feuerheerd firm was founded in 1815 by German Diedrich Matthias Feuerheerd. Initially it exported cattle, fruits, wood and various textiles as well as Port. In 1881, H.L. Feuerheerd, a son of the founder, limited the company to Port. His son Albert ran the house until his death in 1933. It was sold to Barros, Almeida in 1934, although Feuerheerd's Douro estate, Quinta de la Rosa, remained the property of Albert's daughter, the late Claire Bergqvist. La Rosa is still in the Bergqvists' hands.

The firm's vintage Ports are not light due to producing too much wine in a declared year. According to Barros, only about 1,300 cases of the 1985 Feuerheerd were produced — but even such limited quantities cannot ensure excellent quality.

AT A GLANCE
FEUERHEERD BROTHERS
Rua de Leonor de Freitas 182,
C.P. 39
4401 Vila Nova de Gaia,
Portugal
02-30.23.20
Owners: Barros family
Founded: 1815
Average production: 1,000-1,500 cases

TASTING NOTES

1985 FEUERHEERD: There is some fruit here but it still seems extremely light. Barely passable as a vintage. Medium ruby, with a light grape-skin nose, medium-bodied, with round, light tannins, clean fruit flavors and a very simple finish. Last tasted: 1/90. Drink 1991-1992. Release: £10. Current retail: £14. Current auction: NA. **72**

1980 FEUERHEERD: Sweet, simple and aromatic. Medium ruby, almost red, with a fresh black cherry nose, medium-bodied, with pleasant licorice and fruit flavors, quite sweet and round, medium finish. Last tasted: 1/90. Drink 1990. Release: £6. Current retail: £13. Current auction: NA. **74**

1977 FEUERHEERD: This is too mature for such a well-regarded vintage. Medium red with a garnet edge, light black cherry aromas, light-bodied, with round cherry flavors and a simple finish. Last tasted: 1/90. Best to avoid. Release: £5. Current retail: $17 (£15). Current auction: £6. **69**

1970 FEUERHEERD: Decent, with clean, well-focused fruit flavors and a fresh, balanced finish. Medium red with a ruby hue, fresh black cherry aromas, medium-bodied, with very clean cherry flavors and a long, balanced finish. Last tasted: 1/90. Drink 1990. Release: £2. Current retail: $40 (£20). Current auction: £11. **80**

FONSECA

CLASSIFICATION: *FIRST TIER*

COLLECTIBILITY RATING: *AAA*

BEST VINTAGES: *1927, 1948, 1977*

T he vintage Ports of Fonseca are perhaps the most consistently great of them all. Not only do they have a striking fleshiness and powerful richness when young, but they retain that youthfulness for decades.

Some vintage Port aficionados claim that Fonseca no longer makes the massive wines it once did. Bruce Guimaraens, winemaker and vice chairman of Fonseca, has a standard rebuttal: "That is a load of rubbish," he said. "Fonseca is every bit as big as it was. Look at the 1985 or 1977. They are huge wines."

I agree with Guimaraens wholeheartedly. I find Fonseca's young vintages, with the exception of the 1980, to be sublime. They are still hard, powerful and backward wines and need at least 15 years' bottle age to be drinkable.

More mature vintages, such as the 1970 and 1966, still needed another five years of bottle age when I tasted them in December 1989. The 1977 is also a blockbuster wine with monumentally proportioned, chewy, rich raspberry flavors and an impressive tannic backbone. This is one of the greatest Ports made this century.

The big disappointment with Fonseca came in 1980. It is clearly the worst 1980 made by a top house. It is drinkable, but it is much too forward for the superb reputation of Fonseca. There was apparently some rain during the harvest that affected the grapes used in the vintage lots that year.

But even if Fonseca made a string of 1980s, I would still have to put it among the very best houses after tasting the show-stopping 1977, 1948 and 1927. These three wines are at the top of my list of all-time greats.

Fonseca and Taylor share the same owners, but the two houses' vintage Ports couldn't be more different. Fonseca's wines are built like a shot-putter, while Taylor's resemble a javelin thrower. It underlines how Fonseca Guimaraens has retained its individuality since the owners of Taylor bought it in 1948.

Another difference is that the vintage Ports of Fonseca come primarily from the Pinhão Valley, where there are a number of superb vineyard sites. Fonseca owns Quinta do Cruzeiro, bought in 1973, and Quinta do Santo António, bought about six years later. Both are in excellent locations. Guimaraens said the two properties have been used for Fonseca vintage blends since 1912. Cruzeiro includes about 32 acres

AT A GLANCE

FONSECA
Rua Barão de Forrester 404
4400 Vila Nova de Gaia,
  Portugal
02-30.45.05

Owners: Alistair Robertson, Bruce Guimaraens and Huyshe Bower

Founded: 1822

Average production: 12,000-14,000 cases

of vineyards and Santo Antonio, 22 acres.

"The two *quintas* account for about 80 percent of Fonseca's vintages," said Guimaraens. "We buy the rest," primarily from *quintas* not far from Pinhão. All the wines at Cruzeiro and Santo Antonio are produced in *lagares*. "I prefer *lagares*," said Guimaraens. "You have a very, very large surface area giving you great skin contact. We want to get as much color extract as we can before the alcoholic fermentation, and this is the way to do it."

Fonseca bought another property in 1978, Quinta do Panascal, which is on slopes bordering the Tavora River about 5 miles south of Pinhão. It has about 178 acres of vines. The wines from Panascal were intended to go into Fonseca vintages, but only a tiny amount has been of good enough quality to be used, Guimaraens said. He added that new plantings, which represent 80 percent of the *quinta*, should produce wines for top-class Ports.

The Guimaraens family began making Fonseca Ports in 1822, and the company continues to live up to its reputation as a producer of outstanding vintage Port. The only problem in the future will be affording them. Prices for Fonseca vintage Ports have recently skyrocketed.

TASTING NOTES

1985 FONSECA: A hard, take-no-prisoners Port, extremely powerful and closed for the moment. Deep inky color, with concentrated blackberry and raisin aromas, full-bodied, with massive raisin flavors, a superb backbone and a very long finish. Last tasted: 6/90. Drink 1998-2000. Release: $32 (£13). Current retail: $39 (£28). Current auction: $33 (£15). **95**

1983 FONSECA: This is a rough-and-tough wine for laying away. Deep, dark purple-ruby, with an intense, ripe raisin and mint nose, full-bodied, with raisin flavors, full tannins and a long finish. Last tasted: 6/90. Drink 1996-1998. Release: $24 (£10). Current retail: $37 (£21). Current auction: $31 (£11). **90**

1980 FONSECA: I have tasted this numerous times and it just isn't up to par for Fonseca. Medium red with a garnet edge, light plum and brown-sugar nose, medium-bodied, with soft, silky chocolate flavors and not much backbone. Last tasted: 6/90. Drink 1990. Release: $22 (£9). Current retail: $35 (£22). Current auction: $28 (£9). **74**

1977 FONSECA: Until recently this wine was understated and closed. Now it has opened into a mammoth wine with so much fruit that it crushes your palate. Deep ruby, with ripe raspberry and cherry aromas, full-bodied, with layers of concentrated, sweet raspberry flavors, tons of tannin and an incredibly long finish. Perhaps as great as the 1948. Last tasted: 4/90. Drink 1998-2000. Release: $16 (£6.50). Current retail: $65 (£29). Current auction: $55 (£21). **100**

1975 FONSECA: This is one of the better 1975s. It is at its peak, and should stay there for some time. Medium red with a garnet edge, a spicy licorice nose, medium-bodied, with fresh fruit flavors, a round mouth-feel and a medium finish. Last tasted: 8/88. Drink 1990. Release: £4.50. Current retail: $48 (£19). Current auction: $34 (£15). **79**

1970 FONSECA: Some people may enjoy this wine's rather fat, rich and powerful fruit now, but I still find it too young for drinking. Deeply colored, with smoky mint, tar and fruit aromas, full-bodied, with concentrated fruit flavors and plenty of tannins. Last tasted: 12/89. Drink 1992-1995. Release: £2.30. Current retail: $73 (£40). Current auction: $66 (£24). **96**

1966 FONSECA: This is still a monster that needs time. Deep ruby, with a ripe, meaty cassis and berry nose, full-bodied, with tons of velvety fruit flavors, full tannins and a very long finish. Can drink now, but it will be better in 1995. Last tasted: 2/90. Drink 1990-1995. Release: £1.50. Current retail: $84 (£35). Current auction: $69 (£24). **97**

1963 FONSECA: A grand slam. Deep ruby with a slightly red edge, intense black cherry and raspberry nose, full-bodied, with masses of fruit, full tannins and an extremely long finish. This can age indefinitely. Last tasted: 12/89. Drink 1990-1995. Release: £1.15. Current retail: $155 (£69). Current auction: $130 (£53). **98**

1960 FONSECA: Interesting mature fruit flavors, but drying on the finish now. Medium to light red, floral nose, medium-bodied, with floral and berry flavors, light tannins and a short finish. Still quite hard but it may be fading quickly. Last tasted: 8/88. Drink 1990. Release: £.98. Current retail: $84 (£29). Current auction: $60 (£21). **80**

1955 FONSECA: A big wine with tons of rich, luscious fruit. Deep ruby color, with a very ripe, perfumed nose, full-bodied, with great depth of silky berry flavors and a very long finish. Last tasted: 8/88. Drink 1990. Release: £1. Current retail: $170 (£57). Current auction: $175 (£44). **96**

1948 FONSECA: This is astonishingly youthful; it could almost pass as a barrel sample on the palate. The perfect Port? Deep ruby with a slight garnet edge, rich aromas of violets and fruit, extremely full-bodied, with plenty of violet and fruit flavors, full tannins and a long, balanced finish. Can drink now, but it will age for decades. Last tasted: 11/89. Drink 1990. Release: £.48. Current retail: $265 (£95). Current auction: $210 (£72). **100**

1945 FONSECA: A muscular Port with a striking amount of ripe, roasted fruit flavors. Medium garnet with a ruby-red center, intense, roasted coffee, slightly burnt and raisiny nose, full-bodied, with sweet roasted coffee and plum flavors and a balanced, silky finish. Last tasted: 11/89. Drink 1990. Release: £.40. Current retail: $410 (£220). Current auction: $260 (£70). **91**

1934 FONSECA: Robust and decadent, with a multitude of ripe, rich

fruit. Medium red with a garnet edge, vanilla, wild berry and earth aromas, full-bodied, with sweet, smoky vanilla, toffee and fruit flavors, medium tannins and a long finish. Last tasted: 2/90. Drink 1990. Release: £.30. Current retail: $300 (£170). Current auction: $255 (£133). **91**

1927 FONSECA: This Port has so much stuffing it may never die. A truly monumental wine. Red with a garnet edge and ruby center, showing very ripe fruit, black pepper, spice and floral notes on the nose, full-bodied, with tons of velvety, opulent fruit flavors that fill the mouth. It will improve for decades. Last tasted: 12/89. Drink 1990. Release: £.20. Current retail: $400 (£245). Current auction: $380 (£192). **100**

FONSECA-GUIMARAENS
CLASSIFICATION: *FOURTH TIER*

COLLECTIBILITY RATING: A

BEST VINTAGES: *1964, 1967, 1987*

Fonseca-Guimaraens is the second wine of Fonseca, but many other Port houses would be more than happy to produce vintage Ports on the same level as this. Fonseca-Guimaraens is only a notch below the regular Fonseca vintage Ports in quality.

"It is a creature on its own," said Bruce Guimaraens, Fonseca vice chairman and winemaker. "It comes from the same *quintas* as Fonseca but it is made in less good years. You have the same style of Fonseca but less concentration."

I have tasted every vintage of Fonseca-Guimaraens with the exception of 1952, 1954 and 1957, and I question Guimaraens' use of the words "less concentration." In many cases, the wines of Fonseca-Guimaraens have the same intensity of fruit and power as the Fonseca vintage Ports. The raison d'être of Fonseca-Guimaraens is not so much a question of quality but rather one of quantity. In many vintages, Fonseca only has a tiny amount of first-class wine, and rather than declaring a full-fledged vintage, the house bottles it as Fonseca-Guimaraens. This bottling can number from a few hundred to a few thousand cases.

It is interesting to compare these "second" bottlings with declared years of Fonseca. The 1987 Fonseca-Guimaraens will give almost as much pleasure in 10 or 15 years as the 1985 Fonseca. It is an exciting Port with thick, chewy, complex fruit flavors and well-knit tannins. The 1976 Fonseca-Guimaraens is much more youthful and fruity than the 1975 Fonseca. While the 1975 is starting to fade, the 1976 is just beginning to be drinkable. It is a huge wine with tons of fruit and structure.

Another interesting comparison is the 1967 and 1965 Fonseca-Guimaraens with the 1966 Fonseca. The second wines may not have the same monster proportions of fruit, but they are giants in their own right. They are intense and concentrated, with plenty of the chewy raspberry and toffee flavors one expects from Fonseca.

As Guimaraens said above, the wines come primarily from Fonseca's key *quintas*, Quinta do Cruzeiro and Quinta do Santo António in the Pinhão Valley. All are made in *lagares* as well as matured and blended like regular vintages of Fonseca.

I hate to call Fonseca-Guimaraens vintage Port a poor man's Fonseca, but it does tend to sell at substantially lower prices than

AT A GLANCE
FONSECA-GUIMARAENS
Rua Barão de Forrester 404
4400 Vila Nova de Gaia,
Portugal
02-30.45.05
Owner: Fonseca
Average production: 5,000-6,000 cases

Fonseca. For example, the 1967 Guimaraens-Fonseca fetches about £135 to £165 ($249 to $305) a case in British wine auctions, while the 1966 Fonseca sells for more than £300 ($555). Whatever you call it, Fonseca-Guimaraens represents good value.

TASTING NOTES

1987 FONSECA-GUIMARAENS: Extremely racy and classy, well made, with an impressive fruit character and plenty of tannin. Deep purple, with a very ripe, grapy nose, full-bodied, with well-integrated tannins and excellent berry and violet flavors. Long finish. Last tasted: 2/90. Drink after 2000. Not released. **90**

1986 FONSECA-GUIMARAENS: Tight, hard and closed at this stage, but it has very good potential. Inky black-purple, with aromas of perfume and grapes, full-bodied, with tons of tannins and medium berry flavors. Last tasted: 2/90. Drink 1996-1998. Not released. **86**

1984 FONSECA-GUIMARAENS: Lean and tough, a little like a mini-1966. Deep ruby-purple, with licorice and berry aromas, full-bodied, with tough tannins and more than enough black pepper, anise and fruit flavors. Last tasted: 2/90. Drink 1994-1996. Not released. **85**

1982 FONSECA-GUIMARAENS: A very good 1982 with plenty of chewy fruit and a firm backbone holding everything together. Medium ruby with a purple hue, very ripe cherry and grape nose, full-bodied, with medium tannins and a long, sweet finish. Last tasted: 2/90. Drink 1992-1994. Not released. **85**

1978 FONSECA-GUIMARAENS: Very fruity but simple on the palate. Medium ruby with a slight purple hue, fresh mint and cherry nose, medium-bodied, with sweet cassis and cherry flavors, medium tannins and a decent finish. Last tasted: 2/90. Drink 1990-1993. Release: $32 (£5). Current retail: $32 (£15). Current auction: NA. **80**

1976 FONSECA-GUIMARAENS: This is a massive, tough wine that needs more time to come around. Inky color, with ripe raisin and licorice aromas, full-bodied, with tons of fruit flavors and hard tannins and a long finish. Very racy. Last tasted: 2/90. Drink 1993-1995. Release: $32 (£5). Current retail: $38 (£17). Current auction: NA. **89**

1974 FONSECA-GUIMARAENS: A good straightforward vintage Port with attractive, soft fruit. Medium ruby-red, with light violet and pepper aromas, medium-bodied with lovely peppery fruit flavors, light tannins and a medium finish. Last tasted: 1/90. Drink 1990. Release: £3.50. Current retail: $38 (£18). Current auction: NA. **84**

1972 FONSECA-GUIMARAENS: Interesting flavors, but it's fading quickly. Light red with a garnet hue, aromas of mushrooms and earth, medium-bodied, with sweet tobacco and fruit flavors and a light finish. Last tasted: 2/90. Drink 1990. Release: £2. Current retail: $36 (£18). Current auction: NA. **75**

1968 FONSECA-GUIMARAENS: Not as powerful as the three preceding vintages, but shows sweet, ripe fruit. Medium to deep ruby-red, with roasted cassis aromas, medium-bodied, with sweet, velvety fruit flavors and a lovely licorice character on the finish. Last tasted: 2/90. Drink 1990. Release: £1.50. Current retail: $50 (£18). Current auction: NA. **84**

1967 FONSECA-GUIMARAENS: This is almost as good as the 1966 Fonseca. Deep, dark ruby, blackberry aromas, full-bodied, with tons of tannins and blackberry flavors and a long finish. Last tasted: 2/90. Drink 1990-1995. Release: £1.20. Current retail: $56 (£18). Current auction: £12. **90**

1965 FONSECA-GUIMARAENS: Another excellent Port with extremely fresh, youthful fruit. Medium ruby, with black pepper and grape aromas, full-bodied, with plenty of fruit, medium tannins and a very long, ripe finish. Last tasted: 2/90. Drink 1990-1994. Release: £1.20. Current retail: $60 (£20). Current auction: NA. **89**

1964 FONSECA-GUIMARAENS: Superb, with beautiful fruit in an elegant style. Youthful ruby-red, with a black currant and berry nose, medium-bodied, with silky tannins and focused fruit. The slight hardness at the back of the palate gives a racy note. Last tasted: 2/90. Drink 1990. Release: £1.15. Current retail: $60 (£20). Current auction: NA. **90**

1962 FONSECA-GUIMARAENS: A big, tough wine that could still use a couple of years to mellow. Excellent medium red, with a complex nose of cherries and blackberries, medium-bodied, with hard tannins and a firm backbone. Last tasted: 2/90. Drink 1990-1993. Release: £.80. Current retail: $70 (£20). Current auction: NA. **88**

1961 FONSECA-GUIMARAENS: Although quite simple, it shows an impressive amount of fruit for its age. Medium red with a garnet rim and a roasted coffee nose, medium-bodied, with sweet, ripe, roasted fruit flavors and medium tannins. It can improve still. Last tasted: 2/90. Drink 1990. Release: £.80. Current retail: $70 (£20). Current auction: NA. **85**

1958 FONSECA-GUIMARAENS: One of the best Ports of the vintage. Medium red with a ruby center, rich aromas of black cherry and perfume, full-bodied, with lots of elegant fruit flavors, medium tannins and a lingering finish. Last tasted: 2/90. Drink 1990. Release: £.80. Current retail: $90 (£20). Current auction: $35 (£14). **88**

GOULD CAMPBELL
CLASSIFICATION: *FOURTH TIER*

COLLECTIBILITY RATING: A

BEST VINTAGES: *1977, 1983*

Peter Symington, the production director for the Symington Port group, must be half-joking when he calls the Gould Campbell vintage Ports "cheap pouring vintages." Yes, they are relatively inexpensive at 20 percent to 30 percent less than vintage Ports from Graham, Dow or Warre, but no, they are not cheap in quality.

Gould Campbell vintage Ports are very good indeed, and in vintages like 1983 and 1977, they can be outstanding. I have tasted these two vintages in blind tastings against the best names in Port and they have easily held their own. Gould Campbell vintage Ports are rather beefy, with a high level of sweet grapy flavors and tough tannins. Their only imperfection would be a slight coarseness and a sometimes simplistic palate.

Gould Campbell Ports drink well 12 to 14 years after the harvest. The rough-and-tough wines evolve into polished, extremely fruity Ports with a smooth finish. The 1970 Gould is a good example of this, and is wonderful now. The 1980 will very soon be at the same stage of drinkability.

It is difficult to pin down where the wines come from to make up the vintage blends of Gould Campbell. The Symingtons say that this wine is more a creation of the blending room than of any particular vineyard or *quinta*. Nonetheless, a high proportion of the wines comes from the Rio Torto area. Production averages between 4,000 and 8,000 cases.

Founded in 1797, Gould Campbell became part of the Symington Port Shippers in the early 1960s. For most of its existence, Gould Campbell was a brand of Cloude & Baker, Port shippers and wine merchants. During World War II, Offley Forrester managed Gould Campbell for Cloude & Baker. Offley bought the stocks and brand after the war.

Peter Symington said that his family hopes "that clients will buy the vintage Ports of Gould Campbell after they buy Graham or Taylor." Considering the excellent quality and good value of wines like the 1977 and 1983 Gould, it may be wiser for clients simply to buy the Gould and forget the others.

TASTING NOTES

1985 GOULD CAMPBELL: A good, standard 1985, quite lean and angular. Deep purple, with very grapy raspberry aromas, full-bodied, with medium tannins, sweet fruit and a slightly short finish. Last tasted: 6/90. Drink 1995-1997. Release: $23 (£11). Current retail: $29 (£20). Current auction: $23 (£11). **85**

1983 GOULD CAMPBELL: This is right up with the major-league 1983s. It is extremely full and concentrated, with a massive fruit structure. Inky color, very concentrated black currant nose, full-bodied, with tons of tannin, velvety fruit flavors and a closed finish. Truly excellent. Last tasted: 6/90. Drink 1996-1998. Release: $22 (£9). Current retail: $31 (£16). Current auction: £13. **93**

1980 GOULD CAMPBELL: Balanced, with lots of potential for aging. Deep ruby, with a cassis and tomato nose, full-bodied, with full tannins and rich, velvety, sweet cassis flavors on the finish. Last tasted: 2/90. Drink 1992-1994. Release: $15 (£7). Current retail: $30 (£16). Current auction: NA. **86**

1977 GOULD CAMPBELL: This monumental wine proves how underrated this house is. Dark inky color, with very ripe grapy, floral aromas, full-bodied, with plenty of tannins, tons of fruit and a very long finish. Last tasted: 2/90. Drink 1994-1998. Release: $11 (£5). Current retail: $46 (£19). Current auction: $32 (£10). **93**

1975 GOULD CAMPBELL: Decent, but slightly dry on the finish. Medium red, with a chocolate and berry nose, medium-bodied, with light tannins, berry flavors and a dry finish. Lasted tasted: 2/90. Drink 1990. Release: £4.50. Current retail: $32 (£15). Current auction: $22 (£9). **76**

1970 GOULD CAMPBELL: Plenty of stuffing, with layers of elegant berry flavors and silky tannins. Deep ruby-red, with a blackberry and cherry nose, full-bodied, with medium tannins backing up a fine fruit structure, giving the wine an elegant backbone. Last tasted: 2/90. Drink 1990. Release: £2. Current retail: $45 (£22). Current auction: $33 (£12). **88**

1966 GOULD CAMPBELL: Very fresh and youthful for a 1966, but remains slightly one-dimensional. Medium red, with fresh raspberry aromas, medium-bodied, with firm tannins and a balance of cherry and berry flavors. Last tasted: 2/90. Drink 1990. Release: £1.30. Current retail: $70 (£25). Current auction: $45 (£16). **84**

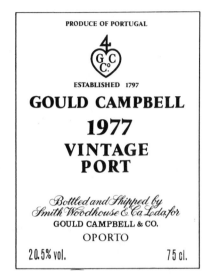

PRODUCE OF PORTUGAL

ESTABLISHED 1797

GOULD CAMPBELL
1977
VINTAGE
PORT

Bottled and Shipped by
Smith Woodhouse & Ca Lda for
GOULD CAMPBELL & CO.
OPORTO

20.5% vol.   75 cl.

W. & J. GRAHAM

CLASSIFICATION: *FIRST TIER*

COLLECTIBILITY RATING: *AAA*

BEST VINTAGES: *1948, 1963, 1985*

AT A GLANCE

W. & J. GRAHAM
Rua Rei Ramiro 514
4400 Vila Nova de Gaia,
   Portugal
02-39.60.65

Owner: Symington Port Shippers

Founded: 1820

Average production: 15,000-
   20,000 cases

The Symington family considers W. & J. Graham its flagship Port house, and in view of the extraordinary quality of Graham's vintage Ports, it is easy to understand why. It is currently producing some of the greatest vintage Port available.

Graham consistently makes remarkable wines in nearly every generally declared vintage. Graham vintage Ports are typically very sweet, with a high concentration of ripe fruit and an iron backbone of tannins. They are wines built for long-term aging and normally come around after about 15 years of bottle age, although they continue to improve for decades in strong years.

The Symingtons have been great advocates of autovinification, even for vintage Ports; however, Peter Symington, production director of the group, said that they still tread most of the best wines for Graham Ports. Most of the wines used for Graham come from growers who prefer using *lagares*, and Symington, like many others in the trade, believes it makes little sense to make them change now, especially considering the extremely high quality of the wines. Graham's vintage Port production ranges from 15,000 to 20,000 cases a vintage.

These wines originate mostly from vineyards near the property of Quinta dos Malvedos, which the Symingtons bought in 1981. Malvedos has always supplied a tiny amount of Port for Graham vintage but the majority has come from nearby vineyards and the Rio Torto Valley. This will change when new plantings come on line at Malvedos in the late 1990s. Quinta das Lajes has traditionally gone into Graham blends and produces massive, chewy wines.

The area just west of the village of Tua on the Douro River, where Malvedos is situated, also has some outstanding vineyard sites. They produce Ports with rich fruit and tannins yet with balance and freshness. This holds true even in extremely hot years, when riverside *quintas* farther west near Pinhão make wines that can taste roasted and overripe.

The Symingtons have only owned Graham since 1970. The Scottish trading company opened a Portuguese branch in 1808, primarily as a merchant in the textile business. It was not until 1820 that Graham began shipping Port. A popular story is that the company never intended to be a Port shipper, but it accepted a few dozen pipes of Port in payment for an outstanding debt and started shipping Port.

Graham may have been started by chance, but today the company is run with great precision. The consistently outstanding quality of its vintage Ports illustrates a passion for making great Port by everyone who has owned the house.

TASTING NOTES

1985 GRAHAM: What more could one want in a young vintage Port? It has great elegance and great power. Brilliant, deep ruby-purple, with boysenberry and licorice aromas, full-bodied, very fleshy, with a firm backbone of tannins. Last tasted: 6/90. Drink 1998-2000. Release: $31 (£13). Current retail: $40 (£18). Current auction: $33 (£16). **96**

1983 GRAHAM: A superb achievement from a very underrated year. Deep, dark ruby-purple, with rich floral and violet aromas, full-bodied, with masses of strawberry flavors, full tannins and a long finish. Last tasted: 6/90. Drink in 1996-1998. Release: $30 (£10). Current retail: $40 (£18). Current auction: $30 (£13). **93**

1980 GRAHAM: This is very impressive, with loads of fruit and tannins. Deep ruby, with a floral, cherry and plum nose, full-bodied, with medium tannins and sweet plum flavors on the finish. Last tasted: 6/90. Drink 1991-1993. Release: $18 (£9). Current retail: $40 (£17). Current auction: $28 (£10). **90**

1977 GRAHAM: This wine is going through a dumb period at the moment. It is closed and not giving much on the palate. It is still a big, hard and tightly knit wine. Deep purple-ruby, with intense floral, cassis and prune aromas, full-bodied, with plenty of fruit and extremely hard tannins. Built for aging. Last tasted: 4/90. Drink 1996-1998. Release: $15 (£6.50). Current retail: $63 (£30). Current auction: $58 (£21). **90**

1975 GRAHAM: Even Graham didn't make a very good wine in this marginal vintage. Medium red with a light edge, it has a grapy, spicy nose, with light, soft fruit on the palate and a rather short finish. Last tasted: 2/89. Drink 1990. Release: £5. Current retail: $44 (£19). Current auction: $33 (£15). **78**

1970 GRAHAM: This is an extremely full-bodied, powerful wine, but it still retains a classy balance. Deep ruby, with chocolate and berry aromas, full-bodied, with anise and dried cherry flavors, full, hard tannins and a long finish. Good now but a few more years of bottle age would improve it. Last tasted: 12/89. Drink 1990-1993. Release: £2.30. Current retail: $73 (£32). Current auction: $55 (£22). **94**

1966 GRAHAM: Elegant, silky and youthful, this is a sexy wine. Medium ruby-red, showing aromas of plums, chocolate and ripe fruit. The palate follows through with a bounty of sweet plum flavors and a fleshy mouth-feel. It should continue to improve with age. Last tasted: 12/89. Drink 1990. Release: £1.50. Current retail: $82 (£45). Current auction: $60 (£27). **93**

GRAHAM'S
1985
VINTAGE
PORT

BOTTLED AND SHIPPED BY
Wm & Graham & Cº
OPORTO

REGISTERED BRAND
GRAHAM
OPORTO
PRODUCE OF PORTUGAL

1963 GRAHAM: This is a monumental wine with a great balance of fruit and tannin. Medium ruby with a garnet edge, enticing nose of bitter chocolate and plums, full-bodied, with chocolate and raspberry flavors, medium tannins and a very long finish. Last tasted: 12/89. Drink 1990-1993. Release: £1.15. Current retail: $150 (£90). Current auction: $130 (£52). **97**

1960 GRAHAM: Like many 1960s, this wine is on its way down, but it was undoubtedly once superb. Two years ago I found it a mature, caressing Port. Medium red with a garnet hue, sweet berry and tobacco aromas, light-bodied, with a silky mouth-feel, delicately rich raspberry flavors and a light finish. Last tasted: 8/88. Drink 1990. Release: £.95. Current retail: $80 (£37). Current auction: $60 (£27). **84**

1955 GRAHAM: A big, rather brutish wine packed to the brim with fruit. Medium ruby-garnet, with a licorice and violet nose, full-bodied, with tough tannins and a balance of generous, sweet fruit flavors. Will improve with age. Last tasted: 11/89. Drink 1990. Release: £.95. Current retail: $190 (£82). Current auction: $175 (£66). **94**

1954 GRAHAM: This is one of the vintage Port surprises of my life. It is a truly excellent wine. It was apparently sold as Harveys vintage 1954 in the United Kingdom. Youthful red-ruby, with a fresh, aromatic nose, medium-bodied, with good tannins, lovely fruit flavors and a long finish. A joy to drink. Last tasted: 2/90. Drink 1990. Release: £.9. Current retail: $155 (£46). Current auction: NA. **91**

1948 GRAHAM: Great class and power. This is an example of how great the 1948s are. Youthful medium ruby with a slight garnet edge, a nose of licorice and ripe plums, with lavish, sweet plum flavors and a firm tannic backbone. There is a wonderful depth of racy fruit here. Good now but will improve. Last tasted: 11/89. Drink 1990. Release: £.48. Current retail: $290 (£135). Current auction: $245 (£99). **95**

1945 GRAHAM: What the 1948 has in power the 1945 has in finesse. It is still very concentrated but extremely well balanced and mellow. Medium ruby with a garnet edge, ripe plum aromas, medium-bodied, with plenty of elegant, delicate plum flavors and a balance of rounded tannins on the finish. Will improve with age. Last tasted: 11/89. Drink 1990. Release: £.40. Current retail: $425 (£220). Current auction: $450 (£103). **95**

1942 GRAHAM: This is a silky, classy, elegant, mature vintage Port with a complex character of fruit on the nose and palate. Medium red with a lighter edge, delicate fresh raspberry and currant aromas, medium-bodied, with silky, elegant fruit flavors, medium tannins and a very sweet finish. Stunning. Last tasted: 4/90. Drink 1990. Release: £.38. Current retail: $330 (£125). Current auction: $210 (£83). **89**

1935 GRAHAM: Incredible richness and wonderful finesse on the nose and palate. Medium red with a garnet edge, ripe, mature licorice aromas, full-bodied, with sweet, velvety, ripe cherry flavors and great balance. A joy to drink. Last tasted: 4/90. Drink 1990. Release: £.30. Current retail: $395 (£120). Current auction: $240 (£116). **94**

1927 GRAHAM: The is a classically structured wine with mountains of ripe fruit and an excellent balance of tannins. Deep red with a brick center, concentrated coffee and plum aromas, full-bodied, with generously thick, ripe plum flavors, medium tannins and a wonderfully rich finish. Last tasted: 2/90. Drink 1990. Release: £.20. Current retail: $400 (£165). Current auction: $250 (£138). **94**

GRAHAM'S MALVEDOS
CLASSIFICATION: *FOURTH TIER*

COLLECTIBILITY RATING: *A*

BEST VINTAGES: *1987, 1982, 1962*

Graham's Malvedos is a very good quality, blended vintage Port. Wine merchants nearly always promote it as a single-*quinta* Port, which it may be in the future but has never been in the past.

James Symington, a director of the Symington Port Shippers, which owns W. & J. Graham, admits to the confusion. "This is always a question with Malvedos," he said. "Is it or isn't it a single *quinta*? The wine is not labeled as a single *quinta* but simply, says Malvedos, like a brand."

Regardless, the vintage Ports of Malvedos have been rather up and down in quality. It can be an excellent, rich, chewy wine, while in some years it is simple and boring. Vintages in the 1980s have been uniformly good. The 1987 and 1982 are particularly noteworthy, packed to the brim with the same sweet cherry flavors and velvety tannins found in Graham vintage Ports. They need about 10 years of bottle age before drinking.

Malvedos vintages are sold about a decade after their harvest date. The exception was the 1986, which was sold in 1989 in the United States. It was a change in policy, but James Symington said the wine was so good and there was such demand that they could justify the change.

The 1970s and late 1960s were not good periods for Malvedos vintages. All the wines from this era were rather one-dimensional and lightly structured. Part of the problem, according to winemaker Peter Symington, was that Malvedos was made by the *movimosto* method in the late 1960s. "The wines were very light and their colors were terrible," he said. I have only tasted the 1968 Malvedos, and it was indeed light and almost over the hill.

The Symingtons took over W. & J. Graham in 1970, when the company was apparently in poor financial condition. It obviously did not invest in making good vintage Ports from Malvedos, although the Graham 1970 and 1966 were excellent. The house of Graham owned Quinta dos Malvedos near the village of Tua, but its production had shrunk to a few dozen pipes. The *quinta* never played an important role in Graham or Malvedos vintages.

When the Symingtons bought Graham, they didn't buy Malvedos until 11 years later. Today, Quinta dos Malvedos includes about

300 acres of vines and should produce about 350 pipes of Port by mid-1990. The *quinta's* grapes are now transported to Quinta do Bomfim and fermented in autovinification tanks.

Despite confusion over Malvedos being sold as a single-*quinta* Port, the Symingtons have no plans to rename the Malvedos Ports. "Why should we change things?" said Symington. "It is not going to make the wine any better by changing the name."

TASTING NOTES

1987 MALVEDOS: Amazing richness and depth of sweet, chewy fruit flavors. Dark inky color, with intense blackberry and cherry aromas, full-bodied, with sweet grape and cherry flavors and an excellent balance of round, ripe tannins. A great density of ripe fruit. Last tasted: 2/90. Drink 2002-2005. Not released. **91**

1986 MALVEDOS: Very well structured, showing attractive, balanced, firm tannins and pleasant fruit flavors. Deep ruby, ripe blackberry aromas, full-bodied, with medium tannins and excellent sweet berry flavors. Last tasted: 2/90. Drink 1996-1998. Release: $35. Current retail: $35. Current auction: NA. **85**

1984 MALVEDOS: Rather one-dimensional, but it is packed to the brim with fruit. Deep purple, with cassis, tomato and berry aromas, full-bodied, with tough tannins and an abundance of sweet cassis flavors. Last tasted: 2/90. Drink 1993-1995. Not released. **83**

1982 MALVEDOS: A big, chewy wine, one of the major-league Malvedos vintages. Deep, dark purple, very ripe cassis aromas, full-bodied, with full tannins and very clean, fresh raspberry flavors. Last tasted: 2/90. Drink 1994-1998. Not released. **90**

1979 MALVEDOS: Too light and too dull. Medium ruby, fresh berry aromas, medium-bodied, with silky, simple fruit flavors and light tannins. Last tasted: 2/90. Drink 1990. Not released. **74**

1978 MALVEDOS: A difficult wine to assess. It seems closed and not ready but there is also a dryness on the finish. Medium ruby-purple, very perfumed berry nose, medium-bodied, with sweet, simple berry flavors, medium tannins and a short finish. Last tasted: 2/90. Drink 1990-1993. Release: $30 (£5). Current retail: $30 (£16). Current auction: NA. **82**

1976 MALVEDOS: Very sweet and earthy, with strange rubbery aromas. Medium red with a garnet hue, meaty and earthy nose, medium-bodied, very sweet, with coffee and fruit flavors on the finish. Last tasted: 2/90. Drink 1990. Release: $17 (£5). Current retail: $30 (£17). Current auction: NA. **74**

GRAHAM'S
MALVEDOS
1978
VINTAGE PORT

BOTTLED AND SHIPPED BY
Wm & Graham & Co
OPORTO

REGISTERED·BRAND
GRAHAM
OPORTO
PRODUCE OF PORTUGAL

1968 MALVEDOS: Starting to fade on the palate. Medium red with a garnet edge, slightly volatile cherry nose, medium-bodied, with sweet fruit flavors but slightly acidic. Drink up soon. Last tasted: 2/90. Drink 1990. Release: £1.50. Current retail: $50 (£18). Current auction: $30 (£17). **70**

1965 MALVEDOS: Not much character here but it's still a most palatable vintage. Deep red with a garnet rim, light aromas of tomato, earth and berries, medium-bodied, with sweet, velvety fruit flavors and a short finish. Last tasted: 2/90. Drink 1990. Release: £1.20. Current retail: $65 (£20). Current auction: $35. **79**

1964 MALVEDOS: Sweet, velvety and simple. Medium red, with a cassis and slightly roasted nose, medium-bodied, with very sweet, velvety fruit flavors and well-integrated tannins. One-dimensional. Last tasted: 2/90. Drink 1990. Release: £1. Current retail: $54 (£20). Current auction: NA. **82**

1962 MALVEDOS: Overflowing with fresh fruit. Medium ruby with a red tint, earthy, grapy aromas, medium-bodied, with black currant flavors, medium tannins and a long finish. Last tasted: 2/90. Drink 1990. Release: £.80. Current retail: $65 (£20). Current auction: £11. **89**

1961 MALVEDOS: Delicate and rather refreshing. Medium red with a garnet edge, a lovely floral, perfumed nose, medium-bodied, with sweet, fresh cherry flavors and a smooth finish. Last tasted: 2/90. Drink 1990. Release: £.80. Current retail: $65 (£21). Current auction: NA. **87**

1958 MALVEDOS: I have had this wine twice. One bottle was extremely tired and fading. Another was better but drying out a bit. Medium ruby-garnet, with a black cherry nose, light-bodied, with good cherry flavors but slightly hot on the finish. Last tasted: 2/90. Drink 1990. Release: £.80. Current retail: $65 (£30). Current auction: $42. **79**

1957 MALVEDOS: Very well balanced, with delicious coffee and berry flavors. Medium to light red with a garnet rim, aromas of chocolate and leather, medium-bodied, with light tar, coffee and fruit flavors and a long finish. Quite hot on the finish. Last tasted: 2/90. Drink 1990. Release: £.80. Current retail: $65 (£31). Current auction: $38. **84**

1952 MALVEDOS: Rich and sweet, with just enough character and style. Light ruby with a garnet rim, lovely cherry nose, medium-bodied, with sweet cherry flavors, a balance of tannins and an elegant finish. Last tasted: 11/89. Drink 1990. Release: £.30. Current retail: $125 (£35). Current auction: NA. **85**

RICHARD HOOPER & SONS

CLASSIFICATION: *Not rated*

COLLECTIBILITY RATING: *Not rated*

The vintage Ports of Richard Hooper & Sons are produced and bottled by Port giant Real Companhia Velha (Real Vinicola). Hooper represents a tiny percentage of the company's annual wine sales of 1.4 million cases.

Until recently, Hooper vintage Ports were in the same league as the rest of Real Companhia's — disappointing. Except for the 1985, all the Hooper vintages I have tasted have been substandard, either extremely light or displaying winemaking flaws. The 1985, however, is pleasant, with sweet fruit and a medium backbone. It seems to be evolving more quickly than expected.

The 1985 was the first vintage of Hooper that was a selection of wines specially bottled for the house. Past vintages of Hooper were simply the Real regular vintage Ports with a different label. Since 1987, Hooper vintage Ports have come primarily from the vineyards at Quinta Nova, which is a few miles downriver from Pinhão.

The wine merchant firm of Hooper was founded in 1771 in London. Real Vinicola bought the company in 1951. Until 1971 Hooper was run independently of Real Vinicola. After 1971 it became a brand of Real Vinicola.

TASTING NOTES

1985 HOOPER: Not a blockbuster, but shows some very pretty fresh fruit character. Medium purple-ruby with fresh raspberry and chocolate aromas, full-bodied with plenty of raspberry flavors, silky medium tannins and a fresh finish. Last tasted: 6/90. Drink 1994-1996. Release: $15 (£10). Current retail: $17 (£13). Current auction: NA. **80**

1983 HOOPER: Some wines fall apart due to poor handling. This could be one of them. Brick red, with acetic, volatile aromas, medium-bodied, with varnish flavors. Last tasted: 3/90. Best to avoid. Release: £7. Current retail: $15 (£12). Current auction: NA. **60**

1982 HOOPER: It is not surprising that this comes from the same lot as the regular 1982 Royal Oporto, another vintage Port brand produced by Real Companhia Vinicola. I tasted it blind with a group of 1982s and 1983s and it was hot and out of balance. Medium ruby with a light red rim, aromas of chocolate, cherry and earth, medium-bodied,

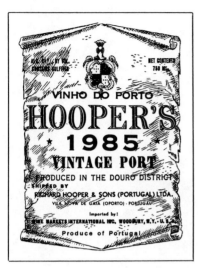

with very sweet earth and berry flavors and medium tannins. Aggressive, hot alcohol shows on the finish. Last tasted: 5/90. Best to avoid. Release: £6.50. Current retail: $18 (£11). Current auction: NA. **68**

1980 HOOPER: Another poor wine. Light brick red, with cherry and cough syrup aromas, medium-bodied, with extremely sweet, cloying fruit flavors and a very sweet finish. Too sugary. Last tasted: 5/90. Best to avoid. Release: £6. Current retail: $22 (£12). Current auction: NA. **67**

HUTCHESON

CLASSIFICATION: *Not rated*

COLLECTIBILITY RATING: *Not rated*

There is not much to say about Hutcheson. It declares few vintages and what is bottled as vintage Port is not very interesting.

Now owned by the Barros, Almeida group, Hutcheson was founded in 1881 by British wine merchants Thomas Page Hutcheson and Alexander Davidson Taylor. It apparently had a good reputation in the last century in Great Britain, but it can only be assumed that it wasn't known for vintage Ports, since its mature vintages never surface in London auction rooms.

Thomas Hutcheson retired from the firm in 1920 and a new partner, Augustus G. Bouttwood, joined. Five years later Taylor died, and Bouttwood quickly became disillusioned with the Port trade. In 1927 he sold to the Barros family. Today the company annually sells about 15,000 to 20,000 cases of Port, mostly fine old tawnies and vintage-dated tawnies. Vintage declarations total about 3,000 cases.

AT A GLANCE

HUTCHESON
Rua de Leonor de Freitas,
  182, C.P. 39
4401 Vila Nova de Gaia,
  Portugal
02-30.23.20
Owner: Barros family
Founded: 1881
Average production: 3,000 cases

TASTING NOTES

1979 HUTCHESON: Probably should not have been declared. It is too light. Ruby-garnet, with an earthy chocolate nose, light-bodied, with slightly nutty chocolate and fruit flavors. Very simple. Last tasted: 1/90. Best to avoid. Release: £5. Current retail: $40 (£10). Current auction: NA. **69**

1970 HUTCHESON: A good, solid wine for current drinking. Deep red, with cherry and red pepper on the nose, medium-bodied, with peppery fruit flavors, medium tannins, good backbone and a long finish. Last tasted: 1/90. Drink 1990. Release: £2. Current retail: $43 (£15). Current auction: NA. **79**

C.N. KOPKE

CLASSIFICATION: *FIFTH TIER*

COLLECTIBILITY RATING: *Not rated*

BEST VINTAGES: *1985, 1960, 1987*

As the oldest Port house, C.N. Kopke should feel some responsibility for making excellent vintage Ports, and in recent years the firm has done just that. Since 1982 Kopke has been making consistently good vintage Ports — its 1985 is exceptional.

Founded in 1638, Kopke was created by German Christiano Kopke and remained in his family's hands until 1870, when the English firm Mason Cately & Co. took control. The firm was sold to the Barros family in 1953.

The Barroses call Kopke "the jewel of the crown of the group" and they are extremely proud of the house. "We have really tried to keep the quality of Kopke's vintage Ports since we bought it," said Manuel Angelo Barros. "It is truly a great name in Port."

Recent vintages prove that the Barroses, indeed, have maintained quality. The house makes rich, full-bodied wine with a profusion of chewy fruit. Vintage Ports like the 1987 and 1985 show a solid backbone of tannins and a superb level of fruit. They need at least eight years of bottle age before drinking.

The only problem with Kopke vintage Ports in recent years is that they sometimes lack the complexity of wines from major houses like Taylor or Graham. This could be due to Kopke's reliance on Quinta da Santa Luiz, where a large part of the Barros group Ports is made. "Kopke is normally sold as a single-*quinta* wine," said Barros.

Quinta da Santa Luiz includes about 640 acres of land, of which 160 acres are planted to vines. It produces about 240 pipes of Port, which should increase to about 300 by mid-1990. The vintage wines are produced half by *lagar* and half by autovinification. A selection of the estate's best wines in a particular year go into the Kopke vintage blend, which averages between 10,000 and 12,000 cases. The Kopke vintage Ports may or may not be labeled Quinta da Santa Luiz.

Vintages in the 1970s and early 1980s were not up to par with the wines from the 1960s and mid-1980s. They are lighter and sweeter and generally lack stuffing. They remind me of the weak wines produced at Barros during the same period.

I have not tasted extremely old vintages of Kopke, although a wine like the 1927 can occasionally be found at auction. A century ago, Kopke shipped the vintage Ports of Quinta do Roriz.

Barros said that the style of Kopke vintage Port changed slightly after they bought the house. "Before it was very English in style, hard and powerful," he said. "But our older winemaker at the time was interested in a different style of vintage" — lighter and more elegant.

Today, Kopke has a young winemaker, Emanuel Rodrigues, who worked nearly a decade for the company before taking charge of the blending in 1982. He wants to return to the English style — big and powerful. He is succeeding, in view of the quality of the wines since he took over. This is a house to watch.

TASTING NOTES

1987 KOPKE: This is an elegant wine with good fruit and structure. Deep purple, with a rich, floral, grapy nose, full-bodied, with a good balance of medium tannins and sweet fruit flavors. Last tasted: 1/90. Drink 1995-1997. Release: $24 (£17). Current retail: $24 (£17). Current auction: NA. **86**

1985 KOPKE: A dark horse that should finish among the top 1985s in years to come. Deep purple, with fresh blackberries and raspberries on the nose, full-bodied, with balanced tannins, a firm structure and a lovely finish. Last tasted: 1/90. Drink 1996-1998. Release: $18 (£11). Current retail: $21 (£14). Current auction: NA. **90**

1983 KOPKE: A bit one-dimensional but wonderfully rich and fruity. Deep purple, with a dense blackberry nose, full-bodied, with intense grapy flavors, medium tannins and a firm backbone. Last tasted: 1/90. Drink 1993-1994. Release: $18 (£9). Current retail: $23 (£23). Current auction: NA. **85**

1982 KOPKE: A very well-made 1982 with lots of finesse. Medium to deep ruby, with a rich strawberry nose, full-bodied, with medium tannins, very good fruit flavors and a medium finish. Slightly one-dimensional. Last tasted: 1/90. Drink 1991-1992. Release: $16 (£8). Current retail: $26 (£21). Current auction: NA. **83**

1980 KOPKE: Quite hot and unbalanced, it is evolving too quickly. Medium ruby-red, with forward alcohol and vanilla aromas, medium-bodied, with decent peppery, spicy fruit flavors, but a little hot on the finish. Last tasted: 1/90. Drink 1990. Release: $16 (£7). Current retail: $31 (£20). Current auction: NA. **71**

1979 KOPKE: Very weak and simple. Medium red, with a sweet cherry nose, light-bodied, with very sweet fruit flavors and a short finish. Drinkable but too simple. Last tasted: 1/90. Best to avoid. Release: £6. Current retail: £16. Current auction: NA. **69**

1978 KOPKE: Past its prime, quite weak. Light to medium red, with spicy berry aromas, light-bodied, light tannins and simple cough syrup flavors. Last tasted: 1/90. Drink 1990. Release: $13 (£6). Current retail: $29 (£20). Current auction: NA. **70**

1977 KOPKE: Too far off the mark for such an excellent vintage. It is simply too mature. Medium red with a garnet edge, slightly nutty cassis aromas, light-bodied, with cassis flavors, light tannins and a very short finish. Last tasted: 1/90. Best to avoid. Release: £7. Current retail: £22. Current auction: NA. **68**

1975 KOPKE: Much better than the 1977 and good for such a weak vintage. Medium red-garnet, grape and chocolate aromas, medium-bodied, with a velvety mouth-feel and earthy, roasted fruit flavors. Last tasted: 1/90. Drink 1990. Release: £4.50. Current retail: $28 (£18). Current auction: $10. **82**

1974 KOPKE: Breaking up a bit but still holding on. Medium red with a garnet rim, chocolate and coffee nose, medium-bodied, with forward coffee and fruit flavors, light tannins and a medium finish. Last tasted: 1/90. Drink 1990. Release: £4. Current retail: £18. Current auction: NA. **74**

1970 KOPKE: A confusing wine. It is quite forward in color but has a youthful nose and palate. Medium red with a garnet edge, excellent fresh fruit aromas, full-bodied, with a good balance of focused fruit flavors and medium tannins. Last tasted: 1/90. Drink 1990. Release: £2. Current retail: $41 (£20). Current auction: $27 (£19). **82**

1966 KOPKE: Rich but rather hard. It has reached its peak. Medium red with a garnet rim, bitter chocolate and walnut aromas, medium-bodied, with walnut flavors, medium tannins and a dry finish. Last tasted: 1/90. Drink 1990. Release: £1.30. Current retail: $65 (£20). Current auction: NA. **81**

1960 KOPKE: A very good, strong 1960. Medium red with a garnet edge, complex cherry and bark nose, medium-bodied, with a rich, round mouth-feel and wonderfully rich fruit flavors on the finish. Last tasted: 1/90. Drink 1990. Release: £1. Current retail: $65 (£31). Current auction: NA. **87**

MARTINEZ GASSIOT
CLASSIFICATION: *THIRD TIER*

COLLECTIBILITY RATING: *A*

BEST VINTAGES: *1967, 1970, 1985*

Martinez Gassiot goes almost unnoticed in vintage Port circles, but the house often makes outstanding Ports that equal or better those of its sister house, Cockburn Smithes.

"People think that Martinez is a second wine of Cockburn, since we don't promote it," said Peter Cobb, who oversees the house as well as working for Cockburn. "The house can obviously stand on its own merits."

The 1967 Martinez is a good example of the vintage Ports this house is capable of producing and it supports those who believe 1967 is a better vintage than 1966. Moreover, the 1967 Martinez is better than the Cockburn from the same vintage. It is a huge wine with masses of tannin and fleshy ripe fruit that expand in the mouth from start to finish. The 1970 Martinez is almost as impressive, but with more finesse and elegance. Its lovely cassis and cherry flavors and integrated tannins should convince anyone that Martinez is a serious contender in vintage Port.

Recent Martinez vintage Ports have also been very good, especially the 1985. It has more than enough strength of fruit and tannin to justify a decade or more of bottle age before opening. The 1987 is slightly leaner, but it is a pretty wine with very attractive, earthy, milk chocolate flavors and a firm backbone.

Production of Martinez vintage Ports is limited, with only about 3,000 cases made in a declaration. "Martinez retains its identity," said Gordon Guimaraens, production director for both Cockburn and Martinez. "We use completely different *quintas* for Martinez." They include Quinta do Bartol, next door to Cockburn's Quinta dos Canais; Quinta da Adega, across the river from Tua; and Quinta da Marcela, in the Pinhão Valley. All the wines are made in *lagares*.

The young Ports are transported to the Martinez lodge in Vila Nova de Gaia the spring after the harvest. The lodge is next door to Cockburn's cellar. Martinez annually sells about 180,000 cases, and makes excellent mature tawnies as well as standard Ports.

Martinez was founded in 1797 in London by D. Sebastian Gonzalez Martinez, a Spaniard who sold cigars, Sherry and Port. John Peter Gassiot joined the firm in 1822. It was not until 1834 that the company took a lodge in Vila Nova de Gaia. For more than a century

AT A GLANCE
MARTINEZ GASSIOT
Rua des Coradas 13
4401 Vila Nova de Gaia, Portugal
02-39.40.31
Owner: Hiram Walker/Allied Vintners
Founded: 1790
Average production: 3,000 cases

the house focused on bulk sales to clients in the United Kingdom who then bottled the wines under their own names. Martinez sold shares on the London stock market in the 1950s, and was bought by British wine merchant John Harvey in 1961. Harvey bought Cockburn a year later. The two houses became part of drinks giant Allied-Lyons in 1971. It is now part of Hiram Walker Allied Vintners.

The vintage Ports of Martinez remain intentionally in very limited supply, according to Guimaraens. "It is not a very well-known vintage house," he said. "That is why really we don't make much."

TASTING NOTES

1987 MARTINEZ: Still very closed, but round, ripe and rich, with extremely attractive fruit flavors and plenty of grip on the finish. Deep ruby with a purple center, aromas of flowers, milk chocolate and earth, full-bodied, with round tannins and a long finish. Should be drinkable sooner than the 1985. Last tasted: 5/90. Drink 1996-1997. Release: £13. Current retail: £13. Current auction: NA. **84**

1985 MARTINEZ: A burly wine with muscles. Deep, dark ruby, with concentrated cherry aromas, full-bodied and tightly structured, with ripe tannins and rich cherry and earth flavors. Last tasted: 6/90. Drink 1996-1997. Release: $21 (£11). Current retail: $26 (£15). Current auction: NA. **89**

1982 MARTINEZ: Nicely balanced and sweet, holding together well. Medium to deep ruby, with a plum, earth and spice nose, full-bodied, with round, ripe tannins, licorice and fruit flavors and a long finish. Last tasted: 6/90. Drink 1992-1994. Release: $17 (£9). Current retail: $28 (£14). Current auction: NA. **82**

1975 MARTINEZ: A typical 1975 — simple and slightly dull. Medium red, with spicy aromas, medium- to light-bodied, with cherry flavors and light tannins that quickly fade. Last tasted: 2/90. Drink 1990. Release: £4.50. Current retail: $40 (£15). Current auction: £11. **75**

1970 MARTINEZ: A tough wine with a lot of class. Medium to deep red, with cassis, cherry and berry aromas, medium-bodied, with good medium tannins and a very good depth of ripe fruit flavors. It still seems a little closed. Decant a few hours before serving. Last tasted: 2/90. Drink 1990-1993. Release: £2. Current retail: $60 (£22). Current auction: $29 (£13). **89**

1967 MARTINEZ: A blockbuster, much better than the 1967 Cockburn. Excellent youthful ruby-red, with rich, ripe cherry aromas, full-bodied, with well-integrated tannins forming a solid backbone for the mass of fleshy fruit flavors. Will improve with more age. Last tasted: 2/90. Drink 1990. Release: £1.30. Current retail: $60 (£20). Current auction: £11. **93**

1963 MARTINEZ: Starting to fade, but it may be just the bottle I tasted. It is elegant all the same. Medium red with a garnet edge, aromas of cherries and spices, medium-bodied, with firm tannins and delicate, sweet berry flavors. Last tasted: 2/90. Drink 1990. Release: £.90. Current retail: $90 (£34). Current auction: $80 (£18). **82**

1955 MARTINEZ: Very rich, delicious and silky sweet. Medium red-garnet with a lighter edge, rich bitter chocolate nose, medium-bodied, with lovely, balanced, sweet chocolate and fruit flavors and a very long, silky finish. Last tasted: 11/89. Drink 1990. Release: £.80. Current retail: $120 (£48). Current auction: $110 (£24). **86**

MESSIAS

CLASSIFICATION: *Not rated*

COLLECTIBILITY RATING: *Not rated*

BEST VINTAGE: *1970*

Sociedade Agricola e Comercial dos Vinhos Messias is perhaps better known for its table wines than for its Ports, vintage or otherwise. While the firm has been selling Port since 1934, it only began shipping vintage Port in the 1950s.

Messias vintage Ports are extremely inconsistent in quality. For example, in 1970 the company produced an excellent wine with a bounty of attractive, sweet silky fruit. Then in 1977 it made a flawed and acetic wine.

"It is new to us, Port wine," said C. Farinha Beirão, a director of Messias. "We are much better known for our (table) wines." Messias sells about 208,000 cases of Port. Its table-wine sales total about 300,000 cases, and include *vinho verde*, Dão, Bairrada and Douro. Messias' vintage Port production totals 10,000 to 12,000 cases.

Most of Messias' vintage Port comes from its own *quintas* near the village of Ferradosa upriver from Tua. Its two *quintas* there, Quinta do Cachão and Quinta do Rei, have about 320 acres of vineyards combined. All the wines are made by autovinification.

Messias was established in 1926 by Messias Baptista and remains family-owned. The founder's son Messias Baptista and son-in-law Adelino Vigàrio are in charge of running the company. The headquarters of Messias is about 40 miles south of Oporto in Mealhada, although it maintains a modern Port lodge in Vila Nova de Gaia.

"It is a question of tradition," said Beirão. "Since we are not a traditional producer of vintage Port, we have to make our own pricing. But we can't sell for prices like Taylor or Fonseca. It is very difficult selling vintage Port."

TASTING NOTES

1985 MESSIAS: An odd, slightly volatile, varnish nose detracts. I asked the winemaker about it and she said it was normally like that. Medium ruby with a light edge, violet and varnish aromas, medium-bodied, with simple fruit flavors and a short finish. Last tasted: 2/90. Best to avoid. Release: $12. Current retail: $14. Current auction: NA. **67**

1984 MESSIAS: Much better than the 1985. Medium ruby with a purple hue, roasted nut and fresh, black currant aromas, medium-bodied, with clean, fresh, sweet fruit flavors, medium tannins and a long finish. Quite chewy. Last tasted: 2/90. Drink 1994-1995. Release: $11. Current retail: $15. Current auction: NA. **78**

1983 MESSIAS QUINTA DO CACHAO: One-dimensional but clean, without the depth of fruit to be a major-league 1983. Medium ruby with a purple hue, cassis and strawberry aromas with a smoky character, medium-bodied, with medium tannins and a short finish. Needs a little more time. Last tasted: 2/90. Drink 1993. Release: $8. Current retail: $11. Current auction: NA. **77**

1982 MESSIAS: This is light and quick-maturing, definitely not a wine for the cellar. Medium-light ruby, with a very ripe raisin and earth nose, medium-bodied, with sweet velvety fruit flavors and an extremely simple finish. Last tasted: 2/90. Drink 1990-1992. Release: $7. Current retail: $12. Current auction: NA. **72**

1977 MESSIAS QUINTA DO CACHAO: The winemaker says that most bottles of this Port are high in volatile acidity. Medium-ruby center turning red, stewed tomato and varnish aromas, medium-bodied, with sweet fruit flavors and very high acidity. Last tasted: 2/90. Best to avoid. Release: $7. Current retail: $19. Current auction: NA. **60**

1970 MESSIAS QUINTA DO CACHAO: This is a good 1970, with layers of focused strawberry and berry flavors. Medium ruby, with ripe strawberry and cherry aromas, medium-bodied, with sweet, silky fruit flavors, medium tannins and a long finish. Nicely balanced. Last tasted: 2/90. Drink 1990. Release: NA. Current retail: $55. Current auction: $20. **87**

1966 MESSIAS QUINTA DO CACHAO: Big and sweet for a 1966, but very good nonetheless. Deep ruby-red, black cherry and strawberry aromas, medium-bodied, with rich, ripe fruit and medium tannins. Very sweet on the finish. Last tasted: 2/90. Drink 1990. Release: NA. Current retail: $30. Current auction: $15. **84**

1963 MESSIAS: This started out fine in the glass but quickly faded. It is over the hill. Medium red with a large garnet rim, light cassis and slight varnish aromas, medium-bodied, with slightly weedy, sweet fruit flavors and a light finish. Rather odd. Last tasted: 2/90. Drink 1990. Release: NA. Current retail: $40. Current auction: NA. **71**

MORGAN BROTHERS

CLASSIFICATION: *FIFTH TIER*

COLLECTIBILITY RATING: *Not rated*

BEST VINTAGES: *1970, 1963*

The oldest bottle of Morgan Brothers vintage Port in Croft's wine library in Vila Nova de Gaia is the 1945. "The old managers of Morgan liked to drink the vintages themselves," said John Burnett, managing director of Croft, which has controlled Morgan since 1952. "We don't have many left."

The style of Morgan vintage Ports is fascinating. They are big, fat and sweet, rather thick and coarse, but with plenty of character. The 1985 is typical, with its sweet, velvety plum flavors and abundant tannins. It needs at least 10 years in the bottle to soften its rough edges. More mature vintages like the 1970 and 1963 are rich, fat Ports with plenty of plum flavors and personality. I have not tasted older vintages, but years such as 1955 and 1948 have good reputations among serious Port tasters.

The only slight disappointment among the Morgan vintage Ports I tasted was the 1977. It was forward and ready to drink, with slightly tired roasted coffee flavors. It's a pleasant drink, but not what one expects from a great vintage like 1977.

Some people say that Morgan is simply a blend of vintage lots of Croft and Delaforce, but David Delaforce assured me that the wines are unique unto themselves. There are no well-known *quintas* that are always used in the Morgan vintage blends, although a large part of its vintage wines come from around the Rio Torto and the Roncão Valley.

Croft handles Morgan virtually the same way the Symington Group makes vintage Ports for Gould Campbell, Smith Woodhouse and Quarles Harris. The best wines not used for their major houses in a great year go into the blends of their secondary houses. Quantities of Morgan remain limited to only a few thousand cases.

"We bottle a little bit of Morgan vintage and only in very good years," said Burnett, who added that most of it is sold in the United Kingdom. "Our intention with Morgan is to keep it going."

Burnett said that Morgan remains primarily a supplier of private-label Port for customers in Europe. The firm makes a complete range of wine, from simple rubies and old tawnies to white Ports. Morgan has always been better known for its good-quality, tawny Ports. One such Morgan Port had a strong reputation during the late 19th century. Charles Dickens in *Nicholas Nickleby* wrote about drinking to the health of Mr. Linkwater with a magnum of Morgan's Double Diamond.

Morgan dates back to 1715, when a London wine merchant named Haughton started a firm trading in Port. It wasn't until the late 1790s that Aaron Morgan joined the company and the name was changed. The company stayed in family hands until 1952, when it was sold to Croft.

"We want to keep Morgan's vintage Ports going," Burnett re-emphasized. "Vintage Port is part of the pedigree and prestige of a company. You always want to make a little bit of it."

TASTING NOTES

1985 MORGAN: Lacks class but is a good, rough-and-tough vintage to lay away. Deep purple-red, with ripe, almost raisiny aromas, full-bodied, with velvety, sweet plum flavors, full tannins and a long finish. Last tasted: 2/90. Drink 1996-1998. Release: £11. Current retail: £20. Current auction: NA. **85**

1977 MORGAN: Ready to drink, with plenty of roasted vanilla and fruit flavors. Not a top-notch 1977, but pleasant nonetheless. Deep red, with coffee, roasted nut and vanilla aromas, full-bodied, with velvety fruit flavors, medium tannins and a very sweet finish. Last tasted: 2/90. Drink 1990. Release: £5. Current retail: £24. Current auction: NA. **78**

1970 MORGAN: A velvety, well-made wine with an abundance of sweet, concentrated fruit flavors. Deep ruby with a brick red hue, concentrated aromas of berries and blackberries, full-bodied, with sweet, velvety fruit flavors, medium tannins and a very sweet finish. Last tasted: 2/90. Drink 1990. Release: £2. Current retail: £22. Current auction: NA. **88**

1966 MORGAN: Very sweet, hard and fruity, but slightly one-dimensional. Deep ruby-brick red, with a slightly earthy, fresh cherry nose, full-bodied, with sweet fruit flavors, medium tannins and a short finish. Last tasted: 2/90. Drink 1990. Release: £1.30. Current retail: £26. Current auction: NA. **80**

1963 MORGAN: Intensely fruity and delicious. Medium to deep brick red, with a bitter chocolate and black cherry nose, medium-bodied, with intensely sweet chocolate and fruit flavors, medium tannins and a long finish. Last tasted: 2/90. Drink 1990. Release: £.90. Current retail: £28. Current auction: £24. **86**

NIEPOORT

CLASSIFICATION: *SECOND TIER*

COLLECTIBILITY RATING: *Not rated*

BEST VINTAGES: *1955, 1927, 1945*

Niepoort is to vintage Port what Krug is to Champagne. They are both small houses in a world dominated by large competitors, but they are producing outstanding wines that very few can match.

For years, the family-owned house of Niepoort often has been inaccurately labeled as only a tawny Port producer, but anyone who has tasted the Niepoort 1955 or 1945 would know that this tiny house belongs in the same league as the major vintage Port houses. It is the most underestimated and underappreciated producer of vintage Ports.

The typical Niepoort vintage Port is an explosion of intensely concentrated grape and raspberry flavors. Its compact tannin structure compresses this overabundance of fruit into a focused masterpiece with superb intensity of flavors. It is this pinpointed, fresh fruit character that makes Niepoort vintage Ports so unique.

The white-haired Rolf van der Niepoort is the driving force behind this family-run shipper, which sells about 40,000 cases of various types of Port each year. Rolf and his son Dirk are constantly blending and tasting their wines with their winemaker, José Nogueira, and his son Zeze in search of the ultimate Port, whether it's a new vintage, a late-bottled vintage or a vintage-dated *colheita* tawny. They never seem satisfied.

"The 1987 is very good but I am not satisfied yet," said Dirk after tasting the young wine in early 1990. "I know that we can make even a better vintage Port one day."

Rolf has a more philosophical bent. "Vintage Port is the king that was born a king," he said. "Since vintage is king, you must make it a beautiful ceremony when drinking it. For example, tasting our 1945 is like going to an opera, not to the movies."

The 1970, 1945, 1955, 1942 and 1927 are breathtaking vintage Ports. They are opulent wines with masses of velvety, sweet, fresh fruit flavors and firm tannins. Most of these wines could pass for a vintage Port 20 or 30 years younger. "The 1945 will last another 50 years. I am sure of it," said Rolf.

The Niepoorts are very cagey about exactly where their vintage wines originate. The wines apparently come from one or two small *quintas* in the Pinhão Valley. They are made by *remontagem*. Vintage production ranges from 3,000 to 6,000 cases.

Niepoort bought two *quintas* in late 1988 that may one day produce excellent Ports. Both are west of Pinhão near the Tedo River. Quinta de Napoles has about 100 acres of vineyards and Quinta do Carril another 25. The two combined should produce about 250 pipes of Port when their new plantings come on line. "However, we are not positive whether we will get vintage quality from these vineyards. We will have to wait and see," said Dirk, who worked for half a year in California's Napa Valley with Cuvaison Winery and has an international wine collection.

The house was established in 1842 by Eduard Kebe, who five years later took on Dutchman F.M. van der Niepoort as a partner. When Kebe died in 1848, Niepoort took complete control of the company, and it has been in family hands ever since. Dirk is the fifth generation to work in the firm.

The tiny Niepoort cellars in Vila Nova de Gaia are difficult to find, and once inside, they are even more difficult to navigate. They are dark, humid cellars with barrels, casks and bottles everywhere. It is as if the contents haven't been moved for 100 years. The Niepoorts like it that way, however, and are keen guardians of their heritage, keeping stocks of old wines in barrel, small glass demijohns and bottles. I have seldom tasted a bad bottle of Port from Niepoort, whether a simple ruby or a glorious mature tawny.

Unfortunately, old bottles of Niepoort vintage Ports are very rare. "There are not a lot of old Niepoort vintages left," said Dirk a few days after tasting his superb 1927 and excellent 1942. "People just drank them up. They kept their Taylors and Fonsecas but thought they should drink their Niepoorts. That makes me a little upset, especially when I think how good the 1945, 1942 and 1927 are now."

TASTING NOTES

1987 NIEPOORT: An impressive example of the vintage, with lots of power and backbone. Inky color, with a very intense, grapy, Syrah-like nose, full-bodied, with full, ripe tannins and plenty of sweet fruit flavors. Extremely long on the finish. Last tasted: 11/89. Drink 2000. Release: $27 (£15). Current retail: $27 (£15). Current auction: NA. **91**

1985 NIEPOORT: I have tasted some inspiring bottles of the 1985, but there may be some bottle variation. Nonetheless, it is a massive wine at its best. Deep purple, with a very jammy, grapy nose, full-bodied, with lots of velvety, sweet fruit flavors, full, tough tannins and a long finish. Last tasted: 6/90. Drink 1998-2000. Release: $25 (£13). Current retail: $33 (£20). Current auction: NA. **92**

1983 NIEPOORT: There is an abundance of fruit, but it finishes a little short. Medium to deep ruby, with very ripe berry and raspberry aromas, medium-bodied, with fresh, sweet fruit flavors, medium tannins and a decent finish. Last tasted: 6/90. Drink 1994-1996. Release: $14 (£10). Current retail: $24 (£17). Current auction: £6. **84**

1982 NIEPOORT: One of the best 1982s produced. Very deep ruby with an inky center, extremely ripe berry and grape aromas, full-bodied, with focused, ripe raspberry flavors, full tannins and a long, long finish. Not too sweet. Last tasted: 6/90. Drink 1994-1996. Release: $13 (£10). Current retail: $22 (£17). Current auction: £8. **90**

1980 NIEPOORT: Lovely, sweet and balanced, a joy to drink. Deep ruby, with a rich raspberry nose, full-bodied, with soft, velvety, sweet fruit flavors, light tannins and a lingering finish. Lovely now but will improve. Last tasted: 6/90. Drink 1990-1993. Release: $12 (£9). Current retail: $30 (£17). Current auction: NA. **87**

1978 NIEPOORT: Quite good for the vintage but a little forward. Medium to deep ruby, with simple fruit aromas, medium-bodied, with integrated tannins, very sweet raspberry flavors and a simple finish. Last tasted: 11/89. Drink 1990. Release: $11 (£7). Current retail: $32 (£17). Current auction: NA. **81**

1977 NIEPOORT: Powerful, yet maintains a round, rich fruit structure that underscores Niepoort's brilliance. Deep ruby, with an intense raspberry nose, full-bodied, with elegant tannins and masses of sweet fruit flavors. Excellent finish. Last tasted: 4/90. Drink 1994-1996. Release: $11 (£6.50). Current retail: $50 (£20). Current auction: $30 (£8). **89**

1975 NIEPOORT: Nice now but losing its fruit, like other 1975s. Medium to light ruby, perfumed cherry nose, medium-bodied, with sweet fruit flavors and light tannins. Drink up. Last tasted: 11/89. Drink 1990. Release: £5. Current retail: $37 (£18). Current auction: $20 (£7). **79**

1970 NIEPOORT: One couldn't hope for a classier or more tightly knit 1970. Great deep ruby color, with very intense cherry and chocolate aromas, full-bodied, with medium tannins and a great balance of ripe, sweet fruit flavors. Wonderful finish. It can go on for decades. Last tasted: 1/90. Drink 1990-1995. Release: £2. Current retail: $55 (£25). Current auction: $33 (£16). **93**

1966 NIEPOORT: This is a live wire of a wine with very strong structure and crisp fruit. Deep ruby, with a bitter chocolate and rich raspberry nose, full-bodied, with plenty of tannins, lovely sweet fruit flavors and a lasting finish. Last tasted: 11/89. Drink 1990-1993. Release: £1.50. Current retail: $70 (£30). Current auction: $40 (£17). **89**

1963 NIEPOORT: Firm, with great harmony of fruit and tannins, this superb Port needs an hour or two of decanting. Medium ruby, with a very ripe, earthy berry nose, medium-bodied, with an excellent backbone of tannins and a stunning amount of grape and violet flavors. Can drink now, but it will improve with age. Last tasted: 11/89. Drink 1990. Release: £1.10. Current retail: $90 (£40). Current auction: $60. **90**

1955 NIEPOORT: This may be the best 1955 made. Medium ruby with a garnet rim, it has incredibly ripe cherry and grape aromas and a profusion of plum flavors, hard tannins, massive structure and a long finish. Will improve for decades more. Last tasted: 8/90. Drink 1990. Release: £1. Current retail: $175 (£65). Current auction: £24. **98**

1945 NIEPOORT: Another Port shipper once mistook this extraordinary wine for one 15 years younger. It is very youthful, with caressing, sweet fruit flavors. Medium garnet with a ruby center, blackberry, black pepper and smoke aromas, medium-bodied, with sweet blackberry and licorice flavors, light tannins and a very long finish. Last tasted: 2/90. Drink 1990. Release: £.40. Current retail: $250 (£125). Current auction: £110. **97**

1942 NIEPOORT: Bottled in its third year, like most other 1942s, this was bottled in 1-liter, hand-blown bottles. I tasted it with four other top 1942s and it finished well ahead of the bunch. It is perhaps the greatest 1942 still in existence. Deep, dark brick red, with a rich roasted coffee and fruit nose, full-bodied, with rich, round, velvety fruit flavors and a very sweet, long finish. Last tasted: 4/90. Drink 1990. Release: £.30. Current retail: $240 (£110). Current auction: £77. **93**

1927 NIEPOORT: I tasted this with 10 other 1927s, and it held its own with the best. On another occasion, I tasted it blind, and many of the tasters thought it was a top 1963. It is still going strong, with a great intensity of rich fruit. Deep brick red with a ruby center, milk chocolate and ripe berry aromas, full-bodied, with sweet, rich chocolate and berry flavors and an extremely long finish. Last tasted: 4/90. Drink 1990. Release: £.20. Current retail: $260 (£140). Current auction: £116. **97**

OFFLEY FORRESTER
CLASSIFICATION: *FOURTH TIER*

COLLECTIBILITY RATING: *A*

BEST VINTAGES: *1983, 1966, 1980*

Offley Forrester remains rather obscure in vintage Port circles, even though its origins are linked to one of the most colorful characters in the history of Port, Baron Joseph James Forrester, who joined his uncle at the firm in 1831. The baron would, nonetheless, be proud of the quality of his firm's current vintages.

Offley was founded in 1737. In 1962 it became part of the Sandeman group, which in 1965 sold 50 percent of Offley to St. Raphael, a French apéritif company owned by Italian drinks group Martini & Rossi. Seagram, which purchased Sandeman in 1980, sold its interest in Offley to Martini & Rossi in 1983. Offley is one of the largest Port brands in the world, selling about 600,000 cases a year, and is particularly strong in the Portuguese and Italian markets.

All of Offley's vintage Ports originate from the company's Quinta Boa Vista, about 5 miles downriver from Pinhão. The exception was 1987, when Offley made both a Boa Vista and a vintage Port blended from various estates in the Cima Corgo. The Boa Vista Ports are labeled as such, while the others carry only the Offley name. According to Jorges Guimaraens, Offley's export manager, his company decided to make two different vintage wines due to the increasing worldwide demand for their vintages, particularly in the United States.

The vintage Ports produced at Boa Vista tend to be well structured and concentrated, but perhaps lacking that extra dimension to make them truly outstanding. There are exceptions, such as the 1983 and 1980, which are two of the best wines made in those vintages. Offley Boa Vistas tend to reach their optimum drinking age 10 to 13 years after the vintage date, and can continue to drink well for another few decades. The 1966 is still wonderfully fresh and firm, with plenty of fruit to keep it going, but the 1963 is beginning to break up, with the alcohol starting to show.

Boa Vista encompasses about 310 acres. The vineyards currently total 160 acres, although they should equal about 235 by the mid-1990s. The vines at Boa Vista are 15 to 20 years old. Annual production currently averages 160 pipes and should increase to about 250 pipes in a few years. Some 8,000 to 10,000 cases of vintage Port should be produced at the property, although production has been slightly less in the past.

The property has not always been part of Offley. It was sold in the mid-1950s to a Portuguese family, but remained under contract to Offley. All the wines were made at Sandeman's winery at Celeirós until 1978, and after that at the *quinta* itself. Offley bought Boa Vista in 1980.

The property is a typical example of a single-*quinta* operation. All the wines are produced in four 180-hectoliter stainless steel fermentation tanks. They are temperature-controlled, with programmable pumping over. *Lagares* were used until 1977. Enologist Alexander Pina Carvalho prefers the current system to the *lagar* because it is much easier to control fermentation. "We want to extract as much as possible through controlling the temperature," he said.

"Our blend for the vintage is very, very easy," Pina Carvalho said. "I simply take a look at the wines from the four different vats, select and blend them together." He said they tried blending in other *quintas'* wines in some vintages but that the samples did not show as well as the unblended Boa Vista.

Baron Forrester was an iconoclast in the Port trade during the early 1800s. He lambasted the trade for a variety of reasons, including what he thought was the adulteration of the product through the addition of alcohol. Luckily, Forrester never put into practice what he preached, considering his house's long tradition for producing quality vintage Ports.

Tasting Notes

1987 OFFLEY: Simple, but has very good fruit structure. Dark purple, with grapy, floral aromas, full-bodied, with round, chewy fruit flavors, medium tannins and a long finish. Last tasted: 1/90. Drink 1995-1996. Not released. **84**

1987 OFFLEY BOA VISTA: Very classy and well crafted. Deep inky color, very ripe black currant aromas, full-bodied, with plenty of racy fruit flavors, a tough backbone and a long finish. Last tasted: 1/90. Drink 1997-1998. Release: £15. Current retail: £15. Current auction: NA. **88**

1985 OFFLEY BOA VISTA: Polished, with good fruit and backbone. Deep inky color, elegant perfumed nose, full-bodied, with silky, elegant fruit flavors, medium tannins and a long finish. Last tasted: 6/90. Drink 1996-1998. Release: $22 (£11). Current retail: $29 (£16). Current auction: NA. **89**

1983 OFFLEY BOA VISTA: This 1983 is one of the best. Black-purple, with very intense grape must aromas, full-bodied, with grapy and peppery flavors, full tannins, good backbone and a long finish. Has good grip. Last tasted: 1/90. Drink 1994-1998. Release: $22 (£10). Current retail: $27 (£15). Current auction: £7. **91**

1982 OFFLEY BOA VISTA: This wine suffers from the 1982 syndrome — too ripe, almost burnt fruit. Very deep ruby, with plum and raisin aromas, full-bodied, with velvety fruit flavors, medium tannins and a long finish. Last tasted: 6/90. Drink 1992-1998. Release: $18 (£10). Current retail: $22 (£17). Current auction: $14. **84**

1980 OFFLEY BOA VISTA: This vintage continues to impress and this is a very good 1980 indeed. Deep ruby, with a ripe plum and blackberry nose, full-bodied, with tons of fruit flavors, good balance, medium tannins and a long finish. Last tasted: 6/90. Drink 1990-1994. Release: $14 (£7). Current retail: $30 (£16). Current auction: NA. **90**

1977 OFFLEY BOA VISTA: Medium ruby, with ripe plum and raisin aromas, full-bodied and ripe, with medium tannins and a long finish. Last tasted: 1/90. Drink 1993-1994. Release: $11 (£5). Current retail: $45 (£25). Current auction: $26 (£11). **88**

1975 OFFLEY BOA VISTA: Decent, but quite light. Light color, rose and plum nose, light-bodied, with fresh flavors and light tannins, slightly dry on the finish. Last tasted: 2/89. Drink 1990. Release: £4.50. Current retail: $27 (£20). Current auction: £8. **75**

1972 OFFLEY BOA VISTA: More enjoyable than the 1975. Light ruby, with a delicate plum and spice nose, medium-bodied, with soft, round fruit flavors, light tannins and a caressing finish. Last tasted: 2/89. Drink 1990. Release: £2. Current retail: $30 (£12). Current auction: £9. **79**

1970 OFFLEY BOA VISTA: A little too simple for a 1970. Medium ruby with a garnet edge, plenty of raspberry aromas, medium-bodied, with one-dimensional raspberry flavors and a medium finish. Last tasted: 2/89. Drink 1990. Release: £2.30. Current retail: $48 (£35). Current auction: $28 (£13). **81**

1966 OFFLEY BOA VISTA: Supports those who believe the 1966s are better than the superb 1963s. It is extremely rich and well structured. Medium red, with a rich plum and raspberry nose, full-bodied, with very sweet plum flavors, medium tannins and a long finish. Can drink now, but it will improve. Last tasted: 2/89. Drink 1990. Release: £1.30. Current retail: $45 (£25). Current auction: $35 (£15). **90**

1963 OFFLEY BOA VISTA: Quite weak for a 1963. Forward medium red, earthy plum nose, medium-bodied, with good fruit flavors, but a little hot on the finish. Last tasted: 2/89. Drink 1990. Release: £.90. Current retail: $97 (£39). Current auction: $50 (£21). **80**

1960 OFFLEY BOA VISTA: Many of the 1960s are folding up and this is no exception. Light red with a garnet edge, delicate cherry aromas, light-bodied, with a silky mouth-feel, but a little dry and hot on the finish. Last tasted: 2/89. Drink 1990. Release: £.80. Current retail: $70 (£18). Current auction: £13. **78**

OSBORNE

CLASSIFICATION: *Not rated*

COLLECTIBILITY RATING: *Not rated*

Osborne has been in the fortified wine business since 1772, when it began trading in Sherry, but only has been in the Port trade since 1967. Originally associated with Quinta do Noval, Osborne now has its own lodges and produces a range of different Ports.

Its vintage Port production is limited, and the house still appears to be trying to find a style. Recent vintages are rather light and uninteresting, although cleanly made. The 1985, for example, shows a lovely peppery nose but falls short on the palate, lacking the concentration one would expect.

Older vintages also leave something to be desired. The 1970 is very drinkable, with a nice, silky mouth-feel, but there is a slightly green and stemmy character to the wine that is off-putting. The 1960, which was bought as bottled wine from Noval, is still very good, with elegant plum flavors and a nice balance.

"The Osborne group wanted to diversify," said José Teles Dias da Silva, the young managing director of the house. "A Port can give prestige and image to a group." Osborne annually sells about 60,000 cases of Port.

Osborne buys all of its Ports from growers, although the house has been actively looking to buy a property. Vintage lots may be made either in *lagar* or by autovinification. Once the wines arrive from the Douro at Osborne's lodge, the vintage lots are kept in large stainless steel vats. They are never held in wood like past vintages, in hopes of reducing oxidation, according to Osborne's winemaker, Francisco Oliveira. He also works for the Port house of C. da Silva. Osborne's vintage production equals a few thousand cases.

"It can be difficult sometimes for us," said da Silva. "Other people have been in the Port trade for years. They may have a tradition going back three generations. We don't have the tradition yet."

AT A GLANCE

OSBORNE
Rua da Cabaça 37
4400 Vila Nova de Gaia,
** Portugal**
02-30.26.48
Owners: Osborne & CIA
  and Bodegas Montecillo
Founded: 1772
Average production: 2,000-
  3,000 cases

TASTING NOTES

1985 OSBORNE: Well made, but much too light for such an excellent vintage. Medium ruby with a red hue, peppery aromas, medium-bodied, with elegant medium tannins and a light finish. Last tasted: 1/90. Drink 1993-1994. Release: $20. Current retail: $21. Current auction: NA. **76**

VINHO   DO PORTO

OPORTO
PORTUGAL

1985
VINTAGE PORT
BOTTLED IN 1888
PRODUCED IN THE DOURO DEMARCATED REGION
OSBORNE
(VINHOS DE PORTUGAL) & Cª. LDA.
VILA NOVA DE GAIA

OSBORNE
PRODUCE OF PORTUGAL

20,4°   75 cl

1982 OSBORNE: Sweet and simple, even a little boring. Medium ruby-red, with earthy, slightly vegetal, coffee-ground aromas, medium-bodied, with sweet fruit flavors, medium tannins and a short finish. Last tasted: 1/90. Drink 1991-1993. Release: $13. Current retail: $26. Current auction: NA. **72**

1970 OSBORNE: Medium to light ruby-red, with slightly stemmy cherry aromas, medium-bodied, with slightly stemmy but silky fruit flavors and a long finish. Last tasted: 1/90. Drink 1990. Release: NA. Current retail: $50. Current auction: NA. **77**

1960 OSBORNE: This is bottled wine bought from Quinta do Noval. It is very sweet, with plenty of fruit flavors. Medium red, with a cassis and cherry nose, medium-bodied, with tons of velvety fruit flavors. Perfect now, but a little hot. Last tasted: 1/90. Drink 1990. Release: NA. Current retail: $60. Current auction: NA. **82**

A. PINTOS DOS SANTOS
CLASSIFICATION: *Not rated*

COLLECTIBILITY RATING: *Not rated*

his may be the weakest of the vintage Ports produced by the Barros, Almeida group. The vintage Ports of A. Pintos dos Santos are extremely light and simple and can be viewed only as vintage-dated rubies for current drinking in most instances.

According to Manuel Angelo Barros, a director of Barros, Almeida, the A. Pintos dos Santos vintage Ports are the same as those shipped under the label of Douro Wine Shippers & Growers Association. Douro Wine Shippers provides private-label Ports for clients primarily in Europe. Some of the buyers' brands are Flagman in West Germany, Rocha in Holland and Maia in Italy.

Although the Ports of Santos and Douro Wine Shippers may make commercial sense for Barros, their vintage Ports hold little interest for serious vintage Port consumers.

AT A GLANCE
A. PINTOS DOS SANTOS
Rua de Leonor de Freitas 182,
C.P. 39
4400 Vila Nova de Gaia,
Portugal
02-30.23.20
Owners: Barros family
Founded: 1872
Average production: 600-1,000 cases

TASTING NOTES

1985 A. PINTOS DOS SANTOS: Maturing too quickly in color and flavor. Medium ruby-red, with a spicy cherry nose, medium-bodied, with round, silky fruit flavors, light tannins and a light finish. Last tasted: 1/90. Best to avoid. Release: £10. Current retail: £14. Current auction: £8. **69**

1982 A. PINTOS DOS SANTOS: Very light and forward. Medium red, black cherry nose, light- to medium-bodied, with clean berry flavors and a light finish. Maturing quickly. Last tasted: 1/90. Drink 1990. Release: £6.50. Current retail: £13. Current auction: £8. **70**

1980 A. PINTOS DOS SANTOS: Slightly out of balance and hot but there are still some decent fruit flavors. Medium ruby going red, with peppery, grapy aromas and flavors, medium-bodied, with medium tannins and a short finish. Too alcoholic. Last tasted: 1/90. Drink 1990. Release: £6. Current retail: £13. Current auction: NA. **70**

1970 A. PINTOS DOS SANTOS: A little hot and past its peak. Medium red with a garnet hue, chestnut and cherry aromas, light- to medium-bodied, with spicy chestnut and fruit flavors and a harsh, hot finish. Last tasted: 1/90. Drink 1990. Release: £2. Current retail: £20. Current auction: £9. **70**

MANOEL D. POCAS JUNIOR
CLASSIFICATION: *FIFTH TIER*

COLLECTIBILITY RATING: *Not rated*

BEST VINTAGE: *1985*

AT A GLANCE

POCAS JUNIOR
Rua Visconde das
  Devesas 186, C.P. 56
4401 Vila Nova de Gaia,
  Portugal
02-30.02.12

Owners: Poças family

Founded: 1918

Average production: 3,000-
  5,000 cases

Acaicio Manoel Poças Maia remembers that his grandfather used to say the vintage Port business was for the British houses and not for them, which explains why his house, Manoel D. Poças Junior, began making good vintage Ports at such a late date.

It was not until 1960 that Poças Junior made its first vintage Port. "I had to continually fight to get some vintage Port made," said Poças Maia, who added that his firm produced tiny amounts before just for his family's consumption. "I finally convinced everyone with the 1960."

I have only tasted five vintages of Poças Junior, but their quality is good. The 1985 was the best of them, showing plenty of interesting black pepper and fruit flavors and a lean tannic backbone. The 1970 was also very good, offering delicious flavors of chocolate and plums rounded off with a velvety mouth-feel. Even the 1960 is holding on well, with more than enough sweet, soft fruit flavors to give pleasant drinking for another decade or so.

Poças annually sells about 200,000 cases of Port, mostly simple tawnies and rubies as well as fine mature wood Ports. Vintage Port remains a very small percentage of the company's total production, from 3,000 to 5,000 cases. Most of these vintages have been sold in European countries other than Great Britain.

Most of the Poças vintage Ports have come from a grower near the village of San João da Pesqueria south of the Douro River, and the company has continued to buy wines from there. The wines were once made by *lagar*, but most are now made by autovinification. Poças also owns three *quintas*: Quartas, Santa Barbara and Vale de Cavalos. The latter is expected to produce vintage-quality wines by mid-1990. Located in the Douro Superior, Vale de Cavalos totals about 125 acres, with about 75 planted to vine. It should produce about 300 pipes of Port in the future.

Poças Junior was established in 1918, and the founding family continues to build the prestige of the firm, which family members are convinced will be enhanced through making first-class vintage Ports. "The possibility of making great vintage Ports is just the same with us as the British houses," said Poças Maia. In some vintages, he has already proved his point.

TASTING NOTES

1985 POCAS JUNIOR: Hard and quite tough for a 1985, with lots of grapy, peppery flavors and a firm backbone. It is still rather lean though. Purple with an inky center, black pepper nose, medium-bodied, with black pepper and fruit flavors, medium tannins and a hard finish. Last tasted: 2/90. Drink 1996-1998. Release: $17 (£11). Current retail: $19 (£13). Current auction: NA. **85**

1975 POCAS JUNIOR: This is starting to dry out and has a slightly unattractive roasted vanilla character. Medium red, with a vanilla, roasted nut and plum nose, light-bodied, with medium tannins and an astringent finish. Last tasted: 2/90. Drink 1990. Release: £4.50. Current retail: $34 (£18). Current auction: NA. **74**

1970 POCAS JUNIOR: I have had this three or four times and it is always a pleasant surprise when served blind. Medium to light ruby, with bitter chocolate and plum aromas, medium-bodied, with sweet, rich chocolate and plum flavors, medium tannins and a sweet, velvety finish. Delicious. Last tasted: 2/90. Drink 1990. Release: £2. Current retail: $52 (£20). Current auction: NA. **84**

1963 POCAS JUNIOR: This is a little simple for a 1963 but it is still attractive. Medium ruby with a light edge, milk chocolate and plum aromas, medium-bodied, with a balance of tannins and a fresh, fruity finish. Last tasted: 2/90. Drink 1990. Release: £.80. Current retail: $100 (£28). Current auction: NA. **82**

1960 POCAS JUNIOR: Some 1960s have dried out, but this is still very sweet, round and savory. Medium to light red with a slight garnet hue, aromas of chocolate and sweet plums, medium-bodied, with sweet, velvety fruit flavors, light tannins and a spicy finish. The alcohol shows a bit on the finish. At its peak now. Last tasted: 2/90. Drink 1990. Release: £.70. Current retail: $80 (£30). Current auction: NA. **82**

QUARLES HARRIS
CLASSIFICATION: *FOURTH TIER*

COLLECTIBILITY RATING: *A*

BEST VINTAGES: *1970, 1977, 1983*

AT A GLANCE
QUARLES HARRIS
Travessado Barão de Forrester, Apartado 26
4401 Vila Nova de Gaia, Portugal
02-39.60.63
Owner: Symington Port Shippers
Founded: 1680
Average production: 4,000-5,000 cases

It's easy to overlook Quarles Harris, since it remains a rather obscure house in the large holdings of the Symington Port Shippers. Its vintage Ports are extremely dependable in quality, however, and should not be missed.

Quarles Harris vintage Ports are like lesser Taylor Ports in style. While hard and firm, with well-focused fruit flavors, they don't have the longevity of the wines from great shippers like Taylor or Dow, but they are pleasant to drink all the same — especially since they sell for about two-thirds the price of similar vintages from the popular houses.

The recent vintages of Quarles Harris are typical of what the house has to offer. They are not blockbuster wines, but are well-crafted, solid vintage Ports for cellaring eight to 10 years. The 1983 is particularly good, with an elegant tannic structure backed up with plenty of raspberry flavor. It needs a little more bottle age than the smoother 1985 to be ready for drinking.

The 1970 is currently at its peak for drinking. It is a lovely wine, with beautiful, caressing, sweet fruit flavors and a balance of ripe tannins. Although it will improve with bottle age, it makes little sense to wait. Older vintages are very nearly past their peaks. The 1966, for example, was fading on the palate, although this could have been due to a poor bottle. The 1963 was good, with mature, soft fruit flavors, very near its peak. Quarles Harris vintage Ports do not seem to be wines to cellar for decades, although I have not evaluated vintages older than the 1963.

Peter Symington, the director of production for the Symington group, has a simple philosophy about Quarles Harris: "Unless they are good we don't bottle them. They are Ports that are sold on sample (meaning merchants want to taste them before buying) and don't sell simply on reputation."

Like the Ports of the Symingtons' other similar houses, Smith Woodhouse and Gould Campbell, Quarles Harris vintage Ports are not tied to any particular *quinta*. They are reflections of the blender's talents. "We know the style of Ports which Quarles Harris should be and we make them accordingly," said Symington, who added that the wines come primarily from the Rio Torto area. Quarles Harris makes 4,000 to 5,000 cases of vintage Port, depending on the year.

Quarles Harris was established in 1680. The house became a subsidiary of Warre in the 18th century, when the name became simply a brand. The Symingtons became associated with Quarles Harris soon after A.J. Symington became a partner in Warre. Quarles Harris has continued making good Ports under the Symington's ownership ever since.

TASTING NOTES

1985 QUARLES HARRIS: Firm and well made, with a sufficient structure of fruit and tannin for long-term aging. Medium to deep ruby, with a light tomato and boysenberry nose, medium- to full-bodied, with medium tannins, spicy, peppery fruit flavors and a lingering finish. Last tasted: 6/90. Drink 1995-1997. Release: $21 (£11). Current retail: $29 (£20). Current auction: £8. **85**

1983 QUARLES HARRIS: More elegance, power and class than the 1985. Deep purple, with enchanting crème de framboise aromas, full-bodied, with an abundance of tannins and concentrated fruit flavors, slightly hard but with a very good, long finish. Last tasted: 2/90. Drink 1996-1998. Release: $18 (£9). Current retail: $33 (£16). Current auction: £8. **89**

1980 QUARLES HARRIS: Another well-crafted, firm wine. Medium ruby-red, with focused aromas of violets and perfume, medium-bodied, with medium tannins and racy, lean fruit flavors. Last tasted: 2/90. Drink 1990-1993. Release: $13 (£7). Current retail: $26 (£16). Current auction: $18 (£7). **83**

1977 QUARLES HARRIS: Incredibly intense fruit flavors make this exciting and attractive. Ruby-red, with a concentrated nose of tomatoes and cassis, full-bodied, with round tannins and tons of velvety fruit flavors. Last tasted: 2/90. Drink 1993-1996. Release: $11 (£5). Current retail: $43 (£19). Current auction: $26 (£9). **89**

1975 QUARLES HARRIS: Both bottles of this wine that I have tasted were poorly corked. One bottle was vinegar and the other was slightly tired. Medium brick red with a garnet edge, a nose of cherries and blackberries, light-bodied, with peppery, medium-sweet fruit flavors, light tannins and a short finish. The alcohol is showing on the finish. Last tasted: 4/90. Drink 1990. Release: £4. Current retail: $35 (£16). Current auction: $28. **73**

1970 QUARLES HARRIS: A complete wine with a bounty of fruit and tannins to give it great longevity. Red with a ruby center, intense black cherry and leather aromas, medium-bodied and full of tannins, with velvety, sweet fruit flavors and a long finish. Very good backbone. Last tasted: 2/90. Drink 1990-1993. Release: £2. Current retail: $60 (£25). Current auction: $27 (£12). **89**

1966 QUARLES HARRIS: Not holding together very well. Decent fruit but starting to fade. Medium red with a garnet hue, slightly volatile

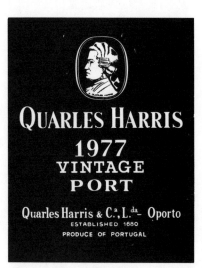

chocolate and spice aromas, medium-bodied, with light tannins and rather hot, spicy fruit flavors on the finish. Last tasted: 2/90. Drink 1990. Release: £1.30. Current retail: $78 (£30). Current auction: NA. **74**

1963 QUARLES HARRIS: This is a sweet, velvety wine that beckons you to drink it. Deep red with a garnet edge, light coffee and berry nose, medium-bodied, with plenty of tannins, but the velvety, ripe fruit flavors soften the wine. Last tasted: 2/90. Drink 1990. Release: £.90. Current retail: $110 (£35). Current auction: $103. **85**

QUINTA DO BOMFIM
CLASSIFICATION: *FIFTH TIER*

COLLECTIBILITY RATING: *Not rated*

BEST VINTAGES: *1965, 1984, 1987*

I t is surprising that Quinta do Bomfim vintage Ports were not commercialized before 1978, considering their obvious quality. For decades, Bomfim Ports have been the backbone for Silva & Cosens' Dow vintage wines.

Quinta do Bomfim vintage Ports exhibit the same exuberant fruit and hard backbones of Dow; they lack only the complexity of the vintage blend. The Symingtons often say that a blend is always better than a single-*quinta* Port, and this is undoubtedly true of the fine vintage Ports their group makes. But single-*quinta* vintage Ports like Quinta do Bomfim are better than many other houses' vintage blends.

In fact, wines like the Bomfim 1984 and 1987 are nearly as good as some recent vintages of Dow. The difference is more than made up for in the wines' relative prices. Quinta do Bomfim vintages usually cost 30 percent less than Dow. The two wines are never made in the same year; when Dow does not declare a vintage, a Quinta do Bomfim Port may be produced, depending on the amount of quality wine made on the property.

All the wines of Bomfim are made at the massive winery on the property, which is the Symingtons' main production facility. It can produce more than 10,000 pipes of Port in a vintage. Bomfim vintage Ports are all made through autovinification — another vote of confidence for the method. I would still like to see what the wines would be like if they were made by *lagar*. Production is 6,000 to 8,000 cases.

Bomfim encompasses about 190 acres, with 90 percent under vine. It produces about 180 pipes of Port, which should double by the mid-1990s. A large part of the vineyards is new plantings.

Quinta do Bomfim was built in the mid-1890s under the direction of George Warre, who owned Silva & Cosens at the time. Warre personally owned Bomfim until he retired in the early 1900s and sold the property to his company. When he died in 1913, the company exchanged shares the following year with the house of Warre. Bomfim has always remained attached to Silva & Cosens.

Quinta do Bomfim has been the relatively unknown key component of Dow vintage Ports. Now, with its own excellent vintage Ports, Quinta do Bomfim will inevitably make a reputation for itself.

AT A GLANCE
QUINTA DO BOMFIM
Travessa Barão de Forrester,
Apartado 14
4401 Vila Nova de Gaia,
Portugal
02-39.60.63

Owner: Symington Port Shippers

Founded: 1890

Average production: 6,000-8,000 cases

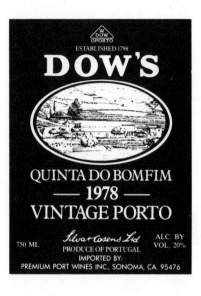

TASTING NOTES

1987 QUINTA DO BOMFIM: Extremely impressive, with generous, rich black cherry notes. Deep inky purple, with ripe black cherry aromas, full-bodied, with full tannins and a great concentration of fruit flavors. Very well structured. Last tasted: 2/90. Drink 1998-2000. Not released. **86**

1986 QUINTA DO BOMFIM: Very hard and closed at the moment, but still shows good fruit flavors and potential. Very dark ruby with a black center, a grape and licorice nose, medium-bodied, with full, hard tannins, blackberry flavors and a closed finish. Last tasted: 2/90. Drink 1996-1997. Not released. **82**

1984 QUINTA DO BOMFIM: Powerful and hard, with a classy dryness, one of the best wines I have tried from this property. Dark ruby-purple, with a lovely grape and raspberry nose, full-bodied, with tons of tannins and lots of medium-sweet fruit flavors. Very solid. Last tasted: 2/90. Drink 1995-1996. Not released. **86**

1982 QUINTA DO BOMFIM: Very smooth and fruity, lacking the disagreeable roasted, raisiny character of many of the wines from this vintage. Medium ruby with a red hue, delicate grape, cherry and raspberry aromas, medium-bodied, with round cherry flavors and medium tannins. Last tasted: 2/90. Drink 1992-1993. Not released. **82**

1979 QUINTA DO BOMFIM: One of of the better 1979s I have tasted. Most are rather watery and diluted, with little interesting fruit. This is fairly exciting, with plenty of fruit and tannin. Medium ruby, with a perfumed black cherry nose, medium-bodied, with medium tannins and lovely floral fruit flavors. Last tasted: 2/90. Drink 1990. Release: $28 (£14). Current retail: $28 (£15). Current auction: NA. **81**

1978 QUINTA DO BOMFIM: All the components, from the rich fruit flavors to the hard tannins, are well integrated. Medium ruby, with a black cherry nose, full-bodied, with medium tannins and very good focused blackberry flavors. Quite dry with a long finish. Last tasted: 2/90. Drink 1990-1992. Release: $27 (£14). Current retail: $29 (£16). Current auction: NA. **85**

1965 QUINTA DO BOMFIM: Only about 50 cases of this wine were made. It has super balance with wonderful raspberry notes on the palate and an extremely firm tannin backbone. This wine will improve with age. Last tasted: 6/90. Drink 1990. Release: £2. Current retail: £17. Current auction: NA. **87**

QUINTA DA CAVADINHA

CLASSIFICATION: *FIFTH TIER*

COLLECTIBILITY RATING: *Not rated*

BEST VINTAGES: *1982, 1987, 1986*

Quinta da Cavadinha recently joined the Symington Port Shippers' stable of fine vintage Ports, but it was already clearly a thoroughbred vineyard site, producing remarkably aromatic and delicately concentrated wines.

The Symingtons bought Cavadinha in 1980, including stocks of the 1978 and 1979 wines. These vintage Ports were already good, but the Symingtons have improved the quality since taking over. The 1987 and 1986 are particularly good, with deep colors and ripe, concentrated aromas. They show an impressive amount of fleshiness while maintaining a good harmony.

The best wines of the *quinta* were used in Warre vintage Port blends in 1985, 1983 and 1980. According to Bruce Guimaraens, of Taylor and Fonseca, Cavadinha was a component of the Fonseca vintage blends in the 1960s and 1970s.

The property is directly opposite Quinta do Noval on the western side of the Pinhão Valley. Quinta da Cavadinha encompasses 87 acres of vineyards and produces about 180 pipes of Port. The *quinta* also has an impressive winery, which houses stainless steel temperature-controlled fermentation tanks designed by the Symingtons. The tanks can be used either as an automated *remontagem* system or for auto-vinification. The five tanks each hold about 12 pipes' worth of must, which is the average size of a traditional *lagar*, and are also squat in shape to ensure a proper ratio of skins to juice to get a strong extraction during the fermentation.

Peter Symington calls the system "the best of two worlds," and plans to use the winery to process wines from only the best *quintas* under contract to his family as well as for Cavadinha's own grapes. Symington believes that many of these *quintas* may not be able to process large crops in coming harvests due to new plantings in the area. The installation, he hopes, will help absorb this oversupply.

Production of Quinta da Cavadinha's single-*quinta* vintage Ports ranges from 8,000 to 10,000 cases. They are usually sold about eight to 10 years after their harvest date. "We want to offer the consumer an excellent drinking vintage Port at a reasonable price when we release these wines," said Johnny Symington. Prices of vintage from Quinta da Cavadinha are relatively reasonable, about $20 to $30 a bottle.

AT A GLANCE

QUINTA DA CAVADINHA
Travessa do Barão de Forrester,
Apartado 26
4401 Vila Nova de Gaia,
Portugal
02-39.60.63
Owner: Symington Port Shippers
Average production: 8,000-10,000 cases

TASTING NOTES

1987 QUINTA DA CAVADINHA: This is quite hard for the normally delicate and fruity wines of Cavadinha. Deep purple, with very grapy, floral aromas, full-bodied, with a hard, tannic backbone and a short finish. Very good level of fruit flavors. Needs time. Last tasted: 2/90. Drink 1998-2000. Not released. **86**

1986 QUINTA DA CAVADINHA: Very fleshy and elegant for a 1986 and as good as the impressive 1987. It may be one of the best 1986s. Excellent deep inky color, with a nose of tar and berries, full-bodied, with ripe, fleshy fruit flavors, full tannins and a gutsy finish. Good grip. Last tasted: 2/90. Drink 1997-1998. Not released. **85**

1984 QUINTA DA CAVADINHA: A little short; perhaps it is simply closed for the moment. Medium purple-red, with aromas of tar, cassis and tomatoes, medium-bodied, with silky, sweet fruit flavors and medium tannins on the finish. Last tasted: 2/90. Drink 1992-1994. Not released. **81**

1982 QUINTA DA CAVADINHA: Extremely tight and well structured, with a hard backbone and rich fruit flavors. Deep ruby, with a cassis and perfume nose, medium- to full-bodied, with medium tannins and a sweet, balanced, fruity finish. Last tasted: 2/90. Drink 1992-1994. Not released. **86**

1979 QUINTA DA CAVADINHA: Sweet, velvety and elegant. Medium ruby with a red hue, fresh aromas of currants and cherries, medium-bodied, with very sweet fruit flavors, medium tannins and a light finish. A little simple, but delicious. Last tasted 2/90. Drink 1990-1992. Release: $25 (£14). Current retail: $25 (£15). Current auction: NA. **82**

1978 QUINTA DA CAVADINHA: Long and silky, with plenty of finesse and mellow fruit flavors. Medium ruby, with a nose of currants and perfume, medium-bodied, with tightly knit tannins, medium sweet currant flavors and a balanced finish. A harmonious wine. Last tasted: 2/90. Drink 1990-1992. Release: $28 (£14). Current retail: $28 (£17). Current auction: NA. **83**

QUINTA DA CORTE
CLASSIFICATION: *FIFTH TIER*

COLLECTIBILITY RATING: *Not rated*

BEST VINTAGES: <u>*1987, 1984*</u>

Quinta da Corte vintage Ports are a relatively recent addition to the Croft-Delaforce group, but they boost the group's image by producing good vintage wines.

Corte is directly tied to Delaforce, Sons & Co. and produces its own vintage Ports in years when its mother house decides against a general declaration. From my tastings, Quinta da Corte is a shining example of how a single property can produce, in some years, vintage Ports better than the blends of other houses. During the 1980s, Corte has made classier, more provocative vintage Ports than the two major houses in the group, Croft and Delaforce.

Corte vintage Ports are firm, elegant wines with the breeding of a fine claret. They may not be in the very upper echelon of vintage Ports, but they are definitely better than those of many other houses and single-*quinta* producers.

The property is owned by the Pacheco and Cyrne families, who contracted Corte's production to Delaforce in 1979. "We had a lot of confidence in them and we made the wines at the *quinta* for many years," said David Delaforce, who set up the deal. He now works in London as Delaforce's managing director. "It is a prime vineyard site and very well managed. We have worked with the families for a long time and we wanted to continue to work with them."

Quinta da Corte, at the mouth of the Rio Torto, encompasses about 90 acres, with most of the property under vine. Its traditional terraced vineyards are some of the most beautiful and well kept in the Cima Corgo. The vines are 25 to 30 years of age. Production equals 120 to 130 pipes of Port, depending on the year. Nearly all the wines are made in autovinification tanks, although a tiny part is still made in *lagares* for experimentation purposes.

The spring after the harvest, all of Corte's wines are moved down to Delaforce's lodges in Vila Nova de Gaia. Depending on the quality of the year, some of the Port may go into Delaforce vintages or be released as a single-*quinta* bottling. Corte is also a main contributor to Delaforce's premium tawnies, such as the Eminence Choice, a 15-year-old blend. Corte's single-*quinta* vintage production ranges from 2,000 to 4,000 cases.

Quinta da Corte makes better vintage Ports every year. The 1987

AT A GLANCE
QUINTA DA CORTE
Pinhão, Portugal

Owners: Pacheco and Cyrne families

Average production: 2,000-4,000 cases

is the best ever. It is a beautiful wine with a graceful balance of ripe blackberry flavors and firm, forceful tannins. Like most Corte vintage, it will be ready to drink after about a decade.

"We have gotten to know the property better over the years," said Delaforce. "Before, we were using the wines more for blending into our own tawnies. After 1978, we started to look at the property as a single-*quinta* wine. One gains from experience."

TASTING NOTES

1987 QUINTA DA CORTE: Classy and silky in the mouth, showing plenty of elegance and power. Deep purple, with a fresh, black olive nose, full-bodied, with medium tannins and balanced tar and blackberry flavors. Last tasted: 2/90. Drink 1997. Not released. **87**

1984 QUINTA DA CORTE: Slightly lean and hard, like many other 1984s, but very well balanced. Medium ruby-purple, with aromas of tar, olives and fruit, full-bodied, with plenty of tannins and a medium depth of fruit flavors. Linear in structure but classy. Last tasted: 2/90. Drink 1994-1996. Not released. **84**

1980 QUINTA DA CORTE: Simple and fruity, but still interesting to drink. Medium to deep ruby with a red hue, milk chocolate and raspberry aromas, medium-bodied and quite tannic and hard, with sweet fruit flavors and a medium finish. Needs some time. Last tasted: 2/90. Drink 1990-1993. Release: £12. Current retail: £14. Current auction: NA. **81**

1978 QUINTA DA CORTE: Another simple wine, perfectly ready to drink. Medium red, with a fruity, black olive nose, medium-bodied, with sweet fruit flavors, medium tannins and a short finish. Last tasted: 2/90. Drink 1990. Release: $24 (£14). Current retail: $24 (£17). Current auction: NA. **80**

QUINTA DO CRASTO

CLASSIFICATION: *Not rated*

COLLECTIBILITY RATING: *Not rated*

BEST VINTAGE: <u>1987</u>

Quinta do Crasto might be a serious entry into the estate-bottled vintage Port market in a few years. Its owners decided to start bottling and selling their own Ports after shipping laws were changed in 1986.

The vintage Ports of Crasto show a gradual, consistent improvement in quality each year. The 1987 is the best yet. It is a well-crafted, balanced wine with pretty black pepper and fruit notes on the nose and palate and a firm tannin backbone. Its only flaw is that it is one-dimensional on the palate.

"We want to develop the concept of a château up the Douro," said Jorge Roquette, an Oporto-based banker and one of five shareholders in the estate. Crasto, about 4 miles west of Pinhão, encompasses 345 acres, with 120 under vine. The property comprises two adjacent *quintas*: Sobreira and Reitor. Roquette said he has records dating Quinta do Crasto back to 1615.

Production is currently about 8,000 cases, although it will increase to about 24,000 when new plantings come on line. Vintage production is much smaller. For example, about 1,000 cases of the 1985 were made. Each bottle of vintage is numbered on the label. Crasto plans to make a small range of Ports, primarily premium styles such as vintage, late-bottled vintage and aged tawnies.

Crasto's production was sold to A.A. Ferreira in the past. Before that, the crop was sold to the house of Constantino, which merged with Ferreira in 1961. Crasto was the source of Constantino's vintage wines — a 1958 Constantino vintage Port's cork was branded with "Crasto." The current shareholders of Crasto are members of the family that originally owned Constantino.

Although Crasto's vintage Ports are clean and fruity, they lack the concentration and complexity of major-league wines. They are made in *lagares* although not trodden; the *movimosto* method is used instead. This method has a tendency to produce lighter Ports, and could be the main reason Crasto's wines are not first class. Crasto plans to revert to treading a portion of their harvest, according to Roquette.

Nonetheless, the owners are very keen on making a château-produced vintage Port. "We are pretty confident," said Roquette. "We

AT A GLANCE

QUINTA DO CRASTO
Gouvinhas Ferrao
5060 Sabrosa, Portugal
05-49.22.07

Owners: Jorge Roquette and four partners

Founded: 1615

Average production: 1,000 cases

think we have a place in the market for our Ports. Before, it was incomprehensible that we were in the oldest demarcated wine region in the world and we couldn't ship our wines ourselves."

TASTING NOTES

1987 QUINTA DO CRASTO: A balanced yet very simple wine. Shows improvement from earlier vintages. Deep purple, with a black pepper nose, medium-bodied, with medium tannins and very grapy, black pepper flavors. One-dimensional. Last tasted: 1/90. Drink 1993-1995. Not released. **80**

1985 QUINTA DO CRASTO: Short, simple and drinkable. Too light for a 1985. Medium ruby, with a light, grapy, Gamay-like nose, medium-bodied, with light tannins and a light, spicy finish. Last tasted: 1/90. Drink 1990. Release: $24 (£15). Current retail: $24 (£13). Current auction: NA. **71**

1978 QUINTA DO CRASTO: Clean but not a vintage Port in structure. Medium ruby with a garnet edge, very strange, perfumed, crème de cassis nose, medium- to light-bodied, with very sweet and simple fruit flavors. Lacks structure. Last tasted: 1/90. Drink 1990. Release: £15. Current retail: £15. Current auction: NA. **70**

1958 QUINTO DO CRASTO (CONSTANTINO): This was shipped as a Constantino vintage Port, although the cork was branded with "Crasto" on its side. Light fruit, with lovely almost tawnylike flavors—not bad for a 1958. Medium garnet, with a chocolate, cherry vanilla nose, light-bodied, with sweet spice, chocolate fruit flavors, light silky tannins and a short finish. Last tasted: 8/90. Drink 1990. Release: £.80. Current retail: £25. Current auction: NA. **79**

QUINTA DA EIRA VELHA

CLASSIFICATION: *FIFTH TIER*

COLLECTIBILITY RATING: *Not rated*

BEST VINTAGE: <u>1987</u>

Quinta da Eira Velha is rich in tradition and history. Its owners have documents that date the property to the beginning of the 16th century, when it was owned by a wealthy Portuguese land-owner in Vila Real.

Today, Englishmen Peter and Richard Newman own the property, which produces some of the most beautiful single-*quinta* vintage Ports available. The wines of Eira Velha may not win blind tastings, but they are a joy to drink, with enchanting aromas of ripe plums and cherries and focused sweet fruit on the palate.

The first vintage of Eira Velha commercially available was the 1978, which was bottled and sold through Cockburn Smithes. The 1978 Eira Velha is a wonderful glass of Port, with a seductive nose of sweet cherries and pleasingly soft, round fruit flavors. The 1987 could prove to be equally impressive, although it is still rather raw. Eira Velha Ports generally need about eight to nine years of bottle age before drinking. Production averages about 5,000 cases.

Since the 1987 vintage, Eira Velha has been bottled and sold through the house of Martinez Gassiot, a member of the Hiram Walker-Allied Vintners Port group. The group buys all of the *quinta's* production. Prior to 1978, Eira Velha's harvest was bought by A.A. Ferreira.

Located west of the Pinhão Valley, Eira Velha encompasses about 120 acres, with 65 under vine. Production averages about 120 pipes of Port, which will increase by another 30 in mid-1990 due to new plantings.

The *lagares* in which all of Eira Velha's wines are made are legendary in the region. In 1949 Peter Newman's father, Tom, had the walls above each *lagar* lined with blue Portuguese tiles depicting various stories relating to the history of the firm. One shows Port wine being unloaded in Newfoundland; another pictures Dartmouth Harbor in England. There is even one of a small sailing ship named Jenny being rammed by a French privateer- in 1804. The four stone *lagares* have rare rounded corners and were built in 1901.

Eira Velha was bought by the Newmans in 1938. It had been owned by Cable Roope, who had been a partner of the Newmans' in the Port house of Hunt Roope. When Cable left in 1918, he took ownership of the *quinta* with him. Cable Roope made the wines at Eira Velha from 1828 to 1918, but Graham took over from 1918 to 1938.

AT A GLANCE
QUNITA DA EIRA VELHA
Pinhão, Portugal
05-47.21.62
Owners: Peter and Richard Newman
Founded: 1978
Average production: 5,000 cases

Hunt Roope had shipped all of its vintage Ports as the brand of Tuke Holdsworth. The company and its vintage brand were sold to Ferreira in 1956.

The Newman family has a centuries-old tradition of trading with Portugal. It began in the 18th century, trading cod from Newfoundland, and soon moved to Port. At one time, the Newmans had a fleet of trading ships and would take Port from Hunt Roope in casks as ballast. The young Port would spend the winter in Newfoundland and then be shipped back to Portugal. "The Canadians got a taste for the wine," said Peter Newman, 46, a co-owner of Eira Velha who lives in England. "We still ship a Port called Newman. The Newfoundland Liquor Corporation sells Newman's Celebrated Port. We find the blend for them."

When the Newmans are at the *quinta*, the white and navy blue checked flag of the firm is still flown along with the Union Jack and flag of Portugal. The very good quality of Eira Velha's vintage Ports adds to its illustrious history.

TASTING NOTES

1987 EIRA VELHA: A good all-around 1987 with excellent fruit and tannins. Dark ruby with a purple center, aromas of grape skins and bitter chocolate, medium- to full-bodied, with grape skin flavors, medium to full tannins and a long finish. Very good potential. Last tasted: 5/90. Drink 1996-1998. Not released. **86**

1982 EIRA VELHA: Not as good as the 1978, slightly forward, but still delicious. Medium brick red, with a rich plum nose, medium-bodied, with plenty of sweet cherry flavors, medium tannins and finish. Last tasted: 3/90. Drink 1990-1993. Release: £10. Current retail: £12. Current auction: NA. **81**

1978 EIRA VELHA: A delicious 1978. Medium red-ruby, with lovely, perfumed cherry aromas, medium-bodied, with sweet, silky fruit flavors, light tannins and a lovely, long finish. Last tasted: 3/90. Drink 1990. Release: $22 (£9). Current retail: $30 (£16). Current auction: £8. **85**

Quinta do Infantado

CLASSIFICATION: *Not rated*

COLLECTIBILITY RATING: *Not rated*

The owners of Quinta do Infantado like to emphasize that they are one of the few producers of estate-grown and bottled vintage Port, and while they are among the few who produce, age and bottle their vintage Port in the Douro, they suffer like many others from what appears to be inexperience in making truly top-quality vintage Ports.

Quinta do Infantado's vintage Ports lack the concentration and structure of those from first-rate producers. They show adequate levels of sweet fruit and decent tannins but they seem to have been left too long in wood.

Nonetheless, the vintage Ports of Quinta do Infantado are perfectly acceptable to drink. They are not made for long-term aging, but wines like the 1985 and 1978 are agreeable on the palate. The 1982, on the other hand, is marginally acceptable due to its odd aromas and very dry finish.

The estate, located near Pinhão, was established in 1816. It was first owned by Prince Pedro IV, son of the Portuguese King El-Rei João VI, who later became King of Portugal. In the late 1800s, the Roseira family bought the property and still runs the estate.

Today, Quinta do Infantado includes about 70 acres of vineyards with an average age of about 20 years. Another 45 acres were grafted in 1989 and 1990. The total annual production of the estate equals about 9,000 cases, although by 1993 it should increase to 14,000.

Infantado makes a range of Ports, from simple rubies and tawnies to wood-aged and vintage Ports. All the wines are made in *lagar*. Until 1979, most of the production was sold in bulk to major shippers, including Sandeman and Taylor, according to João Roseira, the winemaker and manager of the *quinta*. Vintage Port production equals 2,000 to 3,000 cases.

Like a handful of other estate-produced and bottled vintage Port pioneers, the Roseira family is making improvements each year to make better wines. They are serious about what they do, and their wines should inevitably improve in the coming years. "The passion and care that we at Quinta do Infantado put in our wines and the small quantities sold each year make these Ports unique wines," said Roseira. "We aim to make (our) Ports as natural as possible so that they will show the character of the soil and climate where they are grown."

At a Glance

QUINTA DO INFANTADO
Rua Paolo da Gama 550, 8 E
4100 Oporto, Portugal
02-68.62.36

Owners: Roseira family

Founded: 1816

Average production: 2,000-3,000 cases

TASTING NOTES

1985 QUINTA DO INFANTADO: Pleasant on the palate, this 1985 is quite forward at this point. Deep ruby, with a very ripe and roasted nose, medium-bodied, with very sweet fruit flavors and a soft mouth-feel. Last tasted: 7/90. Drink 1992-1993. Release: $33 (£13). Current retail: $33 (£13). Current auction: NA. **76**

1982 QUINTA DO INFANTADO: Not much here; it is very simple and sweet, almost cloying. Medium red-ruby, with a roasted nut and beet nose, medium-bodied with sweet fruit flavors and a light finish. Last tasted: 7/90. Drink 1990. Release: $35 (£15). Current retail: $35 (£15). Current auction: NA. Drink 1990. **70**

1978 QUINTA DO INFANTADO: There are some lovely aromas and nice fruit flavors on the palate but it is really dry on the finish. Medium red with a garnet hue, and simple fresh cherry aromas, medium-bodied, with sweet berry flavors, light tannins and a short dry finish. Last tasted: 7/90. Drink 1990. Release: £16. Current retail: £16. Current auction: NA. **75**

QUINTA DO NOVAL
CLASSIFICATION: *SECOND TIER*

COLLECTIBILITY RATING: *AA*

BEST VINTAGES: *1931, 1934, 1927*

Quinta do Noval has had a bumpy history, which is reflected in the up-and-down quality of its vintage Ports. Drinking a Noval 1931 or 1934 is a once-in-a-lifetime experience, but a bottle of the 1978 or 1982 is a disappointment.

Perhaps these fluctuations in quality are a result of the van Zeller family's continued quest to make something as good as the 1931. Such great quality has proven elusive, and mistakes have been made along the way.

The fact that Noval declared the 1931 vintage exemplifies the house's tradition for taking risks. Most of the world was reeling from the crash of 1929 during that period, and the Port market was extremely depressed. Port shippers had already found it difficult to sell their large crop of the very good 1927, and no one could bear the thought of declaring the 1931.

Luiz Vasconcelos Porto, the great-grandfather of the Noval's current managing director, was running Noval at the time and had strong links in the United Kingdom market, which bought nearly all of Noval's production. Apparently Vasconcelos Porto could see the great quality in this 1931 and asked the opinion of a wine merchant named Butler in London.

"Mr. Butler forced my grandfather to declare the 1931," said Fernando van Zeller, who ran the firm from 1963 to 1982. "He said that the wine was so great that it had to be declared." Van Zeller said about 6,000 cases were made, and a large part was sold through Butler.

Cristiano van Zeller, managing director of Noval, said that the vintage wines are made entirely from vineyards at Quinta do Noval itself. The property of Noval is on the eastern side of the Pinhão Valley, with a perfect southwest exposure. It encompasses nearly 500 acres, with about 300 under vine.

Cristiano's sister Teresa often jokes that the impressive whitewashed terraces of the property were painted with the name "Noval" because Sandeman was wrongly using pictures of the property in the 1950s to publicize where they acquired their grapes. Sandeman knows nothing about this, but the terraces of Noval may be the most impressive in the Douro, reminiscent of terraced vineyards in the northern Rhône Valley.

AT A GLANCE
QUINTA DO NOVAL
Rua Cândido dos Reis 575
4401 Vila Nova de Gaia,
  Portugal
02-30.20.20
Owners: van Zeller family
Founded: 1813
Average production: 8,000-
  12,000 cases

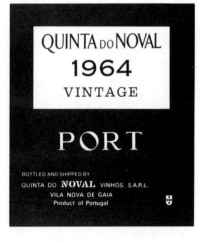

The property is broken up into various parcels of vines. The best known is Quinta do Marco. Noval vintages also include grapes from the neighboring properties of Silval, 49 acres, and Canadas, 74 acres. Noval also owns a *quinta* up the Douro River between Pinhão and Tua, Quinta da Barca, with 71 acres. Van Zeller said that grapes from Barca are not used for Noval's vintage lots.

All the wines are produced in *lagares*. Van Zeller says he will never stop treading his wines, since it is the best way to extract color and fruit during the short fermentation period. "We have no reason to change from treading," said van Zeller during the 1989 harvest. "If we have to increase the price of labor then we will increase the price of our Port. It is not that much more expensive to use a *lagar*."

Noval has a pristine fermentation area on the main property with five granite *lagares*. Two hold 22 pipes, while the others hold 20, 18 and 15. No more than three *lagares* are used at one time. Once the fermentation begins, the treading is switched over to *macacos*, wooden poles 4 or 5 feet long with numerous appendages. A worker walks along the side of the *lagar* and pushes down the cap of grape skins as it floats on top of the must during the fermentation, which helps the extraction process.

The new Port is racked and fortified into *tonéis* on the floor below the *lagares*. In the past, the young Port was moved down to Noval's lodge in Vila Nova de Gaia the spring following the harvest, but it now stays up the Douro until the second spring after the harvest, when preliminary blends are made. Noval normally produces between 8,000 and 12,000 cases of vintage.

The vintage Ports of Noval are usually slightly sweeter and fruitier than the wines from other leading Port houses, with the exception of such top Portuguese firms as Ferreira and Niepoort. The wines emphasize a strong fruit structure and slightly higher sugar content, which allows them to age extremely well. They normally drink well after about 15 years of bottle age but will continue to improve for decades.

Noval has a history of producing both fantastic and mediocre Ports, mostly because of a past policy of declaring a barrage of vintages. For instance, the 1941 Noval was never a serious vintage Port. Vintages such as 1978 and 1982 are more recent examples. These wines are shorter-term Ports — drinking well after about a decade.

Now that Cristiano, his sister and their cousins are settled in at Noval, they are making headway toward producing excellent vintage Ports as in years past, and they promise never to declare weak vintages.

The 1985 was their first step back toward what serious Port collectors expect from Noval, and although the 1987 was not declared by Noval, the small amount made was also a great improvement.

TASTING NOTES

1987 QUINTA DO NOVAL: This was not declared officially by Noval but about 1,200 cases were made. It is an exquisite wine with elegant, sweet fruit flavors. It reminds me of a top 1967. Excellent deep inky color, intense nose of blackberries and tar, full-bodied, with very sweet, round fruit flavors, well-integrated tannins and a long finish. Last tasted: 1/90. Drink 2000-2002. Not released. **89**

1985 QUINTA DO NOVAL: Very good, but seems a little stalky. It should come together with time. Medium ruby-purple, with a plum nose, full-bodied, with concentrated plum flavors, full tannins and a long finish. Last tasted: 6/90. Drink 1996-1998. Release: $22 (£13). Current retail: $33 (£22). Current auction: $24 (£12). **86**

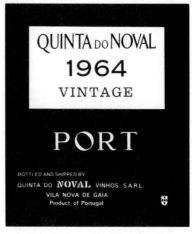

1982 QUINTA DO NOVAL: Like many 1982s, this is slightly forward and quite sweet. Deep red, with prunes and vanilla on the nose, medium-bodied, with light raisin flavors, medium tannins and a long finish. Last tasted: 6/90. Drink 1992-1994. Release: $23 (£10). Current retail: $24 (£16). Current auction: £7. **78**

1978 QUINTA DO NOVAL: Why was this wine declared? It is drinkable but not up to the standards of a top Port shipper. Medium red with a garnet edge, a nose of earth and black pepper, light, sweet plum flavors and an almost untraceable finish. Last tasted: 11/89. Drink 1990. Release: $18 (£9). Current retail: $29 (£13). Current auction: $20 (£7). **72**

1975 QUINTA DO NOVAL: This is one of the better 1975s. Medium ruby-red, with an attractive plum and tobacco nose, medium-bodied, with simple plum flavors and light tannins. The alcohol is starting to show. Last tasted: 11/89. Drink 1990. Release: £5. Current retail: $50 (£16). Current auction: $33 (£13). **81**

1970 QUINTA DO NOVAL: I have had this wine numerous times. Bottles vary from outstanding to disappointing. At its best, it is medium ruby-red, with a ripe fruit and tobacco nose, sweet, fresh plum flavors, a round mouth-feel and a silky finish. Last tasted: 12/89. Drink 1990-1993. Release: £2. Current retail: $68 (£35). Current auction: $50 (£18). **89**

1967 QUINTA DO NOVAL: This was made in very limited quantities but is extremely good. Medium ruby, with black cherry and plum aromas, medium-bodied, with silky fruit flavors, light tannins and a long, cedary, fruity finish. Last tasted: 12/89. Drink 1990. Release: £1.50. Current retail: $70 (£25). Current auction: $30 (£12). **88**

1966 QUINTA DO NOVAL: This is the best Noval made in three decades and is still fairly reasonable in price considering the quality. It is powerful, rich and fruity on the palate — almost raw. Medium ruby, with coffee and plum aromas, full-bodied, with sweet tea, coffee and plum flavors and medium tannins. It will improve with age. Last tasted: 12/89. Drink 1990. Release: £1.50. Current retail: $75 (£30). Current auction: $32 (£21). **91**

1963 QUINTA DO NOVAL: It is surprising Noval could not make a better 1963. It is still nice on the palate for those who want a mature vintage. Medium red-garnet, with smoky plum aromas, medium-bodied, with sweet, mature tobacco and cherry flavors and light, velvety tannins. Last tasted: 12/89. Drink 1990. Release: £1.15. Current retail: $120 (£40). Current auction: $105 (£31). **84**

1960 QUINTA DO NOVAL: This is a delicious example of a mature vintage Port, with lovely leather and plum aromas and sweet, mature flavors of leather, hazelnuts and plums. It is starting to dry out slightly. Last tasted: 11/89. Drink 1990. Release: £.95. Current retail: $78 (£35). Current auction: $40 (£22). **82**

1958 QUINTA DO NOVAL: Some people may find it too light, but I have been enjoying this vintage for the past two or three years. Light ruby-garnet, with lovely, delicate plum notes on the nose and palate. Best to drink up soon. Last tasted: 11/89. Drink 1990. Release: £.90. Current retail: $100 (£30). Current auction: $40 (£19). **82**

1955 QUINTA DO NOVAL: An excellent example of this sublime vintage, this is a lovely, soft, fruity Port with a wonderful balance of fruit and tannin. Medium ruby, with fresh aromas and flavors. Last tasted: 8/90. Drink 1990. Release: £1. Current retail: $150 (£57). Current auction: $100 (£37). **88**

1950 QUINTA DO NOVAL: This is surprisingly good for a 1950. I tasted it with four or five other 1950s and it was one of the best. There are plenty of smoky plum notes on the nose and palate, with a soft balance of tannin and acidity. Perfect now. Last tasted: 11/89. Drink 1990. Release: £.60. Current retail: $240 (£60). Current auction: $70 (£20). **85**

1947 QUINTA DO NOVAL: A wine with superb balance and class. Medium ruby-garnet, with a strawberry and plum nose, medium-bodied, with lovely, sweet strawberry and plum flavors and an elegant finish. Can improve with age. Last tasted: 11/89. Drink 1990. Release: £.45. Current retail: $300 (£62). Current auction: $195 (£48). **93**

1945 QUINTA DO NOVAL: This is as well-made as a fine Swiss watch. Medium ruby with a garnet rim, with aromas of perfume, flowers and oranges, medium-bodied, with sweet floral, orange and plum flavors, a silky mouth-feel and a sweet finish. Delicious. Last tasted: 11/89. Drink 1990. Release: £.40. Current retail: $325 (£92). Current auction: $250 (£72). **92**

1942 QUINTA DO NOVAL: Looks quite tired and tawny but it still retains youthful plum flavors. It needs about two hours of aeration. Medium brick red with a very light amber edge, with a ripe, sweet plum and vanilla nose, full-bodied, with velvety, sweet, round plum flavors. Gentle, sweet and caressing on the finish. Last tasted: 4/90. Drink 1990. Release: £.30. Current retail: $200 (£75). Current auction: NA. **86**

1941 QUINTA DO NOVAL: I have only had this wine once, and it was well past its prime. Not many shippers made a 1941. Already brown, oxidized on the nose and palate. Last tasted: 9/85. Best to avoid. Release: £.30. Current retail: $70 (£25). Current auction: NA. **50**

1938 QUINTA DO NOVAL: It was barely holding on when I tasted it in 1985 but it still showed some interesting spicy leather aromas and flavors. It's more like a mature, light-bodied tawny at this point. Last tasted: 9/85. Drink 1990. Release: £.30. Current retail: $110 (£65). Current auction: NA. **71**

1934 QUINTA DO NOVAL: This wine was a knockout in a recent blind tasting of nearly a dozen 1934s and 1935s. In 1985, however, another bottle was past its prime. The good bottle was in suspended animation; ruby-red with rich raisin and cassis aromas, very ripe, smoky raisin flavors, medium tannins and a lingering finish. Good bottles will improve with age. Last tasted: 2/90. Drink 1990. Release: £.30. Current retail: $305 (£75). Current auction: $240 (£55). **98**

1931 QUINTA DO NOVAL: On most occasions, this wine lives up to its lofty reputation. It has an impressive balance of fruit and tannin, with plenty of fresh, youthful fruit flavors. Deep ruby, with ripe chocolate, berry and cherry aromas, full-bodied, with very round, sweet fruit flavors and silky tannins. Last tasted: 11/89. Drink 1990. Release: £.30. Current retail: $1,000 (£430). Current auction: $700 (£330). **99**

1927 QUINTA DO NOVAL: Still incredibly tough and youthful. It drinks better one or two hours after decanting. Deep ruby-garnet, with ripe raspberry and plum aromas, full-bodied, with thick, chewy fruit flavors and a long finish. Last tasted: 12/89. Drink 1990. Release: £.20. Current retail: $275 (£126). Current auction: $275 (£97). **93**

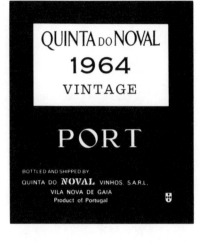

QUINTA DO NOVAL NACIONAL
CLASSIFICATION: *FIRST TIER*

COLLECTIBILITY RATING: *AAAA*

BEST VINTAGES: *1931, 1963, 1966*

AT A GLANCE
QUINTA DO NOVAL NACIONAL
Rua Candido dos Reis 575
4401 Vila Nova de Gaia,
Portugal
02-30.20.20
Owners: van Zeller family
Founded: 1813
Average production: 200-250 cases

No other Port is as collectible as Quinta do Noval Nacional. It consistently sells at auction for two to three times the price of any other well-known vintage Port. Moreover, it holds the record for the most expensive Port ever sold. A bottle of 1931 Nacional went for nearly $6,000 at the Graycliff Restaurant in the Bahamas, although the regular market value is about $3,000 to $4,000.

There is much confusion and mystique surrounding this very rare Port. It is produced entirely from ungrafted vines in a section of Quinta do Noval's 300 acres of vineyards. " 'Nacional' means national, or from the soil," said Cristiano van Zeller, managing director of Noval. "It is from the soil of the nation."

Nacional has little in common with Noval's standard vintage Ports, other than being made on the same property. Van Zeller believes 1931 was Nacional's first vintage, but his uncle Fernando, who ran the property from 1963 to 1982, said that some vintages were made during the 1920s. Regardless of its origins, the 1931 Nacional has always been an extraordinary Port. Many of the Nacional vines were only six years old at the time, since replanting of the parcel began in 1925, but the 1931 was black as ink and as thick and concentrated as molasses when I tasted it in 1989. It is one of the greatest bottles of wine I have ever drunk.

The 1963 is equally amazing and still tastes like a barrel sample. When Bruce Guimaraens of Fonseca tasted it in November 1989, he said, "I am not sure how to evaluate this Port. I have never encountered anything like it."

Nonetheless, like most of the world's great wines, Nacional has had its ups and downs. The vintages in the late 1970s and early 1980s have not been up to Nacional's stellar standards. For example, the 1980 and 1982 Nacionals are good Ports but they clearly are not in the upper echelons of their respective vintages. The 1978 Nacional may have been better left undeclared. But the 1985 Nacional has marked a return to greatness, and the 1987 continues the trend.

Unfortunately, Nacional is almost impossible to buy unless at auction or on a restaurant wine list. The wine has not been sold commercially, but has been offered as an incentive to trade clients, such as United Kingdom and U.S. agents, who buy Noval's regular vintage Ports. The ratio usually has been six bottles of Nacional for every 50 cases of the regular vintage Port. This policy may change, however.

Only about 200 to 250 cases of Nacional are made in any given year. Noval made about five pipes of Port in 1987 and 2.5 pipes in 1989. It is produced each year, but only bottled on its own when Noval declares a vintage. The exceptions are 1962, 1964, 1967, 1980 and 1987. Otherwise, it is used as a component of the firm's other Ports.

There are approximately 5,000 ungrafted vines at Noval with an average age of about 30 years. In 1988 van Zeller planted another 973 vines, primarily Touriga Nacional, Tinta Francisca and Tinta Cão. There is also a substantial amount of Sousão, a less popular variety that makes extremely deep-colored wines.

The Douro Valley, like most vine-growing regions in Europe, is infested with phylloxera, the louse that destroyed European vineyards in the late 1800s. There is little doubt that phylloxera is also in Noval's vineyards, since its soil composition is the same as that of other vineyards in the Douro and is not a soil type in which the pest does not survive, such as those with an extremely high percentage of sand.

"I really don't know if there is phylloxera or not," said van Zeller during the 1989 harvest. "The vines have not been attacked. It is completely fumigated. For many years, the ungrafted vines were treated with sulfur. The treatment lasted for about 30 years during the turn of the century. Perhaps the vineyards are disinfected."

The Nacional vines face southwest, ensuring perfect exposure to the sun. Compared to the grafted vines just adjacent, the foliage of Nacional vines is much less lush and green. This suggests a much less vigorous growing cycle, which may be one reason for the vineyard's low yields, about half the norm. The old age of the vines may also contribute to the low yields.

Van Zeller does periodically replant the Nacional parcel, but only on a plant-by-plant basis. He simply waits for a vine to die from either age or natural causes and replants in its place. He usually plants a shoot from an adjacent vine. All the cultivation in the vineyard is done by hand.

This hands-on approach is carried through to the fermentation of the wine. The three pipes' worth of grapes are fermented in a 15-pipe *lagar* and trodden during the entire two to three days of fermentation. The amount of must only goes up to the ankles of the treaders — a normal *lagar* is filled to midway up their thighs — so the must is extremely well worked, ensuring an outstanding extraction of color and fruit character. After the fermentation and fortification, the wine is handled like any other vintage Port, but it is kept separate. Van Zeller ages it for a year in small lodge pipes and then another year in small stainless steel vats before bottling.

Many other Port shippers claim the wine is simply a gimmick. "If we only made 300 cases of a particular vintage Port, we could do exactly the same," said one neighboring vintner. Others, such as Croft, have gone as far as planting ungrafted vines and making their own rendition of the Nacional. Van Zeller doesn't seem too worried. "Nacional is Nacional. Let the others try to make something like it."

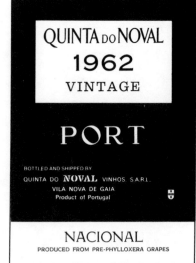

QUINTA DO NOVAL
1962
VINTAGE

PORT

BOTTLED AND SHIPPED BY
QUINTA DO **NOVAL** VINHOS S.A.R.L.
VILA NOVA DE GAIA
Product of Portugal

NACIONAL
PRODUCED FROM PRE-PHYLLOXERA GRAPES

TASTING NOTES

1987 QUINTA DO NOVAL NACIONAL: This Port shows the essence of freshly crushed grapes. It is as dark as black ink, with a very closed nose, very full-bodied and extremely tannic, with masses of fruit flavors. Last tasted: 1/90. Drink 2005-2010. Not released. **94**

1985 QUINTA DO NOVAL NACIONAL: After a few rather weak years, this puts Nacional back on top. Very deep ruby-black, with ripe raisiny aromas, an abundance of fruit and tannin and an extremely thick and viscous finish. Last tasted: 11/89. Drink 2002-2007. Release: NA. Current retail: $200 (£75). Current auction: NA. **95**

1982 QUINTA DO NOVAL NACIONAL: This could have been the best Port made in the often disappointing 1982 vintage, but it seems to have been left in wood too long. Medium ruby, with intense aromas of grape skins and vanilla, full-bodied, with concentrated black cherry flavors and very good structure. Last tasted: 11/89. Drink 1995-1998. Release: NA. Current retail: $190 (£75). Current auction: NA. **86**

1980 QUINTA DO NOVAL NACIONAL: Good, but not what one expects from Nacional. Medium red, with a bouquet of chocolate and roasted coffee, medium-bodied, with roasted flavors, medium tannins and a silky finish. Last tasted: 2/90. Drink 1990-1993. Release: NA. Current retail: $280 (£81). Current auction: NA. **80**

1978 QUINTA DO NOVAL NACIONAL: This should not have been bottled as Nacional. Medium ruby, with chocolate, earth and raisin aromas and flavors, medium-bodied, rather lean and tough and lacking in fruit. Last tasted: 11/89. Drink 1990-1992. Release: NA. Current retail: $235 (£92). Current auction: $155 (£41). **77**

1975 QUINTA DO NOVAL NACIONAL: This is one of the better 1975s, but it shows how weak the vintage is when even Nacional comes out on the light side. Medium ruby-red, with a burnt coffee and chocolate nose, medium-bodied, with a lovely balance of sweet fruit flavors and tannins and a medium finish. Last tasted: 11/89. Drink 1990-1995. Release: NA. Current retail: $285 (£115). Current auction: $170 (£66). **86**

1970 QUINTA DO NOVAL NACIONAL: A massive wine, what one expects from Nacional in a solid vintage. Deep ruby, with an intense ripe berry nose, full-bodied, very tightly knit, with masses of fruit flavors and tannins and a very long finish. Last tasted: 11/89. Drink 1995-2000. Release: NA. Current retail: $370 (£144). Current auction: $190 (£85). **98**

1967 QUINTA DO NOVAL NACIONAL: This is exciting to drink now but try to hold yourself back. Deep ruby, with a ripe cassis and plum nose, lots of cassis, vanilla and fruit flavors, medium tannins and a long finish. Last tasted: 11/89. Drink 1990-1995. Release: NA. Current retail: $375 (£144). Current auction: £55. **95**

1966 QUINTA DO NOVAL NACIONAL: The focused fruit zeros in on the palate. Excellent deep ruby, very intense black cherry and plum aromas, full-bodied, with incredibly focused fruit flavors, full tannins and a balanced finish. Last tasted: 11/89. Drink 1990-1998. Release: NA. Current retail: $300 (£144). Current auction: $240 (£92). **98**

1964 QUINTA DO NOVAL NACIONAL: A bit of a disappointment, coming between the fabulous 1966 and 1963, but it is an elegant Port nonetheless, with silky fruit flavors similar to a mature claret. Medium red with a garnet edge, delicate plum aromas, with light, silky tannins and a lovely balance of fruit flavors on the finish. Last tasted: 2/90. Drink 1990. Release: NA. Current retail: $350 (£144). Current auction: $130. **84**

1963 QUINTA DO NOVAL NACIONAL: This wine is so incredibly youthful, it is hard to believe it isn't a 1985. Still inky black in color, with fresh grapy, earthy aromas, extremely full-bodied, with thick, tough, intense grapy flavors, full tannins and a tight finish. It still seems closed and dumb. Last tasted: 11/89. Drink 2000-2005. Release: NA. Current retail: $750 (£300). Current auction: $660 (£233). **100**

1962 QUINTA DO NOVAL NACIONAL: Very good for an undeclared vintage. Medium ruby, with intense strawberry aromas, medium-bodied, with silky, sweet fruit flavors and a medium finish. Last tasted: 11/89. Drink 1990. Release: NA. Current retail: $350 (£144). Current auction: $260 (£125). **86**

1960 QUINTA DO NOVAL NACIONAL: This is quite good for the vintage, but not a blockbuster. Medium ruby-garnet, with a light cherry and licorice nose, medium-bodied, with sweet, rich fruit flavors that slowly fade on the palate. Last tasted: 11/89. Drink 1990. Release: NA. Current retail: $385 (£173). Current auction: $265 (£100). **84**

1950 QUINTA DO NOVAL NACIONAL: Most of the 1950s are starting to turn to tawnies, but this is still 100 percent vintage. Medium light ruby with a garnet edge, rich sawdust, plum and cedar aromas, full-bodied, with sweet plum and earth flavors and a long finish. Last tasted: 11/89. Drink 1990. Release: NA. Current retail: $850 (£230). Current auction: £130. **90**

1931 QUINTA DO NOVAL NACIONAL: Perhaps one of the greatest wines ever produced. I tasted it with a London collector who bought the wine at auction in 1988. The Port is still incredibly rich and youthful, medium ruby, with a focused chocolate and cherry nose, medium-bodied, with great balance, a superb concentration of fruit and a never-ending finish. Will continue to improve. Last tasted: 11/89. Drink 1990. Release: NA. Current retail: $3,700 (£1,725). Current auction: £700. **100**

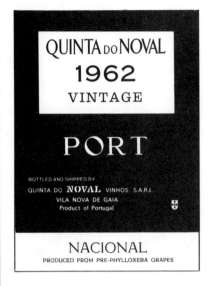

QUINTA DO PANASCAL
CLASSIFICATION: *Not rated*
COLLECTIBILITY RATING: *Not rated*

Making a single-*quinta* vintage Port from Quinta do Panascal seems to be more of an afterthought by Fonseca. It bought the property in 1978, and the wines have apparently not been good enough to go into Fonseca vintage blends. That may change, however.

The quality of the vintage wines produced here has not been spectacular, although they are improving. The 1987 Panascal is the best yet, with a balance of cassis flavors and medium tannins. The 1986 was also a well-crafted, solid single-*quinta* vintage. They both need about eight to nine years of bottle age before drinking.

Early vintages appear out of balance and rather harsh, especially the 1984. It also seems odd to make a single-*quinta* Port in a year like 1985, when Fonseca made a declaration. Bruce Guimaraens, vice chairman and winemaker for Fonseca, said his firm had some good wines from Panascal after the 1985 vintage, so he decided to bottle them.

Located up the Tavora River, the *quinta* has 45 acres of vineyards in full production, which will increase to 178 by mid-1990. Production should reach about 160 pipes of Port. The wines are made in auto-vinification tanks, although Guimaraens plans to return to using *lagares*. Single-*quinta* bottlings of Panascal have totaled just a few thousand cases so far.

Judging from my tastings, the Panascal wines have not yet lived up to Fonseca's great reputation, but there have been extensive plantings at the *quinta* in recent years. Guimaraens remains bullish about the property. "We have planted the vineyards, and those vines will produce top, top quality wines," he said. "I am sure of it."

TASTING NOTES

1987 QUINTA DO PANASCAL: A typical velvety example of the vintage. Medium purple, with cassis and tomato aromas, medium-bodied, with cassis flavors, medium tannins and a long finish. Well balanced. Last tasted: 2/90. Drink 1996-1998. Not released. **82**

1986 QUINTA DO PANASCAL: Very sweet, well-focused fruit flavors and a decent backbone. Medium purple, with earthy, wet leaf aromas, medium-bodied, with medium tannins and a slightly flabby finish. Last tasted: 2/90. Drink 1994-1995. Not released. **79**

1985 QUINTA DO PANASCAL: This was an improvement over the weak 1984. Deep ruby, with aromas of grapes and tar, full-bodied, with very hard, slightly harsh tannins and a lean, hard finish. Lacks balance. Last tasted: 2/90. Drink 1995-1998. Not released. **78**

1984 QUINTA DO PANASCAL: A weak, borderline wine. Medium red, with a floral plum nose, medium-bodied, with sweet, mature, slightly diluted flavors and a medium roasted finish. Last tasted: 2/90. Drink 1990. Not released. **70**

1983 QUINTA DO PANASCAL: A little coarse, but it shows very ripe fruit flavors and powerful tannins. Needs time. Medium ruby with a slightly red hue, roasted coffee and berry aromas, full-bodied, with a very tannic backbone, roasted vanilla and berry flavors and an aggressive finish. Last tasted: 2/90. Drink 1993-1995. Not released. **79**

QUINTA DA ROEDA

CLASSIFICATION: *FIFTH TIER*

COLLECTIBILITY RATING: *Not rated*

BEST VINTAGES: *1967, 1983*

Croft's Quinta da Roêda is situated in one of the Douro Valley's most bucolic settings. The shade of the veranda of its plantation-style house is a relaxing spot during the harvest. Though its setting is tranquil, Roêda is a winemaking machine, producing more than 4,000 pipes of Port in a vintage.

Quinta da Roêda is Croft's key wine production installation in the Douro, where hundreds of area growers bring their crops to be processed each harvest. Roêda is also the backbone of Croft's vintage Ports, and its own 250 acres of vineyards can produce excellent wines.

In undeclared years, Croft occasionally makes a single-*quinta* vintage Port from Roêda, which can be very good. For example, the 1983 Roêda is miles ahead in quality of Croft's declared 1982 vintage. It is rich in black cherry and raspberry flavors, with a lovely structure of integrated tannins. It needs about 10 years of bottle age before drinking.

The 1978 Roêda also compares favorably to the vintage 1977 Croft. It is equally opulent, with lovely roasted nut, chocolate and fruit notes on the nose and palate. The 1978 Roêda is drinkable now, and perhaps does not have the staying power of the 1977, but it is very comparable in overall quality.

Roêda single-*quinta* vintage Ports can be inconsistent, however. The 1980 Roêda has evolved quickly and has a rather boring simple fruit and light tannin structure. The most recent vintage of Roêda, the 1987, is also perplexing. When I first tasted it in early 1989, it was a powerful and rich young wine. Now, it seems to be stripped of much of that character. Maybe the wine is going through a dumb period.

Quinta da Roêda is at the east end of the village of Pinhão. Croft bought the property in 1895. All the wine is made in autovinification tanks. The *quinta's* total production should equal about 400 pipes of Port by mid-1990, when new vineyard plantings come on line. Roêda also has a small plot of 4,000 ungrafted vines, which Croft may one day use to make something comparable to Quinta do Noval's legendary Nacional vintage Port.

"Roêda produces wines with a lot of aromas," said John Burnett, managing director of Croft. "We don't produce the darkest wines from here. Depth of color is not everything. But the quality should be very good."

Roêda single-*quinta* wines may be slightly lighter in color and more elegant than many other big-name vintage Ports, but they still represent solid values for drinking. Production is limited to about 6,000 to 8,000 cases.

TASTING NOTES

1987 QUINTA DA ROEDA: I tasted this Port just after it was blended and it was very impressive. But the last time I tasted it, it had an odd, "off" character on the nose and palate. Medium purple, with a closed, slightly smoky nose, full-bodied, with grapy, earthy fruit flavors, medium tannins and an odd, slightly volatile finish. Final decision pending. Last tasted: 2/90. Drink 1997-2000. Not released. **79**

1983 QUINTA DA ROEDA: Much better than the 1982 Croft, this is rich and well structured with lovely fruit. Medium to deep ruby, with a youthful grape and berry nose, full-bodied, with well-knit medium tannins and more than enough rich raspberry and black cherry flavors to keep it going for years. Last tasted: 2/90. Drink 1995-1997. Release: $22. Current retail: $22. Current auction: NA. **85**

1980 QUINTA DA ROEDA: Evolving quickly; should be drunk very soon. Medium red with a brown edge, chocolate and roasted nut aromas, medium-bodied, with medium tannins and a rather hollow center of the palate. A simple wine. Last tasted: 2/90. Drink 1990. Release: $22 (£8). Current retail: $30 (£16). Current auction: £8. **75**

1978 QUINTA DA ROEDA: Ripe and tough; needs more time. Forward medium to deep ruby, with a garnet rim, ripe bitter chocolate, roasted nut and blackberry aromas, full-bodied, with medium tannins and ripe fruit flavors. Last tasted: 2/90. Drink 1990-1994. Release: $22 (£8). Current retail: $25 (£15). Current auction: $17 (£8). **83**

1967 QUINTA DA ROEDA: I have tasted several bottles and some were extremely tired and high in volatile acidity. The good ones, however, show a nice complexity of cherry flavors with earthy undertones on the nose and palate. Medium red with a brick red hue, attractive nose of cherries and earth, medium-bodied, with silky, soft, ripe fruit flavors and a long finish. Last tasted: 1/90. Drink 1990. Release: £8. Current retail: $60 (£18). Current auction: $25 (£12). **85**

QUINTA DA ROMANEIRA

CLASSIFICATION: *Not rated*

COLLECTIBILITY RATING: *Not rated*

BEST VINTAGE: *1987*

The Vinagre family has been producing Ports at Quinta da Romaneira since the mid-19th century, but has been bottling and selling its own vintage Ports only since 1986. Like a handful of other very good Douro growers, Vinagre decided to take advantage of the change in rules in 1986, which allowed growers in the Douro to ship their wines themselves. Before, the property sold its wines in bulk to other shippers.

"When we were given the opportunity to export our own wines, we thought we had to do it," said owner Antonio Barbosa Vinagre, who had been keeping back stocks of wines in cask since 1967. He also owns a wine property in the *vinho verde* area.

Vinagre is pleased with the outcome of his decision. His wines are selling well in Great Britain, the United States and Portugal. He makes rubies and tawnies as well as vintage. His total production is about 15,000 cases. Vintage equals about 2,000 when declared.

His two most recent vintages, the 1987 and 1985, are good wines, and each year the estate does better. The 1987 shows a good intensity of fruit, good tannins and a medium finish. The 1985 was not quite as good, with strong musty and earthy aromas. Romaneira is honing its style.

Quinta da Romaneira includes about 940 acres of land. Nearly 175 are planted to vineyards. When new plantings come on line in the mid-1990s, production will increase to about 400 pipes. Fermentations are in *lagares*, and the wines are aged on the property in 7,000- to 23,000-liter casks.

The 1935 Romaneira I tasted came from the cellar of Alistair Robertson, the majority shareholder of Taylor Fladgate and Fonseca. Robertson said that his relatives, the Yeatman family, had bought and bottled a pipe of the single-*quinta* wine in 1938. Some of the 1935 Romaneira also went into the Taylor vintage blend.

TASTING NOTES

1987 QUINTA DA ROMANEIRA: Earthy and well structured, showing aging potential. Medium to deep purple, with earthy grape aromas, full-bodied, with lots of tannins and a good depth of earthy fruit flavors. Last tasted: 1/90. Drink 1996-1997. Not released. **81**

1985 QUINTA DA ROMANEIRA: Very rustic in style. Medium ruby, with an earthy licorice nose, medium-bodied, with round tannins, good fruit flavors and some grip on the finish. Last tasted: 1/90. Drink 1992-1994. Release: $29. Current retail: $29. Current auction: NA. **78**

1935 QUINTA DA ROMANEIRA: This bottle came from the owners of Taylor, which formerly used Romaneira's wines in its vintage blends. Deep ruby with a garnet edge, ripe raspberry aromas, medium-bodied, with sweet fruit and earth flavors and a great backbone of tannin and acidity. An impressive wine. Last tasted: 2/90. Drink 1990. Not available. **90**

QUINTA DE LA ROSA

CLASSIFICATION: *Not rated*

COLLECTIBILITY RATING: *Not rated*

BEST VINTAGES: <u>*1960, 1927*</u>

AT A GLANCE

QUINTA DE LA ROSA
5084 Pinhão, Portugal
05-47.22.54

Owners: Bergqvist family

Founded: 1906

Average production: 1,000-2,000 cases

If any new single-*quinta* operation succeeds in making and marketing serious vintage Port, Quinta de la Rosa should; it already has a solid track record for producing very good vintages.

La Rosa for the past three decades has been selling its wines to the Robertson Brothers, now a part of the House of Sandeman. The Bergqvist family, which has owned the *quinta* since 1906, is not very keen on showing people their wines from the mid-1970s and onward, since they are rather light and insipid. Owner Tim Bergqvist attributes the mediocre quality of his wines during those vintages to Robertson's methods of fermentation. Until Bergqvist severed his relationship with Robertson, the company ran the harvest there and made all the wines with the dismal *movimosto* method.

The 1988 Quinta de la Rosa, however, is a giant step in the right direction. It is the first vintage the Bergqvists made themselves with help from their nearby friends, the Symingtons, who produce such Ports as Graham, Warre and Dow. The 1988 is not a great Port, but it shows good potential, with a dark ruby-purple color and clean licorice and black cherry notes on the nose and palate. It just lacks a bit of grip and structure to make it a long-term vintage Port.

Mature vintages of la Rosa are very good indeed. One of the most impressive is the 1960. It is a well-structured, classy wine from a light, elegant year. Many of the 1960s are beginning to fade a bit, but this wine is still going strong. The 1927 la Rosa is also good. I tried it in a blind tasting of 10 other 1927s, all from the top houses, and it easily held its own. The old wines came from Bergqvist's private cellar. Each vintage the family bottled a pipe or two for its own consumption.

"La Rosa was always one of the best *quintas* and we spent a lot of time putting it back together," said Bergqvist, 58, who with Sophia, his energetic, management consultant daughter, is running the property. Sophia, 30, came up with an ingenious idea of selling their coming vintages *en primeur*, as futures. Anyone willing to invest £1,000 receives five cases of Port each year over five years, perhaps even vintage, depending on the quality of the harvest. They have sold the idea to about 156 people.

Bergqvist said that the *quinta* is made up of eight smaller properties. Each has its own microclimate and each batch of wine will be kept separate during the vinification and maturation. The wines will be blended later, in the same manner that a Bordeaux château does its *assemblage*. The *quinta* includes 295 acres of land, and about 100 are under vine. Production should reach 200 pipes of Port by 1995.

The winery at the property is classic in every sense and has a 700-pipe storage capacity. The eight granite *lagares* range in size from 10 to 24 pipes. They feed down to 24 *tonéis*, oval wooden casks ranging in size from 60 to 180 hectoliters. There is also a large 660-hectoliter wooden vat for blending and bottling. The winery's dirt floors retain humidity. Walking through la Rosa's winery, with its wooden beams and whitewashed walls, is like strolling back through time 100 years. Bergqvist plans to modernize the winery, replacing four *lagares* with stainless steel temperature-controlled fermentation tanks.

The main house, where the Bergqvists live when they are in Portugal, is also a wonderful example of an old *quinta*. It is lavishly decorated with antiques, old paintings and drawings of the region. Tim Bergqvist's late mother, Claire, was a legendary figure in the Douro. She was one of the few expatriates who lived virtually full-time in the Douro Valley. She was the only daughter of Albert Feuerheerd, whose family came to the area in 1815 and started a company shipping textiles to Germany. The family also had a Port shipping company with the same name. Feuerheerd Brothers now belongs to Barros, Almeida, the large Portuguese house, which bought the firm in 1933.

TASTING NOTES

1988 QUINTA DE LA ROSA: This was a barrel sample. But this was the first wine the owners made themselves and it was a respectable debut. Medium to deep purple, with intense black cherry and licorice aromas and flavors, full-bodied, with medium tannins and a short finish. A little simple. Last tasted: 5/90. Drink 1996-1998. Not available. **80-84**

1972 QUINTA DE LA ROSA: Light but very drinkable. Ruby-garnet, with a light berry nose, light-bodied, with delicate berry flavors, light tannins and a rather dry, short finish. Last tasted: 10/89. Drink 1990. Not released. **76**

1966 QUINTA DE LA ROSA: Has good backbone, but lacks a bit of flesh. Medium ruby-garnet, with a perfumed berry nose, medium-bodied, with lovely licorice and berry flavors but slightly short on the finish. Last tasted: 10/89. Drink 1990. Not released. **82**

1963 QUINTA DE LA ROSA: Very firm in the mouth, with ample fruit to keep on improving. Medium ruby with an amber edge, concentrated on the nose and palate, with a ripe blackberry character and a rather dry, medium finish. Last tasted: 10/89. Drink 1990. Not released. **85**

1960 QUINTA DE LA ROSA: This is an elegant wine with focused fruit — a very good example of a light vintage. Medium to deep ruby

with a garnet edge, rich raspberry and perfume aromas, medium-bodied, with very good backbone, black pepper and raspberry flavors and a long finish. Drinking well now. Last tasted: 10/89. Drink 1990. Not released. **88**

1927 FEUERHEERD QUINTA DE LA ROSA: As classy as an old Bugatti automobile and probably even harder to find. It was one of three bottles left in the cellars of the owners of the *quinta*. Light ruby-garnet, showing earthy cassis and spice aromas, medium-bodied, with a balance of lovely cassis flavors, good acidity and plenty of sweet fruit on the finish. Last tasted: 12/89. Drink 1990. Not released. **87**

QUINTA DE VAL DA FIGUERIA

CLASSIFICATION: *Not rated*

COLLECTIBILITY RATING: *Not rated*

Quinta de Val da Figueria is one of the newest entries in estate-bottled vintage Ports, and it could very well set an excellent standard, if the quality of the 1987 is any indication of things to come. The 1987 is a well-balanced, well-made wine with elegant fruit flavors and fine tannins. My only criticism is that it could use a little more flesh on the palate. Only about 60 cases were bottled.

Val da Figueria is on the north bank of the Pinhão River next to Quinta de la Rosa on the outskirts of Pinhão village. The property has about 43 acres of vineyards and produces between 100 and 110 pipes of Port. In recent years the wines have been sold to Cálem, although Taylor bought some in the past. All the Ports are made in *lagares*.

The *quinta* is owned by Port veteran Alfredo Cálem Hoelzer, 73, who has worked for decades at the house of Cálem. His son João Filipe, 40, works for Croft in production and quality control. Hoelzer called his 1987 vintage Port a trial to see how his wines would sell under the *quinta* label. He hopes one day to sell most of his *quinta's* production as vintage or other premium Port. Production of the vintage alone could reach 2,500 cases in a good year.

"I want to keep the name on the *quinta* just like anyone else," he said. "We want to sell our own wines."

AT A GLANCE
QUINTA DE VAL DA FIGUERIA
Covas do Duoro
5085 Pinhão, Portugal
05-47.21.59
Owner: Alfredo Cálem Hoelzer
Average production: 1,000-3,000 cases

TASTING NOTES

1987 QUINTA DE VAL DA FIGUERIA: Extremely well crafted, with a firm structure of medium tannins, fresh strawberry flavors and a floral finish. The fruit and tannin are well integrated and focused on the palate. Great potential here for a new Douro shipper. Last tasted: 2/90. Drink 1996. Not released. **83**

QUINTA DE VARGELLAS
CLASSIFICATION: *FOURTH TIER*

COLLECTIBILITY RATING: *A*

BEST VINTAGES: *1987, 1986, 1984*

On one of the walls of an expansive room housing six stone *lagares* at Quinta de Vargellas, a black-and-white illustration shows a group of men in suits and bowler hats standing at the train station at Vargellas. The picture's title reads "Last Outpost of the Empire No. 207."

The caption is not complete fiction. Vargellas is one of the easternmost premium *quintas* in the Douro Valley, and it remains a benchmark for vintage Port. For decades its wines have been key components of Taylor vintages. In undeclared years, Taylor has for centuries made single-*quinta* vintage Ports from Vargellas, which have become extremely popular among vintage Port aficionados.

Tasting a pure Vargellas, it is easy to see where Taylor vintage Ports get their rigid backbones. A wine like the 1984 Vargellas shows the true style of vintage Ports from the *quinta* — very firm in the mouth, with hard tannins and focused violet and berry flavors. Vargellas vintage Ports drink best after about 10 years of bottle age.

Mature bottles of Vargellas last fairly well, although the 1958 and 1961 are both past their primes. The 1964, 1965 and 1967 were all drinking well in 1990, although I think they were probably better about five or six years before.

Bruce Guimaraens, winemaker and vice chairman of Fonseca and estates director for Taylor Fladgate, said that his company has records indicating that the first bottling of Quinta de Vargellas was in 1822, and that some single-*quinta* Ports were shipped to London. The wines were made primarily for family consumption.

The *quinta* dates back to the beginning of the 19th century. It was originally three properties: Quinta do Vale, Quinta de Vargellas do Meio and Quinta de Vargellas de Baixo. When the house of Taylor Fladgate took control of the property in 1893, Vargellas had already been combined with the other two *quintas*. The newly formed *quinta* was in total disarray due to the phylloxera epidemic, and production was down to three pipes. It was the beginning of a long and expensive renovation project. It was not until 1958 that Vargellas went on the market again.

Today the estate includes about 250 acres of vineyards, producing about 300 pipes of Port. Aside from its impressive house, complete with lavish accommodations and swimming pool, Vargellas is one of the most modern wineries in the region, with numerous advanced, temperature-controlled stainless steel fermentation tanks. The seven 15-pipe stone *lagares* are also still used.

The Vargellas winery normally processes about 1,000 pipes of grape must in each harvest. Grapes from neighboring *quintas* are made into Port there. All the grapes from Vargellas' own vineyards are still trodden in *lagares*. The production of a single-*quinta* vintage from Vargellas ranges from 6,000 to 12,000 cases.

"You can control it better with stainless tanks," said Alistair Robertson, managing director of Taylor. "But Vargellas is always done in *lagares*, whether for single-*quinta* or vintage wines. There is a small difference in quality between the two. Six to eight times out of 10, we prefer the *lagar* wines. Why should we change?"

The only change with Quinta de Vargellas wines has been for the better, as the quality of recent vintages suggests. They may not be vintage Taylor, but they represent extremely good quality for the money.

TASTING NOTES

1987 QUINTA DE VARGELLAS: Rich, thick and concentrated, like pure crème de cassis. Deep purple, with a powerful nose of cassis and perfume, full-bodied, with masses of fruit flavors and plenty of tannins. A monumental wine. Last tasted: 2/90. Drink 2000-2005. Not released. **93**

1986 QUINTA DE VARGELLAS: Surprisingly tough and big for a 1986. Deep inky color, with an intense nose of anise and blackberries, full-bodied, with an excellent tannic backbone and long, rich violet and berry flavors on the finish. Last tasted: 2/90. Drink 1997-1999. Not released. **88**

1984 QUINTA DE VARGELLAS: Extremely fresh, with plenty of fruit and an attractive, classy hardness on the finish. Deep inky ruby, with black cherry and anise aromas, full-bodied, with hard tannins and an elegant balance of lovely fruit flavors. Last tasted: 2/90. Drink 1994-1996. Not released. **87**

1982 QUINTA DE VARGELLAS: Forward, but still has rich and beautiful fruit flavors. Medium to deep ruby, with licorice and ripe fruit aromas, full-bodied, with round tannins and plenty of blackberry and violet flavors. Last tasted: 2/90. Drink 1993-1994. Not released. **81**

1978 QUINTA DE VARGELLAS: I have had this wine numerous times, and there seems to be some bottle variation. I have had boring examples, but the last bottle I had was very good. Medium to deep ruby, with an intense floral and grape nose, full-bodied, with hard tannins and a firm backbone. Very good finesse. Last tasted: 2/90. Drink 1990-1995. Release: $29 (£6). Current retail: $29 (£18). Current auction: NA. **85**

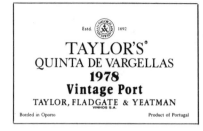

1976 QUINTA DE VARGELLAS: Fresh and fruity, but a bit unexciting. Medium ruby-red, with light tar and floral aromas, medium-bodied, with integrated tannins and fresh fruit flavors. Last tasted: 2/90. Drink 1990. Release: $29 (£5). Current retail: $29 (£19). Current auction: NA. **81**

1974 QUINTA DE VARGELLAS: The nose is attractive, but the wine is rather dull and hard. Deep red, decent perfumed nose, medium-bodied, with hard tannins and a short finish. Last tasted: 2/90. Drink 1990. Release: $27 (£3.50). Current retail: $35 (£20). Current auction: NA. **78**

1972 QUINTA DE VARGELLAS: Delicious, with more than enough fruit to keep a taster occupied. Medium ruby with a red edge, cherry and blackberry nose, medium-bodied, with a silky, elegant mouth-feel and plenty of fresh blackberry flavors. Last tasted: 2/90. Drink 1990. Release: £2. Current retail: $35 (£20). Current auction: $21 (£13). **84**

1969 QUINTA DE VARGELLAS: Delicious now, but has the depth of fruit and strength to keep improving. Red with a deep red center, lovely violet nose, medium-bodied, with silky tannins and a medium finish. Quite hard still. Last tasted: 2/90. Drink 1990. Release: £1.80. Current retail: $50 (£20). Current auction: £19. **85**

1968 QUINTA DE VARGELLAS: A pleasant, simple vintage for current drinking. Medium red with a garnet edge, aromas of milk chocolate and flowers, medium-bodied, with sweet, silky chocolate and fruit flavors and a long, grapy finish. Last tasted: 2/90. Drink 1990. Release: £1.60. Current retail: $55 (£20). Current auction: NA. **82**

1967 QUINTA DE VARGELLAS: Lovely, elegant and balanced. Medium ruby, with a fine violet nose, medium-bodied, with good but slightly simple fruit flavors. Last tasted: 2/90. Drink 1990. Release: £1.50. Current retail: $60 (£20). Current auction: £13. **82**

1965 QUINTA DE VARGELLAS: Well balanced, with an attractive chocolate and roasted nut character. Not a blockbuster. Medium red with a light rim, chocolate and vanilla aromas, medium-bodied, with sweet chocolate and fruit flavors and a sweet, roasted nut finish. Last tasted: 2/90. Drink 1990. Release: £1.20. Current retail: $60 (£20). Current auction: NA. **80**

1964 QUINTA DE VARGELLAS: Starting to dry out, but still shows some interesting earthy, spice aromas which also surface on the palate. Quite simple. Medium ruby garnet, with stemmy, earthy spice aromas, medium-bodied, with rustic herbal flavors, medium tannins and a dry finish. Spirity. Last tasted: 7/90. Drink 1990. Release: £1.15. Current retail: $50 (£22). Current auction: $37 (£15). **75**

1961 QUINTA DE VARGELLAS: There is too much volatile acidity in this one. The palate is better than the nose. Medium red with a garnet edge, aromas of varnish and vinegar, medium-bodied, with sweet, soft fruit flavors and an acidic finish. Last tasted: 2/90. Best to avoid. Release: £.80. Current retail: $45 (£30). Current auction: NA. **68**

1958 QUINTA DE VARGELLAS: Well past its prime, showing a tired, maderized character. Medium brick red with a garnet rim, earthy vanilla and Madeira nose, medium-bodied, with sweet vanilla and chocolate flavors, nutty and oxidized on the finish. Last tasted: 2/90. Best to avoid. Release: £.80. Current retail: $50 (£30). Current auction: £17. **68**

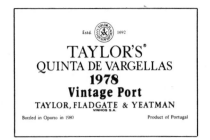

ADRIANO RAMOS-PINTO

CLASSIFICATION: *FIFTH TIER*
COLLECTIBILITY RATING: *Not rated*

BEST VINTAGES: *1983, 1985*

AT A GLANCE

ADRIANO RAMOS-PINTO
380 Avenida Ramos-Pinto,
C.P. 65
4400 Vila Nova de Gaia,
Portugal
02-30.07.16

Owners: Louis Roederer, Rar and Rima

Founded: 1880

Average production: 6,000-8,000 cases

Adriano Ramos-Pinto has a reputation for research and innovation in viticulture and winemaking in the Port trade, so it comes as a surprise to see that the house has only recently focused its attention on producing first-class vintage Ports.

"We cut back the sweetness in our vintage Ports beginning in 1983," said José Ramos-Pinto Rosas, the president of the firm, who has been making Port there for more than 50 years. "Before, we made more traditional Port. They were sweet and round and easier to drink."

One of the main reasons for the change was the insistence of the younger generation at Ramos-Pinto, Ricardo Nicolau de Almeida, commercial director, and João Nicolau de Almeida, production director. The nephews of Rosas, the two brothers are the sons of Fernando Nicolau de Almeida, the respected winemaker at A.A. Ferreira. "My nephews pushed me into it," said Rosas, who keeps two parakeets in his tasting room that fly around freely during meetings. "Especially Ricardo. He said that he couldn't sell our vintages unless we changed."

"Everybody should be able to make a quality vintage Port now," said João. "Many Portuguese houses used to make light vintage Ports. Our markets were primarily places like Brazil, where people preferred lighter wines because of warm weather. Now, since we have gone to northern markets like Britain, we have had to adapt the taste to the consumer there. We must make full-bodied wines and powerful wines."

The 1983 and 1985 are just that. The 1983 is excellent, with an abundance of rich, complex licorice and blackberry aromas and flavors as well as plenty of tannic grip. It is as good as many top 1983s. The 1985 is slightly more elegant and highlights the quality of the vintage, which produced better-balanced and fruitier Ports than 1983. Older vintages are very drinkable but perhaps lack concentration of fruit. The high level of residual sugar dominates everything else in these wines.

While its vintage blend may have been upgraded, Ramos-Pinto remains extremely traditional, and a visit to the firm's offices in Vila Nova de Gaia is like traveling back in time to when it was founded, in 1880. Its orange and yellow lodges along the waterfront are beautifully maintained, with interiors full of ornate, sculptured mahogany woodwork and tiled walls. Producing about 135,000 cases a year of Port, it remains a medium-sized house and sells primarily fine old tawnies in Portugal, Brazil, Belgium and France.

The company was owned by 42 family members until late April 1990, when Champagne Louis Roederer agreed to take a 51 percent interest in the house. The remainder was to be bought by the Oporto-based companies of Rar, sugar brokers, and Rima, a computer firm.

Ramos-Pinto will produce all of its Ports from its own vineyards by mid-1990. The house owns five *quintas*: Santo Domingos, Bom-Retiro, Urtiga, Bons-Ares and Ervamoira. Ramos-Pinto vintage Ports are produced primarily from Bom-Retiro on the Rio Torto and Ervamoira in the Douro Superior on the left bank of the River Coã.

Ramos-Pinto produces 6,000 to 8,000 cases of vintage Port. Its first vintage was 1924. All the wines are made at its modern winemaking center at Quinta dos Bons-Ares. They are made through a modern *remontagem* system in stainless steel temperature-controlled vats, and then aged for two years and bottled at the Ramos-Pinto lodge in Vila Nova de Gaia.

"When people talk about the other houses for vintage Port like Noval, Graham, Warre, Taylor and others, all we want is for them to say Ramos-Pinto in about 10 years," said Ricardo. With recent improvements in Ramos-Pinto's vintage Ports and the savoir faire of Roederer, Nicolau de Almeida's dream may come true.

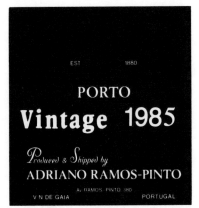

TASTING NOTES

1985 RAMOS-PINTO: Very fine, perhaps a little too elegant for longevity. Deep ruby, with incredibly fresh violet aromas, medium-bodied, with plenty of lovely, elegant, clean raspberry flavors, medium tannins and a balanced finish. Last tasted: 11/89. Drink 1994-1995. Release: $21 (£11). Current retail: $29 (£15). Current auction: NA. **85**

1983 RAMOS-PINTO: Has more grip and power than the 1985, but is still elegant. Deep ruby with a black center, aromas of licorice, blackberries and earth, full-bodied, with ripe blackberry flavors, full tannins and wonderful elegance and balance. Last tasted: 11/89. Drink 1996-1998. Release: $17 (£10). Current retail: $25 (£14). Current auction: £7. **89**

1982 RAMOS-PINTO: A lovely, silky young Port, but a little short on fruit and tannin. Deep to dark ruby, with very ripe blackberry aromas, medium-bodied, with very sweet fruit flavors, medium tannins and a short finish. Too sweet for me. Last tasted: 11/89. Drink 1992-1993. Release: $12 (£8). Current retail: $22 (£14). Current auction: £6. **79**

1980 RAMOS-PINTO: This is so sweet it seems almost flabby. Deep ruby, with a very ripe raisin and raspberry nose, medium-bodied, with very sweet, sugary fruit flavors, slightly harsh and out of balance. Last tasted: 11/89. Drink 1990-1992. Release: $11 (£7). Current retail: $14. Current auction: NA. **74**

1970 RAMOS-PINTO: Well structured, with lovely balanced fruit flavors, like many other 1970s. Medium ruby with a red hue, very ripe cassis nose, medium-bodied, with very sweet cassis flavors and medium tannins. Although this is sugary, it has the backbone to hold everything together. Last tasted: 11/89. Drink 1990-1993. Release: £2. Current retail: $70 (£21). Current auction: $32. **81**

1963 RAMOS-PINTO: A little clumsy but still holding together, with more than enough spicy raspberry flavors and a long finish. Medium red with a slight garnet hue, rich, perfumed berry aromas, medium-bodied, with sweet berry flavors, medium tannins and a balanced finish. Last tasted: 11/89. Drink 1990. Release: £.90. Current retail: $80. Current auction: £6. **83**

REAL COMPANHIA VELHA (ROYAL OPORTO)

CLASSIFICATION: *Not rated*

COLLECTIBILITY RATING: *Not rated*

I f any house should be able to make a great vintage Port, Real Companhia Velha should. The largest Port shipper in the business, it has thousands of acres of vineyards and millions of liters of Port at its disposal each harvest. Alas, such resources have virtually gone to waste.

Real Companhia Velha sells its Ports under many different labels, although Royal Oporto is its main vintage Port brand. Tasting a range of Royal Oporto vintages is a disappointment. With the exception of one or two Ports, most of them are either average or substandard in quality.

The 1987 Royal Oporto shows some effort in producing more than acceptable vintage Port. It has a good balance of violet and fruit aromas, fresh fruit flavors and medium tannins. It should be drinkable in six or seven years.

Nonetheless, vintage Ports like the Royal Oporto 1984 and 1980 are shamefully bad. It is difficult to understand why such vintage Ports were bottled and sold, let alone approved by the Instituto do Vinho do Porto. They can be drinkable, but they are more like rather poor ruby Ports.

For years, the company has been trying to popularize sales of vintage Port, primarily in Europe and the United States. "We have always thought that the vintage Port market should be expanded," said Pedro Silva Reis, 28, administrator of Real Companhia, whose family still owns a large part of the house. "It is necessary to create new markets. Not everyone can afford the prices of vintage Port from the traditional houses. We have a different style of Port. It is lighter."

Real Companhia may make 40,000 to 65,000 cases of a particular vintage Port. Production of the 1985 was about 80,000 cases. Such quantities are two to five times the production of other vintage Port producers. It is sold through a range of brands, including Royal Oporto, Guedes and Hooper. The majority of brands are the same wines, although some, such as Hooper, are a selection of a particular wine.

Competitors say that Real Companhia's large production of average vintage Ports could ruin the market; I view it differently. Royal Oporto is to vintage Port what Mouton Cadet is to Bordeaux. Neither is first class, but merely decent examples of what they are supposed to be. Of course, I am only taking into account the 1985 and 1987

AT A GLANCE

REAL COMPANHIA VELHA (ROYAL OPORTO)
Rue Azevedo Magalhães 314
4401 Vila Nova de Gaia, Portugal
02-30.30.16

Owners: Silva Reis family
Founded: 1756
Average production: 40,000-80,000 cases

Royal Oporto.

The company owns more than 2,700 acres of vineyards in the Douro Valley. Its key *quintas* are Quinta do Carvalhas, near Pinhão, 1,480 acres; Quinta do Boa Vista, near Tua, 865 acres; and Quinta do Nova, downriver from Pinhão, 250 acres. Nearly all the wines are made in autovinification tanks.

Real Companhia Velha was owned in part by Cofipsa, a subsidiary of Italian financier Carlo de Benedetti. Paying about $34 million for the shares, Cofipsa took a 40 percent interest in the Port house in early 1990. The sale was intended to help Real Companhia Velha with investments and renovations. Alain leGrand was named chief executive officer. He was previously a head of Benedictine, the French liqueur company. The deal was reversed in July, however, when Cofipsa sold its interest to the Casa do Douro, due to problems with market sales. The sale to the Casa do Douro sent shock waves through the Port trade. Although the deal was approved by the government, many Port shippers believed that it represented a conflict of interest for the Casa do Douro, which represents 28,000 growers in the Douro Valley, establishes grape prices each harvest and classifies vineyards.

The company is still run by Manuel Silva Reis, 65, who built Real Companhia Velha in four decades into what it is today. He started as a clerk in the house of Souza Guedes and later took control of the company in 1956 after the death of the owner. By 1971 Silva Reis had bought 12 other Port companies. During the revolution in 1974, his company was nationalized and the workers took over the house. Silva Reis fought for nearly four years in court and regained control of the company in 1978. During these years, a large part of Real Companhia Velha's stocks had been sold off to other houses, which Silva Reis never forgave for turning on him.

But nationalization was only a slight stumbling block for Silva Reis. Today, Real Companhia Velha sells more than 1.4 million cases of Port annually, as well as hundreds of thousands of cases of table wines from just about every region of Portugal.

Real Companhia Velha has lofty antecedents, originating from the monopoly company formed by the Marquês de Pombal in 1756 to control the Port trade. At one time, it made stunningly good vintage Ports. The 1871 Real Companhia Velha vintage is one of the greatest Ports I have ever drunk. It was still in perfect condition early in 1990, with fresh fruit and firm structure. One wonders whether Real Companhia Velha will ever make such majestic vintage Ports again.

TASTING NOTES

1987 ROYAL OPORTO: This wine could mark a move toward quality for this house. It's well balanced, with a good depth of fruit that should give it some longevity. Deep purple, with grape and violet aromas, medium-bodied, with elegant violet and fruit flavors, medium tannins and an attractive finish. Last tasted: 11/89. Drink 1995-1996. Release: $12. Current retail: $12. Current auction: NA. **80**

1985 ROYAL OPORTO: This has some fruit but it is too evolved for a 1985. Medium ruby, with a grapy, raisiny nose, medium-bodied, with sweet berry flavors and round tannins. Maturing quickly. Last tasted: 6/90. Drink 1990. Release: $12 (£10). Current retail: $17 (£11). Current auction: NA. **71**

1984 ROYAL OPORTO: Why bottle a Port like this? It's light and earthy, with little class. Light ruby, with light, earthy vanilla and smoke aromas, light-bodied, with a light finish. Last tasted: 11/89. Best to avoid. Release: $11 (£7). Current retail: $16 (£9). Current auction: NA. **65**

1983 ROYAL OPORTO: Some bottles of this are vinegar. Good bottles show some decent fruit and balanced tannins. Deep ruby, with fruit aromas, full-bodied, with raspberry flavors, medium tannins and a long finish. Slightly pedestrian but a decent glass of Port. Last tasted: 6/90. Drink 1990. Release: $9 (£7). Current retail: $13 (£11). Current auction: NA. **76**

1982 ROYAL OPORTO: Hot and out of balance. Strange flavors. Ruby-red color, with an earthy, grassy, raisiny nose, medium-bodied, with very sweet berry flavors and medium tannins, extremely harsh and alcoholic on the finish. Last tasted: 6/90. Best to avoid. Release: $9 (£6.50). Current retail: $19 (£11). Current auction: NA. **60**

1980 ROYAL OPORTO: Short, earthy and poor in quality. Light ruby with a garnet rim, light coffee and earth aromas, light-bodied, short and sweet on the palate. Last tasted: 6/90. Best to avoid. Release: $8 (£6). Current retail: $20 (£6). Current auction: NA. **60**

1978 ROYAL OPORTO: This is just too sweet and simple to be a vintage Port. It is more like a ruby. Light ruby, with an earthy chocolate nose, medium-bodied, with sweet berry flavors and a very dull finish. Last tasted: 11/89. Best to avoid. Release: $8 (£5.50). Current retail: $20 (£5.50). Current auction: NA. **68**

1977 ROYAL OPORTO: Decent fruit and round tannins, but rather light and forward for such a heralded vintage. Medium ruby, with a perfumed raspberry nose, medium- to full-bodied, with clean fruit flavors, light tannins and a long finished. Last tasted: 11/89. Drink 1990-1993. Release: $8 (£6). Current retail: $25 (£17). Current auction: NA. **74**

ROYAL OPORTO
1985
VINTAGE
PORT
PRODUCED IN THE DOURO DISTRICT
PRODUCED AND SHIPPED BY
ROYAL·OPORTO WINE CO.
VILA NOVA DE GAIA (OPORTO) — PORTUGAL
FOUNDED BY ROYAL CHARTER IN 1756
PRODUCE OF PORTUGAL
Imported by WHITWHAMS, USA, SAN FRANCISCO, CALIFORNIA

1970 ROYAL OPORTO: This is sweet and round with clean fruit flavors but lacks the class and grip of the top 1970s. Medium ruby, with a nose of earth, spices and tomato, medium- to full-bodied, with medium tannins and fruity vanilla flavors. Slightly hot on the finish. Last tasted: 11/89. Drink 1990. Release: £1.80. Current retail: $30 (£17). Current auction: NA. **75**

1967 ROYAL OPORTO: Very palatable, but more like a good late-bottled vintage. Medium to light ruby-garnet, with ripe raisin and licorice aromas, medium-bodied, with very sweet, round cherry flavors and a brown sugar finish. Very sugary. Last tasted: 11/89. Drink 1990. Release: £1.30. Current retail: $30. Current auction: NA. **72**

1963 ROYAL OPORTO: This is more like a tawny now than a true vintage. Light ruby-garnet, with a light, nutty cherry nose, medium-bodied, with sweet fruit flavors and light, silky tannins. Last tasted: 11/89. Drink 1990. Release: £1. Current retail: $65 (£29). Current auction: NA. **73**

1871 ROYAL OPORTO: This is a classic pre-phylloxera wine with amazing amounts of fresh fruit for a 120-year-old Port. It is rich and youthful, truly regal. Medium garnet with a light orange edge, light vanilla, anise, spice and leather nose, medium-bodied, with spicy, meaty fruit flavors, balanced, rich and elegant, with well-integrated tannins. Last tasted: 1/90. Drink 1990. Release: £.15. Current retail: $550 (£345). Current auction: NA. **98**

ROBERTSON'S REBELLO VALENTE

CLASSIFICATION: *FOURTH TIER*

COLLECTIBILITY RATING: A

BEST VINTAGES: *1945, 1970, 1967*

Rebello Valente, the brand name of vintage Ports from Robertson Brothers, has almost a cult status among Port collectors. This is due not so much to the outstanding quality of the wines as it is to their tradition and scarcity.

Rebello Valente has been Robertson's vintage Port brand since 1881, and Robertson was one of the few houses besides Quinta do Noval to ship the legendary 1931 vintage. The house is now owned by Seagram through Sandeman.

Recent vintages of Rebello Valente have been rather disappointing compared to the excellent wines of the 1960s and 1970s. The 1985, 1983 and 1980 all suffer from a lack of intensity and structure. These wines are all drinkable after about eight years of bottle age.

By comparison, Rebello Valente 1977, 1970 and 1967 are truly first class. They are muscular vintage Ports with oodles of rich fruit. The 1967 is particularly good and can stand up to most other top 1966s. It is a massive wine with tons of chocolate and ripe raspberry flavors that linger on the palate. The only problem is that it is difficult to find and seldom comes up in auctions.

According to Manuel Ferreira, commercial director of Sandeman, "Rebello Valente is always made from different *quinta* wines than Sandeman." For the past 40 years, Quinta da Tranqueira in the Rio Torto has been the backbone for Rebello Valente vintage Ports, according to Ferreira. Some of the wines of Quinta de la Rosa were also used in the 1960s and 1980s, although the *quinta* is making its own wines now. Production never exceeds 3,000 cases.

Robertson Brothers was established in 1847. It began as a partnership between James Nisbet Robertson and British wine merchants Binder & Gray. In 1855, John Gray died and John Robertson became a partner in the firm; the name was changed to Robertson Brothers. In 1881 it bought the name Rebello Valente from the Allen Co. and began shipping vintage Ports under that brand. Sandeman bought Robertson Brothers in 1953; the purchase did not include Quinta do Roncão, an excellent vineyard east of Pinhão.

Robertson's is popular in the Netherlands, but is a small brand elsewhere. Why does drinks giant Seagram bother with the house and its Ports? "It has a long tradition," said David Sandeman.

AT A GLANCE
ROBERTSON'S REBELLO VALENTE
Dr. Rua Antonio Granjo 207, Apartado
4401 Vila Nova de Gaia, Portugal
02-30.48.36

Owner: Seagram
Founded: 1847
Average production: 3,000 cases

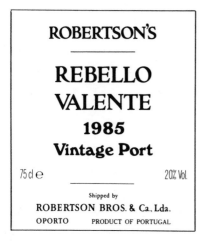

ROBERTSON'S

REBELLO
VALENTE
1985
Vintage Port

75 cl e   20% Vol.

Shipped by
ROBERTSON BROS. & Ca., Lda.
OPORTO   PRODUCT OF PORTUGAL

TASTING NOTES

1985 REBELLO VALENTE: Elegant and light for the vintage. Medium ruby, with a light raisin and black pepper nose, medium-bodied, with black pepper and fruit flavors and medium tannins. Lacks punch on the finish. Last tasted: 6/90. Drink 1994-1996. Release: $23 (£11). Current retail: $38 (£19). Current auction: NA. **81**

1983 REBELLO VALENTE: Another rather light Rebello. Medium ruby-red, with a roasted coffee nose, medium-bodied, with very ripe plum flavors, sweet tannins and a slightly hot and aggressive finish. A bit out of balance. Maybe time in the bottle will help. Last tasted: 6/90. Drink 1993-1994. Release: $23 (£9). Current retail: $36 (£17). Current auction: NA. **78**

1980 REBELLO VALENTE: Starts very slowly on the palate but finishes much better. Medium ruby-red, with a perfumed cherry nose, full-bodied, with sweet fruit flavors, medium tannins and a big, long finish. Last tasted: 2/90. Drink 1993-1995. Release: $16 (£7). Current retail: $40 (£18). Current auction: NA. **80**

1977 REBELLO VALENTE: This is the most recent major-league Rebello Valente. Medium red with a ruby center, intense blackberry nose, full-bodied, with an excellent concentration of ripe blackberry flavors, full tannins and a long finish. Last tasted: 2/90. Drink 1995-1998. Release: $12 (£5). Current retail: $55 (£27). Current auction: $22. **89**

1975 REBELLO VALENTE: I have had this two or three times. One time it looked more like an old Beaujolais Nouveau than a vintage Port. The last bottle I had, however, was clean, simple and delicious. Medium ruby-red, with an aromatic blackberry nose, light- to medium-bodied, with simple, sweet fruit flavors and a medium finish. Drink 1990. Last tasted: 2/90. Release: £4.50. Current retail: $43 (£16). Current auction: $18 (£10). **75**

1972 REBELLO VALENTE: Delicate, with a light balance of fruit and sweetness. It is probably the best 1972 made and is better than most 1975s. Good ruby color, with cassis and black cherry aromas, medium-bodied, with sweet, silky black cherry flavors and a lovely light finish. A refreshing wine. Last tasted: 1/90. Drink 1990. Release: £1.70. Current retail: $40 (£17). Current auction: £8. **83**

1970 REBELLO VALENTE: Drink it alone for dessert. It is like a delicious piece of fruitcake. Medium red, with a roasted, chocolate, earthy nose, medium-bodied, with plenty of tannins and roasted, fruity flavors on the palate. Will improve. Last tasted: 2/90. Drink 1990. Release: £2. Current retail: $50 (£22). Current auction: $27 (£11). **92**

1967 REBELLO VALENTE: Outclasses many 1966s. A complete wine with an abundance of fruit. Deep red with a ruby center, a nose of almonds, chocolate and raspberries, full-bodied, with masses of ripe fruit and an excellent backbone. Will improve. Last tasted: 2/90. Drink 1990. Release: £1.30. Current retail: $50 (£25) Current auction: NA. **91**

1966 REBELLO VALENTE: Clearly not as good as the 1967, but decent. Medium red with a garnet edge, an earthy tomato, slightly volatile nose, medium-bodied, with soft tannins, sweet, roasted chocolate and fruit flavors and a medium finish. Last tasted: 2/90. Drink 1990. Release: £1.30. Current retail: $70 (£28). Current auction: $36 (£14). **82**

1963 REBELLO VALENTE: An elegant, silky wine for current drinking. Not a great 1963 but very good, with interesting flavors. Medium red with a garnet edge, a rather herbal, spicy berry nose, medium-bodied, with medium to full tannins and spicy cinnamon, vanilla and fruit flavors. Last tasted: 2/90. Drink 1990. Release: £.90. Current retail: $92 (£30). Current auction: $38 (£18). **85**

1960 REBELLO VALENTE: Light and balanced, with elegant fruit flavors and a lovely finish. Medium to light ruby, with light berry and black pepper aromas, medium-bodied, with a surprising amount of fresh cherry flavors, light tannins and a silky finish. Last tasted: 11/88. Drink 1990. Release: £.80. Current retail: $55 (£16). Current auction: $35 (£12). **85**

1945 REBELLO VALENTE: For a vintage Port from a bottle that had a level below its mid-shoulder, this was very impressive, with an excellent depth of ripe, concentrated fruit flavors and superb balance. Medium ruby-red, with ripe cherry and vanilla aromas, medium-bodied, with sweet licorice and fruit flavors, silky tannins and a lingering finish. Superb. Last tasted: 5/90. Drink 1990. Release: £.40. Current retail: $245 (£55). Current auction: $185. **92**

1942 REBELLO VALENTE: I have only tasted this once, and it was up the Douro Valley. It was quite tired then. Bottles stored elsewhere may be better. Light ruby with a brown edge, sweet, toasted chocolate and berry aromas, light-bodied, with very sweet vanilla, spice and fruit flavors and a light finish; fading. More like an old tawny. Last tasted: 2/85. Drink 1990. Release: £.38. Current retail: $140 (£50). Current auction: £28. **75**

ROBERTSON'S

REBELLO VALENTE

1985

Vintage Port

75 cl e   20% Vol.

Shipped by
ROBERTSON BROS. & Ca., Lda.
OPORTO   PRODUCT OF PORTUGAL

ROZES

CLASSIFICATION: *Not rated*

COLLECTIBILITY RATING: *Not rated*

BEST VINTAGE: <u>1987</u>

With the clout of the international drinks group Moët-Hennessy-Louis Vuitton, which owns Rozès, one would expect the Port house to produce good vintage Ports. On the whole, it does; however, Rozès' success goes relatively unacknowledged due to the house's reliance on its standard ruby Port sales in France, where Rozès is a leading brand.

The Rozès vintage Ports in the 1980s have shown improvement each declaration. The last year, 1987, is the best Rozès yet — a lovely young vintage Port with an elegant fruit and tannin structure. These Ports tend to be quite Portuguese in style, sweeter and rounder than those from houses with British origins. Rozès vintage Ports are not for long-term aging, but should provide good drinking about eight to 10 years after the vintage date.

Although the company began in the last century, it has only been making vintage Port since 1963. Production of vintage Port totals 1,500 to 2,500 cases in declared years, which include 1963, 1967, 1977, 1978, 1982, 1983, 1985 and 1987. The vintage wines come from the Pinhão area near Covelinhas and are fermented in *lagares*. They are sold primary in Denmark, the United States and Canada. Rozès' total annual sales equal about 125,000 cases, with 64 percent sold in France, 12 percent in Belgium, 9 percent in Italy and the remainder in other markets around the world.

Rozès has considered buying a *quinta* in the Douro Valley, according to Rogerio Leandro da Silva, 41, who has managed the house since 1981. "The company is going through an important reorganization program which envisions investments in Gaia and in the Douro," he said. "It is estimated that for a certain period of time some services will continue to be hired from third parties," but that may change in the future.

The company was established in France in 1855. First known as Maison Ed. Rozès, it traded in Port and soon opened an office in Vila Nova de Gaia. The house was founded by Ostende Rozès, and his son Edmond took over the company in the late 1800s. Edmond passed the business on to his sons, Guy and Yves.

Rozès was shut down during World War II since the two brothers went back to France to fight in the army. When the French Army surrendered, they continued to fight with the Resistance and both later received the Legion d'Honneur Militaire for their heroic efforts behind enemy lines. Just after the war, their Port business was restarted in France, and in 1956 an office in Gaia was opened again. Rozès signed a production contract with Ferreira, which supplied and bottled all the Port for Rozès' brands. The contract lasted until 1962, when Cockburn Smithes began supplying Port for Rozès.

The Rozès family remained owners of the house until 1974, when it was sold to Pedro Domecq International. At the time of the sale, Cockburn no longer wished to carry on its association with Rozès and Domecq started working in 1975 with Taylor Fladgate & Yeatman, which received some equity in the firm. Moët-Hennessy bought the shares from Domecq in 1978, and in 1987 the group's Champagne Moët et Chandon bought the shares from Taylor. Rozès now has its own offices, lodges and stocks of Port in Gaia, although the bottling is done under contract by Quinta do Noval.

TASTING NOTES

1987 ROZES: Elegant, lovely flavors, but early maturing. Inky center with a ruby edge, a slight tar and cassis nose, full-bodied, with fresh, sweet, ripe raspberry flavors, firm tannins and a long, elegant, slightly nutty finish. Last tasted: 6/90. Drink 1995-1996. Not released. **86**

1985 ROZES: A good, rather chewy 1985 with a solid concentration of flavorful fruit and round tannins. Deep ruby with a red hue, pretty, light cherry aromas, full-bodied, with delicious, round, chewy fruit flavors, medium tannins and a sweet finish. Slightly simple but a good bottle of young Port. Last tasted: 5/90. Drink 1995-1997. Release: $16. Current retail: $18. Current auction: NA. **81**

1982 ROZES: Very simple and sugary, with earthy cherry aromas and flavors, but much better than another bottle I tasted in early 1990. Medium ruby center with a lighter rim, earthy cherry and grassy aromas, medium-bodied, with very sweet cherry flavors, sugary tannins and a medium finish. A little hot and unbalanced. Last tasted: 6/90. Drink 1992-1994. Not available. **75**

SANDEMAN

CLASSIFICATION: *THIRD TIER*

COLLECTIBILITY RATING: AA

BEST VINTAGES: *1870, 1963, 1945*

The House of Sandeman may be just a small part of international drinks giant Seagram, but it has played a major role in the Port trade for two centuries, producing consistently good vintage Ports.

The company claims to have shipped one of the first major vintages of Port to Great Britain, the 1790, and Sandeman has reams of invoices documenting its centuries of exporting Port abroad. According to chairman David Sandeman, years ago his company's Ports were shipped in three styles: dry, medium and sweet. "It is always a risk with anything prior to 1904," said Sandeman. "You might get a dry or medium wine. The sweet should be fine, but the others will probably not be very good."

Today's Sandeman vintage Ports are still very good, but they lack that extra concentration of fruit and tannin to be considered in the upper echelon. The 1985 and 1983 are elegant, well-balanced wines and good examples of their vintages, but a little more extract of color, fruit and tannin would put them up with the stars of the vintage. They can be drunk about 10 years after the vintage, but will continue to give drinking pleasure for decades.

It is a shame, however, that the current vintages are not on the same level as wines like 1967, 1966 or 1963. Many of the old vintages of Sandeman illustrate what great talent the company had in making superbly concentrated and powerful vintage Ports. All these wines are still at the top of their vintages, with extremely deep color, concentrated fruit flavors and plenty of backbone.

Judging from my tastings, Sandeman has not produced truly outstanding wines since the 1967 vintage, the last vintage to be produced almost entirely in *lagares*. Since then, most of the vintage lots have been produced in autovinification tanks at the Sandeman production facility in Celeirós. About 75 percent of its vintage Port is made by autovinification and *remontagem*.

The vintage lots are blended by Eduardo Seixas, who has worked since the late 1970s in Sandeman's tasting room. The company also used the talent of freelance taster-blender Federico van Zeller, who also made some of the great wines of Quinta do Noval, until his death in 1988. David Sandeman himself must also approve the vintage lots, as well as other blends such as aged tawnies and Founders Reserve premium ruby.

The grapes for Sandeman vintages come primarily from areas around Pinhão, with an emphasis on the Pinhão Valley and the Rio Torto region. Sandeman has had long-term contracts with growers in this region, which is near its production facilities at Celeirós. Sandeman produces 8,000 to 12,000 cases a vintage, depending on the year.

Sandeman has had a reputation for declaring more vintages than just about any other house, with the possible exception of Quinta do Noval and Offley, although this has not been the case in the 1980s. When there was a split vintage, as in 1966 and 1967 or 1934 and 1935, Sandeman simply made both. Such a policy has lead to some criticism, but the wines have been very good in both vintages. In fact, Sandeman has always made rich wines regardless of the vintage. Its wines from fading vintages like 1960, 1958 and 1950 are still in very good condition.

Sandeman was one of the first houses to try to control the bottling of its vintage Ports. In 1937 it bottled all of its 1935 in London in a specially stenciled bottle to commemorate George V's silver jubilee. "We tried to carry on bottling all of our own vintages, but our customers just didn't accept the idea," said Sandeman.

Older vintages of Sandeman are available in U.S. and United Kingdom wine shops as well as at wine auctions. It is rare, however, to have the opportunity to taste a century's worth of the wines. For the house's 200th anniversary, Sandeman organized just such a tasting in New York on March 17, 1990, which I was fortunate enough to attend. His son George, now managing Sandeman in Vila Nova de Gaia, and his grandson Christopher, then 12, were also there. They toasted one another with a glass of the 1870 Sandeman.

"As long as I am here, I personally feel very uptight about things that are not how I believe they should be for the brand," said David Sandeman a week before the event. "If it was called Seagram's Port, I wouldn't give a damn, but when your name is on the label, there is an entirely different feeling about it."

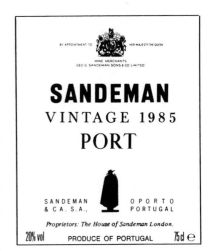

TASTING NOTES

1985 SANDEMAN: Elegant and balanced, but a little short on concentration. Medium ruby-purple, with a spicy plum nose, medium-bodied, with clean fruit flavors, medium tannins and finish. Last tasted: 6/90. Drink 1996-1997. Release: $22 (£13). Current retail: $30 (£20). Current auction: £9. **83**

1982 SANDEMAN: Very much like the 1985, although a bottle I tasted in New York in March 1990 had more pronounced roasted, cooked qualities. Perhaps it was poorly stored. The wine is usually an elegant and youthful Port with a lovely balance of fruit and tannin. Deep ruby, with fresh violet and grape aromas, full-bodied, with a lovely balance of rich, grapy flavors, medium tannins and finish. Last tasted:

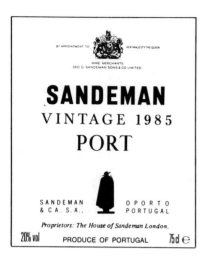

6/90. Drink 1993-1995. Release: $19 (£10). Current retail: $27 (£21). Current auction: £7. **82**

1980 SANDEMAN: Each time I taste this I like it better. It is starting to become an elegant wine. Medium ruby, with fresh berry aromas, plenty of sweet, floral orange flavors, medium ripe tannins and a sweet finish. Last tasted: 6/90. Drink 1990-1993. Release: $19 (£9). Current retail: $35 (£25). Current auction: $28 (£19). **85**

1977 SANDEMAN: Extremely well balanced and supple for a 1977. Medium ruby, with clean berry aromas, full-bodied yet supple, very well balanced, with a long finish. Last tasted: 3/90. Drink 1993-1996. Release: $15 (£6.50). Current retail: $56 (£25). Current auction: $37 (£14). **85**

1975 SANDEMAN: Drying up quickly. Medium to light red, with light tobacco and earth aromas, light-bodied, with earthy anise flavors and a dry finish. The alcohol is quite pronounced. Last tasted: 3/90. Drink 1990. Release: £5. Current retail: $50 (£17). Current auction: $28 (£10). **78**

1970 SANDEMAN: Elegant and balanced, with lovely ripe fruit flavors, but it doesn't quite make it to the heights of other well-known shippers. Medium ruby-red, with a minty chocolate nose, medium-bodied, with cherry flavors, balanced tannins and a short finish. Last tasted: 3/90. Drink 1990-1993. Release: £2.30. Current retail: $70 (£27). Current auction: $38 (£17). **83**

1967 SANDEMAN: Gives credence to the idea that 1967 is a contender with the excellent 1966. Amazingly good, with a superb nose of vanilla, chocolate and blackberries, full-bodied and round, with ripe, velvety fruit flavors and medium tannins that focus the finish. Last tasted: 3/90. Drink 1990-1993. Release: £1.50. Current retail: $65 (£34). Current auction: $38 (£12). **90**

1966 SANDEMAN: I have tasted the 1967 and 1966 wines side by side on various occasions, and I normally prefer the 1966. It is still quite youthful. Deep ruby-red, with a ripe, grapy, perfumed nose, masses of fruit on the palate and plenty of tannins to give the wine balance. It will still improve. Last tasted: 3/90. Drink 1990. Release: £1.50. Current retail: $93 (£35). Current auction: $40 (£21). **92**

1963 SANDEMAN: This may be one of the most underrated 1963s made. Its deep red color gives little indication of the wine's age, and there is an abundance of youthful, rich fruit on the nose and palate. Full tannins and an assertive finish back up everything. Will still improve with age. Last tasted: 3/90. Drink 1990. Release: £1.15. Current retail: $110 (£46). Current auction: $80 (£32). **96**

1960 SANDEMAN: Quite good for a 1960, but starting to fade. Medium red with a garnet rim, mature berry and leather aromas and flavors and a nutty finish. Last tasted: 3/90. Drink 1990. Release: £.95. Current retail: $75 (£45). Current auction: $43 (£23). **79**

1958 SANDEMAN: I have had this wine numerous times and it develops well in the glass after about 20 minutes. It is a very elegant and light Port with plenty of finesse. Light ruby, with fresh berry aromas, light-bodied, with delicate, fruity flavors, slightly hot on the finish. It was probably much better 10 years ago. Last tasted: 3/90. Drink 1990. Release: £.90. Current retail: $70 (£22). Current auction: $47 (£17). **82**

1957 SANDEMAN: This is an undeclared vintage but very good. Only a few hundred cases were bottled for special customers in England. It is quite hard and tough on the palate, but still shows fresh violet aromas and berry flavors. Last tasted: 10/88. Drink 1990. Release: £.80. Current retail: £21. Current auction: £17. **85**

1955 SANDEMAN: This wine can range from very good to sublime. It is always a very sweet, mouthfilling Port with lovely raspberry aromas and rich, round fruit on the palate. It is delicious now but will continue to improve with age. Last tasted: 3/90. Drink 1990. Release: £1. Current retail: $140 (£40). Current auction: $88 (£30). **94**

1950 SANDEMAN: Loosely knit on the palate, it still shows extremely good fruit for a 1950. Many have already fallen by the wayside. Deep ruby-garnet, with rich grapy aromas, full-bodied and rather thick, with plenty of fruit flavors and a long finish. Last tasted: 3/90. Drink 1990. Release: £.60. Current retail: $170 (£35). Current auction: $165 (£19). **87**

1947 SANDEMAN: Well-stored bottles are very well-focused, racy wines. Others are slightly lighter. Medium to deep red-garnet, with raspberry aromas, medium-bodied, with tightly knit layers of fruit flavors, good backbone and a long finish. At its peak now. Last tasted: 3/90. Drink 1990. Release: £.45. Current retail: $180. Current auction: £33. **90**

1945 SANDEMAN: It can't get more enjoyable that this. The color is youthfully ruby-garnet, while the nose shows intense aromas of boysenberries and almonds. Full-bodied, with very focused, sweet fruit flavors, great concentration and a silky mouth-feel. Last tasted: 3/90. Drink 1990. Release: £.40. Current retail: $380 (£59). Current auction: $118 (£46). **95**

1942 SANDEMAN: Although slightly one-dimensional, it shows extremely youthful fruit flavors and a surprising amount of concentration. Cherries and currants on the nose and palate. Still fresh. Last tasted: 3/90. Drink 1990. Release: £.30. Current retail: $175 (£59). Current auction: £46. **88**

1935 SANDEMAN: Bottled in a specially stenciled bottle with purple wax to commemorate King George V's silver jubilee. It may be slightly sexist these days, but the best way to describe this is as a mature, feminine Port. Medium to deep red with a garnet rim, ripe cassis, tomato and berry nose, full-bodied, with lovely, silky, elegant cassis flavors and silky tannins. Last tasted: 3/90. Drink 1990. Release: £.30. Current retail: $450 (£110). Current auction: $250 (£171). **92**

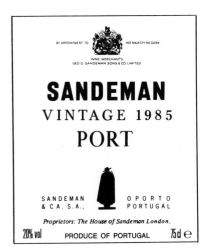

BY APPOINTMENT TO   HER MAJESTY THE QUEEN

WINE MERCHANTS
GEO. G SANDEMAN SONS & CO LIMITED

SANDEMAN
VINTAGE 1985
PORT

SANDEMAN
& CA. S.A.,

OPORTO
PORTUGAL

Proprietors: The House of Sandeman London.

20% vol   PRODUCE OF PORTUGAL   75d e

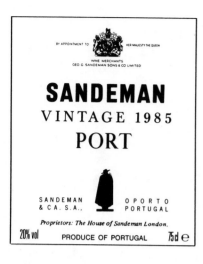

SANDEMAN

VINTAGE 1985

PORT

SANDEMAN & CA. S.A., OPORTO PORTUGAL

Proprietors: The House of Sandeman London.

20% vol   PRODUCE OF PORTUGAL   75cl ℮

1934 SANDEMAN: I first tasted this in a blind tasting of 1935s and 1934s and it was one of the best. It is a ripe blockbuster of a wine. Youthful rich red with a slight garnet rim, focused ripe cherry and toffee nose, with lots of spicy berry flavors and a velvety mouth-feel. Last tasted: 3/90. Drink 1990. Release: £.30. Current retail: $300 (£100). Current auction: NA. **94**

1927 SANDEMAN: This also did well in a blind tasting of 1927s, although the last bottle I had in New York was more forward than those tasted in Britain. It is a wonderful wine, with mature aromas of raspberries and roses, medium-bodied, with lovely, sweet, balanced fruit flavors and a long finish. Last tasted: 3/90. Drink in 1990. Release: £.20. Current retail: $435 (£157). Current auction: $350 (£121). **92**

1920 SANDEMAN: More like a dated tawny than a vintage. Medium amber with a green edge, a remarkably fruity nose of cherries and cassis, medium-bodied, with sweet, nutty vanilla and fruit flavors. Last tasted: 3/90. Drink 1990. Release: £.20. Current retail: $300 (£135). Current auction: $165. **78**

1917 SANDEMAN: Surprisingly good and still holding on to its fruit. Medium brick red, with fresh cherry and berry aromas, light- to medium-bodied, with soft, velvety cherry and toffee flavors. Last tasted: 3/90. Drink 1990. Release: £.21. Current retail: $300 (£160). Current auction: $130 (£66). **88**

1911 SANDEMAN: I tasted this twice in 1990. The first bottle, tasted in New York, was a youthful red color with an amber edge and musty chocolate aromas, but well past its prime and extremely high in volatile acidity. The second bottle, which was actually a half bottle and tasted in London, was delicious. It had a raspberry toffee aroma, with silky, Rye whiskey flavors. Last tasted: 6/90. Drink 1990. Release: £.11. Current retail: $275 (£126). Current auction: $250 (£97). **82**

1908 SANDEMAN: This is more of a novelty than anything else. It has lost most of its fruit and is now a lovely old tawny with nutty vanilla flavors and a bit of fruit on the finish. Last tasted: 3/90. Drink 1990. Release: £.11. Current retail: $320 (£138). Current auction: £106. **75**

1904 SANDEMAN: Not a blockbuster, but still a good vintage Port, with rich cherry aromas, lovely, elegant, sweet fruit flavors and a balance of fine, silky tannins. It is truly elegant. Last tasted: 3/90. Drink 1990. Release: £.11. Current retail: $420 (£263). Current auction: $350 (£203). **88**

1896 SANDEMAN: I tasted two different bottles at a New York tasting. One was completely over the hill, while the second still showed signs of life, with cassis aromas and light, sweet cherry flavors. It was drying out but was still interesting. Last tasted: 3/90. Drink 1990. Release: £.11. Current retail: $600 (£206). Current auction: $340 (£160). **81**

1887 SANDEMAN: Another vintage Port that has turned to tawny. Light garnet, with lovely, delicate vanilla and nut flavors and a sweet finish. Not much fruit left. Last tasted: 3/90. Drink 1990. Release: £.11. Current retail: $600 (£470). Current auction: NA. **74**

1870 SANDEMAN: This bottle is one of nearly two dozen found by a London wine merchant, Richard Torin, in 1989. There was some question as to the wine's authenticity, but David Sandeman has confirmed that the wine was sent in cask to the Glasgow wine merchant David Sandeman & Sons (no family connection.) The wine was absolutely marvelous, with the typical pre-phylloxera stamp of incredibly rich and youthful fruit. Still red with a rich tawny edge, very sweet, grapy floral aromas, with plenty of sweet cherry and light coffee flavors. A truly outstanding Port. Last tasted: 3/90. Drink 1990. Release: £.09. Current retail: $700 (£485). Current auction: NA. **98**

SMITH WOODHOUSE

CLASSIFICATION: *THIRD TIER*

COLLECTIBILITY RATING: *A*

BEST VINTAGES: *1983, 1980*

The 1980s were an excellent decade for Smith Woodhouse, which produced a string of outstanding vintage Ports every declaration. Smith Woodhouse continues to be one of the most underrated houses in vintage Port.

The vintage Ports of Smith Woodhouse, part of the Symington Port group, are halfway between Graham and Dow in style. As young Ports, they are opulent, with the sweet, succulent fruit of Graham and the hard, firm tannins of Dow. The 1983 Smith Woodhouse is a perfect example of this style, exploding with ripe cassis on the nose and palate but holding back a bit due to its excellent tannin structure. The 1983, like other good vintages of Smith Woodhouse, needs 12 to 13 years of bottle age before drinking.

With age, Smith Woodhouse vintage Ports develop an array of flavors ranging from chocolate and anise to tar and earth. There is always a stunning amount of developed fruit flavors in the glass. These mature Ports of Smith Woodhouse, however, may not be indicative of how recent vintages will evolve. Symington Port Shippers has only owned the house since buying W. & J. Graham in 1970. The Symingtons now use different *quintas* for Smith Woodhouse vintages, and blend the wines differently.

It is difficult to say, but I would hazard a guess that today's vintages of Smith Woodhouse are even better than earlier years. Even the Smith Woodhouse 1975, which is a weak vintage for all shippers, is a good bottle of vintage. Adding to its vintage prowess, Smith Woodhouse bottles a traditional late-bottled vintage Port — unfined, unfiltered and bottled after four years in cask — which can compare in quality with many of the full-fledged vintage wines from other houses. The 1974 Smith Woodhouse LBV was still drinking extremely well in late 1989.

Most of the wines for Smith Woodhouse vintages come from the Rio Torto area. Major contributors to the blend are wines from the region's Quinta do Vale Dona Maria. The Symingtons have a 20-year lease on the *quinta*, until 2003. A large part of the wines in Smith Woodhouse vintages are still produced in *lagares*. Production in a vintage year ranges from 6,000 to 8,000 cases.

Londoner Christopher Smith founded Smith Woodhouse in

1784, although he was not active in the firm. Besides being a wine merchant specializing in Port, he was a revered politician, serving as a member of Parliament and as the Lord Mayor of London in the late 1810s. Pressed for time during his political endeavors, he took on partners William, James and Robert Woodhouse, and the firm formally became Smith Woodhouse Bros. in 1828.

The Port house built a strong clientele for more than a century, but after World War II, business became difficult, as it did with other firms. In 1956 Smith Woodhouse was bought by London's Luis Gordon & Sons, who contracted W. & J. Graham to ship the wines. Four years later, Graham bought Smith Woodhouse. As mentioned above, the two houses became part of the Symington group in 1970.

Peter Symington expects Smith Woodhouse vintage Ports to be "up to at least the standards of Ferreira or other similar houses." Could even Symington be underestimating Smith Woodhouse's quality?

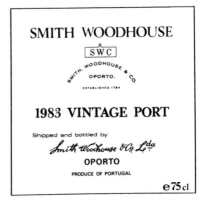

TASTING NOTES

1985 SMITH WOODHOUSE: I have tasted this blind with all the other big-name 1985s and it often holds its own. Medium deep ruby, with lovely violet aromas, full-bodied, with plenty of grip, full tannins and a powerful finish. Last tasted: 6/90. Drink 1996-1998. Release: $11 (£5). Current retail: $32 (£20). Current auction: NA. **89**

1983 SMITH WOODHOUSE: Very impressive for its brute strength. Very deep, dark ruby, with a concentrated cassis nose, full-bodied, rich, powerful and overflowing with fruit flavors and hard tannins. Last tasted: 6/90. Drink 1997-1999. Release: $21 (£9). Current retail: $31 (£17). Current auction: £8. **92**

1980 SMITH WOODHOUSE: Tight, hard and closed, but extremely good for a 1980. Medium deep ruby, with wonderful perfumed berry aromas, full-bodied, very tannic, with lots of grapy flavors. Still closed. Last tasted: 6/90. Drink 1992-1994. Release: $15 (£7). Current retail: $31 (£17). Current auction: NA. **90**

1977 SMITH WOODHOUSE: Another hard wine for laying away but not as outstanding as the other great 1977s. Medium ruby with a red hue, intense ripe cherry aromas, full-bodied and very tannic but well knit, with a background of concentrated berry flavors. Last tasted: 2/90. Drink 1996-1998. Release: $11 (£5). Current retail: $52 (£20). Current auction: $28 (£10). **89**

1975 SMITH WOODHOUSE: Quite good for a 1975, with balanced, clean fruit flavors. Not fading yet. Medium red, with a clean, lightly roasted cherry nose, medium-bodied, with light tannins, silky fruit flavors and a clean finish. Last tasted: 2/90. Drink 1990. Release: £4. Current retail: $38 (£17). Current auction: $23 (£9). **80**

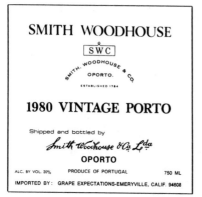

1970 SMITH WOODHOUSE: An example of how this house's young wines lose their hard edge and become elegant and racy. Medium ruby with a red edge, complex, perfumed cherry aromas, medium-bodied, with silky tannins and a lovely balance of very elegant fruit flavors. Last tasted: 2/90. Drink 1990. Release: £2. Current retail: $62 (£22). Current auction: $30 (£13). **86**

1966 SMITH WOODHOUSE: Attractive, but a little simple for a 1966. Medium red with a ruby center, berry and chocolate nose, full-bodied, with medium tannins and more than enough velvety berry flavors. Last tasted: 2/90. Drink 1990. Release: £1.30. Current retail: $80 (£30). Current auction: £15. **83**

1963 SMITH WOODHOUSE: Much more impressive than the 1966, like a mountain built of fruit. Medium deep red, with chocolate, ripe berry and tar aromas, full-bodied, with medium tannins and lots of sweet, ripe berry flavors. Will improve. Last tasted: 2/90. Drink 1990. Release: £.90. Current retail: $110 (£35). Current auction: NA. **89**

TAYLOR, FLADGATE & YEATMAN

CLASSIFICATION: *FIRST TIER*

COLLECTIBILITY RATING: *AAA*

BEST VINTAGES: *1948, 1970, 1977*

T aylor, Fladgate & Yeatman vintage Ports consistently sell for higher prices than any of the other big 10 houses, with the exception of the rare Nacional from Quinta do Noval, which is a reflection of the wines' consistently magnificent quality. What more can one say about Taylor?

Taylor vintage Ports when young are exceedingly tight and subtle, with an underlying almost coarse youthfulness. With age, they become harmonious monuments to their vintages, showing a distinctive power of fruit and tannin. "Taylor is bloody difficult to taste young," said Alistair Robertson, the main shareholder and managing director of Taylor Fladgate. "But it is not supposed to be attractive when young. If it doesn't taste good when young, then it will last for decades."

There is always a slight dryness and hardness to Taylor vintage Ports. This slightly aggressive characteristic in the young Ports turns to a racy elegance with age. "I really prefer a drier style Port," said Robertson, who noted that his other vintage Port, Fonseca, is much sweeter and fuller. "The sweeter style Ports are not as easy to enjoy."

Most of this hard style comes from wine produced at Taylor's Quinta de Vargellas, which is the backbone of its vintage blends. The 250-acre property is about 20 miles up river from Pinhão. It produces about 300 pipes of Port in a good vintage, with a large part going into the vintage blend in a declared year. The production may also be used for a single-*quinta* Port under the property's name. Most of the *quinta's* grapes are still fermented in *lagares*, although the property also has a large modern winery with stainless steel vats.

Taylor owns another property, Quinta de Terra Feita, which is across the Pinhão River from Fonseca's Cruzeiro and Santo Antonio. Terra Feita includes about 120 acres of vineyards, and its wines have been part of the Taylor vintage blend since the last century. The property was bought in 1973. In 1989 it was enlarged slightly after Taylor bought the small neighboring *quinta*. All the wines are made by *lagar*.

"A blend of Vargellas and wines from *quintas* like Terra Feita is what Taylor vintage Port is all about," said Robertson, who added that a small amount of Port bought from other *quintas* may be used in Taylor vintages. "The point of a vintage Port is to have your own special blend."

Taylor produces 15,000 to 20,000 cases of vintage Port in a

AT A GLANCE

TAYLOR, FLADGATE & YEATMAN
Rua do Choupelo 250, C.P. 24
4400 Vila Nova de Gaia,
Portugal
02-30.45.05

Owners: Alistair Robertson, Bruce Guimaraens and Huyshe Bower

Founded: 1692

Average production: 15,000-20,000 cases

declared year. The wines are sold as Taylor Fladgate in the United States to avoid legal problems with the New York wine giant Taylor Wine Co. Everywhere else its wines are sold as Taylor. Nonetheless, some bottles, especially old vintages, find their way to the U.S. market after being re-exported from such places as the United Kingdom.

"I am not sure why Taylor has become so famous," said Robertson. "The success of Taylor over the years must be that people have enjoyed drinking it more than any other vintage Port. It may not win blind tastings, but people like to drink it; that is what counts."

TASTING NOTES

1985 TAYLOR: Extremely understated and closed, it starts out slowly but finishes quickly. Deep ruby-purple, with berry and cherry aromas and flavors, full-bodied, very tannic and hard. Great future. Last tasted: 6/90. Drink 1997-2000. Release: $32 (£14). Current retail: $39 (£19). Current auction: $28 (£17). **90**

1983 TAYLOR: Taylor is always closed and tight when young and this is no exception. Deep ruby-purple, ripe raisin and violet aromas, full-bodied, with sweet raisin and grape flavors, a lovely balance of full tannins and an explosion of fruit on the finish. Last tasted: 6/90. Drink 1996-1998. Release: $25 (£11). Current retail: $45 (£17). Current auction: $28 (£13). **89**

1980 TAYLOR: Once a little rough, the 1980 Taylor has mellowed. Deep ruby, with cherry and berry aromas, full-bodied, with lots of fruit flavors and hard tannins. Very angular. Last tasted: 6/90. Drink 1994. Release: $21 (£9). Current retail: $35 (£14). Current auction: $29 (£11). **88**

1977 TAYLOR: There is an explosion of fruit and tannins in the mouth but at the same time this wine is in total harmony. Deep dark ruby, with blackberries and violets on the nose, full-bodied, with masses of blackberry flavors, full, hard tannins and a very long finish. Will age for decades. Last tasted: 4/90. Drink 1996-1998. Release: $17 (£7). Current retail: $70 (£48). Current auction: $48 (£32). **98**

1975 TAYLOR: Not bad, but more like a good late-bottled vintage. Medium red, with plum and pepper aromas, medium-bodied, with simple fruit flavors. The alcohol is beginning to show. Last tasted: 2/90. Drink 1990. Release: £5.10. Current retail: $44 (£30). Current auction: $35 (£14). **78**

1970 TAYLOR: Clearly lives up to Taylor's superb reputation. Deep ruby, with intense violet and chocolate aromas, full-bodied, with gorgeous fruit flavors, full but well-integrated tannins and an extremely long finish. Amazing balance and finesse. Still needs time. Last tasted: 12/89. Drink 1990-1995. Release: £2.50. Current retail: $73 (£40). Current auction: $60 (£25). **98**

1966 TAYLOR: Rather perplexing, since it is still very hard and coarse. It makes one wonder if it will ever come around. Medium ruby, with a prune and ripe berry nose, medium-bodied, with ripe fruit flavors and rather lean, hard tannins. Last tasted: 12/89. Drink 1990-1993. Release: £1.50. Current retail: $87 (£38). Current auction: $58 (£29). **89**

1963 TAYLOR: A big wine with superb balance, a shining example of this exuberantly fruity vintage. Deep ruby, with violets and coffee on the nose, full-bodied, with dried cherry flavors and plenty of tannin, balanced and long on the finish. Last tasted: 12/89. Drink 1990-1994. Release: £1.15. Current retail: $155 (£78). Current auction: $115 (£57). **97**

1960 TAYLOR: This wine was just hanging on in late 1988, starting to fade, with the alcohol beginning to surface. Medium red with a garnet rim, a developed cedar and tobacco nose, medium-bodied, with intense, sweet plum flavors and a slightly dry finish. Last tasted: 8/88. Drink 1990. Release: £.98. Current retail: $89 (£51). Current auction: $75 (£29). **80**

1955 TAYLOR: Some people may expect more from such a superb vintage, but this is still very good indeed. It is a racy wine with a fruit bowl of flavors. Medium red with a garnet edge, chocolate and vanilla aromas, medium-bodied, with sweet berry flavors and a lovely finish. Last tasted: 11/89. Drink 1990. Release: £1. Current retail: $195 (£105). Current auction: $165 (£86). **88**

1948 TAYLOR: I have had this numerous times and I have always been bowled over by its great quality. It is teeming with plum aromas and flavors. Deep ruby-red, with coffee, cocoa and plum aromas, full-bodied, with ripe fruit flavors, medium tannins and a balanced finish. Will age on and on. Last tasted: 11/89. Drink 1990. Release: £.50. Current retail: $325 (£135). Current auction: $275 (£103). **99**

1945 TAYLOR: Nearly as sublime as the 1948, this is a majestic wine in its own right, with a superb concentration of fruit and a firm structure. Deep, dark ruby with a garnet edge, ripe raisin, almond and cedar aromas, full-bodied, with masses of ripe grape and almond flavors and medium tannins that tickle your palate on the finish. Built to age for centuries but amazing to drink now. Last tasted: 11/89. Drink 1990. Release: £.45. Current retail: $650 (£300). Current auction: $700 (£234). **97**

1942 TAYLOR: This is a nutty vintage Port that has just about metamorphosed into a mature tawny. Medium brick red with an amber edge, slightly musty nut and cherry aromas, medium-bodied, with sweet, velvety nut and fruit flavors with some violets coming from underneath and a medium finish. Last tasted: 4/90. Drink 1990. Release: £.40. Current retail: $275 (£100). Current auction: £75. **78**

Estd. 1692

TAYLOR FLADGATE ®
1983
Vintage Porto

TAYLOR, FLADGATE & YEATMAN

Bottled in Oporto   VINHOS, S.A.R.L.   Product of Portugal

ALCOHOL 20.5%   IMPORTED BY   NET CONTENTS
BY VOLUME   **Charles Lefranc Cellars**   750 ml
SAN JOSE, CALIFORNIA · SOLE AGENTS FOR U.S.A.

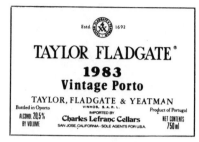

1938 TAYLOR: Not many top houses besides Noval declared 1938. Both this wine and Noval have seen better days. This is more like a tawny at this point. It would have been better about a decade ago, but it's still enjoyable. Medium light garnet, with a nutty, light violet nose, medium-bodied, with sweet violet, nut and fruit flavors and a long finish. A hint of vintage fruit still lingers. Last tasted: 4/90. Drink 1990. Release: £.30. Current retail: $265 (£125). Current auction: £80. **79**

1935 TAYLOR: I tasted two bottles the same night during a blind tasting of 1934s and 1935s. They were bottled by different wine merchants, but they were just about the same in quality and character — delicate and refined, ready to drink. Medium red with a garnet edge, delicate cherry and vanilla aromas, medium-bodied, with balanced, silky, sweet cherry flavors and a long finish. Last tasted: 2/90. Drink 1990. Release: £.30. Current retail: $380 (£206). Current auction: $325 (£171). **88**

1927 TAYLOR: This blows the 1935 off the table. It is incredibly concentrated yet superbly balanced. It lives up to Taylor's lofty reputation. Medium ruby-garnet, with intense raspberry and blackberry aromas, full-bodied, with rich, velvety, ripe raspberry flavors and a long, thick, rich finish. It will continue to improve with age. Last tasted: 12/89. Drink 1990. Release: £.20. Current retail: $440 (£210). Current auction: $385 (£160). **95**

VAN ZELLER

CLASSIFICATION: *Not rated*

COLLECTIBILITY RATING: *Not rated*

Van Zeller & Co. was a well-known Port shipper in the 18th and 19th centuries, but fell into oblivion early this century. Although the owners of Quinta do Noval bought Van Zeller in 1930, it was not until the 1980s that they began to resurrect this historic house.

Cristiano van Zeller, managing director of Noval, has plans for the house, and the fact that his descendants founded Van Zeller & Co. in 1780 only fuels his determination to build the house's reputation as a small, quality producer. In mid-1990, he signed an agreement tying the production of Quinta do Roriz to Van Zeller, and future vintage Port from the property will be called Van Zeller's Quinta do Roriz.

The Quinta do Roriz property, located across the Douro River from Tua, is owned by van Zeller's cousins. It has a centuries-old reputation for producing excellent quality vintage Ports, and has supplied such shippers as Kopke and Gonzales Byass with wine in the past.

Recent vintage Ports from Van Zeller already have been good quality, although all the wines came from various properties in the Pinhão region of the Douro Valley. With its production equaling about 1,000 cases of each vintage, Van Zeller made a particularly good 1983 — which, incidentally, is much better than the 1982 Quinta do Noval. It is a firm vintage Port with plenty of generous fruit and silky tannins. The 1985 is less good but attractive, nonetheless. One can only assume that future vintages of Van Zeller will be even better with the production of Quinta do Roriz now on tap, considering the quality of the *quinta*-produced vintage Ports below.

AT A GLANCE
VAN ZELLER
Rua Candido dos Reis 575
4401 Vila Nova de Gaia,
  Portugal
02-30.20.20
Owners: van Zeller family
Founded: 1780
Average production: 2,000 cases

TASTING NOTES

1985 VAN ZELLER: Not as good as the 1983, but it shows some power and robust fruit. It should be ready sooner than the 1983. Deep purple with a red hue, spicy raisin and plum nose, medium-bodied, with sweet raisin flavors that seem slightly burnt. Good tannic backbone. Last tasted: 1/90. Drink 1996. Release: £11. Current retail: £18. Current auction: NA. **80**

1985 VAN ZELLER QUINTA DO RORIZ: Impressive; this is a tough, tannic young vintage Port. Deep ruby colored with some purple and a nose of black currants and jam, it is full bodied with lots of jammy

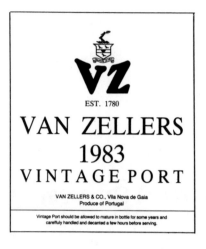

fruit, full tannins and an excellent balance. Last tasted: 7/90. Drink 1996-1998. Not released. **87**

1983 VAN ZELLER: This is much better than the 1982 Quinta do Noval. Deep ruby, with a nose full of violets and perfume, medium-bodied, with elegant, silky fruit flavors, medium tannins and a good finish. Last tasted: 1/90. Drink 1996-1998. Release: $22 (£10). Current retail: $30 (£15). Current auction: NA. **84**

1983 QUINTA DO RORIZ: This is a good all around young vintage Port. Deep dense ruby colored with a dark chocolate, fruity nose, it is full bodied with fleshy fruit, medium tannins, and tons of ripe fruit on the finish. Last tasted: 7/90. Drink 1993-1995. Not available. **84**

1970 QUINTA DO RORIZ: Rather tightly structured, the 1970 Roriz is burly vintage Port with an intriguing ripe blackcherry, pepper nose and flavors. Medium ruby with some garnet on the rim and a peppery, ripe slightly roasted nose, it is full bodied with blackpepper fruit, medium tannins, and a jammy, closed finish. Last tasted: 7/90. Not available. **86**

1960 QUINTA DO RORIZ: This is an elegant understated vintage Port for current drinking. Medium deep garnet with some ruby hue and an understated nose with attractive raspberry, chocolate, berry aromas, it is medium bodied with berry, chocolate fruit flavors, linear structure and medium tannins. Light finish. Last tasted: 7/90. Drink 1990. Not available. **83**

VASCONCELOS
CLASSIFICATION: *Not rated*

COLLECTIBILITY RATING: *Not rated*

BEST VINTAGE: *1963*

While the company of Vasconcelos remains rather mysterious, the vintage Ports it ships under the names of Gonzales Byass and Butler & Nephew are straightforward in style and average to very good in quality. Of course, I have only tasted vintage Ports under those brands when the Vasconcelos firm had nothing to do with them.

After numerous attempts at contacting someone within Vasconcelos, I was only able to get secondhand information from the company's former Belgian agent and other Port shippers. The firm is still owned by the Christie family, a British family with a history in the Port trade; however, all the Vasconcelos' stocks of Port were sold to Sandeman in 1989. Family members are apparently still acting as brokers, trading in bulk Port for various European markets.

Vasconcelos purchased the house of Gonzales Byass in 1983, after the massive Sherry company decided to get out of the Port business. Butler & Nephew had been part of Gonzales Byass since Word War II. Gonzales Byass was founded in Oporto in 1896 and Butler & Nephew in 1789.

The two firms' vintage Ports are quite similar in style. They are rather one-dimensional with a good level of sweet fruit and solid backbones. The Butler & Nephew wines appear to be not quite as good as those from Gonzales Byass. They seem to have been aged in wood longer since a nutty, vanilla character protrudes on the palate.

The 1963 Gonzales Byass is exceptionally good. It is a big, powerful, jammy vintage Port with plenty of tannin and backbone. There have been press reports that the Sherry firm of Gonzales Byass may get back in the Port business, and the firm's French agent confirmed this. Considering the very good quality of the 1963 Gonzales Byass, this would be a good move.

AT A GLANCE
VASCONCELOS
Apartado 60
4401 Vila Nova de Gaia,
   Portugal
02-30.45.54

Owners: Christie family

Founded: Gonzales Byass (1896)
   Butler & Nephew (1789)

Average production: NA

1 9 6 3
VINTAGE PORT

PRODUCED, BOTTLED & SHIPPED
BY
GONZALES, BYASS & C.º
VILA NOVA DE GAIA
PRODUCE OF PORTUGAL

TASTING NOTES

1975 BUTLER & NEPHEW: Light, simple and pleasant, but just too simple to be considered a good vintage Port; it's much more like a ruby. Medium to light red, with lots of garnet, a roasted nut, vanilla, slightly musty nose, light-bodied, with simple berry, vanilla-roast coffee flavors and light tannins. Last tasted: 7/90. Release: £4. Current retail: $37 (£20). Current auction: £11. **74**

1970 BUTLER & NEPHEW: This is not a bad Port but it seems to have been aged in wood much too long for my taste. Very nutty, more like an old style, late-bottled vintage Port. Medium red garnet, with a roasted nut vanilla cherry nose, medium-bodied with round roasted nut and fruit flavors, quite nutty and hot on the finish. Last tasted: 7/90. Release price: £2. Current retail: $50 (£25). Current auction: $24 (£13). **76**

1970 GONZALEZ BYASS: This vintage Port is quite similar in structure to the 1970 Butler & Nephew, but it seems to have spent less in wood. Very ripe and peppery, medium ruby, with a spicy, earthy nose, medium-bodied, with jammy fruit flavors, medium tannins and a long finish. Quite good. Last tasted: 6/90. Drink 1990-1992. Release price: £2. Current retail: $50 (£25). Current auction: $24 (£13). **81**

1963 GONZALEZ BYASS: This is big, fat and rich, with plenty of very sweet, jammy fruit flavors, although a little one-dimensional. Medium to deep garnet-ruby with a garnet edge, a rich plum, raspberry nose, medium- to full-bodied, with very sweet plum and berry fruit flavors and medium-tough tannins. Very sweet finish. Last tasted: 7/90. Drink 1990. Release: £.90. Current retail: $82 (£30). Current auction: $38 (£18). **87**

VIEIRA DE SOUSA

CLASSIFICATION: *Not rated*

COLLECTIBILITY RATING: *Not rated*

About 12 years after Manuel Barros created a Port house bearing his name, he asked a well-regarded Port blender, Alcino Vieira de Sousa, to join his company and start a subsidiary with him. The two men agreed and the House of Vieira de Sousa was founded in 1925.

Unfortunately, what glory that existed then in this house's Ports cannot be found in its wines today. The vintages of Sousa are incredibly light and extremely simplistic. I have never tasted its standard rubies and tawnies sold under the Sousa brand. Perhaps they are more interesting. They apparently sell well in West Germany and Holland.

AT A GLANCE

VIEIRA DE SOUSA
Rua de Leonor de Freitas 182, C.P. 29
4400 Vila Nova de Gaia, Portugal
02-30.23.20

Owners: Barros family

Founded: 1925

Average production: 1,000-2,000 cases

TASTING NOTES

1985 VIEIRA DE SOUSA: Pleasant flavors and aromas, but lacks depth and body. Medium ruby, with a light, earthy beet and berry nose, medium-bodied, with light tannins and advanced flavors. Last tasted: 1/90. Drink 1990-1992. Not available. **70**

1980 VIEIRA DE SOUSA: Beginning to fade, but still drinkable. Medium ruby-red, with a slightly hot, grapy nose, medium-bodied, with cherry flavors and a very simple finish. Quite out of balance. Last tasted: 1/90. Drink 1990. Not available **70**

1978 VIEIRA DE SOUSA: More like a decent, traditional late-bottled vintage with some bottle age. Medium to light ruby, with a simple grapy nose, medium-bodied, with clean, fresh fruit flavors and a short finish. Very easy to drink. Last tasted: 1/90. Drink 1990. Not available. **74**

1970 VIEIRA DE SOUSA: Very light, simple and fruity. Medium red with a deep garnet edge, earthy, grapy aromas, light-bodied, with grapy flavors, light tannins and a short finish. Last tasted: 1/90. Drink 1990. Not available. **71**

WARRE

CLASSIFICATION: *SECOND TIER*

COLLECTIBILITY RATING: *AA*

BEST VINTAGES: *1927, 1963, 1977*

Warre sometimes seems like a forgotten stepchild of the Symington group, since its other vintage Ports, Graham and Dow, often receive the limelight. But Warre vintage Ports can be equally dramatic in quality, with opulent aromas, generous fresh fruit flavors and ripe tannins.

The Warre vintages fall somewhere between Dow and Graham in style, with Dow being the driest and Graham the sweetest. Mature Warre vintage Ports develop beautifully perfumed aromas that carry though to a supple, fruity palate. They are extremely harmonious wines.

Since the 1960s, the quality of Warre vintage Port has been on an upswing. Both the 1963 and 1966 are remarkably good wines, with intense, rich berry and cassis notes on the nose and the palate. They are rather gentle wines that soothe the palate with sweet fruit.

For cellaring, vintages like the 1977 and 1985 are equally impressive, with a great deal of sweet, concentrated fruit and solid tannic backbones. They need 12 to 15 years of aging, and will reward those with patience.

"The Symingtons have been able to pay more attention to Warre since the 1960s," said William Warre, 64, whose family owned part of Warre until 1960 and who still works for the Symingtons in London. "For many years, Warre was always number two to Dow. Now, it has gotten full attention, just like Graham and Dow. It has had new life breathed into it in the last 30 years."

Traditionally, the vintage wines of Warre have come from various *quintas* in the Rio Torto Valley and the Pinhão Valley. A major contributor to the Warre blend has been Quinta do Bom-Retiro, a large vineyard in the Rio Torto Valley. Adriano Ramos-Pinto owns half of the 250-acre Bom-Retiro estate; the rest is owned by the Serdio family, which sells primarily to Warre. All of the Ports from Bom-Retiro are produced in *lagares*.

In 1980 the Symingtons bought Quinta da Cavadinha in the Pinhão Valley and earmarked its production for Warre. Cavadinha encompasses about 86 acres of vineyards, and its best wines are now used for Warre vintages in declared years. The *quinta* also makes a single-*quinta* wine in undeclared years. All the wines there are made through a combined autovinification-*remontagem* system, in stainless steel temperature-controlled vats. Warre's vintage Port production varies between

12,000 and 17,000 cases a year.

Warre is the oldest continuously owned British Port house, with its antecedents dating back to 1670. Warre did not become the company's name until a member of the Warre family joined wine merchant John Clark as a partner in 1729. There were no Warres left in the company by the 1860s. Some Warre family members, however, remained in the Port trade as shareholders in the house of Silva & Cosens. The Symingtons became partners in Warre in 1905, when A.J. Symington joined the company as a shareholder. Symington exchanged shares in 1914 with the Warres at Silva & Cosens so that the Warre family became associated with the house again. The Symingtons bought the Warre shares in both houses by 1960.

Warre remains one of the gems of vintage Port and the Symingtons are continually polishing it. "I am not sure why Warre has been so much better in recent years, but the Symingtons have given it the attention it needs," added William Warre.

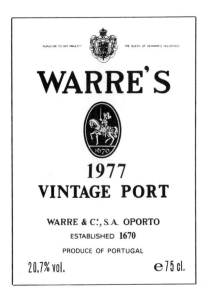

TASTING NOTES

1985 WARRE: There is plenty of grip and backbone here. Deep purple, with concentrated grape and violet aromas, full-bodied, with huge grapy flavors, excellent backbone and a long finish. Last tasted: 6/90. Drink 1998-2000. Release: $28 (£13). Current retail: $35 (£18). Current auction: $33 (£13). **91**

1983 WARRE: Slightly simple and sweet, but still very good. Deep purple, with fresh violet and berry aromas, full-bodied, with very sweet fruit flavors, full tannins and a medium finish. Last tasted: 6/90. Drink 1996-1998. Release: $28 (£10). Current retail: $31 (£15). Current auction: $28 (£11). **88**

1980 WARRE: A solid vintage Port from an unsung vintage. Medium ruby, with clean perfume and black cherry aromas, full-bodied, with silky, sweet concentrated berry flavors and a medium finish. Last tasted: 6/90. Drink 1990-1992. Release: $16 (£9). Current retail: $37 (£14). Current auction: $32 (£10). **88**

1977 WARRE: Rich and highly flavored, starting to open into a superb wine. Deep ruby, with a very perfumed cassis nose, full-bodied, with tons of sweet berry flavors, full, round tannins and a ripe fruit finish. A gentle giant of a wine. Last tasted: 4/90. Drink 1995-1997. Release: $15 (£6.50). Current retail: $56 (£28). Current auction: $38 (£17). **92**

1975 WARRE: Although this wine has attractive mature aromas, it is beginning to dry out. Medium red with a light red rim, chocolate and perfume aromas, light-bodied, with sweet dried cherry flavors and a light finish. Last tasted: 8/88. Drink 1990. Release: £5. Current retail: $40 (£17). Current auction: $32 (£12). **75**

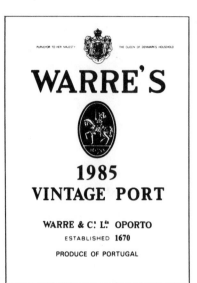

1970 WARRE: Wonderful fruit on the palate, but slightly one-dimensional. Medium deep red, with earthy cassis and tomato aromas, full-bodied, with concentrated black cherry flavors, medium tannins and a long, sweet finish. Quite delicate. Last tasted: 12/89. Drink 1990-1993. Release: £2.30. Current retail: $70 (£30). Current auction: $51 (£22). **88**

1966 WARRE: There is still plenty of fresh, youthful fruit here. Medium ruby-red, with an intense floral and berry nose, medium-bodied, with rich, sweet fruit flavors, medium tannins and a lingering finish. Very good fruit. Last tasted: 6/89. Drink 1990. Release: £1.50. Current retail: $83 (£45). Current auction: $83 (£24). **91**

1963 WARRE: Extremely impressive, with beautifully balanced, harmonious sweet fruit on the palate. Medium ruby-red, ripe cherry and cassis aromas, medium-bodied, with rich, velvety fruit flavors, full, soft tannins and a powerful finish. Last tasted: 12/89. Drink 1990-1992. Release: £1.15. Current retail: $130 (£50). Current auction: $90 (£40). **92**

1960 WARRE: Gentle and rather exotic. Medium red with a garnet edge, a unique nectarine, honey and plum nose, medium- to light-bodied, with sweet, delicate cherry flavors and a supple finish. Drink soon. Last tasted: 8/88. Drink 1990. Release: £.95. Current retail: $85 (£30). Current auction: $85 (£22). **82**

1958 WARRE: A very fresh, clean and delicate Port. Light ruby with a garnet hue, light and peppery on the nose, light-bodied, with fresh cherry flavors, silky light tannins and a sweet finish. Last tasted: 11/89. Drink 1990. Release: £.90. Current retail: $99 (£23). Current auction: $70 (£18). **81**

1955 WARRE: An enchanting wine with soft, sweet cherry flavors. Light to medium red, with a delicate earth and berry nose, medium-bodied, with sweet cherry flavors, a balance of medium tannins and a long, sweet finish. Last tasted: 11/89. Drink 1990. Release: £1. Current retail: $155 (£67). Current auction: $115 (£44). **86**

1947 WARRE: Light and rather fragile. Pale ruby-garnet, with delicate floral aromas, light-bodied, with sweet, soft berry flavors, a firm backbone and a light finish. Last tasted: 11/89. Drink 1990. Release: £.45. Current retail: $225 (£80). Current auction: $160 (£52). **84**

1945 WARRE: This is like a deliciously fresh bowl of fruit. Medium red-ruby with a garnet rim, a nose of cranberries and cherries, full-bodied, with sweet cranberry flavors and a lovely balance of round tannins. A wonderful glass of Port. Last tasted: 11/89. Drink 1990. Release: £.40. Current retail: $345 (£110). Current auction: $235 (£83). **88**

1934 WARRE: The extremely hot 1934 vintage produced some rich, thick and powerful vintage Port, but this one remains extremely elegant. It is a delight to drink now. Light red with a garnet edge, elegant cherry and raspberry aromas, medium-bodied, with light cherry and tomato flavors and a medium finish. Last tasted: 2/90. Drink 1990. Release: £.30. Current retail: $285 (£80). Current auction: $220 (£44). **87**

1927 WARRE: This may be one of the greatest Warre vintages ever produced. It is still amazingly crisp and firm. Medium ruby-garnet, with a unique nose of boysenberry syrup, abundant sweet cassis flavors, an excellent balance of velvety tannins and a long finish. Last tasted: 12/89. Drink 1990. Release: £.20. Current retail: $340 (£130). Current auction: $205 (£88). **93**

1900 WARRE: I have only tasted this wine once, but according to James Symington, whose family owns Warre, the bottle I tried was not a good example. I thought it was more like an old Madeira, slightly oxidized and tired. It was over the hill, but interesting. Garnet with a green edge, slightly nutty aromas with hints of orange peel, very light-bodied, with sweet, nutty fruit flavors and a very light finish. Last tasted: 11/89. Drink 1990. Release: £.10. Current retail: $425 (£140). Current auction: £100. **79**

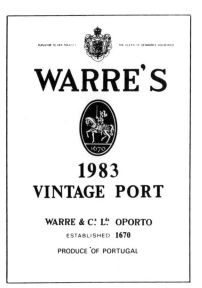

WIESE & KROHN
CLASSIFICATION: *FIFTH TIER*
COLLECTIBILITY RATING: *Not rated*

BEST VINTAGES: *1957, 1960, 1958*

Vintage Port "was a matter of personal pleasure" for the owners of the small premium firm of Wiese & Krohn, according to José Falcão Carneiro. In the past, his family simply made a few hundred cases of vintage Port for its own cellar and focused its commercial attention on fine tawnies and other Ports.

Today there is a growing demand for Krohn's vintages as the firm's reputation increases. "We never had a problem until now for our vintage wines," said Carneiro, 42. "Now, we can't keep up with the demand."

Wiese & Krohn vintage Ports are very rich and sweet, with round tannins and a lingering finish. They soothe one's palate with an abundance of chocolate and grape flavors. The 1984 Wiese & Krohn is a fine example of a recent vintage, with a rather thick, firm structure fleshed out with attractively sweet black pepper and fruit flavors and high alcohol.

Some of the older vintages are very impressive, especially the 1960, 1958 and 1957. All these wines are slightly different, but they share a common richness and sweetness unique to the house of Krohn. "It was our tradition to make this type of vintage Port," said José's father, Fernando, 71. "You must have high alcohol and sweetness. That allows the wine to age."

His vintage Ports from the 1950s and 1960s prove his point, while the exceptions are the 1967 and 1970, which are light and forward. José Carneiro admitted they had some problems with growers during that period, but he also said that they sometimes don't produce good wines in years when other house have good results. "We never follow the general rule," he said. "For example, 1970 was a great year but it was not for us."

All Krohn's vintage Ports come from growers in the Rio Torto Valley who still make them primarily by *lagar*. In 1989 Wiese & Krohn bought a small property in the Rio Torto, Quinta do Retiro Novo, which has about 40 acres of vineyards and produces 60 pipes of Port.

Krohn is one of the few houses whose head blender-taster is a woman. Maria José Aguiar, who resembles singer Bette Midler, has worked at Krohn for 20 years. She makes the final vintage blends, along with father, son and sister Carneiro. The firm's vintage Port production ranges from about 1,250 cases for the young vintages to 400 cases for the older ones.

Wiese & Krohn was established in 1865 by two Norwegians, Theodore Wiese and Dankert Krohn, who had come to trade in codfish. The Carneiro family became shareholders in 1922.

"This is a family business," said José Carneiro. "Everybody does everything. Everyone is linked to the product."

TASTING NOTES

1985 WIESE & KROHN: This has attractive roasted coffee aromas and flavors in a more forward style than many of the top 1985s. Deep ruby with a purple edge, a bitter chocolate and coffee nose, full-bodied, with a velvety mouth-feel, medium tannins and a sweet finish. Last tasted: 1/90. Drink 1994-1995. Release: $21 (£14). Current retail: $32 (£15). Current auction: NA. **81**

1984 WIESE & KROHN: A wonderfully elegant and well-made wine from an unheralded vintage, like a young 1967 Cockburn. Deep ruby, with a lovely grape and violet nose, medium- to full-bodied, with grapy black pepper flavors, medium tannins and a long finish. Very attractive balance. Last tasted: 1/90. Drink 1994-1995. Release: $13 (£10). Current retail: $20 (£11). Current auction: NA. **86**

1982 WIESE & KROHN: Very elegant and well-balanced. Medium ruby with a red hue, lovely chocolate, coffee and mahogany aromas, full-bodied, with round, velvety fruit flavors, medium tannins and a long finish. Much drier than the house's usual vintage. Last tasted: 1/90. Drink 1992-1994. Release: $14 (£8). Current retail: $29 (£15). Current auction: NA. **83**

1978 WIESE & KROHN: A very good 1978 with excellent aromas. Ruby-red, with rich, ripe, grapy, floral aromas, full-bodied, with lots of ripe fruit and black pepper flavors, very sweet, with plenty of backbone. Last tasted: 1/90. Drink 1990-1994. Release: $11 (£6). Current retail: $39 (£24). Current auction: NA. **84**

1975 WIESE & KROHN: A well-made wine from a weak vintage. Medium ruby-red, with a perfumed violet nose, medium-bodied, with very sweet, round fruit flavors, good acidity and lovely balance. Last tasted: 1/90. Drink 1990. Release: £4.50. Current retail: $55 (£27). Current auction: NA. **80**

1970 WIESE & KROHN: Not up to this house's standards. A forward medium garnet, coffee on the nose, medium- to light-bodied, with coffee and slightly burnt fruit flavors and a light tannic finish. Last tasted: 1/90. Drink 1990. Release: £2. Current retail: $81 (£39). Current auction: NA. **74**

PORTO VINTAGE

KROHN'S
1982

SHIPPED BY
WIESE & KROHN, SUCRS., LDA.
OPORTO
ESTABLISHED 1865
PRODUCE OF PORTUGAL

ALC. BY VOL. 20.1%   750 ML

PORT CAN FORM A DEPOSIT. PLEASE TAKE CARE WHEN SERVING
PORTO
PRODUCED IN THE DEMARCATED WINE DOURO REGION

1967 WIESE & KROHN: Starts out well but fades quickly. Medium red-garnet, with a leather and chocolate nose, medium-bodied, with sweet milk chocolate flavors, light tannins and a medium finish. Last tasted: 1/90. Drink 1990. Release: £1.30. Current retail: $81 (£40). Current auction: NA. **75**

1965 WIESE & KROHN: Surprisingly good, with an impressive richness and intensity of fruit on the palate. Medium red with a garnet edge, a lovely spicy berry and chocolate nose, medium-bodied, with very sweet, round fruit flavors and a firm backbone. Will improve with age. Last tasted: 1/90. Drink 1990. Release: £1.30. Current retail: $100 (£50). Current auction: NA. **85**

1963 WIESE & KROHN: This is a gutsy wine with rich, focused fruit flavors. Medium ruby, with a very fresh cassis and black cherry nose, medium-bodied, with sweet coffee and cherry flavors and medium tannins on the finish. Last tasted: 1/90. Drink 1990. Release: £1. Current retail: $165 (£69). Current auction: NA. **87**

1961 WIESE & KROHN: A powerful and lean wine. Medium red, with a slightly roasted coffee nose, medium-bodied, with roasted chocolate and rich fruit flavors, quite tough on the finish. Last tasted: 1/90. Drink 1990. Release: £1. Current retail: $125 (£75). Current auction: NA. **85**

1960 WIESE & KROHN: Full-bodied and rich for the vintage. Light to medium red with a garnet edge, a rich cassis nose, medium-bodied, with very rich flavors, balanced tannins and a lovely, long finish. Last tasted: 1/90. Drink 1990. Release: £.80. Current retail: $144 (£50). Current auction: NA. **89**

1958 WIESE & KROHN: This is one of the very best 1958s available. Medium ruby with a garnet edge, very delicate floral and grapy aromas, light- to medium-bodied, with lovely cherry flavors, great balance and a medium finish. Last tasted: 1/90. Drink 1990. Release: £.80. Current retail: $180 (£75). Current auction: NA. **87**

1957 WIESE & KROHN: Big and youthful, hard and powerful, like an excellent 1966. Medium ruby with a red-garnet rim, rich, complex aromas of berries and earth, full-bodied, with very rich, youthful fruit flavors, medium tannins and a very long finish. A great surprise. Last tasted: 1/90. Drink 1990. Release: £.80. Current retail: $214 (£90). Current auction: NA. **91**

APPENDICES

APPENDIX 1
All Ports Tasted, Listed Alphabetically by House

Score	Vintage	Wine	US Prices Release/Current/Auction			UK Prices Release/Current/Auction			Drink	Last Tasted
BARROS, ALMEIDA										
81	1987	BARROS, ALMEIDA	$28	$28	NA	£14	£14	NA	1995-1996	1/90
80	1985	BARROS, ALMEIDA	24	29	NA	10	14	NA	1994-1996	1/90
76	1983	BARROS, ALMEIDA	8	29	NA	7	15	NA	1990-1993	1/90
75	1978	BARROS, ALMEIDA	7	30	NA	5	13	NA	1990	1/90
74	1974	BARROS, ALMEIDA	NA	40	NA	3	20	NA	1990	1/90
82	1970	BARROS, ALMEIDA	NA	60	NA	2	30	11	1990	1/90
BORGES & IRMAO										
70	1985	BORGES	15	15	NA	10	14	NA	1990	5/90
70	1983	BORGES	12	29	NA	7	15	NA	1990-1992	5/90
79	1982	BORGES	12	30	NA	6	13	NA	1991-1993	5/90
70	1980	BORGES	11	23	NA	6	13	NA	1990	5/90
65	1979	BORGES	11	22	NA	6	12	NA	Avoid	5/90
59	1970	BORGES	NA	60	NA	2	28	11	Avoid	5/90
BURMESTER										
93	1985	BURMESTER	25	25	NA	12	16	NA	1996-1998	1/90
84	1984	BURMESTER	NA	NA	NA	11	14	NA	1993-1995	1/90
88	1980	BURMESTER	18	33	NA	7	15	NA	1993	1/90
82	1977	BURMESTER	11	37	NA	5	28	NA	1991-1993	1/90
86	1970	BURMESTER	NA	55	NA	2	32	NA	1990	1/90
83	1963	BURMESTER	NA	110	NA	0.90	42	NA	1990	1/90
A.A. CALEM & FILHO										
84	1987	CALEM Quinta do Foz	28	28	NA	NR	NR	NR	1995-1996	6/90
88	1985	CALEM	25	36	NA	10	21	NA	1995-1997	6/90
84	1983	CALEM	18	38	NA	9	18	7	1994-1996	6/90
82	1982	CALEM Quinta do Foz	16	34	NA	8	18	NA	1993-1995	6/90
78	1980	CALEM	14	34	NA	7	17	6	1990	6/90
69	1977	CALEM	11	55	23	5	20	12	Avoid	11/89
86	1975	CALEM	NA	50	NA	4.50	25	13	1990	2/90
80	1970	CALEM	NA	50	NA	2	32	13	1990-1994	11/89
82	1966	CALEM	NA	65	40	1.25	40	16	1990	11/89
82	1963	CALEM	NA	85	NA	0.90	42	NA	1990	12/89
CHAMPALIMAUD										
86	1982	CHAMPALIMAUD	20	20	NA	7	15	NA	1992-1994	2/90
CHURCHILL (CHURCHILL GRAHAM)										
83	1987	CHURCHILL Agua Alta	37	37	NA	NR	NR	NR	1995-1997	5/90
78	1986	CHURCHILL Fojo	NR	NR	NR	14	14	NA	1994	2/90
81	1985	CHURCHILL	22	32	NA	12	17	8	1993-1995	6/90
79	1984	CHURCHILL Fojo	NA	NA	NA	12	14	NA	1993	2/90
69	1983	CHURCHILL Agua Alta	22	27	NA	9	15	6	Avoid	7/90
78	1982	CHURCHILL	NA	NA	NA	10	14	10	1990-1992	6/90
COCKBURN SMITHES										
90	1985	COCKBURN	33	37	28	13	20	12	1996-1998	6/90
97	1983	COCKBURN	22	45	28	10	18	12	1998-2000	6/90
77	1975	COCKBURN	NA	44	28	5	18	13	1990	1/90
86	1970	COCKBURN	NA	78	68	2.30	28	20	1990	12/89
85	1967	COCKBURN	NA	55	45	1.50	32	15	1990	12/89
88	1963	COCKBURN	NA	110	85	1.15	40	34	1990	12/89
80	1960	COCKBURN	NA	85	51	0.90	30	24	1990	8/88
84	1958	COCKBURN	NA	NA	NA	NA	NA	NA	1990	11/89
90	1955	COCKBURN	NA	155	110	1	NA	41	1990	11/89
76	1950	COCKBURN	NA	110	90	0.60	65	38	1990	11/89
90	1947	COCKBURN	NA	185	150	0.45	75	45	1990	11/89

NA—not available. NR—not released. Auction prices include 10% buyer's premium (where charged).

Score	Vintage	Wine	US Prices Release/Current/Auction			UK Prices Release/Current/Auction			Drink	Last Tasted
92	1935	COCKBURN	NA	$320	$200	£0.30	£145	£79	1990	2/90
89	1931	COCKBURN	NA	NA	NA	NA	NA	NA	1990	1/90
91	1927	COCKBURN	NA	300	200	0.30	145	146	1990	12/89
91	1912	COCKBURN	NA	350	275	0.40	180	77	1990	10/87
89	1908	COCKBURN	NA	395	325	0.20	185	143	1990	10/87
75	1904	COCKBURN	NA	330	240	0.20	120	94	1990	10/87
82	1896	COCKBURN	NA	400	240	0.15	130	100	1990	2/90

CROFT

Score	Vintage	Wine	US Prices Release/Current/Auction			UK Prices Release/Current/Auction			Drink	Last Tasted
81	1985	CROFT	30	37	29	13	18	14	1995-1997	6/90
69	1982	CROFT	22	37	NA	10	16	8	Avoid	4/90
85	1977	CROFT	14	50	44	6.50	28	16	1992-1994	4/90
76	1975	CROFT	NA	40	28	5	18	13	1990	8/88
89	1970	CROFT	NA	70	55	2.30	25	18	1990	12/89
90	1966	CROFT	NA	68	60	1.50	30	21	1990	12/89
91	1963	CROFT	NA	110	85	1.15	59	33	1990	12/89
90	1960	CROFT	NA	88	57	0.90	30	20	1990	9/89
84	1955	CROFT	NA	145	100	1	45	33	1990	11/89
77	1950	CROFT	NA	170	125	0.60	70	35	1990	4/90
99	1945	CROFT	NA	375	220	0.40	135	94	1990	11/89
93	1935	CROFT	NA	285	240	0.30	95	73	1990	2/90
87	1927	CROFT	NA	350	195	0.20	150	105	1990	12/89

C. DA SILVA

Score	Vintage	Wine	US Prices Release/Current/Auction			UK Prices Release/Current/Auction			Drink	Last Tasted
80	1987	PRESIDENTIAL	NR	NR	NR	NR	NR	NR	1996-1998	2/90
78	1985	PRESIDENTIAL	30	30	NA	10	10	NA	1992-1993	2/90
77	1978	PRESIDENTIAL	NA	34	NA	5	15	NA	1990	2/90
72	1977	PRESIDENTIAL	NA	42	NA	5	20	NA	1991-1993	2/90
75	1970	PRESIDENTIAL	NA	50	18	2	29	NA	1990	2/90

DELAFORCE, SONS & CO.

Score	Vintage	Wine	US Prices Release/Current/Auction			UK Prices Release/Current/Auction			Drink	Last Tasted
81	1985	DELAFORCE	24	27	NA	11	20	NA	1995-1996	6/90
69	1982	DELAFORCE	20	27	NA	10	15	NA	Avoid	6/90
80	1977	DELAFORCE	11	44	28	5	25	12	1990-1993	2/90
76	1975	DELAFORCE	NA	33	22	4.50	17	11	1990	2/90
89	1970	DELAFORCE	NA	40	30	2	24	16	1990	2/90
85	1966	DELAFORCE	NA	65	45	1.30	26	19	1990	2/90
93	1963	DELAFORCE	NA	100	70	0.90	29	19	1990	2/90

DIEZ HERMANOS

Score	Vintage	Wine	US Prices Release/Current/Auction			UK Prices Release/Current/Auction			Drink	Last Tasted
82	1977	DIEZ HERMANOS	NA	NA	NA	4	20	NA	1990-1992	4/90

DOW

Score	Vintage	Wine	US Prices Release/Current/Auction			UK Prices Release/Current/Auction			Drink	Last Tasted
89	1985	DOW	30	35	27	13	22	12	1996-1998	6/90
94	1983	DOW	20	34	25	10	19	12	1996-1998	6/90
90	1980	DOW	15	32	25	9	12	10	1991-1993	6/90
94	1977	DOW	12	60	57	6.50	28	16	1995-1997	4/90
80	1975	DOW	NA	45	30	5	18	15	1990	4/89
79	1972	DOW	NA	39	32	2	20	18	1990	1/90
94	1970	DOW	NA	66	49	2.30	29	20	1990-1993	12/89
94	1966	DOW	NA	90	80	1.50	38	25	1990-1992	12/89
92	1963	DOW	NA	125	108	1.15	42	42	1990-1992	2/90
88	1960	DOW	NA	88	50	0.95	32	26	1990	2/89
91	1955	DOW	NA	190	170	1	85	66	1990	4/90
86	1950	DOW	NA	80	NA	0.60	60	13	1990	11/89
88	1947	DOW	NA	230	209	0.45	80	47	1990	11/89
89	1945	DOW	NA	370	280	0.40	195	116	1990	11/89
79	1935	DOW	NA	300	250	0.30	100	106	1990	6/90
84	1934	DOW	NA	350	285	0.30	100	75	1990	6/90
87	1927	DOW	NA	425	300	0.20	150	150	1990	4/90

H. & C.J. FEIST

Score	Vintage	Wine	US Prices Release/Current/Auction			UK Prices Release/Current/Auction			Drink	Last Tasted
72	1985	FEIST	20	24	NA	10	14	NA	1992	1/90
78	1982	FEIST	NA	NA	NA	6.50	13	NA	1990-1992	1/90

NA—not available. NR—not released. Auction prices include 10% buyer's premium (where charged).

Score	Vintage	Wine	US Prices Release/Current/Auction			UK Prices Release/Current/Auction			Drink	Last Tasted
78	1978	FEIST	NA	NA	NA	£5	£13	NA	1990	1/90

A.A. FERREIRA

Score	Vintage	Wine							Drink	Last Tasted
88	1987	FERREIRA	NR	NR	NR	14	14	NA	1997-1999	11/89
87	1985	FERREIRA	20	26	NA	11	20	NA	1996-1998	11/89
91	1983	FERREIRA Quinta do Seixo	14	22	NA	10	16	NA	1996-1998	11/89
81	1982	FERREIRA	14	25	NA	8	15	NA	1992-1994	11/89
80	1980	FERREIRA	13	21	NA	7	16	NA	1991-1992	11/89
89	1978	FERREIRA	11	28	NA	5	16	NA	1993-1996	11/89
86	1977	FERREIRA	11	35	NA	5	20	22	1992-1995	11/89
81	1975	FERREIRA	NA	32	NA	4.50	16	NA	1990	11/89
86	1970	FERREIRA	NA	40	25	2	23	12	1990-1992	4/89
85	1966	FERREIRA	NA	81	38	1.30	25	12	1990	11/89
85	1963	FERREIRA	NA	110	50	0.90	30	24	1990	8/88
80	1960	FERREIRA	NA	100	35	0.90	20	15	1990	8/88
85	1955	FERREIRA	NA	110	97	1	48	23	1990	11/89
79	1950	FERREIRA	NA	90	NA	0.60	45	NA	1990	11/89
81	1945	FERREIRA	NA	205	150	0.40	75	44	1990	11/89
93	1935	FERREIRA	NA	200	NA	0.30	65	66	1990	2/90

FEUERHEERD BROTHERS

Score	Vintage	Wine							Drink	Last Tasted
72	1985	FEUERHEERD BROTHERS	NA	NA	NA	10	14	NA	1991-1992	1/90
76	1980	FEUERHEERD BROTHERS	NA	NA	NA	6	13	NA	1990	1/90
69	1977	FEUERHEERD BROTHERS	NA	17	NA	5	15	6	Avoid	1/90
80	1970	FEUERHEERD BROTHERS	NA	40	NA	2	20	11	1990	1/90

FONSECA

Score	Vintage	Wine							Drink	Last Tasted
95	1985	FONSECA	32	39	33	13	28	15	1998-2000	6/90
90	1983	FONSECA	24	37	31	10	21	11	1996-1998	6/90
74	1980	FONSECA	22	35	28	9	22	9	1990	6/90
100	1977	FONSECA	16	65	55	6.50	29	21	1998-2000	4/90
79	1975	FONSECA	NA	48	34	4.50	19	15	1990	8/88
96	1970	FONSECA	NA	73	66	2.30	40	24	1992-1995	12/89
97	1966	FONSECA	NA	84	69	1.50	35	24	1990-1995	2/90
98	1963	FONSECA	NA	155	130	1.15	69	53	1990-1995	12/89
80	1960	FONSECA	NA	84	60	0.98	29	21	1990	8/88
96	1955	FONSECA	NA	170	175	1	57	44	1990	8/88
100	1948	FONSECA	NA	265	210	0.48	95	72	1990	11/89
91	1945	FONSECA	NA	410	260	0.40	220	70	1990	11/89
91	1934	FONSECA	NA	300	255	0.30	170	133	1990	2/90
100	1927	FONSECA	NA	400	380	0.20	245	192	1990	12/89

FONSECA-GUIMARAENS

Score	Vintage	Wine							Drink	Last Tasted
90	1987	FONSECA-GUIMARAENS	NR	NR	NR	NR	NR	NR	2000	2/90
86	1986	FONSECA-GUIMARAENS	NR	NR	NR	NR	NR	NR	1996-1998	2/90
85	1984	FONSECA-GUIMARAENS	NR	NR	NR	NR	NR	NR	1994-1996	2/90
82	1982	FONSECA-GUIMARAENS	NR	NR	NR	NR	NR	NR	1992-1994	2/90
80	1978	FONSECA-GUIMARAENS	32	32	NA	5	15	NA	1990-1993	2/90
89	1976	FONSECA-GUIMARAENS	32	38	NA	5	17	NA	1993-1995	2/90
84	1974	FONSECA-GUIMARAENS	NA	38	NA	3.50	18	NA	1990	1/90
75	1972	FONSECA-GUIMARAENS	NA	36	NA	2	18	NA	1990	2/90
84	1968	FONSECA-GUIMARAENS	NA	50	NA	1.50	18	NA	1990	2/90
90	1967	FONSECA-GUIMARAENS	NA	56	NA	1.20	18	12	1990-1995	2/90
89	1965	FONSECA-GUIMARAENS	NA	60	NA	1.20	20	NA	1990-1994	2/90
90	1964	FONSECA-GUIMARAENS	NA	60	NA	1.15	20	NA	1990	2/90
88	1962	FONSECA-GUIMARAENS	NA	70	NA	0.80	20	NA	1990-1993	2/90
85	1961	FONSECA-GUIMARAENS	NA	70	NA	0.80	20	NA	1990	2/90
88	1958	FONSECA-GUIMARAENS	NA	90	35	0.80	20	14	1990	2/90

GOULD CAMPBELL

Score	Vintage	Wine							Drink	Last Tasted
85	1985	GOULD CAMPBELL	23	29	23	11	20	11	1995-1997	6/90
90	1983	GOULD CAMPBELL	22	31	NA	9	16	13	1996-1998	6/90
86	1980	GOULD CAMPBELL	15	30	NA	7	16	NA	1992-1994	2/90

NA—not available. NR—not released. Auction prices include 10% buyer's premium (where charged).

Score	Vintage	Wine	US Prices Release/Current/Auction			UK Prices Release/Current/Auction			Drink	Last Tasted
93	1977	GOULD CAMPBELL	$11	$46	$32	£5	£19	£10	1994-1998	2/90
76	1975	GOULD CAMPBELL	NA	32	22	4.50	15	9	1990	2/90
88	1970	GOULD CAMPBELL	NA	45	33	2	22	12	1990	2/90
84	1966	GOULD CAMPBELL	NA	70	45	1.30	25	16	1990	2/90

W. & J. GRAHAM

Score	Vintage	Wine	Release	Current	Auction	Release	Current	Auction	Drink	Last Tasted
96	1985	GRAHAM	31	40	33	13	23	16	1998-2000	6/90
93	1983	GRAHAM	30	40	30	10	18	13	1996-1998	6/90
90	1980	GRAHAM	18	40	28	9	17	10	1991-1993	6/90
90	1977	GRAHAM	15	63	58	6.50	30	21	1996-1998	4/90
78	1975	GRAHAM	NA	44	33	5	19	15	1990	2/89
94	1970	GRAHAM	NA	73	55	2.30	32	22	1990-1993	12/89
93	1966	GRAHAM	NA	82	60	1.50	45	27	1990	12/89
97	1963	GRAHAM	NA	150	130	1.15	90	52	1990-1993	12/89
84	1960	GRAHAM	NA	80	60	0.95	37	27	1990	8/88
94	1955	GRAHAM	NA	190	175	0.95	82	66	1990	11/89
91	1954	GRAHAM	NA	155	NA	0.90	46	NA	1990	2/90
95	1948	GRAHAM	NA	290	245	0.48	135	99	1990	11/89
95	1945	GRAHAM	NA	425	450	0.40	220	103	1990	11/89
89	1942	GRAHAM	NA	330	210	0.38	125	83	1990	4/90
94	1935	GRAHAM	NA	395	240	0.30	120	116	1990	4/90
94	1927	GRAHAM	NA	400	250	0.20	165	138	1990	2/90

GRAHAM'S MALVEDOS

Score	Vintage	Wine	Release	Current	Auction	Release	Current	Auction	Drink	Last Tasted
91	1987	MALVEDOS	NR	NR	NR	NR	NR	NR	2002-2005	2/90
85	1986	MALVEDOS	35	35	NA	NR	NR	NR	1996-1998	2/90
83	1984	MALVEDOS	NR	NR	NR	NR	NR	NR	1993-1995	2/90
90	1982	MALVEDOS	NR	NR	NR	NR	NR	NR	1994-1998	2/90
74	1979	MALVEDOS	NR	NR	NR	NR	NR	NR	1990	2/90
82	1978	MALVEDOS	30	30	NA	5	16	NA	1990-1993	2/90
74	1976	MALVEDOS	17	30	NA	5	17	NA	1990	2/90
70	1968	MALVEDOS	NA	50	30	1.50	18	17	1990	2/90
79	1965	MALVEDOS	NA	65	35	1.20	20	NA	1990	2/90
82	1964	MALVEDOS	NA	54	NA	1	20	NA	1990	2/90
89	1962	MALVEDOS	NA	65	NA	0.80	20	11	1990	2/90
87	1961	MALVEDOS	NA	65	NA	0.80	21	NA	1990	2/90
79	1958	MALVEDOS	NA	65	42	0.80	30	NA	1990	2/90
84	1957	MALVEDOS	NA	65	38	0.80	31	NA	1990	2/90
85	1952	MALVEDOS	NA	125	NA	0.30	35	NA	1990	11/89

RICHARD HOOPER [SONS

Score	Vintage	Wine	Release	Current	Auction	Release	Current	Auction	Drink	Last Tasted
80	1985	HOOPER	15	17	NA	10	13	NA	1994-1996	6/90
60	1983	HOOPER	NA	15	NA	7	12	NA	Avoid	3/90
68	1982	HOOPER	NA	18	NA	6.50	11	NA	Avoid	5/90
67	1980	HOOPER	NA	22	NA	6	12	NA	Avoid	5/90

HUTCHESON

Score	Vintage	Wine	Release	Current	Auction	Release	Current	Auction	Drink	Last Tasted
69	1979	HUTCHESON	NA	40	NA	5	10	NA	Avoid	1/90
79	1970	HUTCHESON	NA	43	NA	2	15	NA	1990	1/90

C.N. KOPKE

Score	Vintage	Wine	Release	Current	Auction	Release	Current	Auction	Drink	Last Tasted
86	1987	KOPKE	24	24	NA	17	17	NA	1995-1997	1/90
90	1985	KOPKE	18	21	NA	11	14	NA	1996-1998	1/90
85	1983	KOPKE	18	23	NA	9	23	NA	1993-1994	1/90
83	1982	KOPKE	16	26	NA	8	21	NA	1991-1992	1/90
71	1980	KOPKE	16	31	NA	7	20	NA	1990	1/90
69	1979	KOPKE	NA	NA	NA	6	16	NA	Avoid	1/90
70	1978	KOPKE	13	29	NA	6	20	NA	1990	1/90
68	1977	KOPKE	NA	NA	NA	7	22	NA	Avoid	1/90
82	1975	KOPKE	NA	28	10	4.50	18	NA	1990	1/90
74	1974	KOPKE	NA	NA	NA	4	18	NA	1990	1/90
82	1970	KOPKE	NA	41	27	2	20	19	1990	1/90
81	1966	KOPKE	NA	65	NA	1.30	20	NA	1990	1/90

NA—not available. NR—not released. Auction prices include 10% buyer's premium (where charged).

Score	Vintage	Wine	US Prices Release	Current	Auction	UK Prices Release	Current	Auction	Drink	Last Tasted
87	1960	KOPKE	NA	$65	NA	£1	£31	NA	1990	1/90

MARTINEZ GASSIOT

Score	Vintage	Wine	US Prices Release	Current	Auction	UK Prices Release	Current	Auction	Drink	Last Tasted
84	1987	MARTINEZ	NR	NR	NR	13	13	NA	1996-1997	5/90
89	1985	MARTINEZ	21	26	NA	11	15	NA	1996-1997	6/90
82	1982	MARTINEZ	17	28	NA	9	14	NA	1992-1994	6/90
75	1975	MARTINEZ	NA	40	NA	4.50	15	11	1990	2/90
89	1970	MARTINEZ	NA	60	29	2	22	13	1990-1993	2/90
93	1967	MARTINEZ	NA	60	NA	1.30	20	11	1990	2/90
82	1963	MARTINEZ	NA	90	80	0.90	34	18	1990	2/90
86	1955	MARTINEZ	NA	120	110	0.80	48	24	1990	11/89

MESSIAS

Score	Vintage	Wine	US Prices Release	Current	Auction	UK Prices Release	Current	Auction	Drink	Last Tasted
67	1985	MESSIAS	12	14	NA	NA	NA	NA	Avoid	2/90
78	1984	MESSIAS	11	15	NA	NA	NA	NA	1994-1995	2/90
77	1983	MESSIAS Quinta do Cachão	8	11	NA	NA	NA	NA	1993	2/90
72	1982	MESSIAS	7	12	NA	NA	NA	NA	1990-1992	2/90
60	1977	MESSIAS Quinta do Cachão	7	19	NA	NA	NA	NA	Avoid	2/90
87	1970	MESSIAS Quinta do Cachão	NA	55	20	NA	NA	NA	1990	2/90
84	1966	MESSIAS Quinta do Cachão	NA	30	15	NA	NA	NA	1990	2/90
71	1963	MESSIAS	NA	40	NA	NA	NA	NA	1990	2/90

MORGAN BROTHERS

Score	Vintage	Wine	US Prices Release	Current	Auction	UK Prices Release	Current	Auction	Drink	Last Tasted
85	1985	MORGAN BROTHERS	NR	NR	NR	11	20	NA	1996-1998	2/90
78	1977	MORGAN BROTHERS	NR	NR	NR	5	24	NA	1990	1/90
88	1970	MORGAN BROTHERS	NR	NR	NR	2	22	NA	1990	2/90
80	1966	MORGAN BROTHERS	NR	NR	NR	1.30	26	NA	1990	2/90
86	1963	MORGAN BROTHERS	NR	NR	NR	0.90	28	24	1990	2/90

NIEPOORT

Score	Vintage	Wine	US Prices Release	Current	Auction	UK Prices Release	Current	Auction	Drink	Last Tasted
91	1987	NIEPOORT	27	27	NA	15	15	NA	2000	11/89
92	1985	NIEPOORT	25	33	NA	13	20	NA	1998-2000	6/90
84	1983	NIEPOORT	14	24	NA	10	17	6	1994-1996	6/90
90	1982	NIEPOORT	13	22	NA	10	17	8	1994-1996	6/90
87	1980	NIEPOORT	12	30	NA	9	17	NA	1990-1993	6/90
81	1978	NIEPOORT	11	32	NA	7	17	NA	1990	11/89
89	1977	NIEPOORT	11	50	30	6.50	20	8	1994-1996	4/90
79	1975	NIEPOORT	NA	37	20	5	18	7	1990	11/89
93	1970	NIEPOORT	NA	55	33	2	25	16	1990-1995	1/90
89	1966	NIEPOORT	NA	70	40	1.50	30	17	1990-1993	11/89
90	1963	NIEPOORT	NA	90	60	1.10	40	NA	1990	11/89
98	1955	NIEPOORT	NA	175	NA	1	65	24	1990	8/90
97	1945	NIEPOORT	NA	250	NA	0.40	125	110	1990	2/90
93	1942	NIEPOORT	NA	240	NA	0.30	110	77	1990	4/90
97	1927	NIEPOORT	NA	260	NA	0.20	140	116	1990	4/90

OFFLEY FORRESTER

Score	Vintage	Wine	US Prices Release	Current	Auction	UK Prices Release	Current	Auction	Drink	Last Tasted
88	1987	OFFLEY BOA VISTA	NR	NR	NR	15	15	NA	1997-1998	1/90
89	1985	OFFLEY BOA VISTA	22	29	NA	11	16	NA	1996-1998	6/90
84	1987	OFFLEY	NR	NR	NR	NR	NR	NR	1995-1996	1/90
91	1983	OFFLEY BOA VISTA	22	27	NA	10	15	7	1994-1998	1/90
84	1982	OFFLEY BOA VISTA	18	22	14	10	17	NA	1992-1998	6/90
90	1980	OFFLEY BOA VISTA	14	30	NA	7	16	NA	1990-1994	6/90
88	1977	OFFLEY BOA VISTA	11	45	26	5	25	11	1993-1994	1/90
75	1975	OFFLEY BOA VISTA	NA	27	NA	4.50	20	8	1990	2/89
79	1972	OFFLEY BOA VISTA	NA	30	NA	2	12	9	1990	2/89
81	1970	OFFLEY BOA VISTA	NA	48	28	2.30	35	13	1990	2/89
90	1966	OFFLEY BOA VISTA	NA	45	35	1.30	25	15	1990	2/89
80	1963	OFFLEY BOA VISTA	NA	97	50	0.90	39	21	1990	2/89
78	1960	OFFLEY BOA VISTA	NA	70	NA	0.80	18	13	1990	2/89

OSBORNE

Score	Vintage	Wine	US Prices Release	Current	Auction	UK Prices Release	Current	Auction	Drink	Last Tasted
76	1985	OSBORNE	20	21	NA	NA	NA	NA	1993-1994	1/90

NA—not available. NR—not released. Auction prices include 10% buyer's premium (where charged).

Score	Vintage	Wine	US Prices Release/Current/Auction			UK Prices Release/Current/Auction			Drink	Last Tasted
72	1982	OSBORNE	$13	$26	NA	NA	NA	NA	1991-1993	1/90
77	1970	OSBORNE	NA	50	NA	NA	NA	NA	1990	1/90
82	1960	OSBORNE	NA	60	NA	NA	NA	NA	1990	1/90
A. PINTOS DOS SANTOS										
69	1985	A. PINTOS DOS SANTOS	NA	NA	NA	10	14	8	Avoid	1/90
70	1982	A. PINTOS DOS SANTOS	NA	NA	NA	6.50	13	8	1990	1/90
70	1980	A. PINTOS DOS SANTOS	NA	NA	NA	6	13	NA	1990	1/90
70	1970	A. PINTOS DOS SANTOS	NA	NA	NA	2	20	9	1990	1/90
MANOEL D. POCAS JUNIOR										
85	1985	POCAS JUNIOR	17	19	NA	11	13	NA	1996-1998	2/90
74	1975	POCAS JUNIOR	NA	34	NA	4.50	18	NA	1990	2/90
84	1970	POCAS JUNIOR	NA	52	NA	2	20	NA	1990	2/90
82	1963	POCAS JUNIOR	NA	100	NA	0.80	28	NA	1990	2/90
82	1960	POCAS JUNIOR	NA	80	NA	0.70	30	NA	1990	2/90
QUARLES HARRIS										
85	1985	QUARLES HARRIS	21	29	NA	11	20	8	1995-1997	6/90
89	1983	QUARLES HARRIS	18	33	NA	9	16	8	1996-1998	2/90
83	1980	QUARLES HARRIS	13	26	18	7	16	7	1990-1993	2/90
89	1977	QUARLES HARRIS	11	43	26	5	19	9	1993-1996	2/90
73	1975	QUARLES HARRIS	NA	35	28	4	16	NA	1990	4/90
89	1970	QUARLES HARRIS	NA	60	27	2	25	12	1990-1993	2/90
74	1966	QUARLES HARRIS	NA	78	NA	1.30	30	NA	1990	2/90
85	1963	QUARLES HARRIS	NA	110	103	0.90	35	NA	1990	2/90
QUINTA DO BOMFIM										
86	1987	QUINTA DO BOMFIM	NR	NR	NR	NR	NR	NR	1998-2000	2/90
82	1986	QUINTA DO BOMFIM	NR	NR	NR	NR	NR	NR	1996-1997	2/90
86	1984	QUINTA DO BOMFIM	NR	NR	NR	NR	NR	NR	1995-1996	2/90
82	1982	QUINTA DO BOMFIM	NR	NR	NR	NR	NR	NR	1992-1993	2/90
81	1979	QUINTA DO BOMFIM	28	28	NA	14	15	NA	1990	2/90
85	1978	QUINTA DO BOMFIM	27	29	22	14	16	NA	1990-1992	2/90
87	1965	QUINTA DO BOMFIM	NA	NA	NA	2	17	NA	1990	6/90
QUINTA DA CAVADINHA										
86	1987	QUINTA DA CAVADINHA	NR	NR	NR	NR	NR	NR	1998-2000	2/90
85	1986	QUINTA DA CAVADINHA	NR	NR	NR	NR	NR	NR	1997-1998	2/90
81	1984	QUINTA DA CAVADINHA	NR	NR	NR	NR	NR	NR	1992-1994	2/90
86	1982	QUINTA DA CAVADINHA	NR	NR	NR	NR	NR	NR	1992-1994	2/90
82	1979	QUINTA DA CAVADINHA	25	25	NA	14	15	NA	1990-1992	2/90
83	1978	QUINTA DA CAVADINHA	28	28	NA	14	17	NA	1990-1992	2/90
QUINTA DA CORTE										
87	1987	QUINTA DA CORTE	NR	NR	NR	NR	NR	NR	1997	2/90
84	1984	QUINTA DA CORTE	NR	NR	NR	NR	NR	NR	1994-1996	2/90
81	1980	QUINTA DA CORTE	NR	NR	NR	12	14	NA	1990-1993	2/90
80	1978	QUINTA DA CORTE	24	24	NA	14	17	NA	1990	2/90
QUINTA DO CRASTO										
80	1987	QUINTA DO CRASTO	NR	NR	NR	NR	NR	NR	1993-1995	1/90
71	1985	QUINTA DO CRASTO	24	24	NA	13	15	NA	1990	1/90
70	1978	QUINTA DO CRASTO	NA	NA	NA	15	15	NA	1990	1/90
79	1958	CONSTANTINO	NA	NA	NA	0.80	25	NA	1990	8/90
QUINTA DA EIRA VELHA										
86	1987	QUINTA DA EIRA VELHA	NR	NR	NR	NR	NR	NR	1996-1998	5/90
81	1982	QUINTA DA EIRA VELHA	NR	NR	NR	10	12	NA	1990-1993	3/90
85	1978	QUINTA DA EIRA VELHA	22	30	NA	9	16	8	1990	3/90
QUINTA DO INFANTADO										
76	1985	QUINTA DO INFANTADO	33	33	NA	13	13	NA	1992-1993	7/90
70	1982	QUINTA DO INFANTADO	35	35	NA	15	15	NA	1990	7/90
75	1978	QUINTA DO INFANTADO	NA	NA	NA	16	16	NA	1990	7/90

NA—not available. NR—not released. Auction prices include 10% buyer's premium (where charged).

Score	Vintage	Wine	US Prices Release/Current/Auction			UK Prices Release/Current/Auction			Drink	Last Tasted
QUINTA DO NOVAL										
89	1987	QUINTA DO NOVAL	NR	NR	NR	NR	NR	NR	2000-2002	1/90
86	1985	QUINTA DO NOVAL	22	33	24	13	22	12	1996-1998	6/90
78	1982	QUINTA DO NOVAL	23	24	NA	10	16	7	1992-1994	6/90
72	1978	QUINTA DO NOVAL	18	29	20	9	13	7	1990	11/89
81	1975	QUINTA DO NOVAL	NA	50	33	5	16	13	1990	11/89
89	1970	QUINTA DO NOVAL	NA	68	50	2	35	18	1990-1993	12/89
88	1967	QUINTA DO NOVAL	NA	70	30	1.50	25	12	1990	12/89
91	1966	QUINTA DO NOVAL	NA	75	32	1.50	30	21	1990	12/89
84	1963	QUINTA DO NOVAL	NA	120	105	1.15	40	31	1990	12/89
82	1960	QUINTA DO NOVAL	NA	78	40	0.95	35	22	1990	11/89
82	1958	QUINTA DO NOVAL	NA	100	40	0.90	30	19	1990	11/89
88	1955	QUINTA DO NOVAL	NA	150	100	1	57	37	1990	8/90
85	1950	QUINTA DO NOVAL	NA	240	70	0.60	60	20	1990	11/89
93	1947	QUINTA DO NOVAL	NA	300	195	0.45	62	48	1990	11/89
92	1945	QUINTA DO NOVAL	NA	325	250	0.40	92	72	1990	11/89
86	1942	QUINTA DO NOVAL	NA	200	NA	0.30	75	NA	1990	4/90
50	1941	QUINTA DO NOVAL	NA	70	NA	0.30	25	NA	Avoid	9/85
71	1938	QUINTA DO NOVAL	NA	110	NA	0.30	65	NA	1990	9/85
98	1934	QUINTA DO NOVAL	NA	305	240	0.30	75	55	1990	2/90
99	1931	QUINTA DO NOVAL	NA	1000	700	0.30	430	330	1990	11/89
93	1927	QUINTA DO NOVAL	NA	275	275	0.20	126	97	1990	12/89
QUINTA DO NOVAL NACIONAL										
94	1987	QUINTA DO NOVAL NACIONAL	NR	NR	NR	NR	NR	NR	2005-2010	1/90
95	1985	QUINTA DO NOVAL NACIONAL	NA	200	NA	NA	75	NA	2002-2007	11/89
86	1982	QUINTA DO NOVAL NACIONAL	NA	190	NA	NA	75	NA	1995-1998	11/89
80	1980	QUINTA DO NOVAL NACIONAL	NA	280	NA	NA	81	NA	1990-1993	2/90
77	1978	QUINTA DO NOVAL NACIONAL	NA	235	155	NA	92	41	1990-1992	11/89
86	1975	QUINTA DO NOVAL NACIONAL	NA	285	170	NA	115	66	1990-1995	11/89
98	1970	QUINTA DO NOVAL NACIONAL	NA	370	190	NA	144	85	1995-2000	11/89
95	1967	QUINTA DO NOVAL NACIONAL	NA	375	NA	NA	144	55	1990-1995	11/89
98	1966	QUINTA DO NOVAL NACIONAL	NA	300	240	NA	144	92	1990-1998	11/89
84	1964	QUINTA DO NOVAL NACIONAL	NA	350	130	NA	144	NA	1990	2/90
100	1963	QUINTA DO NOVAL NACIONAL	NA	750	660	NA	300	233	2000-2005	11/89
86	1962	QUINTA DO NOVAL NACIONAL	NA	350	260	NA	144	125	1990	11/89
84	1960	QUINTA DO NOVAL NACIONAL	NA	385	265	NA	173	100	1990	11/89
90	1950	QUINTA DO NOVAL NACIONAL	NA	850	NA	NA	230	130	1990	11/89
100	1931	QUINTA DO NOVAL NACIONAL	NA	3,700	NA	NA	1,725	700	1,990	11/89
QUINTA DO PANASCAL										
82	1987	QUINTA DO PANASCAL	NR	NR	NR	NR	NR	NR	1996-1998	2/90
79	1986	QUINTA DO PANASCAL	NR	NR	NR	NR	NR	NR	1994-1995	2/90
78	1985	QUINTA DO PANASCAL	NR	NR	NR	NR	NR	NR	1995-1998	2/90
70	1984	QUINTA DO PANASCAL	NR	NR	NR	NR	NR	NR	1990	2/90
79	1983	QUINTA DO PANASCAL	NR	NR	NR	NR	NR	NR	1993-1995	2/90
QUINTA DA ROEDA										
79	1987	QUINTA DA ROEDA	NR	NR	NR	NR	NR	NR	1997-2000	2/90
85	1983	QUINTA DA ROEDA	22	22	NA	NR	NR	NR	1995-1997	2/90
75	1980	QUINTA DA ROEDA	22	30	NA	8	16	8	1990	2/90
83	1978	QUINTA DA ROEDA	22	25	17	8	15	8	1990-1994	2/90
85	1967	QUINTA DA ROEDA	NA	60	25	8	18	12	1990	1/90
QUINTA DA ROMANEIRA										
81	1987	QUINTA DA ROMANEIRA	NR	NR	NR	NR	NR	NR	1996-1997	1/90
78	1985	QUINTA DA ROMANEIRA	29	29	NA	NR	NR	NR	1992-1994	1/90
90	1935	QUINTA DA ROMANEIRA	NA	NA	NA	NA	NA	NA	1990	2/90
QUINTA DE LA ROSA										
78	1988	QUINTA DE LA ROSA	NR	NR	NR	NR	NR	NR	1996-1998	5/90
76	1972	QUINTA DE LA ROSA	NA	NA	NA	NA	NA	NA	1990	10/89
82	1966	QUINTA DE LA ROSA	NA	NA	NA	NA	NA	NA	1990	10/89
85	1963	QUINTA DE LA ROSA	NA	NA	NA	NA	NA	NA	1990	10/89

NA—not available. NR—not released. Auction prices include 10% buyer's premium (where charged).

Score	Vintage	Wine	US Prices Release/Current/Auction			UK Prices Release/Current/Auction			Drink	Last Tasted
88	1960	QUINTA DE LA ROSA	NA	NA	NA	NA	NA	NA	1990	10/89
87	1927	FEUERHEERD QUINTA DE LA ROSA	NA	NA	NA	NA	NA	NA	1990	12/89

QUINTA DE VAL DA FIGUERIA

Score	Vintage	Wine							Drink	Last Tasted
83	1987	QUINTA DE VAL DA FIGUERIA	NR	NR	NR	NR	NR	NR	1996	2/90

QUINTA DE VARGELLAS

Score	Vintage	Wine							Drink	Last Tasted
93	1987	QUINTA DE VARGELLAS	NR	NR	NR	NR	NR	NR	2000-2005	2/90
88	1986	QUINTA DE VARGELLAS	NR	NR	NR	NR	NR	NR	1997-1999	2/90
87	1984	QUINTA DE VARGELLAS	NR	NR	NR	NR	NR	NR	1994-1996	2/90
81	1982	QUINTA DE VARGELLAS	NR	NR	NR	NR	NR	NR	1993-1994	2/90
85	1978	QUINTA DE VARGELLAS	29	29	NA	6	18	NA	1990-1995	2/90
81	1976	QUINTA DE VARGELLAS	29	29	NA	5	19	NA	1990	2/90
78	1974	QUINTA DE VARGELLAS	27	35	NA	3.50	20	NA	1990	2/90
84	1972	QUINTA DE VARGELLAS	NA	35	21	2	20	13	1990	2/90
85	1969	QUINTA DE VARGELLAS	NA	50	NA	1.80	20	19	1990	2/90
82	1968	QUINTA DE VARGELLAS	NA	55	NA	1.60	20	NA	1990	2/90
82	1967	QUINTA DE VARGELLAS	NA	60	NA	1.50	20	13	1990	2/90
80	1965	QUINTA DE VARGELLAS	NA	60	NA	1.20	20	NA	1990	2/90
75	1964	QUINTA DE VARGELLAS	NA	50	37	1.15	22	15	1990	7/90
68	1961	QUINTA DE VARGELLAS	NA	45	NA	0.80	30	NA	Avoid	2/90
68	1958	QUINTA DE VARGELLAS	NA	50	NA	0.80	30	17	Avoid	2/90

ADRIANO RAMOS-PINTO

Score	Vintage	Wine							Drink	Last Tasted
85	1985	RAMOS-PINTO	21	29	NA	11	15	NA	1994-1995	11/89
89	1983	RAMOS-PINTO	17	25	NA	10	14	7	1996-1998	11/89
79	1982	RAMOS-PINTO	12	22	NA	8	14	6	1992-1993	11/89
74	1980	RAMOS-PINTO	11	14	NA	7	NA	NA	1990-1992	11/89
81	1970	RAMOS-PINTO	NA	70	32	2	21	NA	1990-1993	11/89
83	1963	RAMOS-PINTO	NA	80	NA	0.90	NA	6	1990	11/89

REAL COMPANHIA VELHA (ROYAL OPORTO)

Score	Vintage	Wine							Drink	Last Tasted
80	1987	ROYAL OPORTO	12	12	NA	NR	NR	NR	1995-1996	11/89
71	1985	ROYAL OPORTO	12	17	NA	10	11	NA	1990	6/90
65	1984	ROYAL OPORTO	11	16	NA	7	9	NA	Avoid	11/89
76	1983	ROYAL OPORTO	9	13	NA	7	11	NA	1990	6/90
60	1982	ROYAL OPORTO	9	19	NA	6.50	11	NA	Avoid	6/90
60	1980	ROYAL OPORTO	8	20	NA	6	6	NA	Avoid	6/90
68	1978	ROYAL OPORTO	8	20	NA	5.50	13	NA	Avoid	11/89
74	1977	ROYAL OPORTO	8	25	NA	6	17	NA	1990-1993	11/89
75	1970	ROYAL OPORTO	NA	30	NA	1.80	17	NA	1990	11/89
72	1967	ROYAL OPORTO	NA	30	NA	1.30	NA	NA	1990	11/89
73	1963	ROYAL OPORTO	NA	65	NA	1	29	NA	1990	11/89
98	1871	ROYAL OPORTO	NA	550	NA	0.15	345	NA	1990	11/89

ROBERTSON'S REBELLO VALENTE

Score	Vintage	Wine							Drink	Last Tasted
81	1985	REBELLO VALENTE	23	38	NA	11	19	NA	1994-1996	6/90
78	1983	REBELLO VALENTE	23	36	NA	9	17	NA	1993-1994	6/90
80	1980	REBELLO VALENTE	16	40	NA	7	18	NA	1993-1995	2/90
89	1977	REBELLO VALENTE	12	55	22	5	27	NA	1995-1998	2/90
75	1975	REBELLO VALENTE	NA	43	18	4.50	16	10	1990	2/90
83	1972	REBELLO VALENTE	NA	40	NA	1.70	17	8	1990	1/90
92	1970	REBELLO VALENTE	NA	50	27	2	22	11	1990	2/90
91	1967	REBELLO VALENTE	NA	50	NA	1.30	25	NA	1990	2/90
82	1966	REBELLO VALENTE	NA	70	36	1.30	28	14	1990	2/90
85	1963	REBELLO VALENTE	NA	92	38	0.90	38	18	1990	2/90
85	1960	REBELLO VALENTE	NA	55	35	0.80	16	12	1990	11/88
92	1945	REBELLO VALENTE	NA	245	185	0.40	55	NA	1990	5/90

NA—not available. NR—not released. Auction prices include 10% buyer's premium (where charged).

Score	Vintage	Wine	US Prices Release / Current / Auction			UK Prices Release / Current / Auction			Drink	Last Tasted
75	1942	REBELLO VALENTE	NA	$140	NA	£0.38	£50	£28	1990	2/85
ROZES										
86	1987	ROZES	NR	NR	NR	NR	NR	NR	1995-1996	6/90
81	1985	ROZES	16	18	NA	NR	NR	NR	1995-1997	5/90
75	1982	ROZES	NR	NR	NR	NR	NR	NR	1992-1994	6/90
SANDEMAN										
83	1985	SANDEMAN	22	33	NA	13	20	9	1996-1997	6/90
82	1982	SANDEMAN	19	27	NA	10	21	7	1993-1995	6/90
85	1980	SANDEMAN	19	35	28	9	25	19	1990-1993	6/90
85	1977	SANDEMAN	15	56	37	6.50	25	14	1993-1996	6/90
78	1975	SANDEMAN	NA	50	28	5	17	10	1990	3/90
83	1970	SANDEMAN	NA	70	38	2.30	27	17	1990-1993	3/90
90	1967	SANDEMAN	NA	65	38	1.50	34	12	1990-1993	3/90
92	1966	SANDEMAN	NA	93	40	1.50	35	21	1990	3/90
96	1963	SANDEMAN	NA	110	80	1.15	46	32	1990	3/90
79	1960	SANDEMAN	NA	75	43	0.95	45	23	1990	3/90
82	1958	SANDEMAN	NA	70	47	0.90	22	17	1990	3/90
85	1957	SANDEMAN	NA	NA	NA	0.80	21	17	1990	10/88
94	1955	SANDEMAN	NA	140	88	1	40	30	1990	3/90
87	1950	SANDEMAN	NA	170	165	0.60	35	19	1990	3/90
90	1947	SANDEMAN	NA	180	NA	0.45	NA	33	1990	3/90
95	1945	SANDEMAN	NA	380	370	0.40	118	87	1990	3/90
88	1942	SANDEMAN	NA	175	NA	0.30	59	46	1990	3/90
92	1935	SANDEMAN	NA	450	250	0.30	110	171	1990	3/90
94	1934	SANDEMAN	NA	300	NA	0.30	100	NA	1990	3/90
92	1927	SANDEMAN	NA	435	350	0.20	157	121	1990	3/90
78	1920	SANDEMAN	NA	300	165	0.20	135	NA	1990	3/90
88	1917	SANDEMAN	NA	300	130	0.21	160	66	1990	3/90
82	1911	SANDEMAN	NA	275	250	0.11	126	97	1990	6/90
75	1908	SANDEMAN	NA	320	NA	0.11	138	106	1990	3/90
88	1904	SANDEMAN	NA	420	350	0.11	263	203	1990	3/90
81	1896	SANDEMAN	NA	600	340	0.11	206	160	1990	3/90
74	1887	SANDEMAN	NA	600	NA	0.11	470	NA	1990	3/90
98	1870	SANDEMAN	NA	700	NA	0.09	485	NA	1990	3/90
SMITH WOODHOUSE										
89	1985	SMITH WOODHOUSE	22	32	NA	11	20	NA	1996-1998	6/90
92	1983	SMITH WOODHOUSE	22	31	NA	9	17	8	1997-1999	6/90
90	1980	SMITH WOODHOUSE	15	31	NA	7	17	NA	1992-1994	6/90
89	1977	SMITH WOODHOUSE	11	52	28	5	20	10	1996-1998	2/90
80	1975	SMITH WOODHOUSE	NA	38	23	4	17	9	1990	2/90
86	1970	SMITH WOODHOUSE	NA	62	30	2	22	13	1990	2/90
83	1966	SMITH WOODHOUSE	NA	80	NA	1.30	30	15	1990	2/90
89	1963	SMITH WOODHOUSE	NA	110	NA	0.90	35	NA	1990	2/90
TAYLOR, FLADGATE & YEATMAN										
90	1985	TAYLOR	32	39	28	14	19	17	1997-2000	6/90
89	1983	TAYLOR	25	45	28	11	17	13	1996-1998	6/90
88	1980	TAYLOR	21	35	29	9	14	11	1994	6/90
98	1977	TAYLOR	17	70	58	7	48	32	1996-1998	4/90
78	1975	TAYLOR	NA	44	35	5.10	30	14	1990-1995	12/89
98	1970	TAYLOR	NA	73	60	2.50	40	25	1990-1995	12/89
89	1966	TAYLOR	NA	87	58	1.50	38	29	1990-1993	12/89
97	1963	TAYLOR	NA	160	115	1.15	78	57	1990-1994	12/89
80	1960	TAYLOR	NA	89	75	0.98	51	29	1990	8/88
88	1955	TAYLOR	NA	195	165	1	105	86	1990	11/89
99	1948	TAYLOR	NA	325	275	0.50	135	103	1990	11/89
97	1945	TAYLOR	NA	650	700	0.45	300	234	1990	11/89
78	1942	TAYLOR	NA	275	NA	0.40	100	75	1990	4/90
79	1938	TAYLOR	NA	265	NA	0.30	125	80	1990	4/90
88	1935	TAYLOR	NA	380	325	0.30	206	171	1990	2/90

NA—not available. NR—not released. Auction prices include 10% buyer's premium (where charged).

Score	Vintage	Wine	US Prices Release	Current	Auction	UK Prices Release	Current	Auction	Drink	Last Tasted
95	1927	TAYLOR	NA	$440	$385	£0.20	£210	£160	1990	12/89
VAN ZELLER										
80	1985	VAN ZELLER	NR	NR	NR	11	18	NA	1996	1/90
84	1983	VAN ZELLER	22	30	NA	10	15	NA	1996-1998	1/90
87	1985	VAN ZELLER QUINTA DO RORIZ	NR	NR	NR	NR	NR	NR	1996-1998	7/90
84	1983	VAN ZELLER QUINTA DO RORIZ	NA	NA	NA	NA	NA	NA	1993-1995	7/90
86	1970	VAN ZELLER QUINTA DO RORIZ	NA	NA	NA	NA	NA	NA	1990	7/90
83	1960	VAN ZELLER QUINTA DO RORIZ	NA	NA	NA	NA	NA	NA	1990	7/90
VASCONCELOS BUTLER & NEPHEW										
74	1975	BUTLER & NEPHEW	NA	37	NA	4	20	11	1992	7/90
76	1970	BUTLER & NEPHEW	NA	50	24	2	25	13	1992	7/90
VASCONCELOS GONZALEZ BYASS										
81	1970	GONZALEZ BYASS	NA	50	24	2	25	13	1990-1992	6/90
87	1963	GONZALEZ BYASS	NA	82	38	0.90	30	18	1990	7/90
VIEIRA DE SOUSA										
70	1985	VIEIRA DE SOUSA	NA	NA	NA	NA	NA	NA	1990-1992	1/90
70	1980	VIEIRA DE SOUSA	NA	NA	NA	NA	NA	NA	1990	1/90
74	1978	VIEIRA DE SOUSA	NA	NA	NA	NA	NA	NA	1990	1/90
71	1970	VIEIRA DE SOUSA	NA	NA	NA	NA	NA	NA	1990	1/90
WARRE										
91	1985	WARRE	28	35	33	13	18	13	1998-2000	6/90
88	1983	WARRE	28	31	28	10	15	11	1996-1998	6/90
88	1980	WARRE	16	37	30	9	14	10	1990-1992	6/90
92	1977	WARRE	15	56	38	6.50	28	17	1995-1997	4/90
75	1975	WARRE	NA	40	32	5	17	12	1990	8/88
88	1970	WARRE	NA	70	51	2.30	30	22	1990-1993	12/89
91	1966	WARRE	NA	83	83	1.50	45	24	1990	6/89
92	1963	WARRE	NA	130	90	1.15	50	40	1990-1992	12/89
82	1960	WARRE	NA	85	85	0.95	30	22	1990	8/88
81	1958	WARRE	NA	99	70	0.90	23	18	1990	11/89
86	1955	WARRE	NA	155	115	1	67	44	1990	11/89
88	1947	WARRE	NA	225	160	0.45	80	52	1990	11/89
87	1945	WARRE	NA	345	235	0.40	110	83	1990	11/89
87	1934	WARRE	NA	285	220	0.30	80	44	1990	2/90
93	1927	WARRE	NA	340	205	0.20	130	88	1990	12/89
79	1900	WARRE	NA	425	NA	0.10	140	100	1990	11/89
WIESE & KROHN										
81	1985	WIESE & KROHN	21	32	NA	14	15	NA	1994-1995	1/90
86	1984	WIESE & KROHN	13	20	NA	10	11	NA	1994-1995	1/90
83	1982	WIESE & KROHN	13	29	NA	8	15	NA	1992-1994	1/90
84	1978	WIESE & KROHN	11	39	NA	6	24	NA	1990-1994	1/90
80	1975	WIESE & KROHN	NA	55	NA	4.50	27	NA	1990	1/90
74	1970	WIESE & KROHN	NA	81	NA	2	29	NA	1990	1/90
75	1967	WIESE & KROHN	NA	81	NA	1.30	40	NA	1990	1/90
85	1965	WIESE & KROHN	NA	100	NA	1.30	50	NA	1990	1/90
87	1963	WIESE & KROHN	NA	165	NA	1	69	NA	1990	1/90
85	1961	WIESE & KROHN	NA	125	NA	1	75	NA	1990	1/90
89	1960	WIESE & KROHN	NA	144	NA	0.80	50	NA	1990	1/90
87	1958	WIESE & KROHN	NA	180	NA	0.80	75	NA	1990	1/90
91	1957	WIESE & KROHN	NA	214	NA	0.80	90	NA	1990	1/90

NA—not available. NR—not released. Auction prices include 10% buyer's premium (where charged).

APPENDIX 2
All Ports Tasted, Listed by Score

Vintage	Wine	US Prices Release / Current / Auction			UK Prices Release / Current / Auction			Drink	Last Tasted
100									
1977	FONSECA	$16	$65	$55	£6.50	£29	£21	1998-2000	4/90
1948	FONSECA	NA	265	210	0.48	95	72	1990	11/89
1927	FONSECA	NA	400	380	0.20	245	192	1990	12/89
1963	QUINTA DO NOVAL NACIONAL	NA	750	660	NA	300	233	2000-2005	11/89
1931	QUINTA DO NOVAL NACIONAL	NA	3,700	NA	NA	1,725	700	1990	11/89
99									
1945	CROFT	NA	375	220	0.40	135	94	1990	11/89
1931	QUINTA DO NOVAL	NA	1,000	700	0.30	430	330	1990	11/89
1948	TAYLOR FLADGATE	NA	325	275	0.50	135	103	1990	11/89
98									
1963	FONSECA	NA	155	130	1.15	69	53	1990-1995	12/89
1955	NIEPOORT	NA	175	NA	1	65	24	1990	8/90
1934	QUINTA DO NOVAL	NA	305	240	0.30	75	55	1990	2/90
1970	QUINTA DO NOVAL NACIONAL	NA	370	190	NA	144	85	1995-2000	11/89
1966	QUINTA DO NOVAL NACIONAL	NA	300	240	NA	144	92	1990-1998	11/89
1871	ROYAL OPORTO	NA	550	NA	0.15	345	NA	1990	11/89
1870	SANDEMAN	NA	700	NA	0.09	485	NA	1990	3/90
1977	TAYLOR	17	70	58	7	48	32	1996-1998	4/90
1970	TAYLOR	NA	73	60	2.50	40	25	1990-1995	12/89
97									
1983	COCKBURN	22	45	28	10	18	12	1998-2000	6/90
1966	FONSECA	NA	84	69	1.50	35	24	1990-1995	2/90
1963	GRAHAM	NA	150	130	1.15	90	52	1990-1993	12/89
1945	NIEPOORT	NA	250	NA	0.40	125	110	1990	2/90
1927	NIEPOORT	NA	260	NA	0.20	140	116	1990	4/90
1963	TAYLOR	NA	160	115	1.15	78	57	1990-1994	12/89
1945	TAYLOR	NA	675	700	0.45	300	234	1990	11/89
96									
1970	FONSECA	NA	73	66	2.30	40	24	1992-1995	12/89
1955	FONSECA	NA	170	175	1	57	44	1990	8/88
1985	GRAHAM	31	40	33	13	23	16	1998-2000	6/90
1963	SANDEMAN	NA	110	80	1.15	46	32	1990	3/90
95									
1985	FONSECA	32	39	33	13	28	15	1998-2000	6/90
1948	GRAHAM	NA	290	245	0.48	135	99	1990	11/89
1945	GRAHAM	NA	425	450	0.40	220	103	1990	11/89
1985	QUINTA DO NOVAL NACIONAL	NA	200	NA	NA	75	NA	2002-2007	11/89
1967	QUINTA DO NOVAL NACIONAL	NA	375	NA	NA	144	55	1990-1995	11/89
1945	SANDEMAN	NA	380	370	0.40	118	87	1990	3/90
1927	TAYLOR	NA	440	400	0.20	210	160	1990	12/89
94									
1983	DOW	20	34	25	10	19	12	1996-1998	6/90
1977	DOW	12	60	57	6.50	28	16	1995-1997	4/90
1970	DOW	NA	66	49	2.30	29	20	1990-1993	1/90
1966	DOW	NA	90	80	1.50	38	25	1990-1992	12/89
1970	GRAHAM	NA	73	55	2.30	32	22	1990-1993	12/89
1955	GRAHAM	NA	190	175	0.95	82	66	1990	11/89
1935	GRAHAM	NA	395	240	0.30	120	116	1990	4/90
1927	GRAHAM	NA	400	250	0.20	165	138	1990	2/90
1987	QUINTA DO NOVAL NACIONAL	NA	NA	NA	NA	NA	NA	2005-2010	1/90
1955	SANDEMAN	NA	140	88	1	40	30	1990	3/90
1934	SANDEMAN	NA	300	NA	0.30	100	NA	1990	3/90

NA—not available. NR—not released. Auction prices include 10% buyer's premium where charged.

Vintage	Wine	US Prices Release/Current/Auction			UK Prices Release/Current/Auction			Drink	Last Tasted
93									
1985	BURMESTER	$25	$25	NA	£12	£16	NA	1996-1998	1/90
1935	CROFT	NA	285	240	0.30	95	73	1990	2/90
1963	DELAFORCE	NA	100	70	0.90	29	19	1990	2/90
1935	FERREIRA	NA	200	NA	0.30	65	66	1990	2/90
1983	GOULD CAMPBELL	22	31	NA	9	16	13	1996-1998	6/90
1977	GOULD CAMPBELL	11	46	32	5	19	10	1994-1998	2/90
1983	GRAHAM	30	40	30	10	18	13	1996-1998	6/90
1966	GRAHAM	NA	82	60	1.50	45	27	1990	12/89
1967	MARTINEZ	NA	60	NA	1.30	20	11	1990	2/90
1970	NIEPOORT	NA	55	33	2	25	16	1990-1995	1/90
1942	NIEPOORT	NA	240	NA	0.30	110	77	1990	4/90
1947	QUINTA DO NOVAL	NA	300	195	0.45	62	48	1990	11/89
1927	QUINTA DO NOVAL	NA	450	275	0.20	126	97	1990	12/89
1987	QUINTA DE VARGELLAS	NA	NA	NA	NA	NA	NA	2000-2005	2/90
1927	WARRE	NA	340	205	0.20	130	88	1990	12/89
92									
1935	COCKBURN	NA	320	200	0.30	145	79	1990	2/90
1963	DOW	NA	125	108	1.15	42	42	1990-1992	2/90
1985	NIEPOORT	25	33	NA	13	20	NA	1998-2000	6/90
1945	QUINTA DO NOVAL	NA	325	250	0.40	92	72	1990	11/89
1970	REBELLO VALENTE	NA	50	27	2	22	11	1990	2/90
1945	REBELLO VALENTE	NA	245	185	0.40	55	NA	1990	5/90
1966	SANDEMAN	NA	93	40	1.50	35	21	1990	3/90
1935	SANDEMAN	NA	400	250	0.30	110	171	1990	3/90
1927	SANDEMAN	NA	375	350	0.20	157	121	1990	3/90
1983	SMITH WOODHOUSE	22	31	NA	9	17	8	1997-1999	6/90
1977	WARRE	15	56	38	6.50	28	17	1995-1997	4/90
1963	WARRE	NA	130	90	1.15	50	40	1990-1992	12/89
91									
1927	COCKBURN	NA	300	200	0.30	145	146	1990	12/89
1912	COCKBURN	NA	350	275	0.40	180	77	1990	10/87
1963	CROFT	NA	110	85	1.15	59	33	1990	12/89
1955	DOW	NA	190	170	1	85	66	1990	4/90
1983	FERREIRA Quinta do Seixo	14	22	NA	10	16	NA	199 -1998	11/89
1945	FONSECA	NA	410	260	0.40	220	70	1990	11/89
1934	FONSECA	NA	300	255	0.30	170	133	1990	2/90
1954	GRAHAM	NA	155	NA	0.90	46	NA	1990	2/90
1987	MALVEDOS	NA	NA	NA	NA	NA	NA	2002-2005	2/90
1987	NIEPOORT	27	27	NA	15	15	NA	2000	11/89
1983	OFFLEY BOA VISTA	22	27	NA	10	15	7	1994-1998	1/90
1966	QUINTA DO NOVAL	NA	75	32	1.50	36	21	1990	12/89
1967	REBELLO VALENTE	NA	50	NA	1.30	25	NA	1990	2/90
1985	WARRE	28	35	33	13	18	13	1996-1998	6/90
1966	WARRE	NA	83	83	1.50	45	24	1990	6/89
1957	WIESE & KROHN	NA	214	NA	0.70	90	NA	1990	1/90
90									
1985	COCKBURN	33	37	28	13	20	12	1996-1998	6/90
1955	COCKBURN	NA	155	110	1	0	41	1990	11/89
1947	COCKBURN	NA	185	150	0.45	75	45	1990	11/89
1966	CROFT	NA	68	60	1.50	30	21	1990	12/89
1960	CROFT	NA	88	57	0.90	30	20	1990	9/89
1980	DOW	15	32	25	9	12	10	1991-1993	6/90
1983	FONSECA	24	37	31	10	21	11	1996-1998	6/90
1987	FONSECA-GUIMARAENS	NA	NA	NA	NA	NA	NA	2000	2/90
1967	FONSECA-GUIMARAENS	NA	56	NA	1.20	18	12	1990	2/90
1964	FONSECA-GUIMARAENS	NA	60	NA	1.15	20	NA	1990	2/90
1980	GRAHAM	18	40	28	9	17	10	1991-1993	6/90
1977	GRAHAM	15	63	58	6.50	30	21	1996-1998	4/90

NA—not available. NR—not released. Auction prices include 10% buyer's premium where charged.

Vintage	Wine	US Prices Release / Current / Auction			UK Prices Release / Current / Auction			Drink	Last Tasted
1982	MALVEDOS	NA	NA	NA	NA	NA	NA	1994-1998	2/90
1985	KOPKE	18	21	NA	11	14	NA	1996-1998	1/90
1982	NIEPOORT	13	22	NA	10	17	8	1994-1996	6/90
1963	NIEPOORT	NA	$90	$60	£1.10	£40	NA	1990	11/89
1980	OFFLEY BOA VISTA	14	30	NA	7	16	NA	1990-1994	6/90
1966	OFFLEY BOA VISTA	NA	45	35	1.30	25	15	1990	2/89
1950	QUINTA DO NOVAL NACIONAL	NA	850	NA	NA	230	130	1990	11/89
1935	QUINTA DA ROMANEIRA	NA	NA	NA	NA	NA	NA	1990	2/90
1967	SANDEMAN	NA	65	38	1.50	34	12	1990-1993	3/90
1947	SANDEMAN	NA	180	NA	0.45	NA	33	1990	3/90
1980	SMITH WOODHOUSE	15	31	NA	7	17	NA	1992-1994	6/90
1985	TAYLOR	32	40	28	14	19	17	1997-2000	6/90
89									
1931	COCKBURN	NA	NA	NA	NA	NA	NA	1990	1/90
1908	COCKBURN	NA	395	325	0.20	185	143	1990	10/87
1970	CROFT	NA	70	55	2.30	25	18	1990	12/89
1970	DELAFORCE	NA	40	30	2	24	16	1990	2/90
1985	DOW	30	35	27	13	22	12	1996-1998	6/90
1945	DOW	NA	370	280	0.40	195	116	1990	11/89
1978	FERREIRA	11	28	NA	5	16	NA	1993-1996	11/89
1976	FONSECA-GUIMARAENS	32	38	NA	5	17	NA	1993-1995	2/90
1965	FONSECA-GUIMARAENS	NA	60	NA	1.20	20	NA	1990	2/90
1942	GRAHAM	NA	330	210	0.38	125	83	1990	4/90
1962	MALVEDOS	NA	65	NA	0.80	20	11	1990	2/90
1985	MARTINEZ	21	26	NA	11	15	NA	1995-1997	6/90
1970	MARTINEZ	NA	60	29	2	22	13	1990-1993	2/90
1977	NIEPOORT	11	50	30	6.50	20	8	1994-1996	4/90
1966	NIEPOORT	NA	70	40	1.50	30	17	1990-1993	11/89
1985	OFFLEY BOA VISTA	22	29	NA	11	16	NA	1996-1997	6/90
1983	QUARLES HARRIS	18	33	NA	9	16	8	1996-1998	2/90
1977	QUARLES HARRIS	11	43	26	5	19	9	1993-1996	2/90
1970	QUARLES HARRIS	NA	60	27	2	25	12	1990-1993	2/90
1987	QUINTA DO NOVAL	NA	NA	NA	NA	NA	NA	2000-2002	1/90
1970	QUINTA DO NOVAL	NA	68	50	2	35	18	1990-1993	11/89
1955	QUINTA DO NOVAL	NA	150	100	1	57	37	1990	8/90
1983	RAMOS-PINTO	17	25	NA	10	14	7	1996-1998	11/89
1977	REBELLO VALENTE	12	55	22	5	27	NA	1995-1998	2/90
1985	SMITH WOODHOUSE	22	32	NA	11	20	NA	1996-1998	6/90
1977	SMITH WOODHOUSE	11	52	28	5	20	10	1996-1998	2/90
1963	SMITH WOODHOUSE	NA	110	NA	0.90	35	NA	1990	2/90
1983	TAYLOR	25	45	28	11	17	13	1996-1998	6/90
1966	TAYLOR	NA	87	58	1.50	38	29	1990-1993	12/89
1960	WIESE & KROHN	NA	144	NA	0.80	50	NA	1990	1/90
88									
1980	BURMESTER	18	33	NA	7	15	NA	1992-1993	1/90
1985	CALEM	25	36	NA	10	21	NA	1995-1996	6/90
1963	COCKBURN	NA	110	85	1.15	40	34	1990	12/89
1960	DOW	NA	88	50	0.95	32	26	1990-1992	2/90
1947	DOW	NA	230	209	0.45	80	47	1990	11/89
1987	FERREIRA	NA	NA	NA	14	14	NA	1997-1999	11/89
1962	FONSECA-GUIMARAENS	NA	70	NA	0.80	20	NA	1990-1993	2/90
1958	FONSECA-GUIMARAENS	NA	90	35	0.80	20	14	1990	2/90
1970	GOULD CAMPBELL	NA	45	33	2	22	12	1990	2/90
1970	MORGAN	NA	NA	NA	2	22	NA	1990	2/90
1987	OFFLEY BOA VISTA	NA	NA	NA	15	15	NA	1997-1998	1/90
1977	OFFLEY BOA VISTA	11	45	26	5	25	11	1993-1994	1/90
1967	QUINTA DO NOVAL	NA	70	30	1.50	25	12	1990	12/89
1960	QUINTA DE LA ROSA	NA	NA	NA	NA	NA	NA	1990	10/89
1986	QUINTA DE VARGELLAS	NA	NA	NA	NA	NA	NA	1997-1999	2/90
1942	SANDEMAN	NA	175	NA	0.30	59	46	1990	3/90

NA—not available. NR—not released. Auction prices include 10% buyer's premium where charged.

Vintage	Wine	US Prices Release / Current / Auction			UK Prices Release / Current / Auction			Drink	Last Tasted
1917	SANDEMAN	NA	300	130	0.21	160	66	1990	3/90
1904	SANDEMAN	NA	420	350	0.11	263	203	1990	3/90
1980	TAYLOR	21	35	29	9.50	14	11	1994	6/90
1955	TAYLOR	NA	195	165	1	105	86	1990	11/89
1935	TAYLOR	NA	380	325	0.30	206	171	1990	2/90
1983	WARRE	28	31	28	10	15	11	1996-1998	6/90
1980	WARRE	$16	$37	$30	£9	£14	£10	1990-1992	6/90
1970	WARRE	NA	70	51	2.30	30	22	1990-1993	12/89
1947	WARRE	NA	225	160	0.45	80	52	1990	11/89

87

Vintage	Wine	US Prices Release / Current / Auction			UK Prices Release / Current / Auction			Drink	Last Tasted
1927	CROFT	NA	350	195	0.20	150	105	1990	12/89
1927	DOW	NA	425	300	0.20	150	150	1990	4/90
1985	FERREIRA	20	26	NA	11	20	NA	1996-1998	11/89
1961	MALVEDOS	NA	65	NA	0.80	21	NA	1990	2/90
1960	KOPKE	NA	65	NA	1	31	NA	1990	1/90
1970	MESSIAS Quinta do Cachão	NA	55	20	NA	NA	NA	1990	2/90
1980	NIEPOORT	12	30	NA	9	17	NA	1990-1993	6/90
1965	QUINTA DO BOMFIM	NA	NA	NA	2	17	NA	1990	6/90
1987	QUINTA DA CORTE	NA	NA	NA	NA	NA	NA	1997	2/90
1927	FEUERHEERD QUINTA DE LA ROSA	NA	NA	NA	NA	NA	NA	1990	12/89
1984	QUINTA DE VARGELLAS	NA	NA	NA	NA	NA	NA	1994-1996	2/90
1950	SANDEMAN	NA	170	165	0.60	35	19	1990	3/90
1985	VAN ZELLER QUINTA DO RORIZ	NA	NA	NA	NA	NA	NA	1996-1998	7/90
1963	VASCONCELOS GONZALEZ BYASS	NA	82	38	0.90	30	18	1990	7/90
1945	WARRE	NA	345	235	0.40	110	83	1990	2/90
1934	WARRE	NA	285	220	0.30	80	44	1990	2/90
1963	WIESE & KROHN	NA	165	NA	1	69	NA	1990	1/90
1958	WIESE & KROHN	NA	180	NA	0.80	75	NA	1990	1/90

86

Vintage	Wine	US Prices Release / Current / Auction			UK Prices Release / Current / Auction			Drink	Last Tasted
1970	BURMESTER	NA	55	NA	2	32	NA	1990	1/90
1975	CALEM	NA	50	NA	4.50	25	13	1990	2/90
1982	CHAMPALIMAUD	20	20	NA	7	15	NA	1992-1994	2/90
1970	COCKBURN	NA	78	68	2.30	28	20	1990	12/89
1950	DOW	NA	80	NA	0.60	60	13	1990	11/89
1977	FERREIRA	11	35	NA	5	20	22	1992-1995	11/89
1970	FERREIRA	NA	40	25	2	23	12	1990-1992	4/89
1986	FONSECA-GUIMARAENS	NA	NA	NA	NA	NA	NA	1996-1998	2/90
1980	GOULD CAMPBELL	15	30	NA	7	16	NA	1992-1994	2/90
1987	KOPKE	24	24	NA	17	17	NA	1995-1997	1/90
1955	MARTINEZ	NA	120	110	0.80	48	24	1990	11/89
1963	MORGAN	NA	NA	NA	0.90	28	24	1990	2/90
1987	QUINTA DO BOMFIM	NA	NA	NA	NA	NA	NA	1998-2000	2/90
1984	QUINTA DO BOMFIM	NA	NA	NA	NA	NA	NA	1995-1996	2/90
1987	QUINTA DA CAVADINHA	NA	NA	NA	NA	NA	NA	1998-2000	2/90
1982	QUINTA DA CAVADINHA	NA	NA	NA	NA	NA	NA	1992-1994	2/90
1985	QUINTA DO NOVAL	22	33	24	13	22	12	1996-1998	6/90
1942	QUINTA DO NOVAL	NA	200	NA	0.30	75	NA	1990	4/90
1982	QUINTA DO NOVAL NACIONAL	NA	190	NA	NA	75	NA	1995	11/89
1975	QUINTA DO NOVAL NACIONAL	NA	285	170	NA	115	66	1990-1995	11/89
1962	QUINTA DO NOVAL NACIONAL	NA	350	260	NA	144	125	1990	1/89
1987	ROZES	NA	NA	NA	NA	NA	NA	1995-1996	6/90
1970	SMITH WOODHOUSE	NA	62	30	2	22	13	1990	2/90
1970	VAN ZELLER QUINTA DO RORIZ	NA	NA	NA	NA	NA	NA	1990	7/90
1955	WARRE	NA	155	115	1	67	44	1990	11/89
1984	WIESE & KROHN	13	20	NA	10	11	NA	1994-1995	1/90

85

Vintage	Wine	US Prices Release / Current / Auction			UK Prices Release / Current / Auction			Drink	Last Tasted
1967	COCKBURN	NA	55	45	1.50	32	15	1990	12/89
1977	CROFT	14	50	44	6.50	28	16	1992-1994	4/90
1966	DELAFORCE	NA	65	45	1.30	26	19	1990	2/90
1966	FERREIRA	NA	81	38	1.30	25	12	1990	8/88

NA—not available. NR—not released. Auction prices include 10% buyer's premium where charged.

Vintage	Wine	US Prices Release / Current / Auction			UK Prices Release / Current / Auction			Drink	Last Tasted
1963	FERREIRA	NA	110	50	0.90	30	24	1990	8/88
1955	FERREIRA	NA	110	97	1	48	23	1990	11/89
1984	FONSECA-GUIMARAENS	NA	NA	NA	NA	NA	NA	1994-1996	2/90
1961	FONSECA-GUIMARAENS	NA	70	NA	0.80	20	NA	1990	2/90
1985	GOULD CAMPBELL	23	29	23	11	20	11	1995-1997	6/90
1986	MALVEDOS	35	35	NA	NA	NA	NA	1996-1998	2/90
1952	MALVEDOS	NA	125	NA	0.30	35	NA	1990	11/89
1983	KOPKE	18	23	NA	9	23	NA	1993-1994	1/90
1985	MORGAN	NA	NA	NA	£11	£20	NA	1996-1998	2/90
1985	POCAS JUNIOR	17	19	NA	11	13	NA	1996-1998	2/90
1985	QUARLES HARRIS	21	29	NA	11	20	8	1995-1997	6/90
1963	QUARLES HARRIS	NA	110	103	0.90	35	NA	1990	2/90
1978	QUINTA DO BOMFIM	27	29	22	14	16	NA	1990-1992	2/90
1986	QUINTA DA CAVADINHA	NA	NA	NA	NA	NA	NA	1997-1998	2/90
1978	QUINTA DA EIRA VELHA	22	30	NA	9	16	8	1990	3/90
1950	QUINTA DO NOVAL	NA	240	70	0.60	60	20	1990	11/89
1983	QUINTA DA ROEDA	22	22	NA	NA	NA	NA	1995-1997	2/90
1967	QUINTA DA ROEDA	NA	60	25	5	18	12	1990	1/90
1963	QUINTA DE LA ROSA	NA	NA	NA	NA	NA	NA	1990	10/89
1978	QUINTA DE VARGELLAS	29	29	NA	6	18	NA	1990-1995	2/90
1969	QUINTA DE VARGELLAS	NA	50	NA	1.80	20	19	1990	2/90
1985	RAMOS-PINTO	21	27	NA	11	15	NA	1994-1995	11/89
1963	REBELLO VALENTE	NA	92	38	0.90	30	18	1990	2/90
1960	REBELLO VALENTE	NA	55	35	0.80	16	12	1990	11/88
1980	SANDEMAN	19	35	28	9	25	19	1990-1993	6/90
1977	SANDEMAN	15	56	37	6.50	25	14	1993-1996	6/90
1957	SANDEMAN	NA	NA	NA	0.80	21	17	1990	10/88
1965	WIESE & KROHN	NA	100	NA	1.30	50	NA	1990	1/90
1961	WIESE & KROHN	NA	125	NA	1	69	NA	1990	1/90
84									
1984	BURMESTER	NA	NA	NA	11	14	NA	1993-1995	1/90
1987	CALEM Quinta do Foz	28	28	NA	NA	NA	NA	1995-1996	
1983	CALEM	18	38	NA	9	18	7	1994-1996	6/90
1958	COCKBURN	NA	NA	NA	NA	NA	NA	1990	11/89
1955	CROFT	NA	145	100	1	45	33	1990	11/89
1934	DOW	NA	350	285	0.30	100	75	1990	6/90
1974	FONSECA-GUIMARAENS	NA	38	NA	3.50	18	NA	1990	1/90
1968	FONSECA-GUIMARAENS	NA	50	NA	1.50	18	NA	1990	2/90
1966	GOULD CAMPBELL	NA	70	45	1.30	25	16	1990	2/90
1960	GRAHAM	NA	80	60	0.95	37	27	1990	8/88
1957	MALVEDOS	NA	65	38	0.80	31	NA	1990	2/90
1987	MARTINEZ	NA	NA	NA	13	13	NA	1996-1997	5/90
1966	MESSIAS Quinta do Cachão	NA	30	15	NA	NA	NA	1990	2/90
1983	NIEPOORT	14	24	NA	10	17	6	1994-1996	6/90
1982	OFFLEY BOA VISTA	18	22	14	10	17	NA	1992-1993	6/90
1987	OFFLEY	NA	NA	NA	NA	NA	NA	1995-1996	1/90
1970	POCAS JUNIOR	NA	52	NA	2	20	NA	1990	2/90
1984	QUINTA DA CORTE	NA	NA	NA	NA	NA	NA	1994-1996	2/90
1963	QUINTA DO NOVAL	NA	120	105	1.15	40	31	1990	12/89
1964	QUINTA DO NOVAL NACIONAL	NA	350	130	NA	144	NA	1990	11/89
1960	QUINTA DO NOVAL NACIONAL	NA	385	265	NA	173	100	1990	11/89
1972	QUINTA DE VARGELLAS	NA	35	21	2	20	13	1990	2/90
1983	VAN ZELLER	22	30	NA	10	15	NA	1996-1998	1/90
1983	VAN ZELLER QUINTA DO RORIZ	NA	NA	NA	NA	NA	NA	1993-1995	7/90
1978	WIESE & KROHN	11	39	NA	6	24	NA	1990-1994	1/90
83									
1963	BURMESTER	NA	110	NA	0.90	42	NA	1990	1/90
1987	CHURCHILL Agua Alta	37	37	NA	NA	NA	NA	1995-1997	5/90
1984	MALVEDOS	NA	NA	NA	NA	NA	NA	1993-1995	2/90
1982	KOPKE	16	26	NA	8	21	NA	1992	1/90

NA—not available. NR—not released. Auction prices include 10% buyer's premium where charged.

Vintage	Wine	US Prices Release / Current / Auction			UK Prices Release / Current / Auction			Drink	Last Tasted
1980	QUARLES HARRIS	13	26	18	7	16	7	1990-1993	2/90
1978	QUINTA DA CAVADINHA	28	28	NA	14	17	NA	1990-1992	2/90
1978	QUINTA DA ROEDA	22	25	17	8	15	8	1990-1994	2/90
1987	QUINTA DE VAL DA FIGUERIA	NA	NA	NA	NA	NA	NA	1996	2/90
1963	RAMOS-PINTO	NA	80	NA	0.90	NA	6	1990	11/89
1972	REBELLO VALENTE	NA	40	NA	1.70	17	8	1990	1/90
1985	SANDEMAN	22	33	NA	13	20	9	1996-1997	6/90
1970	SANDEMAN	NA	70	38	2.30	27	17	1990-1993	3/90
1966	SMITH WOODHOUSE	NA	80	NA	1.30	30	15	1990	2/90
1960	VAN ZELLER QUINTA DO RORIZ	NA	NA	NA	NA	NA	NA	1990	7/90
1982	WIESE & KROHN	13	29	NA	8	15	NA	1994	1/90
82									
1970	BARROS, ALMEIDA	NA	$60	NA	£2	£30	£11	1990	1/90
1977	BURMESTER	11	37	NA	5	28	NA	1991-1993	1/90
1982	CALEM	16	34	NA	8	18	NA	1994-1996	6/90
1966	CALEM	NA	65	40	1.25	40	16	1990	11/89
1963	CALEM	NA	85	NA	0.90	42	NA	1990	12/89
1896	COCKBURN	NA	400	240	0.15	130	100	1990	2/90
1977	DIEZ HERMANOS	NA	NA	NA	4	20	NA	1990-1992	4/90
1982	FONSECA-GUIMARAENS	NA	NA	NA	NA	NA	NA	1994-1995	2/90
1978	MALVEDOS	30	30	NA	5	16	NA	1990-1993	2/90
1964	MALVEDOS	NA	54	NA	1	20	NA	1990	2/90
1975	KOPKE	NA	28	10	4.50	18	NA	1990	1/90
1970	KOPKE	NA	41	27	2	20	19	1990	1/90
1982	MARTINEZ	17	28	NA	9	14	NA	1992-1994	6/90
1963	MARTINEZ	NA	90	80	0.90	34	18	1990	2/90
1960	OSBORNE	NA	60	NA	NA	NA	NA	1990	1/90
1963	POCAS JUNIOR	NA	100	NA	0.80	28	NA	1990	2/90
1960	POCAS JUNIOR	NA	80	NA	0.70	30	NA	1990	2/90
1986	QUINTA DO BOMFIM	NA	NA	NA	NA	NA	NA	1996-1997	2/90
1982	QUINTA DO BOMFIM	NA	NA	NA	NA	NA	NA	1992-1993	2/90
1979	QUINTA DA CAVADINHA	25	25	NA	14	15	NA	1990-1992	2/90
1960	QUINTA DO NOVAL	NA	78	40	0.95	35	22	1990	11/89
1958	QUINTA DO NOVAL	NA	100	40	0.90	30	19	1990	11/89
1987	QUINTA DO PANASCAL	NA	NA	NA	NA	NA	NA	1996-1998	2/90
1966	QUINTA DE LA ROSA	NA	NA	NA	NA	NA	NA	1990	10/89
1968	QUINTA DE VARGELLAS	NA	55	NA	1.60	20	NA	1990	2/90
1967	QUINTA DE VARGELLAS	NA	60	NA	1.50	20	13	1990	2/90
1966	REBELLO VALENTE	NA	70	36	1.30	28	14	1990	2/90
1982	SANDEMAN	19	27	NA	10	21	7	1993-1995	6/90
1958	SANDEMAN	NA	70	47	0.90	22	17	1990	3/90
1911	SANDEMAN	NA	275	250	0.11	126	97	1990	6/90
1960	WARRE	NA	85	85	0.95	30	22	1990	8/88
81									
1987	BARROS, ALMEIDA	28	28	NA	14	14	NA	1995-1996	1/90
1985	CHURCHILL	22	32	NA	12	17	8	1993-1995	2/90
1982	CHURCHILL	NA	NA	NA	10	14	10	1990-1992	6/90
1985	CROFT	30	37	29	13	18	14	1995-1997	6/90
1985	DELAFORCE	24	27	NA	11	20	NA	1995-1996	6/90
1982	FERREIRA	14	25	NA	8	15	NA	1992-1994	11/89
1975	FERREIRA	NA	32	NA	4.50	16	NA	1990	11/89
1945	FERREIRA	NA	205	150	0.40	75	44	1990	11/89
1966	KOPKE	NA	65	NA	1.30	20	NA	1990	1/90
1978	NIEPOORT	11	32	NA	7	17	NA	1990	11/89
1970	OFFLEY BOA VISTA	NA	48	28	2.30	35	13	1990	2/89
1979	QUINTA DO BOMFIM	28	28	NA	14	15	NA	1990	2/90
1984	QUINTA DA CAVADINHA	NA	NA	NA	NA	NA	NA	1992-1994	2/90
1982	QUINTA DA EIRA VELHA	NA	NA	NA	10	12	NA	1990-1993	3/90
1975	QUINTA DO NOVAL	NA	50	33	5	16	13	1990	11/89
1987	QUINTA DA ROMANEIRA	NA	NA	NA	NA	NA	NA	1996-1997	1/90

NA—not available. NR—not released. Auction prices include 10% buyer's premium where charged.

Vintage	Wine	US Prices Release / Current / Auction			UK Prices Release / Current / Auction			Drink	Last Tasted
1982	QUINTA DE VARGELLAS	NA	NA	NA	NA	NA	NA	1994	2/90
1976	QUINTA DE VARGELLAS	29	29	NA	5	19	NA	1990	2/90
1970	RAMOS-PINTO	NA	70	32	2	21	NA	1990-1993	11/89
1985	REBELLO VALENTE	23	38	NA	11	19	NA	1994-1996	6/90
1985	ROZES	16	18	NA	NA	NA	NA	1995-1997	5/90
1896	SANDEMAN	NA	600	340	0.11	206	160	1990	3/90
1970	VASCONCELOS GONZALEZ BYASS	NA	50	24	2	25	13		6/90
1958	WARRE	NA	99	70	0.90	23	18	1990	11/89
1985	WIESE & KROHN	21	32	NA	14	15	NA	1994-1995	1/90

80

Vintage	Wine	US Prices Release / Current / Auction			UK Prices Release / Current / Auction			Drink	Last Tasted
1985	BARROS, ALMEIDA	24	29	NA	10	14	NA	1994-1996	1/90
1970	CALEM	NA	50	NA	2	32	13	1990-1994	11/89
1960	COCKBURN	NA	85	51	0.90	30	24	1990	8/88
1987	C. DA SILVA PRESIDENTIAL	NA	NA	NA	NA	NA	NA	1996-1998	2/90
1977	DELAFORCE	11	44	28	5	25	12	1990-1993	2/90
1975	DOW	NA	45	30	5	18	15	1990	4/89
1980	FERREIRA	13	21	NA	7	16	NA	1991-1992	11/89
1960	FERREIRA	NA	100	35	0.90	20	15	1990	8/88
1970	FEUERHEERD	NA	40	NA	2	20	11	1990	1/90
1960	FONSECA	NA	84	60	0.98	29	21	1990	8/88
1978	FONSECA-GUIMARAENS	32	32	NA	5	15	NA	1990-1993	2/90
1985	HOOPER	15	17	NA	10	13	NA	1994-1996	6/90
1966	MORGAN	NA	NA	NA	1.30	26	NA	1990	2/90
1963	OFFLEY BOA VISTA	NA	97	50	0.90	39	21	1990	2/89
1980	QUINTA DA CORTE	NA	NA	NA	12	14	NA	1990-1993	2/90
1978	QUINTA DA CORTE	24	24	NA	14	17	NA	1990	2/90
1987	QUINTA DO CRASTO	NA	NA	NA	NA	NA	NA	1993-1995	1/90
1987	QUINTA DA EIRA VELHA	NA	NA	NA	NA	NA	NA	1996-1998	5/90
1980	QUINTA DO NOVAL NACIONAL	NA	280	NA	NA	81	NA	1990-1993	2/90
1988	QUINTA DE LA ROSA	NA	NA	NA	NA	NA	NA	1996-1998	5/90
1965	QUINTA DE VARGELLAS	NA	60	NA	1.20	20	NA	1990	2/90
1987	ROYAL OPORTO	12	12	NA	NA	NA	NA	1995-1996	11/89
1980	REBELLO VALENTE	16	40	NA	7	18	NA	1993-1995	2/90
1975	SMITH WOODHOUSE	NA	38	23	4	17	9	1990	2/90
1960	TAYLOR	NA	89	75	0.98	51	29	1990	8/88
1985	VAN ZELLER	NA	NA	NA	11	18	NA	1996	1/90
1975	WIESE & KROHN	NA	55	NA	4.50	27	NA	1990	1/90

79

Vintage	Wine	US Prices Release / Current / Auction			UK Prices Release / Current / Auction			Drink	Last Tasted
1982	BORGES	12	30	NA	6.50	13	NA	1991-1993	5/90
1984	CHURCHILL Fojo	NA	NA	NA	12	14	NA	1992-1993	2/90
1972	DOW	NA	39	32	2	20	18	1990	1/89
1935	DOW	NA	300	250	0.30	100	106	1990	6/90
1950	FERREIRA	NA	90	NA	0.60	45	NA	1990	11/89
1975	FONSECA	NA	48	34	4.50	19	15	1990	8/88
1965	MALVEDOS	NA	65	35	1.20	20	NA	1990	2/90
1958	MALVEDOS	NA	65	42	0.80	30	NA	1990	2/90
1970	HUTCHESON	NA	43	NA	2	15	NA	1990	1/90
1975	NIEPOORT	NA	37	20	5	18	7	1990	11/89
1972	OFFLEY BOA VISTA	NA	30	NA	2	12	9	1990	2/89
1958	CONSTANTINO	NA	NA	NA	0.80	25	NA	1990	8/90
1986	QUINTA DO PANASCAL	NA	NA	NA	NA	NA	NA	1995	2/90
1987	QUINTA DA ROEDA	NA	NA	NA	NA	NA	NA	1997-2000	2/90
1982	RAMOS-PINTO	12	22	NA	8	14	6	1992-1993	11/89
1960	SANDEMAN	NA	75	43	0.95	45	23	1990	3/90
1938	TAYLOR	NA	265	NA	0.30	125	80	1990	4/90
1900	WARRE	NA	425	NA	0.10	140	100	1990	11/89

78

Vintage	Wine	US Prices Release / Current / Auction			UK Prices Release / Current / Auction			Drink	Last Tasted
1980	CALEM	14	34	NA	7	17	6	1990	6/90
1986	CHURCHILL Fojo	NA	NA	NA	14	14	NA	1993-1994	2/90
1985	C. DA SILVA PRESIDENTIAL	30	30	NA	10	10	NA	1992-1993	2/90

NA—not available. NR—not released. Auction prices include 10% buyer's premium where charged.

Vintage	Wine	US Prices Release / Current / Auction			UK Prices Release / Current / Auction			Drink	Last Tasted
1982	FEIST	NA	NA	NA	6.50	13	NA	1990-1992	1/90
1978	FEIST	NA	NA	NA	5	13	NA	1990	1/90
1975	GRAHAM	NA	44	33	5	19	15	1990	2/89
1984	MESSIAS	11	15	NA	NA	NA	NA	1994-1995	2/90
1977	MORGAN	NA	NA	NA	5	24	NA	1990	1/90
1960	OFFLEY BOA VISTA	NA	70	NA	0.80	18	13	1990	2/89
1982	QUINTA DO NOVAL	23	24	NA	10	16	7	1994-1996	6/90
1985	QUINTA DO PANASCAL	NA	NA	NA	NA	NA	NA	1995-1998	2/90
1983	QUINTA DO PANASCAL	NA	NA	NA	NA	NA	NA	1993-1995	2/90
1985	QUINTA DA ROMANEIRA	29	29	NA	NA	NA	NA	1994	1/90
1974	QUINTA DE VARGELLAS	27	35	NA	3.50	20	NA	1990	2/90
1983	REBELLO VALENTE	23	36	NA	9	17	NA	1993-1994	6/90
1975	SANDEMAN	NA	50	28	5	17	10	1990	3/90
1920	SANDEMAN	NA	300	165	0.20	135	NA	1990	3/90
1975	TAYLOR	NA	44	35	5.10	30	14	1990-1995	12/89
1942	TAYLOR	NA	275	NA	0.40	100	75	1990	4/90
77									
1975	COCKBURN	NA	$44	$28	£5	£18	£13	1990	1/90
1950	CROFT	NA	170	125	0.60	70	35	1990	4/90
1978	C. DA SILVA PRESIDENTIAL	NA	34	NA	5	15	NA	1990	2/90
1983	MESSIAS Quinta do Cachão	8	11	NA	NA	NA	NA	1993	2/90
1970	OSBORNE	NA	50	NA	NA	NA	NA	1990	1/90
1978	QUINTA DO NOVAL NACIONAL	NA	235	155	NA	92	41	1990-1992	11/89
76									
1983	BARROS, ALMEIDA	8	29	NA	7	15	NA	1990-1993	1/90
1950	COCKBURN	NA	110	90	0.60	65	38	1990	11/89
1975	CROFT	NA	40	28	5	18	13	1990	8/88
1975	DELAFORCE	NA	33	22	4.50	17	11	1990	2/90
1980	FEUERHEERD	NA	NA	NA	6	13	NA	1990	1/90
1975	GOULD CAMPBELL	NA	32	22	4.50	15	9	1990	2/90
1985	OSBORNE	20	21	NA	NA	NA	NA	1993-1994	2/89
1985	QUINTA DO INFANTADO	33	33	NA	13	13	NA	1992-1993	7/90
1972	QUINTA DE LA ROSA	NA	NA	NA	NA	NA	NA	1990	10/89
1970	VASCONCELOS BUTLER & NEPHEW	NA	50	24	2	25	13	1990	7/90
75									
1978	BARROS, ALMEIDA	7	30	NA	5	13	NA	1990	1/90
1904	COCKBURN	NA	330	240	0.20	120	94	1990	10/87
1970	C. DA SILVA PRESIDENTIAL	NA	50	18	2	29	NA	1990	2/90
1972	FONSECA-GUIMARAENS	NA	36	NA	2	18	NA	1990	2/90
1975	MARTINEZ	NA	40	NA	4.50	15	11	1990	2/90
1975	OFFLEY BOA VISTA	NA	27	NA	4.50	20	8	1990	2/89
1978	QUINTA DO INFANTADO	NA	NA	NA	16	16	NA	1990	7/90
1980	QUINTA DA ROEDA	25	30	NA	8	16	8	1990	2/90
1964	QUINTA DE VARGELLAS	NA	50	37	1.15	22	15	1990	7/90
1975	REBELLO VALENTE	NA	43	18	4.50	16	10	1990	2/90
1942	REBELLO VALENTE	NA	140	NA	0.38	50	28	1990	2/85
1970	ROYAL OPORTO	NA	30	NA	1.80	17	NA	1990	11/89
1982	ROZES	NA	NA	NA	NA	NA	NA	1992-1994	6/90
1908	SANDEMAN	NA	320	NA	0.11	138	106	1990	3/90
1975	WARRE	NA	40	32	5	17	12	1990	8/88
1967	WIESE & KROHN	NA	81	NA	1.30	40	NA	1990	1/90
74									
1974	BARROS, ALMEIDA	NA	40	NA	3	20	NA	1990	1/90
1980	FONSECA	22	35	28	9	22	9	1990	6/90
1979	MALVEDOS	NA	NA	NA	NA	NA	NA	1990	2/90
1976	MALVEDOS	17	30	NA	5	17	NA	1990	2/90
1974	KOPKE	NA	NA	NA	4	18	NA	1990	1/90
1970	A. PINTOS DOS SANTOS	NA	NA	NA	2	20	9	1990	1/90
1975	POCAS JUNIOR	NA	34	NA	4.50	18	NA	1990	2/90
1966	QUARLES HARRIS	NA	78	NA	1.30	30	NA	1990	2/90

NA—not available. NR—not released. Auction prices include 10% buyer's premium where charged.

Vintage	Wine	US Prices Release/Current/Auction			UK Prices Release/Current/Auction			Drink	Last Tasted
1980	RAMOS-PINTO	11	14	NA	7	NA	NA	1990-1992	11/89
1977	ROYAL OPORTO	8	25	NA	6	17	NA	1990-1993	11/89
1887	SANDEMAN	NA	600	NA	0.11	470	NA	1990	3/90
1975	VASCONCELOS BUTLER & NEPHEW	NA	37	NA	4	20	11	1990	7/90
1978	VIEIRA DE SOUSA	NA	NA	NA	NA	NA	NA	1990	1/90
1970	WIESE & KROHN	NA	81	NA	2	29	NA	1990	1/90
73									
1980	A. PINTOS DOS SANTOS	NA	NA	NA	6	13	NA	1990	1/90
1975	QUARLES HARRIS	NA	35	28	4	16	NA	1990	4/90
1963	ROYAL OPORTO	NA	65	NA	1	29	NA	1990	11/89
72									
1977	C. DA SILVA PRESIDENTIAL	NA	42	NA	5	20	NA	1991-1993	2/90
1985	FEIST	20	24	NA	10	14	NA	1991-1992	1/90
1985	FEUERHEERD	NA	NA	NA	10	14	NA	1991-1992	1/90
1982	MESSIAS Quinta do Cachão	7	12	NA	NA	NA	NA	1990-1992	2/90
1982	OSBORNE	13	26	NA	NA	NA	NA	1991-1993	1/90
1978	QUINTA DO NOVAL	18	29	20	9	13	7	1990	11/89
1967	ROYAL OPORTO	NA	30	NA	1.30	NA	NA	1990	11/89
71									
1980	KOPKE	16	31	NA	7	20	NA	1990	1/90
1963	MESSIAS	NA	40	NA	NA	NA	NA	1990	2/90
1982	A. PINTOS DOS SANTOS	NA	NA	NA	6.50	13	8	1990	1/90
1985	QUINTA DO CRASTO	24	24	NA	13	13	NA	1990	1/90
1938	QUINTA DO NOVAL	NA	110	NA	0.30	65	NA	1990	9/85
1985	ROYAL OPORTO	12	17	NA	10	11	NA	1990	6/90
1970	VIEIRA DE SOUSA	NA	NA	NA	NA	NA	NA	1990	1/90
70									
1985	BORGES	15	15	NA	10	14	NA	1990	5/90
1983	BORGES	12	15	NA	7	14	NA	1990-1992	5/90
1980	BORGES	11	23	NA	6	13	NA	1990	5/90
1968	MALVEDOS	NA	50	NA	1.50	18	NA	1990	2/90
1978	KOPKE	NA	29	NA	6	20	NA	1990	1/90
1978	QUINTA DO CRASTO	NA	NA	NA	15	15	NA	1990	1/90
1982	QUINTA DO INFANTADO	35	35	NA	15	15	NA	1990	7/90
1984	QUINTA DO PANASCAL	NA	NA	NA	NA	NA	NA	1990	2/90
1983	ROYAL OPORTO	9	13	NA	7	11	NA	1990	6/90
1985	VIEIRA DE SOUSA	NA	NA	NA	NA	NA	NA	1990-1992	1/90
1980	VIEIRA DE SOUSA	NA	NA	NA	NA	NA	NA	1990	1/90
69									
1977	CALEM	11	55	23	5	20	12	Avoid	11/89
1983	CHURCHILL Agua Alta	22	27	NA	9	15	6	Avoid	7/90
1982	CROFT	22	37	NA	10	16	8	Avoid	4/90
1982	DELAFORCE	20	27	NA	10	15	NA	Avoid	6/90
1977	FEUERHEERD	NA	17	NA	5	15	6	Avoid	1/90
1979	HUTCHESON	NA	40	NA	5	10	NA	Avoid	1/90
1979	KOPKE	NA	NA	NA	6	16	NA	Avoid	1/90
1985	A. PINTOS DOS SANTOS	NA	NA	NA	10	14	8	Avoid	1/90
68									
1982	HOOPER	NA	18	NA	6.50	11	NA	Avoid	5/90
1977	KOPKE	NA	NA	NA	7	22	NA	Avoid	1/90
1961	QUINTA DE VARGELLAS	NA	45	NA	0.80	30	NA	Avoid	2/90
1958	QUINTA DE VARGELLAS	NA	50	NA	0.80	30	17	Avoid	2/90
1978	ROYAL OPORTO	8	20	NA	5.50	13	NA	Avoid	11/89
67									
1980	HOOPER	NA	22	NA	6	12	NA	Avoid	5/90
1985	MESSIAS	12	14	NA	NA	NA	NA	Avoid	2/90

NA—not available. NR—not released. Auction prices include 10% buyer's premium where charged.

Vintage	Wine	US Prices Release / Current / Auction			UK Prices Release / Current / Auction			Drink	Last Tasted
65									
1979	BORGES	11	22	NA	6	12	NA	Avoid	5/90
1984	ROYAL OPORTO	11	16	NA	7	9	NA	Avoid	11/89
60									
1983	HOOPER	NA	15	NA	7	12	NA	Avoid	3/90
1977	MESSIAS Quinta do Cachão	7	19	NA	NA	NA	NA	Avoid	2/90
1982	ROYAL OPORTO	9	19	NA	6.50	11	NA	Avoid	6/90
1980	ROYAL OPORTO	8	20	NA	6	11	NA	Avoid	6/90
59									
1970	BORGES	NA	60	NA	2	28	11	Avoid	5/90
50									
1941	QUINTA DO NOVAL	NA	70	NA	0.30	25	NA	Avoid	9/85

NA—not available. NR—not released. Auction prices include 10% buyer's premium where charged.

APPENDIX 3
All Ports Tasted, Listed by Vintage, Score and House

Score	House	US Prices Release/Current/Auction			UK Prices Release/Current/Auction			Drink	Last Tasted
1988									
80	QUINTA DE LA ROSA	NR	NR	NR	NR	NR	NR	1996-1998	5/90
1987									
94	QUINTA DO NOVAL NACIONAL	NR	NR	NR	NR	NR	NR	2005-2010	1/90
93	QUINTA DE VARGELLAS	NR	NR	NR	NR	NR	NR	2000-2005	2/90
91	MALVEDOS	NR	NR	NR	NR	NR	NR	2002-2005	2/90
91	NIEPOORT	27	27	NA	15	15	NA	2000	11/89
90	FONSECA-GUIMARAENS	NR	NR	NR	NR	NR	NR	2000	2/90
89	QUINTA DO NOVAL	NR	NR	NR	NR	NR	NR	2000-2002	1/90
88	FERREIRA	NR	NR	NR	14	14	NA	1997-1999	11/89
88	OFFLEY BOA VISTA	NR	NR	NR	15	15	NA	1997-1998	1/90
87	QUINTA DA CORTE	NR	NR	NR	NR	NR	NR	1997	2/90
86	KOPKE	24	24	NA	17	17	NA	1995-1997	1/90
86	QUINTA DO BOMFIM	NR	NR	NR	NR	NR	NR	1998-2000	2/90
86	QUINTA DA CAVADINHA	NR	NR	NR	NR	NR	NR	1998-2000	2/90
86	ROZES	NR	NR	NR	NR	NR	NR	1995-1996	6/90
84	CALEM Quinta do Foz	28	28	NA	NR	NR	NR	1995-1996	6/90
84	MARTINEZ	NR	NR	NR	13	13	NA	1996-1997	5/90
84	OFFLEY	NR	NR	NR	NR	NR	NR	1995-1996	1/90
83	CHURCHILL Agua Alta	37	37	NA	NR	NR	NR	1995-1997	5/90
83	QUINTA DE VAL DA FIGUERIA	NR	NR	NR	NR	NR	NR	1996	2/90
82	QUINTA DO PANASCAL	NR	NR	NR	NR	NR	NR	1996-1998	2/90
81	BARROS, ALMEIDA	28	28	NA	14	14	NA	1995-1996	1/90
81	QUINTA DA ROMANEIRA	NR	NR	NR	NR	NR	NR	1996-1997	1/90
80	C. DA SILVA	NR	NR	NR	NR	NR	NR	1996-1998	2/90
80	QUINTA DO CRASTO	NR	NR	NR	NR	NR	NR	1993-1995	1/90
80	QUINTA DA EIRA VELHA	NR	NR	NR	NR	NR	NR	1996-1998	5/90
80	ROYAL OPORTO	12	12	NA	NR	NR	NR	1995-1996	11/89
79	QUINTA DA ROEDA	NR	NR	NR	NR	NR	NR	1997-2000	2/90
1986									
88	QUINTA DE VARGELLAS	NR	NR	NR	NR	NR	NR	1997-1999	2/90
86	FONSECA-GUIMARAENS	NR	NR	NR	NR	NR	NR	1996-1998	2/90
85	MALVEDOS	35	35	NA	NR	NR	NR	1996-1998	2/90
85	QUINTA DA CAVADINHA	NR	NR	NR	NR	NR	NR	1997-1998	2/90
82	QUINTA DO BOMFIM	NR	NR	NR	NR	NR	NR	1996-1997	2/90
79	QUINTA DO PANASCAL	NR	NR	NR	NR	NR	NR	1995	2/90
78	CHURCHILL Fojo	NR	NR	NR	14	14	NA	1993-1994	2/90
1985									
96	GRAHAM	31	40	33	13	23	16	1998-2000	6/90
95	FONSECA	32	39	33	13	28	15	1998-2000	6/90
95	QUINTA DO NOVAL NACIONAL	NA	200	NA	NA	75	NA	2002-2007	11/89
93	BURMESTER	25	25	NA	12	16	NA	1996-1998	1/90
92	NIEPOORT	25	33	NA	13	20	NA	1998-2000	6/90
91	WARRE	28	35	33	13	18	13	1996-1998	6/90
90	COCKBURN	33	37	28	13	20	12	1996-1998	6/90
90	KOPKE	18	21	NA	11	14	NA	1996-1998	1/90
90	TAYLOR	32	40	28	14	19	17	1997-2000	6/90
89	DOW	30	35	27	13	22	12	1996-1998	6/90
89	MARTINEZ	21	26	NA	11	15	NA	1995-1997	6/90
89	OFFLEY BOA VISTA	22	29	NA	11	16	NA	1996-1997	6/90
89	SMITH WOODHOUSE	22	32	NA	11	20	NA	1996-1998	6/90
88	CALEM	25	36	NA	10	21	NA	1995-1996	6/90
87	FERREIRA	20	26	NA	11	20	NA	1996-1998	11/89
87	VAN ZELLER QUINTA DO RORIZ	NR	NR	NR	NR	NR	NR	1996-1998	7/90

NA—not available. NR—not released. Auction prices include 10% buyer's premium where charged.

Score	House	US Prices Release/Current/Auction			UK Prices Release/Current/Auction			Drink	Last Tasted
86	QUINTA DO NOVAL	$22	$33	$24	£13	£22	£12	1996-1998	6/90
85	GOULD CAMPBELL	23	29	23	11	20	11	1995-1997	6/90
85	MORGAN	NR	NR	NR	11	20	NA	1996-1998	2/90
85	POCAS JUNIOR	17	19	NA	11	13	NA	1996-1998	2/90
85	QUARLES HARRIS	21	29	NA	11	20	8	1995-1997	6/90
85	RAMOS-PINTO	21	27	NA	11	15	NA	1994-1995	11/89
83	SANDEMAN	22	33	NA	13	20	9	1996-1997	6/90
81	CHURCHILL	22	32	NA	12	17	8	1993-1995	2/90
81	CROFT	30	37	29	13	18	14	1995-1997	6/90
81	DELAFORCE	24	27	NA	11	20	NA	1995-1996	6/90
81	ROBERTSON'S REBELLO VALENTE	23	38	NA	11	19	NA	1994-1996	6/90
81	ROZES	16	18	NA	NR	NR	NR	1995-1997	5/90
81	KROHN	21	32	NA	14	15	NA	1994-1995	1/90
80	BARROS, ALMEIDA	24	29	NA	10	14	NA	1994-1996	1/90
80	HOOPER	15	17	NA	10	13	NA	1994-1996	6/90
80	VAN ZELLER	NR	NR	NR	11	18	NA	1996	1/90
78	C. DA SILVA	30	30	NA	10	10	NA	1992-1993	2/90
78	QUINTA DO PANASCAL	NR	NR	NR	NR	NR	NR	1995-1998	2/90
78	QUINTA DA ROMANEIRA	29	29	NA	NR	NR	NR	1994	1/90
76	OSBORNE	20	21	NA	NA	NA	NA	1993-1994	2/89
76	QUINTA DO INFANTADO	33	33	NA	13	13	NA	1992-1993	7/90
72	FEIST	20	24	NA	10	14	NA	1991-1992	1/90
72	FEUERHEERD	NA	NA	NA	10	14	NA	1991-1992	1/90
71	QUINTA DO CRASTO	24	24	NA	13	13	NA	1990	1/90
71	ROYAL OPORTO	12	17	NA	10	11	NA	1990	6/90
70	BORGES	15	15	NA	10	14	NA	1990	5/90
70	VIEIRA DE SOUSA	NA	NA	NA	NA	NA	NA	1990-1992	1/90
69	A. PINTOS DOS SANTOS	NA	NA	NA	10	14	8	Avoid	1/90
67	MESSIAS	12	14	NA	NA	NA	NA	Avoid	2/90
1984									
87	QUINTA DE VARGELLAS	NR	NR	NR	NR	NR	NR	1994-1996	2/90
86	QUINTA DO BOMFIM	NR	NR	NR	NR	NR	NR	1995-1996	2/90
86	KROHN	13	20	NA	10	11	NA	1994-1995	1/90
85	FONSECA-GUIMARAENS	NR	NR	NR	NR	NR	NR	1994-1996	2/90
84	BURMESTER	NA	NA	NA	11	14	NA	1993-1995	1/90
84	QUINTA DA CORTE	NR	NR	NR	NR	NR	NR	1994-1996	2/90
83	MALVEDOS	NR	NR	NR	NR	NR	NR	1993-1995	2/90
81	QUINTA DA CAVADINHA	NR	NR	NR	NR	NR	NR	1992-1994	2/90
79	CHURCHILL Fojo	NA	NA	NA	12	14	NA	1992-1993	2/90
78	MESSIAS	11	15	NA	NA	NA	NA	1994-1995	2/90
70	QUINTA DO PANASCAL	NR	NR	NR	NR	NR	NR	1990	2/90
65	ROYAL OPORTO	11	16	NA	7	9	NA	Avoid	11/89
1983									
97	COCKBURN	22	45	28	10	18	12	1998-2000	6/90
94	DOW	20	34	25	10	19	12	1996-1998	6/90
93	GOULD CAMPBELL	22	31	NA	9	16	13	1996-1998	6/90
93	GRAHAM	30	40	30	10	18	13	1996-1998	6/90
92	SMITH WOODHOUSE	22	31	NA	9	17	8	1997-1999	6/90
91	FERREIRA Quinta do Seixo	14	22	NA	10	16	NA	199 -1998	11/89
91	OFFLEY BOA VISTA	22	27	NA	10	15	7	1994-1998	1/90
90	FONSECA	24	37	31	10	21	11	1996-1998	6/90
89	QUARLES HARRIS	18	33	NA	9	16	8	1996-1998	2/90
89	RAMOS-PINTO	17	25	NA	10	14	7	1996-1998	11/89
89	TAYLOR	25	45	28	11	17	13	1996-1998	6/90
88	WARRE	28	31	28	10	15	11	1996-1998	6/90
85	KOPKE	18	23	NA	9	23	NA	1993-1994	1/90
85	QUINTA DA ROEDA	22	22	NA	NR	NR	NR	1995-1997	2/90
84	CALEM	18	38	NA	9	18	7	1994-1996	6/90
84	NIEPOORT	14	24	NA	10	17	6	1994-1996	6/90
84	VAN ZELLER QUINTA DO RORIZ	NA	NA	NA	NA	NA	NA	1993-1995	7/90

NA—not available. NR—not released. Auction prices include 10% buyer's premium where charged.

Score	House	US Prices Release / Current / Auction			UK Prices Release / Current / Auction			Drink	Last Tasted
84	VAN ZELLER	$22	$30	NA	£10	£15	NA	1996-1998	1/90
78	QUINTA DO PANASCAL	NR	NR	NR	NR	NR	NR	1993-1995	2/90
78	ROBERTSON'S REBELLO VALENTE	23	36	NA	9	17	NA	1993-1994	6/90
77	MESSIAS Quinta do Cachão	8	11	NA	NA	NA	NA	1993	2/90
76	BARROS, ALMEIDA	8	29	NA	7	15	NA	1990-1993	1/90
70	BORGES	12	15	NA	7	14	NA	1990-1992	5/90
70	ROYAL OPORTO	9	13	NA	7	11	NA	1990	6/90
69	CHURCHILL Agua Alta	22	27	NA	9	15	6	Avoid	7/90
60	HOOPER	NA	15	NA	7	12	NA	Avoid	3/90

1982

Score	House	US Prices Release / Current / Auction			UK Prices Release / Current / Auction			Drink	Last Tasted
90	MALVEDOS	NR	NR	NR	NR	NR	NR	1994-1998	2/90
90	NIEPOORT	13	22	NA	10	17	8	1994-1996	6/90
86	CHAMPALIMAUD	20	20	NA	7	15	NA	1992-1994	2/90
86	QUINTA DA CAVADINHA	NR	NR	NR	NR	NR	NR	1992-1994	2/90
86	QUINTA DO NOVAL NACIONAL	NA	190	NA	NA	75	NA	1995	11/89
84	OFFLEY BOA VISTA	18	22	14	10	17	NA	1992-1993	6/90
83	KOPKE	16	26	NA	8	21	NA	1992	1/90
83	KROHN	13	29	NA	8	15	NA	1994	1/90
82	CALEM Quinta da Foz	16	34	NA	8	18	NA	1994-1996	6/90
82	FONSECA-GUIMARAENS	NR	NR	NR	NR	NR	NR	1994-1995	2/90
82	MARTINEZ	17	28	NA	9	14	NA	1992-1994	6/90
82	QUINTA DO BOMFIM	NR	NR	NR	NR	NR	NR	1992-1993	2/90
82	SANDEMAN	19	27	NA	10	21	7	1993-1995	6/90
81	CHURCHILL	NA	NA	NA	10	14	10	1990-1992	6/90
81	FERREIRA	14	25	NA	8	15	NA	1992-1994	11/89
81	QUINTA DA EIRA VELHA	NR	NR	NR	10	12	NA	1990-1993	3/90
81	QUINTA DE VARGELLAS	NR	NR	NR	NR	NR	NR	1994	2/90
79	BORGES	12	30	NA	6.50	13	NA	1991-1993	5/90
79	RAMOS-PINTO	12	22	NA	8	14	6	1992-1993	11/89
78	FEIST	NA	NA	NA	6.50	13	NA	1990-1992	1/90
78	QUINTA DO NOVAL	23	24	NA	10	16	7	1994-1996	6/90
75	ROZES	NR	NR	NR	NR	NR	NR	1992-1994	6/90
72	MESSIAS Quinta do Cachão	7	12	NA	NA	NA	NA	1990-1992	2/90
72	OSBORNE	13	26	NA	NA	NA	NA	1991-1993	1/90
71	A. PINTOS DOS SANTOS	NA	NA	NA	6.50	13	8	1990	1/90
70	QUINTA DO INFANTADO	35	35	NA	15	15	NA	1990	7/90
69	CROFT	22	37	NA	10	16	8	Avoid	4/90
69	DELAFORCE	20	27	NA	10	15	NA	Avoid	6/90
68	HOOPER	NA	18	NA	6.50	11	NA	Avoid	5/90
60	ROYAL OPORTO	9	19	NA	6.50	11	NA	Avoid	6/90

1980

Score	House	US Prices Release / Current / Auction			UK Prices Release / Current / Auction			Drink	Last Tasted
90	DOW	15	32	25	9	12	10	1991-1993	6/90
90	GRAHAM	18	40	28	9	17	10	1991-1993	6/90
90	OFFLEY BOA VISTA	14	30	NA	7	16	NA	1990-1994	6/90
90	SMITH WOODHOUSE	15	31	NA	7	17	NA	1992-1994	6/90
88	BURMESTER	18	33	NA	7	15	NA	1992-1993	1/90
88	TAYLOR	21	35	29	9.50	14	11	1994	6/90
88	WARRE	16	37	30	9	14	10	1990-1992	6/90
87	NIEPOORT	12	30	NA	9	17	NA	1990-1993	6/90
86	GOULD CAMPBELL	15	30	NA	7	16	NA	1992-1994	2/90
85	SANDEMAN	19	35	28	9	25	19	1990-1993	6/90
83	QUARLES HARRIS	13	26	18	7	16	7	1990-1993	2/90
80	FERREIRA	13	21	NA	7	16	NA	1991-1992	11/89
80	QUINTA DA CORTE	NR	NR	NR	12	14	NA	1990-1993	2/90
80	QUINTA DO NOVAL NACIONAL	NA	280	NA	NA	81	NA	1990-1993	2/90
80	ROBERTSON'S REBELLO VALENTE	16	40	NA	7	18	NA	1993-1995	2/90
78	CALEM	14	34	NA	7	17	6	1990	6/90
76	FEUERHEERD	NA	NA	NA	6	13	NA	1990	1/90
75	QUINTA DA ROEDA	25	30	NA	8	16	8	1990	2/90
74	FONSECA		23	28	9	22	9	1990	6/90

NA—not available. NR—not released. Auction prices include 10% buyer's premium where charged.

Score	House	US Prices Release / Current / Auction			UK Prices Release / Current / Auction			Drink	Last Tasted
74	RAMOS-PINTO	$11	$14	NA	£7	NA	NA	1990-1992	11/89
73	A. PINTOS DOS SANTOS	NA	NA	NA	6	13	NA	1990	1/90
71	KOPKE	16	31	NA	7	20	NA	1990	1/90
70	BORGES	11	23	NA	6	13	NA	1990	5/90
70	VIEIRA DE SOUSA	NA	NA	NA	NA	NA	NA	1990	1/90
67	HOOPER	NA	22	NA	6	12	NA	Avoid	5/90
60	ROYAL OPORTO	8	20	NA	6	11	NA	Avoid	6/90
1979									
82	QUINTA DA CAVADINHA	25	25	NA	14	15	NA	1990-1992	2/90
81	QUINTA DO BOMFIM	28	28	NA	14	15	NA	1990	2/90
74	MALVEDOS	NR	NR	NR	NR	NR	NR	1990	2/90
69	HUTCHESON	NA	40	NA	5	10	NA	Avoid	1/90
69	KOPKE	NA	NA	NA	6	16	NA	Avoid	1/90
65	BORGES	11	22	NA	6	12	NA	Avoid	5/90
1978									
89	FERREIRA	11	28	NA	5	16	NA	1993-1996	11/89
85	QUINTA DO BOMFIM	27	29	22	14	16	NA	1990-1992	2/90
85	QUINTA DA EIRA VELHA	22	30	NA	9	16	8	1990	3/90
85	QUINTA DE VARGELLAS	29	29	NA	6	18	NA	1990-1995	2/90
84	KROHN	11	39	NA	6	24	NA	1990-1994	1/90
83	QUINTA DA CAVADINHA	28	28	NA	14	17	NA	1990-1992	2/90
83	QUINTA DA ROEDA	22	25	17	8	15	8	1990-1994	2/90
82	MALVEDOS	30	30	NA	5	16	NA	1990-1993	2/90
81	NIEPOORT	11	32	NA	7	17	NA	1990	11/89
80	FONSECA-GUIMARAENS	32	32	NA	5	15	NA	1990-1993	2/90
80	QUINTA DA CORTE	24	24	NA	14	17	NA	1990	2/90
78	FEIST	NA	NA	NA	5	13	NA	1990	1/90
77	C. DA SILVA	NA	34	NA	5	15	NA	1990	2/90
77	QUINTA DO NOVAL NACIONAL	NA	235	155	NA	92	41	1990-1992	11/89
75	BARROS, ALMEIDA	7	30	NA	5	13	NA	1990	1/90
75	QUINTA DO INFANTADO	NA	NA	NA	16	16	NA		7/90
74	VIEIRA DE SOUSA	NA	NA	NA	NA	NA	NA	1990	1/90
72	QUINTA DO NOVAL	18	29	20	9	13	7	1990	11/89
70	KOPKE	NA	29	NA	6	20	NA	1990	1/90
70	QUINTA DO CRASTO	NA	NA	NA	15	15	NA	1990	1/90
68	ROYAL OPORTO	8	20	NA	5.50	13	NA	Avoid	11/89
1977									
100	FONSECA	16	65	55	6.50	29	21	1998-2000	4/90
98	TAYLOR	17	70	58	7	48	32	1996-1998	4/90
94	DOW	12	60	57	6.50	28	16	1995-1997	4/90
93	GOULD CAMPBELL	11	46	32	5	19	10	1994-1998	2/90
92	WARRE	15	56	38	6.50	28	17	1995-1997	4/90
90	GRAHAM	15	63	58	6.50	30	21	1996-1998	4/90
89	NIEPOORT	11	50	30	6.50	20	8	1994-1996	4/90
89	QUARLES HARRIS	11	43	26	5	19	9	1993-1996	2/90
89	ROBERTSON'S REBELLO VALENTE	12	55	22	5	27	NA	1995-1998	2/90
89	SMITH WOODHOUSE	11	52	28	5	20	10	1996-1998	2/90
88	OFFLEY BOA VISTA	11	45	26	5	25	11	1993-1994	1/90
86	FERREIRA	11	35	NA	5	20	22	1992-1995	11/89
85	CROFT	14	50	44	6.50	28	16	1992-1994	4/90
85	SANDEMAN	15	56	37	6.50	25	14	1993-1996	6/90
82	BURMESTER	11	37	NA	5	28	NA	1991-1993	1/90
82	DIEZ HERMANOS	NA	NA	NA	4	20	NA	1990-1992	4/90
80	DELAFORCE	11	44	28	5	25	12	1990-1993	2/90
78	MORGAN	NR	NR	NR	5	24	NA	1990	1/90
74	ROYAL OPORTO	8	25	NA	6	17	NA	1990-1993	11/89
72	C. DA SILVA	NA	42	NA	5	20	NA	1991-1993	2/90
69	CALEM	11	55	23	5	20	12	Avoid	11/89
69	FEUERHEERD	NA	17	NA	5	15	6	Avoid	1/90
68	KOPKE	NA	NA	NA	7	22	NA	Avoid	1/90

NA—not available. NR—not released. Auction prices include 10% buyer's premium where charged.

Score	House	US Prices Release	Current	Auction	UK Prices Release	Current	Auction	Drink	Last Tasted
60	MESSIAS Quinta do Cachão	$7	$19	NA	NA	NA	NA	Avoid	2/90
1976									
89	FONSECA-GUIMARAENS	32	38	NA	5	17	NA	1993-1995	2/90
81	QUINTA DE VARGELLAS	29	29	NA	5	19	NA	1990	2/90
74	MALVEDOS	17	30	NA	5	17	NA	1990	2/90
1975									
86	CALEM	NA	50	NA	4.50	25	13	1990	2/90
86	QUINTA DO NOVAL NACIONAL	NA	285	170	NA	115	66	1990-1995	11/89
82	KOPKE	NA	28	10	4.50	18	NA	1990	1/90
81	FERREIRA	NA	32	NA	4.50	16	NA	1990	11/89
81	QUINTA DO NOVAL	NA	50	33	5	16	13	1990	11/89
80	DOW	NA	45	30	5	18	15	1990	4/89
80	SMITH WOODHOUSE	NA	38	23	4	17	9	1990	2/90
80	KROHN	NA	55	NA	4.50	27	NA	1990	1/90
79	FONSECA	NA	48	34	4.50	19	15	1990	8/88
79	NIEPOORT	NA	37	20	5	18	7	1990	11/89
78	GRAHAM	NA	44	33	5	19	15	1990	2/89
78	SANDEMAN	NA	50	28	5	17	10	1990	3/90
78	TAYLOR	NA	44	35	5.10	30	14	1990-1995	12/89
77	COCKBURN	NA	44	28	5	18	13	1990	1/90
76	CROFT	NA	40	28	5	18	13	1990	8/88
76	DELAFORCE	NA	33	22	4.50	17	11	1990	2/90
76	GOULD CAMPBELL	NA	32	22	4.50	15	9	1990	2/90
75	MARTINEZ	NA	40	NA	4.50	15	11	1990	2/90
75	OFFLEY BOA VISTA	NA	27	NA	4.50	20	8	1990	2/89
75	ROBERTSON'S REBELLO VALENTE	NA	43	18	4.50	16	10	1990	2/90
75	WARRE	NA	40	32	5	17	12	1990	8/88
74	POCAS JUNIOR	NA	34	NA	4.50	18	NA	1990	2/90
74	VASCONCELOS BUTLER & NEPHEW	NA	37	NA	4	20	11	1990	7/90
73	QUARLES HARRIS	NA	35	28	4	16	NA	1990	4/90
1974									
84	FONSECA-GUIMARAENS	NA	38	NA	3.50	18	NA	1990	1/90
78	QUINTA DE VARGELLAS	27	35	NA	3.50	20	NA	1990	2/90
74	BARROS, ALMEIDA	NA	40	NA	3	20	NA	1990	1/90
74	KOPKE	NA	NA	NA	4	18	NA	1990	1/90
1972									
84	QUINTA DE VARGELLAS	NA	35	21	2	20	13	1990	2/90
83	ROBERTSON'S REBELLO VALENTE	NA	40	NA	1.70	17	8	1990	1/90
79	DOW	NA	39	32	2	20	18	1990	1/89
79	OFFLEY BOA VISTA	NA	30	NA	2	12	9	1990	2/89
76	QUINTA DE LA ROSA	NA	NA	NA	NA	NA	NA	1990	10/89
75	FONSECA-GUIMARAENS	NA	36	NA	2	18	NA	1990	2/90
1970									
98	QUINTA DO NOVAL NACIONAL	NA	370	190	NA	144	85	1995-2000	11/89
98	TAYLOR	NA	73	60	2.50	40	25	1990-1995	12/89
96	FONSECA	NA	73	66	2.30	40	24	1992-1995	12/89
94	DOW	NA	66	49	2.30	29	20	1990-1993	1/90
94	GRAHAM	NA	73	55	2.30	32	22	1990-1993	12/89
93	NIEPOORT	NA	55	33	2	25	16	1990-1995	1/90
92	ROBERTSON'S REBELLO VALENTE	NA	50	27	2	22	11	1990	2/90
89	CROFT	NA	70	55	2.30	25	18	1990	12/89
89	DELAFORCE	NA	40	30	2	24	16	1990	2/90
89	MARTINEZ	NA	60	29	2	22	13	1990-1993	2/90
89	QUARLES HARRIS	NA	60	27	2	25	12	1990-1993	2/90
89	QUINTA DO NOVAL	NA	68	50	2	35	18	1990-1993	11/89
88	GOULD CAMPBELL	NA	45	33	2	22	12	1990	2/90
88	MORGAN	NR	NR	NR	2	22	NA	1990	2/90
88	WARRE	NA	70	51	2.30	30	22	1990-1993	12/89
87	MESSIAS Quinta do Cachão	NA	55	20	NA	NA	NA	1990	2/90

NA—not available. NR—not released. Auction prices include 10% buyer's premium where charged.

Score	House	US Prices Release/Current/Auction			UK Prices Release/Current/Auction			Drink	Last Tasted
86	BURMESTER	NA	$55	NA	£2	£32	NA	1990	1/90
86	COCKBURN	NA	78	68	2.30	28	20	1990	12/89
86	FERREIRA	NA	40	25	2	23	12	1990-1992	4/89
86	VAN ZELLER QUINTA DO RORIZ	NA	NA	NA	NA	NA	NA		7/90
86	SMITH WOODHOUSE	NA	62	30	2	22	13	1990	2/90
84	POCAS JUNIOR	NA	52	NA	2	20	NA	1990	2/90
83	SANDEMAN	NA	70	38	2.30	27	17	1990-1993	3/90
82	BARROS, ALMEIDA	NA	60	NA	2	30	11	1990	1/90
82	KOPKE	NA	41	27	2	20	19	1990	1/90
81	OFFLEY BOA VISTA	NA	48	28	2.30	35	13	1990	2/89
81	RAMOS-PINTO	NA	70	32	2	21	NA	1990-1993	11/89
81	VASCONCELOS GONZALEZ BYASS	NA	50	24	2	25	13	1990-1992	6/90
80	CALEM	NA	50	NA	2	32	13	1990-1994	11/89
80	FEUERHEERD	NA	40	NA	2	20	11	1990	1/90
79	HUTCHESON	NA	43	NA	2	15	NA	1990	1/90
77	OSBORNE	NA	50	NA	NA	NA	NA	1990	1/90
76	VASCONCELOS BUTLER & NEPHEW	NA	50	24	2	25	13	1990	7/90
75	C. DA SILVA	NA	50	18	2	29	NA	1990	2/90
75	ROYAL OPORTO	NA	30	NA	1.80	17	NA	1990	11/89
74	A. PINTOS DOS SANTOS	NA	NA	NA	2	20	9	1990	1/90
74	KROHN	NA	81	NA	2	29	NA	1990	1/90
71	VIEIRA DE SOUSA	NA	NA	NA	NA	NA	NA	1990	1/90
59	BORGES	NA	60	NA	2	28	11	Avoid	5/90
1969									
85	QUINTA DE VARGELLAS	NA	50	NA	1.80	20	19	1990	2/90
1968									
84	FONSECA-GUIMARAENS	NA	50	NA	1.50	18	NA	1990	2/90
82	QUINTA DE VARGELLAS	NA	55	NA	1.60	20	NA	1990	2/90
70	MALVEDOS	NA	50	NA	1.50	18	NA	1990	2/90
1967									
95	QUINTA DO NOVAL NACIONAL	NA	375	NA	NA	144	55	1990-1995	11/89
93	MARTINEZ	NA	60	NA	1.30	20	11	1990	2/90
91	ROBERTSON'S REBELLO VALENTE	NA	50	NA	1.30	25	NA	1990	2/90
90	FONSECA-GUIMARAENS	NA	56	NA	1.20	18	12	1990	2/90
90	SANDEMAN	NA	65	38	1.50	34	12	1990-1993	3/90
88	QUINTA DO NOVAL	NA	70	30	1.50	25	12	1990	12/89
85	COCKBURN	NA	55	45	1.50	32	15	1990	12/89
85	QUINTA DA ROEDA	NA	60	25	5	18	12	1990	1/90
82	QUINTA DE VARGELLAS	NA	60	NA	1.50	20	13	1990	2/90
75	KROHN	NA	81	NA	1.30	40	NA	1990	1/90
72	ROYAL OPORTO	NA	30	NA	1.30	NA	NA	1990	11/89
1966									
98	QUINTA DO NOVAL NACIONAL	NA	300	240	NA	144	92	1990-1998	11/89
97	FONSECA	NA	84	69	1.50	35	24	1990-1995	2/90
94	DOW	NA	90	80	1.50	38	25	1990-1992	12/89
93	GRAHAM	NA	82	60	1.50	45	27	1990	12/89
92	SANDEMAN	NA	93	40	1.50	35	21	1990	3/90
91	QUINTA DO NOVAL	NA	75	32	1.50	36	21	1990	12/89
91	WARRE	NA	83	83	1.50	45	24	1990	6/89
90	CROFT	NA	68	60	1.50	30	21	1990	12/89
90	OFFLEY BOA VISTA	NA	45	35	1.30	25	15	1990	2/89
89	NIEPOORT	NA	70	40	1.50	30	17	1990-1993	11/89
89	TAYLOR	NA	87	58	1.50	38	29	1990-1993	12/89
85	DELAFORCE	NA	65	45	1.30	26	19	1990	2/90
85	FERREIRA	NA	81	38	1.30	25	12	1990	8/88
84	GOULD CAMPBELL	NA	70	45	1.30	25	16	1990	2/90
84	MESSIAS Quinta do Cachão	NA	30	15	NA	NA	NA	1990	2/90
83	SMITH WOODHOUSE	NA	80	NA	1.30	30	15	1990	2/90
82	CALEM	NA	65	40	1.25	40	16	1990	11/89

NA—not available. NR—not released. Auction prices include 10% buyer's premium where charged.

Score	House	US Prices Release/Current/Auction			UK Prices Release/Current/Auction			Drink	Last Tasted
82	QUINTA DE LA ROSA	NA	NA	NA	NA	NA	NA	1990	10/89
82	ROBERTSON'S REBELLO VALENTE	NA	70	36	1.30	28	14	1990	2/90
81	KOPKE	NA	65	NA	1.30	20	NA	1990	1/90
80	MORGAN	NR	NR	NR	1.30	26	NA	1990	2/90
74	QUARLES HARRIS	NA	78	NA	1.30	30	NA	1990	2/90
1965									
89	FONSECA-GUIMARAENS	NA	60	NA	1.20	20	NA	1990	2/90
87	QUINTA DO BOMFIM	NA	NA	NA	2	17	NA	1990	6/90
85	KROHN	NA	100	NA	1.30	50	NA	1990	1/90
80	QUINTA DE VARGELLAS	NA	60	NA	1.20	20	NA	1990	2/90
79	MALVEDOS	NA	65	35	1.20	20	NA	1990	2/90
1964									
90	FONSECA-GUIMARAENS	NA	60	NA	1.15	20	NA	1990	2/90
84	QUINTA DO NOVAL NACIONAL	NA	350	130	NA	144	NA	1990	11/89
82	MALVEDOS	NA	54	NA	1	20	NA	1990	2/90
75	QUINTA DE VARGELLAS	NA	50	37	1.15	22	15	1990	7/90
1963									
100	QUINTA DO NOVAL NACIONAL	NA	750	660	NA	300	233	2000-2005	11/89
98	FONSECA	NA	155	130	1.15	69	53	1990-1995	12/89
97	GRAHAM	NA	150	130	1.15	90	52	1990-1993	12/89
97	TAYLOR	NA	160	115	1.15	78	57	1990-1994	12/89
96	SANDEMAN	NA	110	80	1.15	46	32	1990	3/90
93	DELAFORCE	NA	100	70	0.90	29	19	1990	2/90
92	DOW	NA	125	108	1.15	42	42	1990-1992	2/90
92	WARRE	NA	130	90	1.15	50	40	1990-1992	12/89
91	CROFT	NA	110	85	1.15	59	33	1990	12/89
90	NIEPOORT	NA	90	60	1.10	40	NA	1990	11/89
89	SMITH WOODHOUSE	NA	110	NA	0.90	35	NA	1990	2/90
88	COCKBURN	NA	110	85	1.15	40	34	1990	12/89
87	VASCONCELOS GONZALEZ BYASS	NA	82	38	0.90	30	18	1990	7/90
87	KROHN	NA	165	NA	1	69	NA	1990	1/90
86	MORGAN	NR	NR	NR	0.90	28	24	1990	2/90
85	FERREIRA	NA	110	50	0.90	30	24	1990	8/88
85	QUARLES HARRIS	NA	110	103	0.90	35	NA	1990	2/90
85	QUINTA DE LA ROSA	NA	NA	NA	NA	NA	NA	1990	10/89
85	ROBERTSON'S REBELLO VALENTE	NA	92	38	0.90	30	18	1990	2/90
84	QUINTA DO NOVAL	NA	120	105	1.15	40	31	1990	12/89
83	BURMESTER	NA	110	NA	0.90	42	NA	1990	1/90
83	RAMOS-PINTO	NA	80	NA	0.90	NA	6	1990	11/89
82	CALEM	NA	85	NA	0.90	42	NA	1990	12/89
82	MARTINEZ	NA	90	80	0.90	34	18	1990	2/90
82	POCAS JUNIOR	NA	100	NA	0.80	28	NA	1990	2/90
80	OFFLEY BOA VISTA	NA	97	50	0.90	39	21	1990	2/89
73	ROYAL OPORTO	NA	65	NA	1	29	NA	1990	11/89
71	MESSIAS	NA	40	NA	NA	NA	NA	1990	2/90
1962									
89	MALVEDOS	NA	65	NA	0.80	20	11	1990	2/90
88	FONSECA-GUIMARAENS	NA	70	NA	0.80	20	NA	1990-1993	2/90
86	QUINTA DO NOVAL NACIONAL	NA	350	260	NA	144	125	1990	1/89
1961									
87	MALVEDOS	NA	65	NA	0.80	21	NA	1990	2/90
85	FONSECA-GUIMARAENS	NA	70	NA	0.80	20	NA	1990	2/90
85	KROHN	NA	125	NA	1	69	NA	1990	1/90
68	QUINTA DE VARGELLAS	NA	45	NA	0.80	30	NA	Avoid	2/90
1960									
90	CROFT	NA	88	57	0.90	30	20	1990	9/89
89	KROHN	NA	144	NA	0.80	50	NA	1990	1/90
88	DOW	NA	88	50	0.95	32	26	1990-1992	2/90

NA—not available. NR—not released. Auction prices include 10% buyer's premium where charged.

Score	House	US Prices Release/Current/Auction			UK Prices Release/Current/Auction			Drink	Last Tasted
88	QUINTA DE LA ROSA	NA	NA	NA	NA	NA	NA	1990	10/89
87	KOPKE	NA	65	NA	1	31	NA	1990	1/90
85	ROBERTSON'S REBELLO VALENTE	NA	55	35	0.80	16	12	1990	11/88
84	GRAHAM	NA	80	60	0.95	37	27	1990	8/88
84	QUINTA DO NOVAL NACIONAL	NA	385	265	NA	173	100	1990	11/89
83	VAN ZELLER QUINTA DO RORIZ	NA	NA	NA	NA	NA	NA	1990	7/90
82	OSBORNE	NA	60	NA	NA	NA	NA	1990	1/90
82	POCAS JUNIOR	NA	80	NA	0.70	30	NA	1990	2/90
82	QUINTA DO NOVAL	NA	78	40	0.95	35	22	1990	11/89
82	WARRE	NA	85	85	0.95	30	22	1990	8/88
80	COCKBURN	NA	85	51	0.90	30	24	1990	8/88
80	FERREIRA	NA	100	35	0.90	20	15	1990	8/88
80	FONSECA	NA	84	60	0.98	29	21	1990	8/88
80	TAYLOR	NA	89	75	0.98	51	29	1990	8/88
79	SANDEMAN	NA	75	43	0.95	45	23	1990	3/90
78	OFFLEY BOA VISTA	NA	70	NA	0.80	18	13	1990	2/89
1958									
88	FONSECA-GUIMARAENS	NA	90	35	0.80	20	14	1990	2/90
87	KROHN	NA	180	NA	0.80	75	NA	1990	1/90
84	COCKBURN	NA	NA	NA	NA	NA	NA	1990	11/89
82	QUINTA DO NOVAL	NA	100	40	0.90	30	19	1990	11/89
82	SANDEMAN	NA	70	47	0.90	22	17	1990	3/90
81	WARRE	NA	99	70	0.90	23	18	1990	11/89
79	MALVEDOS	NA	65	42	0.80	30	NA	1990	2/90
79	CONSTANTINO	NA	NA	NA	0.80	25	NA	1990	8/90
68	QUINTA DE VARGELLAS	NA	50	NA	0.80	30	17	Avoid	2/90
1957									
91	KROHN	NA	214	NA	0.70	90	NA	1990	1/90
85	SANDEMAN	NA	NA	NA	0.80	21	17	1990	10/88
84	MALVEDOS	NA	65	38	0.80	31	NA	1990	2/90
1955									
98	NIEPOORT	NA	175	NA	1	65	24	1990	8/90
96	FONSECA	NA	170	175	1	57	44	1990	8/88
94	GRAHAM	NA	190	175	0.95	82	66	1990	11/89
94	SANDEMAN	NA	140	88	1	40	30	1990	3/90
91	DOW	NA	190	170	1	85	66	1990	4/90
90	COCKBURN	NA	155	110	1	0	41	1990	11/89
89	QUINTA DO NOVAL	NA	150	100	1	57	37	1990	8/90
88	TAYLOR	NA	195	165	1	105	86	1990	11/89
86	MARTINEZ	NA	120	110	0.80	48	24	1990	11/89
86	WARRE	NA	155	115	1	67	44	1990	11/89
85	FERREIRA	NA	110	97	1	48	23	1990	11/89
84	CROFT	NA	145	100	1	45	33	1990	11/89
1954									
91	GRAHAM	NA	155	NA	0.90	46	NA	1990	2/90
1952									
85	MALVEDOS	NA	125	NA	0.30	35	NA	1990	11/89
1950									
90	QUINTA DO NOVAL NACIONAL	NA	850	NA	NA	230	130	1990	11/89
87	SANDEMAN	NA	170	165	0.60	35	19	1990	3/90
86	DOW	NA	80	NA	0.60	60	13	1990	11/89
85	QUINTA DO NOVAL	NA	240	70	0.60	60	20	1990	11/89
79	FERREIRA	NA	90	NA	0.60	45	NA	1990	11/89
77	CROFT	NA	170	125	0.60	70	35	1990	4/90
76	COCKBURN	NA	110	90	0.60	65	38	1990	11/89
1948									
100	FONSECA	NA	265	210	0.48	95	72	1990	11/89
99	TAYLOR	NA	325	275	0.50	135	103	1990	11/89

NA—not available. NR—not released. Auction prices include 10% buyer's premium where charged.

Score	House	US Prices Release/Current/Auction			UK Prices Release/Current/Auction			Drink	Last Tasted
95	GRAHAM	NA	$290	$245	£0.48	£135	£99	1990	11/89
1947									
93	QUINTA DO NOVAL	NA	300	195	0.45	62	48	1990	11/89
90	COCKBURN	NA	185	150	0.45	75	45	1990	11/89
90	SANDEMAN	NA	180	NA	0.45	NA	33	1990	3/90
88	DOW	NA	230	209	0.45	80	47	1990	11/89
88	WARRE	NA	225	160	0.45	80	52	1990	11/89
1945									
99	CROFT	NA	375	220	0.40	135	94	1990	11/89
97	NIEPOORT	NA	250	NA	0.40	125	110	1990	2/90
97	TAYLOR	NA	675	700	0.45	300	234	1990	11/89
95	GRAHAM	NA	425	450	0.40	220	103	1990	11/89
95	SANDEMAN	NA	380	370	0.40	118	87	1990	3/90
92	QUINTA DO NOVAL	NA	325	250	0.40	92	72	1990	11/89
92	ROBERTSON'S REBELLO VALENTE	NA	245	185	0.40	55	NA	1990	5/90
91	FONSECA	NA	410	260	0.40	220	70	1990	11/89
89	DOW	NA	370	280	0.40	195	116	1990	11/89
87	WARRE	NA	345	235	0.40	110	83	1990	2/90
81	FERREIRA	NA	205	150	0.40	75	44	1990	11/89
1942									
93	NIEPOORT	NA	240	NA	0.30	110	77	1990	4/90
89	GRAHAM	NA	330	210	0.38	125	83	1990	4/90
88	SANDEMAN	NA	175	NA	0.30	59	46	1990	3/90
86	QUINTA DO NOVAL	NA	200	NA	0.30	75	NA	1990	4/90
78	TAYLOR	NA	275	NA	0.40	100	75	1990	4/90
75	ROBERTSON'S REBELLO VALENTE	NA	140	NA	0.38	50	28	1990	2/85
1941									
50	QUINTA DO NOVAL	NA	70	NA	0.30	25	NA	Avoid	9/85
1938									
79	TAYLOR	NA	265	NA	0.30	125	80	1990	4/90
71	QUINTA DO NOVAL	NA	110	NA	0.30	65	NA	1990	9/85
1935									
94	GRAHAM	NA	395	240	0.30	120	116	1990	4/90
93	CROFT	NA	285	240	0.30	95	73	1990	2/90
93	FERREIRA	NA	200	NA	0.30	65	66	1990	2/90
92	COCKBURN	NA	320	200	0.30	145	79	1990	2/90
92	SANDEMAN	NA	400	250	0.30	110	171	1990	3/90
90	QUINTA DA ROMANEIRA	NA	NA	NA	NA	NA	NA	1990	2/90
88	TAYLOR	NA	380	325	0.30	206	171	1990	2/90
79	DOW	NA	300	250	0.30	100	106	1990	6/90
1934									
98	QUINTA DO NOVAL	NA	305	240	0.30	75	55	1990	2/90
94	SANDEMAN	NA	300	NA	0.30	100	NA	1990	3/90
91	FONSECA	NA	300	255	0.30	170	133	1990	2/90
87	WARRE	NA	285	220	0.30	80	44	1990	2/90
84	DOW	NA	350	285	0.30	100	75	1990	6/90
1931									
100	QUINTA DO NOVAL NACIONAL	NA	3700	NA	.80	700	1990	1990	11/89
99	QUINTA DO NOVAL	NA	1000	700	.30	430	330	1990	11/89
89	COCKBURN	NA	NA	NA	NA	NA	NA	1990	1/90
1927									
100	FONSECA	NA	400	380	0.20	245	192	1990	12/89
97	NIEPOORT	NA	260	NA	0.20	140	116	1990	4/90
95	TAYLOR	NA	440	400	0.20	210	160	1990	12/89
94	GRAHAM	NA	400	250	0.20	165	138	1990	2/90
93	QUINTA DO NOVAL	NA	450	275	0.20	126	97	1990	12/89
93	WARRE	NA	340	205	0.20	130	88	1990	12/89

NA—not available. NR—not released. Auction prices include 10% buyer's premium where charged.

Score	House	US Prices Release / Current / Auction			UK Prices Release / Current / Auction			Drink	Last Tasted
92	SANDEMAN	NA	$375	$350	£0.20	£157	£121	1990	3/90
91	COCKBURN	NA	300	200	0.30	145	146	1990	12/89
87	CROFT	NA	350	195	0.20	150	105	1990	12/89
87	DOW	NA	425	300	0.20	150	150	1990	4/90
87	FEUERHEERD'S QUINTA DE LA ROSA	NA	NA	NA	NA	NA	NA	1990	12/89
1920									
78	SANDEMAN	NA	300	165	0.20	135	NA	1990	3/90
1917									
88	SANDEMAN	NA	300	130	0.21	160	66	1990	3/90
1912									
91	COCKBURN	NA	350	275	0.40	180	77	1990	10/87
1911									
82	SANDEMAN	NA	275	250	0.11	126	97	1990	6/90
1908									
89	COCKBURN	NA	395	325	0.20	185	143	1990	10/87
75	SANDEMAN	NA	320	NA	0.11	138	106	1990	3/90
1904									
88	SANDEMAN	NA	420	350	0.11	263	203	1990	3/90
75	COCKBURN	NA	330	240	0.20	120	94	1990	10/87
1900									
79	WARRE	NA	425	NA	0.10	140	100	1990	11/89
1896									
82	COCKBURN	NA	400	240	0.15	130	100	1990	2/90
81	SANDEMAN	NA	600	340	0.11	206	160	1990	3/90
1887									
74	SANDEMAN	NA	600	NA	0.11	470	NA	1990	3/90
1871									
98	ROYAL OPORTO	NA	550	NA	0.15	345	NA	1990	11/89
1870									
98	SANDEMAN	NA	700	NA	0.09	485	NA	1990	3/90

APPENDIX 4

Port Vintage Chart, 1900-1987

The following is a list of all vintages reviewed between 1900 and 1987 in chronological order. The number next to the vintage is its score based on *The Wine Spectator* 100-point scale.

1980s

1987	88	Very Good
1986	80	Good
1985	96	Classic
1984	81	Good
1983	92	Outstanding
1982	84	Good
1980	87	Very Good

1970s

1979	74	Average
1978	84	Good
1977	97	Classic
1976	76	Average
1975	80	Good
1974	74	Average
1972	79	Average
1970	95	Classic

1960s

1969	72	Average
1968	77	Average
1967	88	Very Good
1966	93	Outstanding
1965	80	Good
1964	81	Good
1963	98	Classic
1962	82	Good
1961	80	Good
1960	87	Very Good

1950s

1958	84	Good
1957	85	Very Good
1955	94	Outstanding
1954	85	Very Good
1952	80	Good
1950	86	Very Good

1940s

1949	70	Average
1948	99	Classic
1947	93	Outstanding
1946	70	Average
1945	98	Classic
1944	70	Average
1943	70	Average
1942	86	Very Good
1941	70	Average
1940	70	Average

1930s

1938	80	Good
1937	70	Average
1935	95	Classic
1934	93	Outstanding
1931	95	Classic

1920s

1929	80	Good
1927	100	Classic
1926	70	Average
1925	70	Average
1924	85	Very Good
1923	70	Average
1922	85	Very Good
1920	85	Very Good

1910s

1919	75	Average
1917	88	Very Good
1912	99	Classic
1911	80	Good

1900s

1908	94	Outstanding
1904	90	Outstanding
1900	90	Outstanding

Classic	(95-100 points)
Outstanding	(90-94)
Good to Very Good	(80-89)
Average	(70-79)
Below Average	(60-69)
Poor	(50-59

APPENDIX 5
Port Vintages by Score

The following is a list of all vintages reviewed between 1900 and 1987, ranked in order by score. The number next to the vintage is its score based on *The Wine Spectator* 100-point scale.

Classic (95-100 points)

1.	1927	100	Classic
2.	1948	99	Classic
3.	1912	99	Classic
4.	1963	98	Classic
5.	1945	98	Classic
6.	1977	97	Classic
7.	1931	95	Classic
8.	1985	96	Classic
9.	1970	95	Classic
10.	1935	95	Classic

Outstanding (90-94)

11.	1955	94	Outstanding
12.	1908	94	Outstanding
13.	1966	93	Outstanding
14.	1947	93	Outstanding
15.	1934	93	Outstanding
16.	1983	92	Outstanding
17.	1904	90	Outstanding
18.	1900	90	Outstanding

Good to Very Good (80-89)

19.	1987	88	Very Good
20.	1967	88	Very Good
21.	1917	88	Very Good
22.	1980	87	Very Good
23.	1960	87	Very Good
24.	1950	86	Very Good
25.	1957	85	Very Good
26.	1942	86	Very Good
27.	1982	84	Very Good
28.	1962	82	Very Good
29.	1954	85	Very Good
30.	1924	85	Very Good
31.	1922	85	Very Good
32.	1920	85	Very Good
33.	1978	84	Good
34.	1958	84	Good
35.	1984	81	Good
36.	1964	81	Good
37.	1986	80	Good
38.	1975	80	Good
39.	1965	80	Good
40.	1961	80	Good
41.	1952	80	Good
42.	1938	80	Good
43.	1929	80	Good
44.	1911	80	Good

Average (70-79)

45.	1972	79	Average
46.	1968	77	Average
47.	1976	76	Average
48.	1949	70	Average
49.	1944	70	Average
50.	1943	70	Average
51.	1941	70	Average
52.	1940	70	Average
53.	1937	70	Average
54.	1926	70	Average
55.	1925	70	Average
56.	1923	70	Average
57.	1919	75	Average
58.	1979	74	Average
59.	1974	74	Average
60.	1969	72	Average

Classic	(95-100 points)
Outstanding	(90-94)
Good to Very Good	(80-89)
Average	(70-79)
Below Average	(60-69)
Poor	(50-59

SELECTED BIBLIOGRAPHY

Bradford, Sarah. *The Story of Port: The Englishman's Wine*. New and Revised Edition. London: Christie's Wine Publications, 1983.

Broadbent, Michael. *Christie's Price Index of Vintage Wine*. London: Christie's Wine Publications. 1989.

Christie's. *Price Index of Vintage Wine, 1989 Edition*.

Cockburn, Ernest. *Port Wine and Oporto*. London: Wine and Spirit Publications Ltd.

Croft, John. *Treatise on the Wines of Portugal Since the Establishment of the English Factory at Oporto*.

Da Costa Lima, Jose Joaquim. *A Word or Two About Port*. English version. Oporto: Instituto do Vinho do Porto, 1939.

A.A. Ferreira. *A Portuguese in London*.

Fletcher, Wyndham. *Port: An Introduction to Its History and Delights*. London: Sotheby Publications, 1978.

Forrester, Baron Joseph James. *Portugal, Its Capabilities*.

Howkins, Ben. *Rich, Rare & Red*. London: William Heinemann Ltd., 1982.

Jefford, Andrew. *Port: An Essential Guide to the Classic Drink*. New York: Exeter Books, 1988.

Johnson, Hugh. *Modern Encyclopedia of Wine*. New York: Simon and Schuster, 1983.

Johnson, Hugh. *The Story of Wine*. London: Mitchell Beazley Publishers, 1989.

Lichine, Alexis. *New Encyclopedia of Wines and Spirits*. New York: Alfred A. Knopf, 1987.

Metcalfe, Charles, and McWhirter, Kathryn. *The Wines of Spain & Portugal*. London: Salamander Books, Ltd., 1988.

A. Moreira de Fonseca, A. Galhano, E. Serpa Pimental, and J.R.-P. Rosas. *Port Wine: Notes on Its History, Production, & Technology*. Second Edition. Oporto: Instituto do Vinho do Porto, 1984.

Penning-Rowsell, Edmund. *The Wine of Bordeaux*.

Peynaud, Emile. *Knowing and Making Wine*. English Edition. New York: John Wiley & Sons, Inc., 1984.

Redding, Cyrus. *A History and Description of Modern Wines*, London. 1833.

Robertson, George. *Port*. Revised Edition. London: Faber and Faber Limited, 1982.

Robinson, Jancis. *Vines, Grapes and Wines*. London: Mitchell Beazley, 1986.

Saintsbury, George. *Notes on a Cellar-Book*. Sixth Edition. London: MacMillan and Co., Limited, 1924.

Sellers, Charles. *Oporto Old and New*. London. 1899.

Shaw, T.G. *Wine, The Vine and the Cellar*. London. 1863.

Stanislawski, Dan. *Landscapes of Bacchus: The Vine in Portugal*. Austin, Texas: University of Texas Press, 1970.

Valente-Perfeito, J.C. *Let's Talk About Port*. Oporto: Instituto do Vinho do Porto, 1948.

Virginario, J.M. *A Portuguese in London: Letter from J.M. Virginianò, correspondent of the Ferreira family of Regua in the post-Napolenoic period*. Oporto: A.A. Ferreira S.A., 1988.

Vizatelly, Henry. *Facts about Port and Madeira*. London. 1880.

GLOSSARY

Autovinification: a method of fermentation for producing Port in closed-off stainless steel or concrete vats with pressure locks. When the pressure inside the vats reaches a particular level the locks open and juice is pumped from the bottom of the tank to the top and over the cap of skins, seeds and stems. This ensures proper extraction of color, tannins and fruit from the cap during fermentation.

Barcos rabelos: wooden, single-sail, flat-bottom riverboats widely used until the late 1950s to transport casks of young Port down the Douro River to Vila Nova de Gaia.

Baume: a winemaking term, used mostly in Europe, describing the sugar content of grapes, must and wines. One degree Baume is equal to about 1.8 degrees Brix.

Botrytis cinerea: a mold that grows on the skins of grapes, usually after a damp period just before or during the harvest. Small amounts of Botrytis can benefit certain wines, such as Sauternes, reducing the water content of the grapes and increasing the natural sugars. The rot in its advanced stages, however, can damage and sometimes ruin the grapes.

Brix: similar to Baume, but used primarily by U.S. winemakers to describe the sugar content of their grapes.

Colheita: a tawny Port produced from a single vintage.

Crusted Port: a blend of young, rich Ports from various years, which has been bottled after three or four years of aging in large wooden casks. These Ports are not treated, and they throw a crust like a vintage Port, improving with age in the bottle.

Engarrafadores: producers of estate-bottled Port.

Grip: a tasting term usually used to describe a young vintage Port with a good intensity of fruit and tannins.

Hogshead: an oak barrel with a capacity of 267 liters, one-half the size of a shipping pipe.

Lagar: the traditional vessel for fermenting Port. Made of stone, it is a large, rectangular, shallow and open vat, where a handful of workers tread the cap of the must down into the juice to assure proper extraction during fermentation.

Late-bottled vintage Port: a premium ruby from a single vintage that spends from three to four years aging in wooden casks before being bottled. Traditional LBVs — very rare today — are never fined or filtered and therefore throw a crust and improve with age in the bottle. Modern LBVs are treated to remove solids and do not require decanting before service.

Movimosto: a method of fermentation in *lagares* devised by Cockburn in the 1960s to reduce the necessity of treading. Juice is pumped from the *lagar* during fermentation and sprayed over the floating cap, which pushes it down into the juice.

Must meter: a winemaking apparatus that measures the sugar content and potential alcohol of the fermenting must.

Négociant: a French word for merchants or shippers who buy grapes or wines from growers and use them to make their own wines.

Oidium: a fungus that attacks all the green parts of the vines, producing a light powder. Also known as powdery mildew, it can badly affect the development of the berries in its advanced form.

Phylloxera: a root louse that arrived in Europe in the 1860s and proceeded to decimate the majority of European vineyards over more than 30 years. The insect damages a vine by destroying its root system.

Pipe: elongated wooden cask used as a traditional measure for buying, storing and selling Port. A pipe in the Douro Valley is usually 500 liters in size, while in Vila Nova de Gaia it comprises 534 liters.

Quinta: a vineyard site or estate that may equal from one or two to thousands of acres. Wines from the very best *quintas* in the Douro Valley serve as the backbones of vintage Ports.

Refractometer: a winemaking instrument used to measure the sugar content of grapes and must.

Vila Nova de Gaia: a city located across the Douro River from Oporto. It is the center of the Port trade, where most shippers blend, age, bottle, stock and sell their wines.

Vinho verde: a simple, light red or white wine produced in the Minho district of Portugal characterized by low alcohol, high acidity and a slight sparkle.

Wood-aged Port: a wine made from Ports that have been aged in wooden casks or vats including white, ruby, tawny, old tawny, vintage character, late-bottled vintage and *colheita.*

White Port: a wine made from a range of white grape varities grown in the Douro Valley. It is consumed primarily as an apértif.

Vintage Port: a wine produced from the wine of a single vintage, usually from several different vineyards, and bottled after aging two to two and a half years in wooden casks or vats. It is never fined or filtered, and so it throws a crust and needs to be decanted before serving. Most vintage Ports are drinkable after 10 to 15 years of bottle age, but some will improve for decades in the bottle.

INDEX

INDEX

Tasting and Inventory Notes

WINE	VINTAGE	NOTES	RATING

TASTING AND INVENTORY NOTES

WINE	VINTAGE	NOTES	RATING

TASTING AND INVENTORY NOTES

WINE	VINTAGE	NOTES	RATING

Tasting and Inventory Notes

WINE	VINTAGE	NOTES	RATING

TASTING AND INVENTORY NOTES

WINE	VINTAGE	NOTES	RATING

TASTING AND INVENTORY NOTES

WINE	VINTAGE	NOTES	RATING

Tasting and Inventory Notes

WINE	VINTAGE	NOTES	RATING

TASTING AND INVENTORY NOTES

WINE	VINTAGE	NOTES	RATING

TASTING AND INVENTORY NOTES

WINE	VINTAGE	NOTES	RATING